Karin Luttermann, Jan Engberg (Hrsg. / Eds.)

Digitalisierung und multimodale Ressourcen in diskursiven juristischen Prozessen

Digitalisation and Multimodal Resources in Discursive Legal Processes

Rechtslinguistik

Studien zu Text und Kommunikation
Studies on Text and Communication

Herausgegeben von

Claire Kramsch (Berkeley)
Claus Luttermann (Eichstätt-Ingolstadt)
Karin Luttermann (Eichstätt-Ingolstadt)

Band 14

LIT

Digitalisierung und multimodale Ressourcen in diskursiven juristischen Prozessen

Digitalisation and Multimodal Resources in Discursive Legal Processes

Herausgegeben von / Edited by

Karin Luttermann
Jan Engberg

LIT

Die Drucklegung haben freundlich unterstützt:
Dekanat der Sprach- und Literaturwissenschaftlichen Fakultät
der Katholischen Universität Eichstätt-Ingolstadt
Institut für Kommunikation und Kultur der Universität Aarhus

○

Gedruckt auf alterungsbeständigem Werkdruckpapier entsprechend
ANSI Z3948 DIN ISO 9706

Bibliografische Information der Deutschen Nationalbibliothek
Die Deutsche Nationalbibliothek verzeichnet diese Publikation in der Deutschen Nationalbibliografie; detaillierte bibliografische Daten sind im Internet über https://dnb.dnb.de abrufbar.

ISBN 978-3-643-15496-5 (gb.)
ISBN 978-3-643-35496-9 (PDF)

Verlagskontakt:
Fresnostr. 2 D-48159 Münster
Tel. +49 (0) 2 51-62 03 20
E-Mail: lit@lit-verlag.de https://www.lit-verlag.de

Auslieferung:
Deutschland: LIT Verlag, Fresnostr. 2, D-48159 Münster
Tel. +49 (0) 2 51-620 32 22, E-Mail: vertrieb@lit-verlag.de

Geleitwort der Herausgeber zur Reihe

Sprache verbindet Menschen – auch in rechtlichen Dingen. Recht lebt in und durch Sprache. Von Rechtsetzung und Rechtsanwendung bis zu Begegnungen mit anderen Rechts- und Sprachkulturen im heimischen Recht wie im internationalen Rahmen, in Text und Kommunikation: Sprache ist das Medium.

Sprachgebrauch knüpft dabei an Alltagswissen an, das im juristischen Umfeld modifiziert wird. Jeder etwa hat eine Vorstellung von „Treue" und verbindet etwas mit „Glauben", aber was bedeutet „Treu und Glauben" als juristischer Begriff? – Ruft der Dichter Emile Zola: „J'accuse!", dann mag man manchen Gedanken daran binden. Tritt vor Gericht der Staatsanwalt mit „Angeklagt wird …!" auf und führt dies weiter aus, ist das eine gesetzlich bestimmte Handlung im Eingang von Hauptverhandlungen in Strafsachen. Recht hat also eigenartige Muster sprachlichen Handelns. Das berührt Verständlichkeit und Verständnis. Wie Sprache hier im Kontext wirkt, ist eine Aufgabe, die interdisziplinäre Arbeit fordert.

Die Reihe *Rechtslinguistik – Studien zu Text und Kommunikation* spannt zum Dialog einen Bogen zwischen Fakultäten, die Sprache und Recht behandeln. Das Untersuchungsspektrum umfasst etwa Gesetzestexte, mündliches und schriftliches Handeln in Rechtsinstitutionen wie Behörden und Gerichten, anwaltliche Beratungsgespräche, Fragen des Stils sowie bei internationalen Sachverhalten auch der Übersetzung. Versuche der Rechtsharmonisierung in der Europäischen Union sowie Handel und Kommunikation in globalen Netzen zeigen, wie notwendig hier vertiefende Betrachtung ist. Die Reihe bietet ein Forum für Begegnung und gemeinsame Projekte.

Berkeley / Kalifornien, im Mai 1996

Claire Kramsch Claus Luttermann Karin Luttermann

Editorial Introduction to the Series

Language unites people – also in the realm of law. Law lives in and through language. In the writing and in the application of the law, in the interpretation and transmission of legal texts, in the contact between legal culture and vernacular culture, in national and international law: language is the medium.

Language use in the legal realm is linked to everyday knowledge, modified to fit the legal setting. For instance, every German knows the meaning of „Treue" (faith) and „Glauben" (belief), but what does „Treu und Glauben" (in good faith) mean in legal terms? When the writer Emile Zola says: „J'accuse!", various meanings may come to mind. But when the prosecutor in a German court utters the words: „Angeklagt wird …!" (is accused) and strengthens this utterance with incriminatory details, this can only be heard as a conventionalized speech act, fixed by statute at the beginning of a German criminal procedure. The language of the law has specific linguistic patterns that affect intelligibility and comprehension. How language works in this context can be investigated through interdisciplinary collaboration.

The series *Rechtslinguistik – Studies on Text and Communication* brings together researchers from various disciplines that deal with language and the law: jurisprudence, sociology, anthropology, linguistics, literary and cultural studies. It explores the discourse of legal texts, the use of oral and written language in legal institutions and courts of law, the discourse of counselling, legal stylistics, translation and interpretation in multilingual settings, issues of language and power. Current attempts at the legal harmonization of the European Union and at solving cross-cultural problems of communication between trading partners point to the urgent need for such research. This series offers a forum for the exchange of ideas and for joint projects in this field.

Berkeley / California, May 1996

Claire Kramsch   Claus Luttermann   Karin Luttermann

Inhaltsverzeichnis / Table of Contents

Introduction

Jan Engberg / Karin Luttermann

I. Digitisation of expert communication in the field of law

The term *digitisation* is ambiguous. Digitisation is basically regarded as assemblages of digital technologies. 'Being digital' is seen as a form that enables communication with the help of digital media. In linguistics, digital communication goes beyond mere transmission via technical media. Rather, digital practice is linked to socio-cultural and behavioural aspects and, above all, to communicative practices. In line with the pragmatic turn in linguistics and recent research on theoretical and methodological aspects of the dissemination and mediation of law to citizens unfamiliar with the law by lawyers and legal institutions, the topic connecting the contributions to this edited volume is the digitisation of expert communication in the field of law. The internet has grown ever more important as a medium of communication in today's world, also in the area of law. To name just two instances up front, already at an early stage of the development of the internet many jurisdictions began publishing their legislation online. In many cases the next imminent step is to make all court decisions available to the general public via the internet.

Where the publication of legislation was ethically unproblematic (legislation must be made available to the public anyway in order for it to fulfill its purpose), severe problems emerge due to the personal character of court decisions. Hence, we can already deduct two of the central types of problems in connection with law and the internet: firstly, it is very useful for making legal information available to citizens – but availability does not necessarily equal intelligibility; secondly, how do we protect the personal privacy of citizens, when legal communication with private elements becomes publically available? These two problems are part of the discussions in most of the contributions in this edited volume. In other words: language use in law and its multimodal manifestations, its embedding in and interweaving with secure data exchange, citizen services, suitable secure procedures for communication as well as cognitive aspects and comprehensibility issues are of fundamental interest here.

The communication of legal matters in digital formats and in online settings has increasingly become an object of study in legal linguistics. For the purposes of legal linguistics, it plays a major role that the internet as a medium of communication is characterised by a high degree of accessibility. What citizens need in order to access information on the internet is an internet connection and some kind of technical device with a browser – and then all information in the world is available, if it has not been locked down by its authors or publishers. This means that this channel of communication is generally extremely apt for making specialised information available for the wider public (cf. Bondi / Cacchiani 2021). In the field of law, it means that legal experts and legal authorities and institutions have here a very useful and efficient means for channelling information to citizens (in the case of jurisdictional institutions, as in the examples above), but also to customers of private legal agents like law firms.

Over the last 10 years, much research in legal linguistcs has investigated this type of communicative efforts (cf., e.g., contributions in Engberg / Luttermann / Cacchiani / Preite 2018; Luttermann / Engberg 2023 with further references). For as was to be expected, it is not enough to make information available on the internet for citizens to find it, get interested in it, let alone understand it adequately. In this volume, we intend to pursue further this general topic of what the communicative conditions in a broad sense are for non-experts in the field of law that want to or need to gain insight into legal matters with relevance for their daily life. The focus of the book, however, is on the special conditions created by digitisation. In this regard, we are interested in the role of digitisation for the way legal institutions relate to addressees and how such institutions organise their communicative work. But we are equally interested in, for instance, how lawyers use the internet to acquire customers or staff. In this context, the popularity of the internet and its affordances have, e.g., created new digitally mediated subtypes of the genre 'biographic presentations' (cf., e.g., Lombardi / Luttermann 2023). However, legal internet forums and so-called blawgs, i.e. typically blogs by lawyers in which they act as advisors for legal laypersons, are also examples of communicative arenas that have emerged due to the development of digital communication and are therefore a frequent object of study (cf. Anesa 2016; Diani 2023; Garzone 2014; Tessuto 2015; Turnbull 2023). The contributions to be presented in the following belong to this part of the general framework of legal linguistics.

II. Contributions to this volume

The first group of contributions in this book shares an interest in the basic ideas and questions of law in the context of digitsation. The first contribution by Daniel Green (*Legal Linguistics and Transformative Change through the Lens of the Sustainable Development Goals*) makes a case for a more critical approach to the study of language in law. Following the general approach of Gerlinde Mautner (2016), he proposes what he calls 'critical applied legal linguistics' as a way of supporting transformative change in fields of legal practice connected to sustainability. Using the example of the concept of sustainability in legal texts among other issues concerning the digital field, he demonstrates how legal linguistic insights like the vagueness and openness of legal terms and the context dependence of any linguistic meaning are important to include as conceptual lenses in order to achieve actual sustainable development along the lines of UN's Sustainable Development Goals. In this way, he lays out the basics of this novel approach to the study of language in law.

The second contribution with the title *The European Union Governance in the Regulation of Digital Data* by Antonio Lazari zooms in on the legal framework for working with digital data in the EU. He is interested in comparing the aspects of how digital security is handled at the macro level of different states, ideological visions, and legal systems in the world, as the challenges of securing access and exploitation of the giant data repositories resulting from today's digital possibilities are global. After presenting the regulations in a number of countries around the world, he specifically discusses the basic principles of the regulations in China and the U.S.A., seeing both as problematic due to their lack of focus on the fundamental rights of citizens. Here, he sees the regulations of the EU as a relevant alternative, especially due to their respect for the EU's own Charter of Fundamental Rights, with a consequential potential of preventing developments towards digital service providers and states becoming all-devouring giants, endangering citizens' digital lives.

After these more basic contributions, the next section looks at law in digital settings in national contexts. Chiara Preite's contribution (*"Vos amis notaires vous répondent" – Popularising Legal Knowledge for Citizens on the* Notaires.fr *Website*) studies how the Association des Notaires de France on its website popularises knowledge of the practice of French notaries. She talks about popularisation rather than mere information because her analyses demonstrate that the website author intends to guide users into the world of notaryship and thus create a relation of confidence with them. In her study, she focuses on forms of definitional reformulation, fostering the cognitive process of constructing relevant knowledge about notaries. The investigation is carried out based on verbal text in the context of the website as well as on embedded videos. A specifically important function of the videos is that of engaging the audience and hence intending to influence the image of notaries held by the users of the website.

In their contribution *„Justiz verstehen!" – Kulturkontrastive Analysen digitaler Rechtskommunikation auf ministeriellen Webseiten in Deutschland und Dänemark*, Karin Luttermann and Jan Engberg compare the official websites of the German and Danish Ministries of Justice, respectively. As indicated above, the digital setting in principle opens a communicative arena for coming into actual contact with citizens at large and thus popularising the institution and its expertise. However, the analysis reveals a clear difference between the two. Based, for example, on assessment of the structure of the website, the elements included, the depths of explanation, and the chosen visuals, the comparative analysis demonstrates that the digital communication of the German Ministry seems far more interested in coherent information about itself and its expertise and thus in creating an image as an open institution than the Danish Ministry. Hence, the strategy of popularisation appears more prominent in the German Federal Ministry of Justice.

In the third contribution, Patricia Rawinsky (*Multimodalität und Popularisierung – eine Beispielanalyse von Erklärvideos zur Erstellung der Steuererklärung*) analyses how multimodal elements are exploited in order to popularise legal knowledge in explanatory videos. In the analysis, aspects of verbal intelligibility and depth of explanation are combined with aspects of the intended relationship with the users of the video as well as with aspects like choice of multimodal elements and their expected recognisability for non-expert users. Among the central results is the fact that the main intention behind the explanatory videos is to disseminate know-how about how to perform specific tasks, rather than to popularise the underlying expert knowledge in itself. However, in the second video there are clear traces of an intention to convey the expert knowledge more to the users, especially through functional use of multimodal and multimedial characteristics.

As the final contribution to the second section, the contribution with the title *Klare und digitalisierungsfreundliche Gesetze in Norwegen – Möglichkeiten und Grenzen der Begriffsarbeit* by Jon Christian Fløysvik Nordrum, Torunn Reksten, Janine Schaller-Bøyum, and Ole Våge presents principles for the work on legislation that are clear and easy to implement in digital settings in a Norwegian context. There are clear relations between the topic of this contribution and the contribution by Antonio Lazari: both are interested in the conditions of using and gathering data in the current digital setting. However, where Antonio Lazari focuses on the principles behind the overall normative regulation in different jurisdictions, this contribution has its focus on how the language used in legislation may help ensure a more precisely automated data processing of legislative texts and thus a more efficient use of digital procedures in large-scale public administration. Focus is upon how work on differentiating and harmonising concepts in legislative processes can be systematically structured and planned in order to diminish the risk of conceptual overlaps and gaps that are highly problematic for digital processing (and in actual fact also for human processing). Furthermore, the special conditions for such conceptual work that are rooted in the general characteristics of any legal language (e.g., vagueness) are discussed as a basis for the necessity of a specific kind of conceptual work.

The final section consists of contributions with a more international focus. Karin Luttermann and Alessandra Lombardi (*Anwälte adressieren Klienten. Eine vergleichende Analyse von Berufsbiographien deutscher und italie-nischer Anwaltsvideos auf Kanzlei-Webseiten*) compare the websites of so-called boutique law firms, i.e., highly specialised firms, with a predominantly international orientation, in Italy and Germany. The object of the studies are video presentations (audio-visual CVs) of key lawyers at these firms which have now become a common feature on law firm websites. Focus is on the role of these videos in the website's broader context, on the strategies concerning relationship management visible in the videos, as well as on the choice of multimodal means. The authors are specifically interested in the potential influence of the focused aspects concerning image, perceived credibility, and professional and personal life values projected by the lawyers. The analyses show that there are many transcultural overlaps between the presentations, for instance concerning the part of professional ethos and specific experience in the fields of legal expertise, whereas differences are visible, e.g., in the importance of personal expertise (Germany) vs. expertise of the team (Italy).

Next, in her contribution titled *Les marqueurs introduisant un «ailleurs» discursif dans les publications de l'UE destinées au grand public, aux adolescents et aux enfants*, Alida Maria Silletti analyses digital information publications oriented towards adults, young people or children, respectively. Attention is directed at a specific verbal characteristic, the so-called parenthetic connectives of reformulation and interpretation, which is a frequent indicator of explanations at different levels. It indicates that something more is said about the topic introduced earlier in a text. Its use is interesting as one of the indicators of the presence of explanations of the legal concepts from the field of the EU, which are necessary due to the knowledge asymmetry in relation to the addressees. Based on the analyses, the contribution suggests a set of principles for the use of the elements in the chosen part of the French language system, depending mainly upon the relations to be indicated between concepts and their reformulations.

Finally, carrying on with a similar object of study, Giuliana Diani (*"All Brexplained!" – Popularising Brexit to Younger Generations*) investigates two information-oriented books for children (on Brexit from the point of view of discourse analysis and aspects of multimodality). The author is especially interested in the influence of the age of the targeted children on the strategic choices of the authors. The discourse analysis focuses on types of explanation following the approach by Helena Calsamiglia and Teun van Dijk (2004), but it has a special interest in the combination of verbal and visual elements in this context. The results of the analysis shows that there is quite a number of overlaps between the character of the popularisation effort in the two books, e.g., in the explanatory strategies chosen, but that the book for the small children is fundamentally different from the other book in that it relies far more heavily on an integrated visual mode in the form of comic-like visual stories with humanised animal characters.

III. Acknowledgements

We would like to thank all the authors for their contributions, which provide an excellent basis to foster discussion within the scientific community of legal linguistics, as well as between science and the general public on the complex topic of language and law in the field of digitisation. We would also like to thank our colleagues for their agreement to undertake the peer review, without which this volume would not have been possible to print. Special thanks go to the sponsors, in particular the Dean's Office of the Faculty of Languages and Literatures at the Catholic University of Eichstätt-Ingolstadt, and the University of Aarhus for their generous financial support of the printing costs, as well as to all the helping hands for proofreading and designing the layout. We would also like to thank the publisher Dr. Wilhelm Hopf for including the book in the publishing programme and the lector Guido Bellmann for his competent and professional support and his great commitment.

IV. References

Anesa, Patrizia. 2016. The Deconstruction and Reconstruction of Legal Information in Expert-Lay Online Interaction. *ESP today* 4 (1), 69-86. https://www.esptodayjournal.org/esp_today_back_issues_vol6.html. Last accessed 3.9.2024.

Bondi, Marina / Silvia Cacchiani. 2021. Knowledge Communication and Knowledge Dissemination in a Digital World. *Journal of Pragmatics* 186, 117-123. https://doi.org/10.1016/j.pragma.2021.10.003. Last accessed 3.9.2024.

Calsamiglia, Helena / Teun A. van Dijk. 2004. Popularization Discourse and Knowledge about the Genome. *Discourse & Society* 15 (4), 369-389. https://doi.org/10.1177/0957926504043705. Last accessed 3.9. 2024.

Diani, Giuliana. 2023. Disseminating Legal Information on Online Law Forums in English and Italian. *Ibérica* 46, 299-320. https://doi.org/10.17398/2340-2784.46.299. Last accessed 3.9. 2024.

Engberg, Jan / Karin Luttermann / Silvia Cacchiani / Chiara Preite (Eds.). 2018. *Popularization and Knowledge Mediation in the Law / Popularisierung und Wissensvermittlung im Recht*. Wien: Lit.

Garzone, Giuliana. 2014. Investigating Blawgs through Corpus Linguistics – Issues of Generic Integrity. In: Maurizio Gotti / Davide S. Giannoni (Eds.), *Corpus Analysis for Descriptive and Pedagogical Purposes. ESP Perspectives*. Bern: Peter Lang, 167-188.

Lombardi, Alessandra / Karin Luttermann. 2023. Legal Specialists Telling their Stories on the Internet. A Comparative Analysis of Professional Self-Portrayals on German and Italian Law Firm Websites. In: Patrizia Anesa / Jan Engberg (Eds.), *The Digital (R)evolution of Legal Discourse. New Genres, Media, and Linguistic Practices*. Berlin: de Gruyter, 53-66.

Luttermann, Karin / Jan Engberg (Eds.). 2023. *Popularisierung als Methode der Wissensvermittlung in der Rechtslinguistik / Popularisation as a Method of Knowledge Mediation in Legal Linguistics*. Berlin: Lit.

Mautner, Gerlinde. 2016. *Discourse and Management*. London: Palgrave.

Tessuto, Girolamo. 2015. "Posted by …". Scholarly Legal Blogs as Part of Academic Discourse and Site for Stance and Engagement. *Textus* 15 (2), 85-106.

Turnbull, Judith. 2023. "Where do I stand?". Online Legal Information for Children and Adolescents. In: Karin Luttermann / Jan Engberg (Eds.), *Popularisierung als Methode der Wissensvermittlung in der Rechtslinguistik / Popularisation as a Method of Knowledge Mediation in Legal Linguistics.* Berlin: Lit, 313-338.

Section I

Digitalisierung im Recht – Grundlegende Ideen /

Digitisation in Law – Basic Ideas

Daniel Green

Legal Linguistics and Transformative Change through the Lens of the Sustainable Development Goals

Abstract

This contribution makes some suggestions as to how Critical Applied Legal Linguistics (CrALL) can be conceived through the lens of the Sustainable Development Goals (SDGs). It seeks to make a case that legal linguists can and should assume an active role in addressing and critically engaging with the various global challenges, as laid out in the 2030 Agenda. The question this contribution pursues is how CrALL can allow for transformative change by providing effective monitoring, evaluation and critique of sustainability discourses around the globe. Building on Mautner (2016), it presents various arguments in support of the view that legal linguists should engage critically with questions of what is and what ought to be (Hart 2012) in relation to legislative discourses in and around sustainability. It is argued that CrALL can contribute to transformative change by laying bare real social issues that arise from the creation and interpretation of rules and regulations worldwide, and by highlighting the significance of the "practice-related quality" (Reisigl 2017: 49), contextuality and constituting/constitutive nature of legislative discourse worldwide, and finally, by offering a data-based evaluation of inequalities concerning social, historical, political, and economic factors at local, regional and global levels. The contribution concludes that critical, interdisciplinary, and systematic analyses of sustainability legislation through the lens of legal linguistics may offer a fruitful pathway towards transformative change.

I. Introduction

This contribution argues that Critical Applied Legal Linguistics (CrALL) can contribute to and help implement transformative change by providing methodologies for effective monitoring, evaluation and critique of sustainability discourses around the globe. It assumes transformative change to be an ongoing process through which "a more just and sustainable world" can be created (Gass 2011: 13). It seeks to introduce various arguments in support of the view that legal linguists can and should engage critically with questions of what is and what ought to be (Hart 2012) in relation to legislation in and around sustainability. By reference to the UN's Sustainable Development Goals (SDGs), this contribution argues that legal linguistics can deepen our understanding of how sustainability is translated across legal cultures which, in turn, shapes how legal language is used to express, enact and transform concepts of sustainability in local, regional and global contexts.

In 2015, the UN General Assembly (UNGA) formulated seventeen common objectives intended to serve as a "blueprint for peace and prosperity for people and the planet now and into the future" (United Nations 2015). These SDGs are described as "an urgent call for action by all countries – developed and developing – in a global partnership" and include the following:

1 No poverty	2 Zero hunger	3 Good health and well-being	4 Quality education
5 Gender equality	6 Clean water and sanitation	7 Affordable and clean energy	8 Decent work and economic growth
9 Industry, innovation and infrastructure	10 Reducing inequality	11 Sustainable cities and communities	12 Responsible consumption and production
13 Climate action	14 Life below water	15 Life on land	16 Peace, justice and strong institutions
17 Partnerships for the goals			

Tab. 1: The 17 Sustainable Development Goals (United Nations 2015)

The SDGs have been described as a "universal political agenda" adopted with a view to achieving "a better and more sustainable future for all" and "solving the social, economic, and environmental issues that hinder global progress towards sustainability intended to be achieved by the year 2030" (Yamaguchi / Bernardino / Ferreira / Lima / Pascotini / Yamaguchi 2023: 5502). Though there is no such thing as an 'orthodox definition' of sustainability, this contribution approaches the concept drawing on a definition provided by the Encyclopaedia Britannica (2023):

> the long-term viability of a community, set of social institutions, or societal practice. In general, sustainability is understood as a form of intergenerational ethics in which the environmental and economic actions taken by present persons do not diminish the opportunities of future persons to enjoy similar levels of wealth, utility, or welfare.

Evidently, sustainability lies at the heart of the 17 SDGs, and the associated 169 targets and 213 indicators (as of 2023), which are the foundation of this global endeavour. As noted by Harding-Esch / Hywel (2021: 8), "languages are invisible in the SDGs" and, one may add, that legislative discourse and communication remain equally unnamed. This is surprising given that legislative discourse and communication are of central significance in achieving the SDGs in all the 193 UN Member States. It is international players' communicative practices, such as interpreting, accepting, rejecting, and renegotiating language in and around legislative texts and agreements that bring about global, regional and local discourses of sustainability.

This argument is built on the assumption that language and communication should be placed "centre-stage, while not losing sight of the socio-economic context that language use is embedded in" (Mautner 2016: 1). Indeed, generally speaking, for the international community to address, negotiate and act upon regulations of the "Global Public Goods" (cf. Buchholz / Sandler 2021: 488), language is not merely tool, not merely a medium of discourse, but it rather constitutes and is constitutive of the legal realities forged in international law by the players involved (cf. Mautner

2016: 178). Some authors go as far as claiming that the international community "does not exist beyond the discursive level, namely that it materialises only when political agents talk about it, refer to it, and attribute to it certain values, rules, and virtues" (Mitrani 2017: 3).

It should at this point be emphasised that neither the architecture of international law nor the allocation of power across the international community is arbitrary, but at least co-created by discourse. In fact, both the international community and the body of international law could also be organised and discursively realised differently. The status quo is a direct and / or indirect consequence of the socio-historical context out of which the current situation and the identities of its players have emerged. The discursive construction of sustainability by different players across different contexts shows how context-dependent the meaning of the term appears to be and how the indeterminacy of sustainability has meant and continues to mean different things in different contexts.

Being mindful of the context-dependence of sustainability, this contribution stresses the role of language and legislative discourse in realising the SDGs across the UN Member States and argues that language serves not only as a mere instrument of discourse in international law but actively molds the legal frameworks established by its players. Critical analyses of the discursive formations of and around sustainability may reveal the contextual (inter)dependence of the concept's meaning and the indeterminacy resulting from its use across different contexts. In this vein, critical legal linguistics can make recommendations and develop multi-faceted and innovative methodologies on effective ways of monitoring, evaluation and critique of sustainability discourses in local, national and / or regional settings. In doing so, as this contribution will argue, critical legal linguistics could provide questions and answers to the challenges arising from the interaction between the abstract notion of sustainability and the regulatory force of the law.

Section II deals with the challenge of defining sustainability and the inherent indeterminacy associated with the use of the concept in different contexts. Section III will then turn to the power dynamics at play in the incorporation, interpretation and application of sustainability within international law, and how through a systematic analysis of legislative discourse, critical legal linguistics can contribute to a better understanding of how sustainability is translated into legal cultures and policy at the national level. Section IV will finally provide some concluding remarks regarding the interdependence of sustainability norms, legislative discourse, and the socio-political contexts in which international players operate, reiterating the potential for critical legal linguistics to contribute to transformative change and with it to justice and sustainability around the globe.

II. The many faces of sustainability

1. Vagueness and conceptualisation

As mentioned in the previous section, sustainability is notoriously difficult to define for those who look for an all-encompassing meaning of the term. It seems that when a significant term cannot be pinned down to an exclusive and generalisable meaning (cf. Gansel / Luttermann 2020; Endicott 2000), when there seems to be a dispute regarding the meaning of sustainability in relation to a specific scenario, the arena of semantic struggles (Felder 2006) in international law is open. In short, the following discussion should begin with the acknowledgement of the inherent indeterminacy residing in the use and application of the concept of sustainability.

Endicott (2005: 27) has eloquently argued for embracing the "value of vagueness" in normative texts and has raised numerous points, many of which also seem relevant to consider when seeking to discern the many faces of sustainability in the context of the SDGs. He argues that "vagueness is of central importance to the very idea of guiding conduct by norms" (Endicott 2005: 28; cf. Felder 2023), which may particularly hold true for the context of international law and the partly conflicting interests of the parties involved. This communicative indeterminacy arises in the translation of the normative stance of sustainability into the specific legal orders around the globe.

Notably, some players seem to have more power to define a term, such as sustainability, than others do. For instance, the negotiation of trade agreements as is visible in the United States-Mexico-Canada Agreement (USMCA) may reflect power imbalances, with one player pushing towards their preferred interpretation of sustainability by demanding the inclusion of specific provisions related to environmental protection (cf. Congressional Research Service 2023). Or, in Kritsiotis' (1998: 400) words,

> [o]ne does not need to cast the net too far afield in the life time of the United Nations to retrieve evidence which suggests that international law is a language subsued-by power.

Some actors hold a greater degree of power over others, not only in terms of their ability to select specific linguistic items included in agreements, but also in their capacity to determine the interpretation and application of such language. This power of strong players to veto on or to override the inclusion and interpretation of linguistic items may have real-life consequences regarding the sensitive architecture of international obligations towards sustainability. For instance, power imbalances between players may lead to strong players insisting on the inclusion of specific linguistic expressions, while objecting to incorporating others.

In doing so, strong players are able to use legal language with a view to steering the interpretation of individual terms or entire provisions in trade agreements and similar legal frameworks to exert control over the regional sustainability discourses so that expected outcomes in interpretation align more closely with their own political and economic interests in a specific region. This, in turn, can lead to less powerful players being forced to accept terms and / or interpretations of sustainability that may not align with their own political and economic priorities. It is therefore reasonable to assume that the relationship between language and power is one of mutual reinforcement, bringing about dependencies in international relations.

At this point, we may wish to pause and reflect whether the use and the application of sustainability in the light of the SDGs could be arbitrary in the context of international law, that both the (in)determinacy and the (im)precision associated with it could even "bring with them forms of arbitrariness" (Endicott 2005: 37; cf. Endicott 2014). Those who can unilaterally offset the indeterminacy or precision of sustainability in a given context can therefore be assumed to do so from a position of power. Sustainability in action manifests itself in a space where players are in constant struggle with one another, entering into and withdrawing from alliances. Importantly, rivalries between strong players, such as the United States (US) and the People's Republic of China, are palpable despite or perhaps precisely because of the shared goal of sustainable development.

The question, one may argue, is not necessarily, whether the concept of sustainability will make the race, but *whose* interpretation of sustainability in action will prevail, permeate, and perhaps dominate the international community. Traditionally, while the US have prioritised policies that support industries and businesses while also implementing measures to mitigate environmental impact, China's notion of sustainability is strongly influenced by achieving economic development whilst also addressing social and environmental concerns. That is to say that the notion of sustainability as a common ground of national policies can also be used as a justification for pursuing national interests at the expense of weaker players. The degree to which a specific definition of sustainability is implemented and which measures are adopted at home and overseas is co-modulated by national interests. China's Belt and Road Initiative (BRI) is a fine example of how the notion of sustainability can be utilised by strong players, such as China, by providing sustainable solutions to less powerful players and bringing about dependence of those players through the backdoor:

> To realize the SDGs, we need not only firm commitments, but more importantly, concrete actions. In 2013, President Xi Jinping proposed the Belt and Road Initiative, which offered China's wisdom and solutions to the implementation of the 2030 Agenda. The BRI is committed to enhancing policy, infrastructure, trade, finance, and people-to-people connectivity among countries. The Initiative is highly compatible with the 2030 Agenda in terms of visions, goals and measures, and provides strong support and impetus for the implementation of the SDGs. (Permanent Mission of the People's Republic of China to the UN 2022)

This contribution is not concerned with any one particular player or the bilateral relations across players. However, it is noteworthy that one of the faces of sustainability may be identified with national interests. These interests need not be driven by a selfish pursuit of power only, but by what a certain player deems necessary in accordance to meet certain local needs and requirements. The (in)determinacy and (im)precision of sustainability in action is therefore continuously discursively constructed, both at home and within the international community. This can be best illustrated by comparing unequal players, such as Finland and Pakistan, both of which engage in the interpretation of environmental treaties such as the Paris Agreement and seek to implement concrete measures to respond to different context-specific challenges.

As a consequence of this ubiquity of context-dependence of sustainability measures, the focus of this contribution is therefore necessarily limited. It is limited to the discursive links between the 2030 Agenda for Sustainable Development, the SDGs and the normative texts in force within the various national jurisdictions. It seeks to provide some answers to the following questions:

i. Can CrALL provide effective monitoring, evaluation and critique of sustainability discourses around the globe?
ii. If so, how?

In my attempt to answer these questions, many of my considerations are influenced by *Legal Linguistics beyond Borders*, a volume edited by Friedemann Vogel (2019), which shows the diversity but also the fragmentation of the field in Europe and beyond. Sustainability is a multidimensional concept. Paradoxically, its application can bring about social, historical, political and / or economic inequality. For instance, the implementation of a one-size-fits-all approach of sustainability could lead to social conflict, political tensions and economic dependence of players in a particular region. Therefore, any implementation of sustainability in action should, inter alia, be accompanied by a careful assessment of the social, political, historical and economic context.

2. Critical Applied Legal Linguistics (CrALL)

This may require critical legal linguists to take a position towards inequality around the globe and not merely to describe those contextual parameters specific to certain regions. The question therefore subsists whether legal linguists should be exclusively concerned with the description of bilateral, plurilateral and / or multilateral treaties and the results of their implementation in any given national jurisdiction. Or whether it would also be reasonable to take into consideration the specific idiosyncrasies of both the legal system at hand, the letter of the law as well as the social realities of the society in which these norms shall be in effect. As previously mentioned, the concept of sustainability becomes meaningful and thus actionable by reference to a specific context. However, the context in which the sustainability of an entity or a process is negotiated,

> rests on the legal fiction of sovereign parity and autonomy, a fiction that collapses in the face of persistent material inequalities and relations of dependence traceable to colonial and neo-colonial pasts and presents […]. (Rajah 2012: 485)

Legal linguistics should not be reduced to an ancillary discipline of law and jurisprudence, it is just as much *legal* linguistics as it is legal *linguistics*. The reason why it seems reasonable to argue for CrALL on the relationship between law and language is best expressed by reference to the distinction between "rule of law" and "rule by law". Jothie Rajah (2012: 487) elaborates that:

> 'Rule by law' is a shorthand signifying the absence of law's capacity to be autonomous from power. If 'rule of law' is, in general, held as exalted, representing an ideal 'law' that operates as a bulwark against power, then 'rule by law' is treated as an instrumentalist deployment of law by power; law in the service of power rather than in the service of 'the people' or 'justice'.

Legal linguistics deals with law. Law, in turn, is at the heart of the social order. It follows that all schools of legal linguistics in one way or another are concerned with the social order, the very fabric of which societies are made. This also means that legal linguists cannot escape questions about what is and what ought to be (cf. Hart 2012) in international law. This is because the use of a specific term or stretch of language can never be autonomous from the power relations out of which language emerges. In fact, language use is often the very result of such power asymmetries. Its interpretation can also never be short of compromise. Legislative incorporation is in itself a process of translation. Translating the notion of sustainability into a national jurisdiction is co-influenced by a nexus of competing social, political and economic interests across more powerful and less powerful groups. Therefore, no one translation, and, importantly, no one interpretation of normative texts can be the same across different jurisdictions even if they were to deal with the same issue, i.e. sustainable food production.

For instance, a recent study conducted by Brumer / Wezel / Dauber / Breland / Grard (2023: 3) found that Austria and Germany differ, inter alia, with regard to the respective implementation of "organic agriculture, which is very developed in Austria and to a lesser extent in Germany." The many faces of sustainability also become visible in prescriptive discourses in which sustainability can be learned like the Queen's English:

> Small and medium food companies need support to learn the 'grammar' of sustainability as well as to integrate sustainability principles at the management level. The sharing and valorisation of best practices could help them in this process (Lafortune / Puch / Mosnier / Fuller / Diaz / Riccaboni / Kloke-Lesch / Zachariadis / Carli / Oger 2021: xii).

Again, sustainability as an overarching concept and sustainability principles as a more (or less) specified basis for action only becomes meaningful in relation to a specific context. Discourses of sustainability are therefore decontextualised from the landscape of international law and recontextualised into a specific national jurisdiction thus allowing for new discourses to emerge (cf. Blommaert 2005: 251). Legal language and communication are not simply a by-product of text trajectories across the players (in)directly involved in legislative incorporation. This is why effective discursive monitoring of the conversion process from the abstract notion of sustainability into the many faces of sustainability on the level of national legislation is reasonable and merits further reflection.

The debate surrounding the measurability of sustainability (cf. Wühle 2023) shows that there is a lack of consenus as to how degrees of sustainability should be operationalised and measured. This is also reflected in the divergent research trends and emphases that have emerged within the (sub)field(s) of sustainability research, e.g., in relation to the social, economic and environmental aspects of sustainability (cf. Ozili 2022).

III. Discourse makes the world go round: monitoring, evaluating and critiquing constructions of sustainability

1. Legal linguistics and the construction of sustainability

The indeterminacy of sustainability also strikes roots in academic research. In their bibliometric analysis of literature reviews, Yamaguchi / Bernardino / Ferreira / Lima / Pascotini / Yamaguchi (2023: 5513f.) found "growing diversification in research areas", with artificial intelligence being the "SDG with the greatest relevance". They also found that while players such as the United Kingdom, the United States and Australia were "the most productive countries in SDG review articles", it was those players who engaged in "intercontinental collaboration" and in "collaboration with developing countries" that showed greater relevance than those who did not. The SDGs "with the highest values of keywords occurrences were health (SDG 3), climate change (SDG 13), food (SDG 2), energy (SDG 7), and water (SDG 6)." In the co-occurrence analysis of keywords such as "technology (SDG 9) and economic growth (SDG 8)" were singled out "as hidden key elements […] with the greatest relevance among the analyzed keywords."

Finally, the authors point out that they were able to observe an "imbalance between the different SDG" with "the main gaps found were for literature reviews on reduced inequalities (SDG 10)", "gender equality (SDG 5)," "oceans, seas and maritime environments (SDG 14) […] and related to peace, justice, and strong institutions (SDG 16)". Yamaguchi / Bernardino / Ferreira / Lima / Pascotini / Yamaguchi (2023: 5513) conclude that "more effective and reliable methods" should be developed in order to allow for the verifying of the evolution of SDG in each area of research." Legal linguistics could provide such methods if it remains mindful of its methodological scope as well as of its limitations. The field has the potential to examine and evaluate systematically how the concept of sustainability is conceptualised, intratextually and contextually represented, and executed in normative texts. This includes investigating the ways in which sustainability is constructed and interpreted by the players, as well as exploring the impacts and consequences of sustainability legislation on various stakeholders.

Introducing the term "jurimetrics", Loevinger (1949: 486) suggested investigating "the patterns of legislative behavior", amongst various other proposals. More than seventy years later, Loevinger's idea could serve as a basis for jurimetric analyses of the complex interdependence of the discursive processes operative in legislative drafting around the globe. Similarly to Yamaguchi / Bernardino / Ferreira / Lima / Pascotini / Yamaguchi (2023: 5513f.)'s bibliometric analysis, systematic analyses of legislative discourse would enable those working in sustainability law and related areas to gain deeper insights into how normative content is incorporated into national jurisdictions. The pervasiveness of sustainability law and sustainability in law is evident in the intertextual embeddedness of sustainability in legal practice, policy-making and organisation discourse (cf. Mautner 2017). In this context, the role of supranational organisations, such as the European Union and related initiatives, such as the Green Deal, should be considered as well as the political discourses reflected in the legislative efforts implementing a specific interpretation of sustainability. It seems that any argument to the contrary is quickly challenged by the difficulty in identifying a single area of law that does not have some connection to the pursuit of sustainable outcomes.

The indeterminacy surrounding sustainability in action brings about chances as well as challenges both of which are relatable to ways of investigating, and perhaps measuring, the discursive construction of sustainability-related legislation. In short, the question is how exactly the normative content of sustainability is lifted out of the global 17 SDGs and, after such decontextualisation, is recontextualised into the concrete local context of the Member State. The words of the SDGs and the respective indicators

> do not themselves tell the whole story. It is only when we look around [...] that a fuller picture of the text's function emerges; when we consider its multimodal quality, including its materiality, when we relate those words to their physical surroundings [...]; and when we trace the links between the text in question and the many other texts and interactions that brought it into being. (Mautner 2016: 48)

Close reading of the references made to the attributive adjective *sustainable* in the indicators reveals that Mautner's point of the embeddedness of texts also very much applies to the concept of sustainability in the SDGs. Consider, for instance, the following uses of sustainable as used in the indicators:

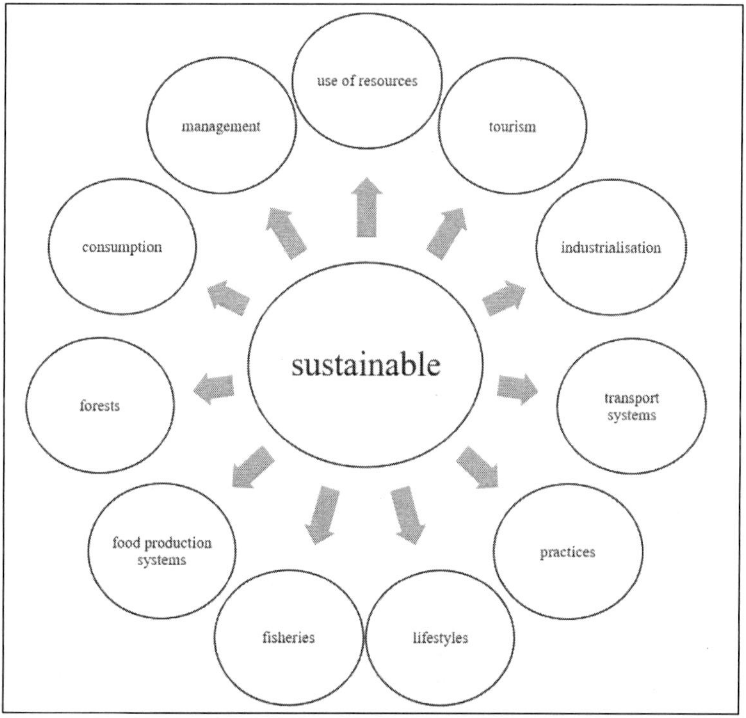

Fig. 1: Use of sustainable in the SDG indicators (United Nations 2023)

2. The role of digitalisation

It becomes clear in the examples above that due to its multi-facetedness sustainability cannot be viewed as a universally applicable concept that is self-explanatory and self-evident. Other terms such as digital sustainability and sustainable digitalisation can also be used to illustrate how the concept of sustainability lacks specificity and how context does not necessarily provide more clarity. It could be argued that the abstract concept of sustainability is first translated into a specific legal culture, which, in turn, shapes the language used to express, enact and transform sustainability in action.

For instance, the notion of *sustainable* digitalisation may, inter alia, be associated in one legal culture with the maintenance of harmonised standards of data collection, processing, and storage with a view to protecting individuals' privacy rights, e.g., in the European Union. While the US seem to take a more decentralised approach which is more open to balancing privacy protection with business interests and the prospect of innovation (cf. U.S. Chamber of Commerce 2019), Chinese legal culture focuses on national security and state control over data management rather than the protection of citizens' privacy rights (cf. He 2023). Based on this divergence of interests, one may argue that the notion of sustainability is translated into European, American, or Chinese legal cultures (cf. Piszcz / Sierocka 2020: 535), inter alia, and subsequently contextualised in relation to digitalisation and privacy rights.

In addition, it could be argued that language shapes players' understanding and interpretation of the concept of sustainability, by framing it in particular ways and imbuing it with certain values and meanings pretextually operative (cf. Widdowson 2004). This highlights the significance of examining the interplay between the discursive and the cultural dimensions of sustainability as well as the ways in which language use and interpretation can influence sustainability in action with regard to a specific context, such as digitalisation. Şerban / Stefan / Potočnik / Moxon (2020) describe digitalisation as "the use of digital tools and opportunities, but also to the social phenomenon of the increasing importance of digital technology, mass communication and online spaces and communities". This may also raise questions and concerns relating to the varying degrees of digitalisation around the globe and the issues associated with it.

On a global level, the road towards digitalisation should therefore have speed limits, such as safeguard mechanisms to protect the environment, human rights, democracy, data control, quality of life and more. In a nutshell, the language-law nexus should shift to the forefront of the discussion. While many may agree on what constitutes a sustainable entity or a sustainable practice, it remains unclear how digitalisation as a process (or as a product) should be expressed to achieve a specific sustainable outcome through legislative norm setting. There is a justifiable need for sustainable practices and management of digital resources and systems to ensure their long-term viability and minimise negative impacts on both the environment and society. However, the issues remain that certain players in the international community are simply more powerful than others, and that certain areas tend to be focused on more frequently or more substantially. What is more, the benefits enjoyed and the challenges faced by players in a specific local, national and / or regional setting can vary greatly, which is also reflected in political compromise forged in legislative drafting.

3. Exploring sustainability legislation through the legal linguistics lens

Broadly speaking, legal linguistics is concerned with the use of legal language and the legal language user in a plethora of contexts. But what exactly is it that legal linguistics can contribute to the task of tracing the links between the SDGs and the legislative texts in the respective national jurisdictions? How, if at all, can legal linguistics provide toolkits to explore the interplay between the legislative texts and the bundles of interactions that emerge in relation to a Member State's specific needs and social, historical, political and / or economic realities? And, how should such insights be put to practical use? The arena in which all of these aspects meet is the law, be it in a house of parliament, in a court or in any other context in which the law is operative, since nothing and no one can escape the Midas touch of the law: "Just as everything King Midas touched turned into gold, everything to which the law refers becomes law, i.e. something legally e x i s t i n g" (Kelsen 1945: 161, original emphasis). Building on Laclau / Mouffe (1985), one may argue that within legislative discourse in and around sustainability the construction of meaning is an ongoing and unstable process, which results in identity being contingent to change.

In this context, Hollway (1984: 233) contends that various positions become available to individuals as they engage with one another through the meanings generated in discourse. The possible meanings of sustainability in relation to actors and practices can thus never arrive at an absolute, factual, foundational, objective, real or correct endpoint but are, inter alia, constantly (re-)negotiated on the basis of the social, historical, political and / or economic parameters. The reduction of sustainability to a binary distinction between sustainable and unsustainable oversimplifies the complex and interconnected nature of sustainability challenges. To fully grasp the complexities reflected in legislation in and around sustainability, it is essential to examine the multifaceted ways in which these factors intersect and influence each other in legislative drafting and interpretation.

So what can legal linguistics do? In order to answer this question, we should carefully consider the individual components of the term CrALL legal linguistics. First, there seems to be a consensus that legal linguistics one way or another focuses on language-related issues in the law. Research in legal linguistics can thus be relevant to any legal context and is not tied to legal texts and practices only. However, a distinction may be made between theoretical legal linguists and applied legal linguists. While those working in Theoretical Legal Linguistics (TLL) tend to focus more on the development of abstract descriptive models of language in and around law, applied legal linguists (ALL) usually take an interest in actual issues and practical solutions at the law-language interface (cf. Green / Green 2022).

As with many other fields and disciplines, fragmentation and / or diversification is common in the course of which certain aspects of academic inquiry are moved to the front. It seems that in legal linguistics there are three trends observable with regard to the use of the term legal linguistics, which merits further discussion, i.e.:

i. Retention of the term legal linguistics
ii. Modification of the term by adding *theoretical* or *applied*
iii. Specification of Critical to Applied Legal Linguistics (i.e. CrALL)

Let us reflect on the use of the terms legal linguistics, Applied Legal Linguistics and CrALL and how these terms may be understood in relation to the constructs of sustainability listed above.

4. Reflection of terms: *Legal* linguistics or legal *linguistics*?

Legal linguistics is an umbrella term and its use may refer to both theoretical and empirical approaches to the study of legal language in context. It remains unclear whether legal linguists are more concerned with theoretical abstraction or empirical analysis, or both, and where / if a line should be drawn. It is also difficult to discern whether legal linguistics should be conceived as *legal* linguistics or legal *linguistics*. Or, in other words, how much weight should be given to the study of language and how much to the study of law and where and how exactly the interdisciplinary characteristics of the discipline comes in. In contrast, the term Applied Legal Linguistics seems to be more suitable in that it captures, inter alia, the hands-on practical perspective on legal language in use. For instance, it may be argued that applied legal linguists do not ponder on legal language use in the comfortability of the ivory tower, but venture off into the unknown territory of the law as enacted, applied and fought over. Applied legal linguists work with real-life language data in legal settings and contexts where the law is negotiated, e.g., in hospitality law, regulating "a global, multilingual, and diverse sector in which territorial legislation meets cross-border interactions" (Green / Varburgh 2024: 289).

Theoretical legal linguists tend to stay in, but the work they do is not less valuable. The success of legal linguistics as a field hinges on its ability to foster collaboration between those who are engaged in theoretical inquiry and those who are committed to practical implementation. To achieve its goals, legal linguistics must not only generate innovative ideas and theoretical frameworks but also develop practical tools that can actually be used by legal practitioners, policymakers, and other stakeholders. For instance, the Konstanz Information Miner (KNIME), a data analytics, reporting and integration platform (cf. Berthold / Cebron / Dill / Gabriel / Kötter / Meinl / Ohl / Thiel / Wiswedel 2009), could be used to produce a more holistic perspective on sustainability in legislation. The global sustainability discourse is not only tangible linguistically by which statements find their way into it but also where there are "breaches, boundaries, and restrictions" (Spitzmüller / Warnke 2011: 63) across legal cultures and national jurisdictions that influence which processes and products are constructed as sustainable.

Such comparative discourse analyses of legislation and other relevant materials also requires a willingness to bridge the gap between theory and practice, and to adapt to the evolving needs and contexts of legal decision-making in relation to sustainability and other key concepts. What sets CrALL apart is the assumption that there is no such thing as legal language and communication without power relationships, and where power relationships emerge there is potential for inequality to arise. Finally, critical legal linguists usually accept the challenge to explore and detect how ideologies and power structures are obscured and / or disguised in legal language and communication and what the real-life effects of such asymmetries may be. By upholding rigorous ethical standards and conducting research with integrity, legal linguists can help to ensure that their work contributes to positive social change and the advancement of human rights. Returning to the question to which extent legal linguistics can provide toolkits in relation to legislative drafting in the context of the SDGs and the 2030 Agenda (cf. United Nations 2015, 2023), one's conclusion could be that it heavily depends on the perspective a legal linguist adopts. Mautner (2016: 37f.) has provided a helpful list of junctures for those who wish to follow a critical approach:

i. Defining a problem
ii. Declaring an interest

iii. Collecting data and preparing data
iv. Examining linguistic detail
v. Interpreting findings
vi. Applying findings

5. Sustainable research on sustainability in legal linguistics

From the perspective of critical legal linguistics, the problem in relation to sustainability is complex in many a regard. First, the concept is open to interpretation and the divergence in its use across UN Member States can yield very different results. Therefore, the implementation of sustainable food production systems materialise differently in Ethiopia than in the United Kingdom, because the UK takes an interest in high-tech solutions, such as weeding robots, granular drones and advanced satellite imaging, inter alia (cf. Department for International Trade 2019). What may be considered a sustainable use of resources, a sustainable forest, sustainable tourism or sustainable consumption in one Member State can barely be used as a blueprint for another. Secondly, it is challenging to define the specific context-dependent issues at hand and to develop a clear understanding of the multi-facetted nature of sustainability in the rich contexts available. What is more, it remains a challenge to determine those actions or practices, which align with sustainability in one Member State that are perhaps not regarded as sustainable in another.

The collection and preparation of data in sustainability research generally and critical discourse analysis specifically might also pose a challenge. This is because the varying interpretations of the concept could make it harder to develop a consistent and standardised framework to measure the sustainable and tell it from the unsustainable. As some of the examples in previous sections have shown, the different interpretations of sustainability across different Member States are brought about by different political priorities set by Member States, which could, in turn, affect how data is collected, prepared and analysed. This might also hold true for analyses in CrALL, since different legal orders do not only conceptualise sustainability differently, but they also apply different standards of sustainability within the different subdomains. The many faces of sustainability tend to be realised within the idiosyncrasies of a specific legal culture but they also manifest in the characteristics of the legal language system operative in a specific local, national and / or regional setting.

Critical legal linguists can not only make a contribution to "ensuring a high quality standard of the law throughout its creation" (Lorz 2019: 7) by aiding the legislation process, but they can also assist in monitoring, evaluating and critiquing discourses in and around the law in relation to specific issues. One promising avenue toward achieving this aim might involve drawing on insights from "corpus-assisted discourse studies," an interdisciplinary approach that can shed light on the underlying mechanisms driving discourses (Gillings / Mautner / Baker 2023: 1). In addition to methodological considerations, legal linguistics should join hands around the globe, regardless with which school of legal linguistics they identify. This also entails that future legal linguists should commit to and engage in global partnership and cooperation in research networks, such as the International Language and Law Association (ILLA), the Austrian Association for Legal Linguistics (AALL) or the International Association for Forensic and Legal Linguistics (IAFLL). Finally, in conducting research in legal linguistics across UN Member states, it is important to ensure that such research is sustainable in the sense that it does not lead to a depletion of resources or have a negative impact on society.

IV. Concluding remarks

Critical legal linguistics can contribute to sustainability research in various ways. The most promising prospect being that it can monitor, describe and evaluate the construction of sustainability-related legislation, and provide systematic analysis of legislative discourse on a local, regional and global level. It can also provide deeper insights into how normative content is incorporated into national jurisdictions, by making legislative discourses comparable. Critical legal linguistics has the potential to unravel the discursive processes underlying the context-based interpretation and application of local, regional and global level sustainability norms.

In doing so, legal linguists should not only be concerned with a structural description of legal language, but should be mindful of data available on different players' social, technological, economic and political priorities as well as factual capabilities. The contribution also sought to demonstrate how the multifaceted concept of sustainability with its diverse applications across Member States shows the interconnectedness of different actors, different factors and contexts. It discussed some issues with defining sustainability and how the indeterminacy of the term can be a basis for both co-operation and conflict within the international community. It was argued that the many meanings of sustainability are central to the idea of guiding conduct by norms, and that powerful players are likely to define sustainability in a way that reflects their interests.

China's Belt and Road Initiative was used as an example to illustrate how sustainability in action can be repurposed in this way. It was argued that sustainability in action should be accompanied by careful assessments of the social, political, historical, and economic context to avoid causing conflicts, social inequality, and economic dependence of developing countries. This is why it was questioned whether legal linguists should be exclusively concerned with the description of treaties or also consider the different legal systems and the social realities at hand. The incorporation of the concept of sustainability into national jurisdictions is complex. It involves translating this abstract notion into a specific context and is influenced by a nexus of at times competing social, political, and economic interests on various levels, which are interdependent.

Critical legal linguistics can make a valuable contribution to transformative change by tracing and making explicit the links between the SDGs and legislative texts in national jurisdictions. Research perspectives differ with regard to research focus and this also applies to legal linguistics. When using the terms *legal linguistics*, *Applied Legal Linguistics*, and *Critical Applied Legal Linguistics* in relation to sustainability it is therefore important to take into consideration the role of power relationships in legislative discourse and communication. In this context, it was suggested to carefully consider "power over" and "power of discourse" (Mautner 2016:

178) in relation to sustainability and how the struggle for sustainability is also embedded and reflected in power struggles. It is concluded that critical, interdisciplinary and systematic analyses of sustainability legislation through the lens of legal linguistics may offer a fruitful pathway towards transformative change.

V. References

Berthold, Michael R. / Nicolas Cebron / Fabian Dill / Thomas R. Gabriel / Tobias Kötter / Thorsten Meinl / Peter Ohl / Kilian Thiel / Bernd Wiswedel. 2009. KNIME – The Konstanz Information Miner Version 2.0 and Beyond. *ACM SIGKDD Explorations Newsletter* 11, 26-31.

Blommaert, Jan. 2005. *Discourse. A Critical Introduction.* Cambridge: Cambridge University Press.

Buchholz, Wolfgang / Todd Sandler. 2021. Global Public Goods. A Survey. *Journal of Economic Literature* 59 (2), 488-545.

Congressional Research Service. 2023. *U.S.-Mexico-Canada (USMCA) Trade Agreement*. https://sgp.fas.org/crs/row/IF10997.pdf. Last accessed 20.12.2023.

Department of International Trade. 2019. *UK Capability in Agri-Tech Engineering*. https://www.greaterlincolnshirelep.co.uk/assets/documents/UK-Capability-Agri-Tech-Final_%281%29.pdf. Last accessed 20.12.2023.

Encyclopaedia Britannica. 2023. *Sustainability*. https://www.britannica.com/science/sustainability. Last accessed 20.12.2023.

Endicott, Timothy. 2000. *Vagueness in Law*. Oxford: Oxford University Press.

Endicott, Timothy. 2005. The Value of Vagueness. In: Vijay Bhatia / Jan Engberg / Maurizio Gotti / Dorothee Heller (Eds.), *Vagueness in Normative Texts*. Bern: Peter Lang, 27-48.

Endicott, Timothy. 2014. The Coxford Lecture. Arbitrariness. *Canadian Journal of Law and Jurisprudence* 27 (1), 49-71.

Felder, Ekkehard (Ed.). 2006. *Semantische Kämpfe. Macht und Sprache in den Wissenschaften*. Berlin: de Gruyter.

Felder, Ekkehard. 2023. Empathie und Vagheit in der Rechtssprache. In: Karin Luttermann / Jan Engberg (Eds.), *Popularisierung als Methode der Wissensvermittlung in der Rechtslinguistik / Popularisation as a Method of Knowledge Mediation in Legal Linguistics*. Berlin: Lit, 83-97.

Gansel, Christina / Karin Luttermann (Eds.). 2020. *Nachhaltigkeit. Konzept, Kommunikation, Textsorten*. Berlin: Lit.

Gass, Robert. 2011. *What is Transformation? And how it advances Social Change*, 1-48. http://stproject.org/wp-content/uploads/2012/03/What_is_Transformation.pdf. Last accessed 20.12.2023.

Gillings, Mathew / Gerlinde Mautner / Paul Baker. 2023. *Corpus-Assisted Discourse Studies*. Cambridge University Press. Cambridge.

Green, Daniel / Luke Green (Eds.). 2022. *Contemporary Approaches to Legal Linguistics*. Vienna: Lit.

Green, Daniel / Januš Chaim Varburgh. 2024. Review Article of Hospitality Law. Managing Legal Issues in the Hospitality Industry (Wiley 2017). *Journal for the Semiotics of Law – Revue internationale de Sémiotique juridique* 37, 283-291.

Harding-Esch, Philip / Coleman Hywel. 2021. Introduction. Languages and the Sustainable Development Goals after Covid-19. In: Philip Harding-Esch / Coleman Hywel (Eds.), *Language and the Sustainable Development Goals*. London: British Council. 64-76. https://www.teachingenglish.org.uk/sites/teacheng/files/ L024_EnglishforEducation Systems_DakarConferenceProceedings_Web_FINAL_April2021.pdf. Last accessed 20.12.2023.

Hart, Herbert L. A. 2012. *The Concept of Law*. Oxford: Oxford University Press.

He, Alex. 2023. State-Centric Data Governance in China. *Centre for International Governance Innovation Papers* 282, vi-20. https://www.cigionline. org/static/documents/no.282.pdf. Last accessed 20.12.2023.

Hollway, Wendy. 1984. Gender Difference and the Production of Subjectivity. In: Julian Henriques / Wendy Hollway / Cathy Urwin / Couze Venn / Valerie Walkerdine (Eds.), *Changing the Subject. Psychology, Social Regulation and Subjectivity*. London: Methuen, 227-263.

Kelsen, Hans. 1945. *General Theory of Law and State*. Cambridge: Harvard University Press.

Kritsiotis, Dino. 1998. The Power of International Law as Language. *California Western Law Review* 34 (2), 398-409.

Laclau, Ernesto / Chantal Mouffe. 1985. *Hegemony and Socialist Strategy*. London: Verso.

Lafortune, Guillaume / María Cortés Puch / Aline Mosnier / Grayson Fuller / María Diaz / Angelo Riccaboni / Adolf Kloke-Lesch / Theodoros Zachariadis / Eugenio Carli / Antoine Oger. 2021. *Europe Sustainable Development Report 2021. Transforming the European Union to Achieve the Sustainable Development Goals. SDSN, SDSN Europe and IEEP*. Paris. https://www.idos-research.de/en/others-publications/article/europe-sustainable-development-report-2021-transforming-the-european-union-to-achieve-the-sustainable-development-goals/. Last accessed 20.12.2023.

Loevinger, Lee. 1949. Jurimetrics. The Next Step Forward. *Minnesota Law Review* 33 (5), 455-493. https://scholarship.law.umn.edu/mlr/1796. Last accessed 20.12.2023.

Lorz, Alexander. 2019. Creating Law with Language. Crossing Borders and Connecting Disciplines from the Perspective of Legislative Practice. In: Friedemann Vogel (Ed.), *Legal Linguistics Beyond Borders. Language and Law in a World of Media, Globalisation and Social Conflicts Relaunching the International Language and Law Association (ILLA)*. Berlin: Drucker & Humblot, 5-8.

Mautner, Gerlinde. 2016. *Discourse and Management*. London: Palgrave.

Mautner, Gerlinde. 2017. Organizational Discourse. In: Gerlinde Mautner / Franz Rainer (Eds.), *Business Communication. Linguistic Approaches*. Berlin: de Gruyter, 609-628.

Mitrani, Mor. 2017. The Discursive Construction of the International Community. Evidence from the United Nations General Assembly. *KFG Working Paper Series* 78, 1-29. https://www.polsoz.fu-berlin.de/en/v/transformeurope/publications/workingpaper/wp/wp78/WP_78_WEB_new.pdf. Last accessed 20.12.2023.

Ozili, Peterson K. 2022. Sustainability and Sustainable Development Research around the World. *MPRA Paper* 115767, 1-27. https://mpra.ub.uni-muenchen.de/115767/1/MPRA_paper_115767.pdf. Last accessed 20.12.2023.

Permanent Mission of the People's Republic of China to the UN. 2022. *Jointly Advancing the Belt and Road Initiative and the 2030 Agenda for Global Sustainable Development.* http://un.chinamission.gov.cn/eng/chinaandun/economicdevelopment/202209/t2020915_10766230.htm. Last accessed 20.12.2023.

Piszcz, Anna / Halina Sierocka. 2020. The Role of Culture in Legal Languages, Legal Interpretation and Legal Translation. *International Journal for the Semiotics of Law – Revue internationale de Sémiotique juridique* 33, 533-542.

Rajah, Jothie. 2012. *Authoritarian Rule of Law Legislation, Discourse and Legitimacy in Singapore*. Cambridge: Cambridge University Press.

Reisigl, Martin. 2017. The Discourse-Historical Approach. In: John Flowerdew / John Richardson (Eds.), *The Routledge Handbook of Critical Discourse Studies*. London: Routledge, 44-59.

Șerban, Adina Marina / Veronica Stefan / Dunja Potočnik / Dan Moxon. 2020. *Social Inclusion, Digitalisation and Young People*. https://pjpeu.coe.int/documents/42128013/47261953/053120+Study+on+SID+Web.pdf/0057379c-2180-dd3e-7537-71c468f3cf9d. Last accessed 20.12.2023.

Spitzmüller, Jürgen / Ingo Warnke. 2011. *Diskurslinguistik. Eine Einführung in Theorien und Methoden der transtextuellen Sprachanalyse*. Berlin: de Gruyter.

United Nations. 2015. *The 17 Goals*. https://sdgs.un.org/goals. Last accessed 20.12.2023.

United Nations. 2023. *SDG Indicators. Global Indicator Framework for the Sustainable Development Goals and Targets of the 2030 Agenda for Sustainable Development*. https://unstats.un.org/sdgs/indicators/indicators-list/. Last accessed 20.12.2023.

U.S. Chamber of Commerce. 2019. *U.S. Chamber's Model Data Privacy Legislation.* https://www.uschamber.com/technology/data-privacy/us-chambers-model-data-privacy-legislation. Last accessed 20.12.2023.

Vogel, Friedemann (Ed.). 2019. *Legal Linguistics Beyond Borders. Language and Law in a World of Media, Globalisation and Social Conflicts Relaunching the International Language and Law Association (ILLA).* Berlin: Drucker & Humblot, 5-8.

Widdowson, Henry G. 2004. *Text, Context, Pretext. Critical Issues in Discourse Analysis*. Oxford: Blackwell.

Wühle, Michael. 2023. *Making Sustainability Measurable. A Practical Book for Sustainable Living and Working*. Cham: Springer.

Yamaguchi, Natália Ueda / Eduarda Gameleira Bernardino / Maria Eliana Camargo Ferreira / Bruna Pietroski de Lima / Mauro Renato Pascotini / Mirian Ueda Yamaguchi. 2023. Sustainable Development Goals. A Bibliometric Analysis of Literature Reviews. *Environmental Science and Pollution Research* 30 (3), 5502-5515.

Zerssa, Gebeyanesh / Debela Feyssa / Dong-Gill Kim / Bettina Eichler-Löbermann. 2021. Challenges of Smallholder Farming in Ethiopia and Opportunities by Adopting Climate-Smart Agriculture. *Agriculture* (11), 1-25.

List of abbreviations

AALL	Austrian Association for Legal Linguistics
ALL	Applied Legal Linguistics
BRI	Belt and Road Initiative
CrALL	Critical Applied Legal Linguistics
ILLA	International Language and Law Association
KNIME	Konstanz Information Miner
SDG	Sustainable Development Goals
TLL	Theoretical Legal Linguistics
UN	United Nations
UNGA	United Nations General Assembly
US	United States

Antonio Lazari

The European Union Governance in the Regulation of Digital Data

Abstract

The heralded 'digital tsunami' is the result not only of the opportunities provided by technology but also the fact that personal data are drawn into the omnivorous orbit of security companies and organisations. A new space has been constituted which is hard to define according to the traditional frames of public / private reference. In this contribution we will comparatively analyse some solutions offered by the great political and legal models. Ultimately, the new giant repositories of information increase social vulnerability, not merely in the manner that is frequently flagged, as tools to control people. The concentration of growing databases of information organised by various public and private entities offers the opportunity to utilise this information for purposes other than which they were created for. This is not a question of the traditional individual aspects of personal privacy. As we have seen in this study, it covers a further, wider social and political spectrum concerning democratic life.

Compared to the Chinese sovereignist vision and the jagged and mercantilist US idea of digital security, the European Union proposes a conception closely linked to the jurisprudence of the CJEU about the essence of fundamental rights. Consequently, the primordial questions which emerge when studying cybersecurity ("Two questions always hang in the air either explicitly or implicitly: Security of what? And security from whom?") must be approached in a complex, comparative and axiological way, underlining that cybersecurity refers public goods in opposite to private properties and that the organisations and bodies designated to protect them must be subject to the scrutiny of constitutionally relevant rules, lest they become genuine Cyber Leviathans.

I. Prologue

In the light of recent events concerning coronavirus contagion containment measures, the importance of the security issue, understood as safeguarding of life on the one hand, and security applied to the personal identity of citizens on the other, has been emphasised. The arguments and conclusions here concerning cybersecurity may be applied and are also valid *mutatis mutandis* to the comparative dynamics of the protection of individual rights before public and / or private powers: "*a new form of (digital) private power has now arisen due to the massive capability of organizing content and processing data*" (De Gregorio 2021: 42; italics in original). Initially, the issue was about cybersecurity. The large-scale attack of the WannaCry virus infected over 230,000 computers in more than 150 countries, affecting the operations of railways, healthcare systems, telecommunications operators, and businesses throughout Europe. One month later, there was another major cyber-attack, NotPetya, and at the beginning of 2020, critical hardware vulnerabilities were reported.

In addition to these highly visible events, a huge army of individuals are constantly trawling the web in search of weaknesses with a view to undermining the confidentiality, integrity and availability of our valuable digital assets. The level of complexity and the scale of such attacks are constantly increasing. The vulnerability of our personal devices is also linked to collective and state vulnerability, requiring complex cybersecurity systems. Hybrid threats have been used, combining cyber-attacks with online misinformation to interfere in the decision-making processes of our liberal democracies. Today, cyber-attacks have the injurious capacity to cause loss of human life, as critical security systems, such as planes or cars, become dependent on digital technologies.

There are two focal points to this contribution: on the one hand, the need to defend the cybernetic community from so-called cyber-attacks, portrayed in the edifying documentary film "The Defenders" in 2017. Another coordinate that is closely linked to this first need emerges in another film:

"Snowden" by Oliver Stone, from 2016. In his speech to the European Parliament, Edward Snowden described the *Five Eyes Network* as a supranational intelligence organisation that did not respond to state laws in their respective countries. The 2019 film "The Great Hack" depicts another tableau from the dark side of social media following the 2016 US Presidential Elections. Unless greater scrutiny and control are developed alongside increased technological capacities in the application of law and intelligence services, freedom and democracy are in danger because this unchecked increase in technology constitutes a true shift in power, and even an anthropological one (cf. Zuboff 2019: 23), beyond the control of parliaments and constitutional systems, which traditionally protect people against state actions.

This contribution deals with aspects of comparative and European law related to the issue of cybersecurity and cyber-attacks, and is divided into two sections: The first will deal with the heterogeneous panorama of state legislation from a comparative and empirical-descriptive perspective. In this context, it should be pointed out that a situation of intrinsic transnationality of the data flow must be matched by a transnational legal solutions. The second section, based on the acknowledged impossibility of tackling the intrinsically transnational issue of cybersecurity by means of exclusively national regulation, will examine normative laws and the underlying governance pursued by the European Union and the Council of Europe, which represents the core argument of this contribution.

Once again, the transnational nature of the protected good, either national security in the Chinese model, or the protection of fundamental rights in the European conception, has to be shaped into an openness of dialogue if it is not to run the risk of building cybernetic Golems (cf. Bygrave 2014: 108f.). Firstly, we shall analyse the non-viability of a purely national solution that offers only a limited horizon with regard to an issue without borders *per se*.

II. National Legislation within the European Union

Within the European Union, and European territory in general, the legal situation was extremely heterogeneous prior to the intervention of European legislators and judges. A brief comparison highlights the scarce and generally incomplete legislation prior to EU regulation. Comparative research also reveals progressive convergence in the issue of cybersecurity and the protection of digital data, originating in EU legislation, in addition to a greater degree of coherence and internal effectiveness for each national system.

In France, the most relevant act in this issue passed on 15 January 1988, *Loi Informatique et Libertés* n. 78, of January 1978, was repealed by Act 2018/273 of 20 June 2018, which transposes the General Data Protection Regulation 2016/679 (hereinafter GPDR);[1] and *La loi sur la securité des réseaux et systèmes d'information*, n. 2018/133 transposes the Network Information Service Directive 2016/1148 (hereinafter NIS).[2] The preceding regulation was based on a set of administrative and criminal laws, wherein complaints for damage were regulated by article 1240 of the *Code Civil*. In reality, national regulations with regard to cybersecurity are based on two key texts: the 2013 White Paper on security and national defence on the one hand, and the 2015 national strategy for digital security on the other. The transposition of the GDPR has already led to several sentences: on 16 November 2016, the Paris Court of Appeal sentenced a hacker for obtaining, using and selling another user's personal data; on 12 August 2016, the Paris Regional Court sentenced an individual for supplanting another user's identity. Furthermore, the *Commission Nationale de l'Informatique et des Libertés* has multiple investigations underway and has demanded vast sums in compensation.[3]

---

[1] LOI No. 2018-493 de 20 June 2018, *relative à la protection des données personnelle.*

[2] LOI No. 2018-133 de 26 de February de 2018, *sur la securité des réseaux et systèmes d'information.*

[3] The most relevant fine has been undertaken against Google for an amount of fifty million euros. https://www.cnil.fr/sites/default/files/atoms/files/san-2019-001_21-01-2019.pdf (Last access 12.12.2022).

In Italy, potential damages compensation lawsuits are regulated in accordance with article 2050 of the *Codice Civile*. In terms of criminal law, Legislative Decree 231/2001 and *Legge* 48/2008 have been passed with regard to cybercrimes. The General Data Protection Regulation was transposed by means of Act 101/2018,[4] whereas the NIS Directive was enacted by means of a Law passed on 18 May 2018.[5] As a consequence of the transposition of the key EU legislation, up to five ministries (economic development, infrastructure and transport, economy, health, and the environment) have been designated as "NIS competent authorities", each one responsible for one or more areas of specialisation. This model is halfway between the highly centralised French system, with just one competent authority, and the decentralised schemes of Scandinavian countries such as Sweden, where regulatory and supervisory tasks related to cybersecurity are attributed to a series of major public sector agencies. One significant figure is the 960,000 € fine imposed by the *Autorità Garante della Privacy* on the country's largest telephone company TIM for illegally processing a customer's personal details and failing to report an incident in the data protection of its customers in the year 2013.[6] The second civil section of the Court of Cassation, in its decree 17665 published on 5 July 2018, explained the distinction between personal data and merely identification data, clarifying that the scope of the reporting obligation encompasses the data collection form.[7]

---

[4] "Disposizioni per l'adeguamento della normativa nazionale alle disposizioni del Regolamento (UE) 2016/679 del Parlamento europeo e del Consiglio, del 27 aprile 2016, relativo alla protezione delle persone fisiche con riguardo al trattamento dei dati personali, nonché alla libera circolazione di tali dati, e che abroga la direttiva 95/46/CE (Regolamento generale sulla protezione dei dati)", d.lgs. n. 101 del 2018, published on 4 September 2018, has entered into force on 19 September 2018.

[5] D.Lgs. 65/2018 – Attuazione Direttiva (UE) NIS 2016/1148, Attuazione della direttiva (UE) 2016/1148 del Parlamento europeo e del Consiglio, del 6 luglio 2016, recante misure per un livello comune elevato di sicurezza delle reti e dei sistemi informativi nell'Unione.

[6] Two are the main measures adopted by the Guarantor: Ordinanza ingiunzione nei confronti di Telecom Italia S.p.A., 16 maggio 2018, n. 297 del 16 maggio 2018, and Ordinanza ingiunzione nei confronti di Telecom Italia s.p.a. – 16 maggio 2018, n. 296 del 16 maggio 2018.

[7] Civile Ord. Sez. 2 Num. 17665/2018, 05/07/2018.

Within the context of Britain, current regulations are once again governed by the European Union: the 2018 Data Protection Act, which transposes the GDPR; the 2013 Communication Act; and the 2018 Network and Information System Regulation, which complies with the obligations derived from the NIS directive. The UK's Information Commissioner's Office has issued cautions and hefty fines, as in the case of Bounty (ICO 2019).

In Germany, cybersecurity is regulated by means of the IT-*Sicherheitsgesetz* of 25 July 2015, the *Kreditwesengesetz* of 1998, and the Wertpapierhandelsgesetz of 2016, and by a series of military protocols. The Federal Law *Bundesdatenschutzgesetz* (known as BDSG), which transposed the GDPR, was enacted in July of 2017, coming into force on 25 May 2018. Of particular importance is the decision of the Bonn Regional Court regarding the application of the GDPR issued on 30 May 2018 No. 10 O 171/18,[8] in which it holds that the GDPR fundamentally applies a principle of minimisation of data collection and, therefore, the obligations established by the policy of ICANN of gathering data even from third parties, who perform purely technical functions, breaches EU legislation.

In Spain, a raft of regulations has been brought in, comprising chiefly Decree Law 12/2018 transposing the NIS Directive, encompassed in the Cybersecurity Code of Law, published by INCIBE on 8 January 2019, which has 48 normative interventions of varying order,[9] following the recent entry into force of Organic Act 3/2018, of 5 December, governing Personal Data Protection and the guarantee of digital rights.

As the analysis of the extreme inconsistency of single municipal laws in the European Union showed, there was an urgent need for a uniform supranational regulation mainly in the legislative form, as we will see below.

---

[8] Tribunal Regional de Bonn, 30 May 2018 No. 10 O 171/18. Before the entry into force of the GDPR Regulation, the Administrative Court of Karlsruhe had already ruled on its scope (judgment of 6 July 2017, No. 10 K 7698/16).

[9] For a more comprehensive view of the degree of compliance with the GPDR see the report of the European Data Protection Board: http://www.europarl.europa.eu/meetdocs//2014_2019/plmrep/COMMITTEES/LIBE/DV/2019/02-25/9_EDPB_report_EN.pdf (Last access 12.2.2022).

III. National Regulations on Cybersecurity outside the European Union

1. Regulation in the United States system

At the end of 2015, after years of long negotiations, Congress passed legislation that allowed companies to voluntarily share information about cybersecurity threats against the federal government and other companies: the Cybersecurity Act. In spite of the requirements for private entities to take measures to eliminate personal information before sharing cybernetic threat indicators, there are critical aspects of the law with regard to companies that potentially violate the privacy rights of people, whilst not necessarily enhancing cybersecurity. Similarly, because the discipline of cybersecurity is not coordinated with the protection of citizens' privacy, American regulations tend not to view cybersecurity as a matter of national security, as we have seen more recently in the reports on Russian interference in the 2016 elections. A broader approach based on national interest will require closer cooperation between the US and other nations, a strategy that did not emerge in the recent adoption of the Cybersecurity and Infrastructure Security Agency Act of November 2018.[10]

This lack of legislative coordination has emerged in the case law of the Supreme Court. The recent Microsoft cases of 17 April 2018, *United States v. Microsoft Corp and Google* in 2017, and *Carpenter v. United States* in 2018,[11] stressed that the original coincidence of interests between the federal government and multinationals has been disintegrating, making way for a progressive conflict between the interests of American multinationals and the aims of the US government in the prosecution of serious crimes. In the Carpenter case, the court held, in a very tight decision drafted by Judge Roberts, that the government had violated the Fourth Amendment of the United States Constitution by accessing records containing the physical locations of cellular telephones without a search warrant. The recent class

---

[10] H.R.3359 – Cybersecurity and Infrastructure Security Agency Act of 2018.
[11] Carpenter vs. United States (2018), No. 16-402, 585.

action lawsuits brought against *Yahoo!*[12], *PayPal*[13], *Chegg*[14] and, in particular, the ruling of 28 January 2019 in the *In re Equifax Securities Litigation*[15], which allowed the majority of claims brought by plaintiffs to survive a motion for dismissal, are signs that cyber-attacks can also be the subject of litigation *inter privatos*.

Furthermore, the case of America cannot be decoded by means of a simplistic approach. In 2018 alone, some states continued to re-evaluate and modify their regulations governing privacy and cybersecurity. In May of that year, the State of Vermont passed an initial law that required data brokers (companies that gather and sell or licence personal information about consumers with whom said companies do not maintain a direct relationship to third parties) to implement an information security programme, inform people that their data are being collected, and give users the option not to participate in data collection. In September, Colorado reinforced its consumer data protection law with a new innovative bill that required "reasonable security procedures and practices" to protect personal identification information. In November, the Ohio Data Protection Act entered into effect (2018 SB 220) as part of the broader CyberOhio initiative aimed at helping companies in Ohio to defend themselves against cybersecurity threats. The Ohio act provides a safe port for companies that implement and maintain "reasonable" cybersecurity controls.

Of particular interest to us is the California Consumer Privacy Act. California's State Legislature passed the California Consumer Privacy Act in 2018, which most experts consider to be the foundation of a future US federal law inspired by the European GDPR model. This legislative measure, which will enter into force on January 1st, 2023, may be considered the strongest piece of US legislation in terms of guaranteeing civil liberties, and it must be read in a broader context that also encompasses the intention of the Supreme Court in its ruling in the Carpenter case of 2018 to limit the

[12] In re Yahoo! Inc. Shareholder Litig., Case No. 17-CV-307054, (Cal. Supp. Ct Jan. 4, 2019).

[13] Sgarlata v. Paypal Holdings, Inc., No. 3:17-cv-06956 (N.D. Cal.).

[14] In re Heartland Payment Sys. Sec. Litig., No. 09-1043, (D. N.J. December 7, 2009).

[15] In re Equifax, Inc. Secur. Litig., Case No. (N.D. Ga. Jan. 28, 2019).

interventions of state authorities in the private lives of citizens, which in the court case pertained to records of the locations of mobile devices.

2. Regulation in the Chinese system

Firstly, the Chinese Government's Strategy of International Cooperation on Cyberspace, published for the first time by *Xinhua News* in March 2017, sets out the Government's objectives with regard to cybersecurity, international cooperation and the means to achieve its objectives.[16] The first point, although it expresses a progressive stance on sovereignty and security in cyberspace through the permanence of international sovereignty, affirms a partially protectionist vision contrary to any supranational interference in regulations regarding national cyberspace. The fourth section shows the Chinese Government's support for a free and open web, in which all citizens enjoy full rights, access to information, and participation within the parameters established by the laws of cyberspace governance. In other words, China promotes the free movement of information as long as public and national interests are assured.[17] The six points could shape a highly contradictory scenario, but they tend to fairly promote Chinese interests in cyberspace, especially where they allow for possible international governance as long as there is no direct or indirect interference with the citizens of each state, in other words nationally.

Some time ago, the Chinese Government decided to become involved in "control of the narrative over [...] China's rise" (Chi / Dou 2016: 1). China seeks to be fully independent of other countries, gradually developing an idea of cyber-sovereignty. China's Cybersecurity Act of 2016 is designed chiefly to strengthen local networks against malicious pirating and all kinds of cyber-attacks, especially from US servers (cf. Parasol 2018: 69). However, from the view of foreign businesses, this part of the legislation

---

[16] Cybersecurity Administration of China. "International Strategy of Cooperation on Cyberspace", published on 1 march 2017. http://new.xinhuanet.com/english/china/2017-03/01/c1360943715.htm (Last access 12.12.2022).

[17] Cybersecurity Administration of China. "International Strategy of Cooperation on Cyberspace", published on 1 march 2017. http://new.xinhuanet.com/english/china/2017-03/01/c1360943715.htm (Last access 12.12.2022).

would appear to be "a techno-nationalist Trojan horse" (Tiezzi / Shanno 2014: 54). The power given to state authorities by this legislation seems to find weak limits in relation to the protection of key information infrastructure (article 31 of the Cybersecurity Act) and the information and data storage requirements of trading companies (article 37 of that same law).

> China's Cybersecurity Law is masquerading as an attempt to enhance cybersecurity, but it is so much more. The danger is that other countries may adopt a similar approach, in a brazen attempt to gain commercial advantage for indigenous firms, while clearly crossing a legal and regulatory boundary that far surpasses what is required to be considered consistent with best practices. That has already occurred in countries across the world where China has shared its surveillance methodology, especially in Africa. So there are two sides of the cybersecurity legal pendulum – the Chinese version and the EU version. (Wagner 2019)

This legislative measure explicitly sets out the intentions of the Beijing Government to prevent foreign companies from exporting personal data outside its borders, whilst simultaneously putting themselves forward as the only guarantor of protection, which leads to a clear loss of privacy for the sensitive data of China's citizens. The aim of the Government is, therefore, to develop a colossal evaluation network capable of exerting indiscriminate control over personal data (cf. Shakelford / Alexander 2018). Within the Trade in Services Board of GATS (General Agreement on Trade in Services), a complex map has emerged of the different cybersecurity (cf. Lee 2019: 34) strategies regarding (the criticisms levelled against) China's cybersecurity act, and in particular the definitions and rules applied to manage critical information structures, personal information and important data (cf. Mishra 2019). Members of the World Trade Organisation have adopted markedly different stances to criticise China's cybersecurity regulations.

Delegates from the US and Japan have been the most eloquent in their critiques. Japan highlighted the restrictions placed on the data mobility of personal information and the important data compiled by operators of critical information infrastructures. The country's representative pointed out that the definition of critical information infrastructure was excessively broad and vague, which could affect the operations of foreign businesses operating within China's industries, deemed to be open on its GATS list. Japan also held that "foreign operators could be forced to take on the additional burden of setting up a separate server within China in order to store personal information and important data" in violation of China's national treaty of obligations. The Japanese representative raised a series of more specific concerns including uncertainty in terms of the inspection criteria and the scope of the responsibility of web operators. These concerns reflect the criticisms of the US articulated in a separate White Paper published in September, demanding that China does not implement its cybersecurity law (cf. Blume 2018: 804ff.).

The representative of the European Union expressed far more serious concerns. He began by considering that China's cybersecurity law would need to be evaluated with regard to the protection of certain rights. The EU delegates took this opportunity to remind other members that the protection of personal data was a fundamental right enshrined in article 8 of the EU's Charter of Fundamental Rights. Bearing in mind these principles, the European Union only objected to the concept of sensitive data, which its representative claimed was defined in an excessively broad way.[18]

[18] The Brazilian delegate said that "it was very important to examine whether issues such as cybersecurity, data flows or privacy could be addressed under existing WTO rules or whether new rules were needed." China responded to these criticisms by arguing that "the protection of cybersecurity to ensure national security and protect the immediate interests of the general public was of crucial importance and a legitimate regulatory right to which any member was entitled." More specifically, the Chinese representative argued that the previous criticism reflected widespread misunderstandings of its cybersecurity regime. For example, China noted that data localisation was only necessary for critical information infrastructure; security reviews were only required for personal information or important data collected in mainland China; important data only included data important for the Chinese state; mechanisms were in place to allow the cross-border transfer of data; personal information could be transferred after consent had been given; and consent was presumed for international calls, emails and cross-border purchases. Finally, China also objected to the fact that all of its laws were open to comment during the drafting process and that in creating its cybersecurity review system "China had relied on the practice of other WTO members."

3. Regulation in the Socialist Republic of Vietnam

During the meeting of the Services Council in October 2018, various members also criticised Vietnam's cybersecurity bill which came into effect on 1 January 2019. The government of Japan expressed its opposition to the provisions requiring foreign companies to set up an office and a local data server in order to operate in the country, establishing ulterior obligations of national treatment in favour of Vietnam. The US also argued that "it was unclear what types of service providers would be affected or what measures they would have to take to comply". In response, the Vietnamese delegation largely swept aside the question, arguing that they "did not wish to distort the outcome of the discussions in the National Assembly". In its definitive version, the very broad provision regarding the location of servers was replaced by a requirement that only the data of Vietnamese users and "other important data" compiled or generated by Vietnam's cybernetic infrastructure would be stored in the country, along very similar lines to the provisions of Chinese legislation.

Debates about the cybersecurity laws of China and Vietnam within the World Trade Organisation reflect a global conflict between divergent visions with regard to data privacy. On the one hand, there are countries such as China and Vietnam which use an expansive understanding of cyber-sovereignty to justify a more restrictive treatment of cross-border data flows (cf. Kokas 2019). Furthermore, there are countries such as the US which do not contemplate a unified federal legal regime regarding data privacy and cybersecurity. And finally, there are organisations such as the European Union that, in accordance with the General Data Protection Regulation, have acted as guardians – even in the trial phase, as we have seen – of the rights of EU citizens regarding their digital footprint and identity. China's statement that its cybersecurity review system "is based on the practice of other WTO members" uses the European Union's regime to legitimise the more restrictive provisions of its own legislation. Since these debates go far beyond adhesion to GATS lists, it might be worth exploring whether broader dialogue about digital privacy is required, without being disguised in the language of trade law (cf. Kokas 2019: 12).

4. Regulation in the Russian Federation

Finally, along the same strategic line of creating national cyber-sovereignty, the Russian Federation is moving towards constructing a digital iron curtain.

> Certain governments advance strong policy rationales to justify data localisation. Countries such as China and Russia propagate the need for increased sovereign control over domestic cyberspace (or what China has re-branded as cyber sovereignty). (Mishra 2019: 6)

In order to tackle cybernetic threats, and in response to the US's cybersecurity strategy, in April 2019, the Russian Parliament approved the creation of a sovereign internet known as Runet.[19] The controversial project not only involves setting up a domestic web that can function autonomously, but it would also allow the Russian authorities to filter external information and block any content they deem to be undesirable or dangerous. The core plan entails creating a national infrastructure so that, in the event of a cyber-attack, digital walls could be deployed.

5. Legislation in the MENA zone (Middle Eastern and North African Countries)

The majority of Middle Eastern and North African Countries (MENA) are currently embroiled in various conflicts that are leading to economic, social and political decline. The Internet has represented one of the main drivers and tools contributing to the crystallisation of the political situation and the possible diffusion of internal problems. The broad and far-reaching use of social media has not only contributed to regime changes in some cases but has also facilitated the spread of misinformation in critical situations (cf. Finnemore / Hollis 2016). Firstly, the tremendous vulnerability of this area has been broadly shown.

> The history of cyber-attacks reflects the importance of cyber interactions for international relations within the MENA region. One cannot dissociate cybersecurity from geopolitics; and this is especially true for the MENA region,

---

[19] For more information https://tass.com/politics/1053917 (Last access 12.12.2022).

> where cybered conflict is just one of the symptoms of wider geopolitical tensions. (von Finckenstein 2019: 6)

Governments, companies and individuals in the MENA zone have adopted new technologies and digital applications on a large scale in a process known as digitalisation. In order to prevent cyber-attacks, Middle Eastern governments have closed the online space through the application of harsh and oppressive cybercrime laws. Governments throughout the region are drafting such legislation which simply deprives internet users of their basic human rights.

> As demonstrations usually took place on the streets, the virtual space was not a security concern for governments. In this sense, the Arab spring presented the tipping point in MENA media development. To keep the population in check, many governments resorted to restricting online platforms or using new technologies as surveillance tools. (von Finckenstein 2019: 8)

For example, Bahrain's Cybercrime Act, passed in 2014, gives various governmental organisations, including the Interior Ministry and the Public Information Ministry, the capacity to block and censor a wide range of websites (cf. Kausch 2019). No court order is required to censor websites that host content considered to pose a challenge to the government, such as any content published that is critical of Bahrain's government, the royal family, or the status quo in general. A similar form of censorship is found in Egypt's cybercrime law passed in 2018. In accordance with its article 7, any website can be blocked if its content is considered to be a crime by virtue of the law, whenever it is a threat to national security, or endangers the security of the country or its national economy, effectively legalising the blocking of websites.

These laws also facilitate and legalise mass surveillance by the state and foreign governments (cf. Finnemore / Hollis 2016: 470). For example, Egyptian law allows for the violation of its citizens' privacy rights by foreign governments. Article 4 of the law tackles the exchange of data and information between Egypt and foreign countries through foreign affairs and international cooperation ministries within the framework of international, regional or bilateral agreements, or the application of the principle of reciprocity. The article does not include any requirement for the exchange of said information such as the existence of data protection laws in the requesting country or requirements regarding scope, how long information can be held, or the processing of that information.

Some cybercrime laws take things even further, not only criminalising the activities of individuals but also imposing criminal liability on internet service providers (ISP), telecommunications companies and online platforms for the content uploaded by users. Article 2 of Egypt's cybercrime law, for example, requires telecommunications companies to retain and store user data for 180 days. This includes data that allow for the identification of users' "metadata" about the content of their communications, the IP address of their computer and the devices they use. This means that telecommunications providers could be asked to turn detailed information over to the authorities about the communications of users, including information about voice calls, text messages, visits to websites and the use of applications on computers and smartphones. The same article requires telecommunications companies to comply with regulations for any "other data decided by the National Telecommunications Regulatory Authority Board (NTRA)" which means that, based on a decision of the NTRA, companies could be required to compile and retain data not set out by law (cf. Al-Sisi 2018).

The article also broadens the legal entitlement of telecommunications service providers to collect user data, extending this to agents and distributors responsible for commercialising their services. Furthermore, article 2 gives national security authorities the right to access these data, and telecommunications service providers are obliged to offer the technical assistance required to facilitate this access. In other words, the act provides security services with sweeping powers to obtain user data, without limitations or standards.

IV. From Empirical Analysis to Analytical Considerations: Models of Governance

A brief comparison of the different national legal systems has shown the extreme variety – and even fragmentation – of solutions associated with different legal cultures and underlying political strategies. Within the European Union and in Europe in general, the legal situation was extremely heterogeneous before the intervention of European legislators and judges. However, the need for international regulation in relation to such a transnational issue cannot be tackled through a range of legal solutions that are municipal in their scope. Very briefly, there are two emerging tendencies within state legislation: the first tends to offer global solutions by adopting an *omnibus* kind of legislation (this is the case, for example, in the Cybersecurity Act enacted in the People's Republic of China in 2016); the second approach, in contrast, disciplines the issue of cybersecurity by means of a closely articulated raft of rules of several categories, from administrative to trade and even criminal law. In the context of the European Union, the progressive move towards legal harmonisation has implied a simplification of national regulations. It has avoided the balkanisation of such heterogeneous national systems, as in the United States regulations.

Furthermore, this consideration only deals with technical legislative factors. Several indicators point to a crisis at the heart of the emerging area of international law on cybersecurity. Proposals for binding international agreements for the key stakeholders, including China and Russia, have received little enthusiasm from other states and, in general, it seems that they have a limited chance of success. At present, the deficient implementation of the Council of Europe Convention on Cybercrime of 2001[20] and its future updates in a Protocol[21] or other initiatives undertaken by the African Union (the African Union Convention on Cybersecurity and Personal Data

---

[20] Cf. Daskal (2016).

[21] Enhanced International Cooperation on Cybercrime and Electronic Evidence (2019). https://rn.coe.int/summary-towards-a-protocol-to-the-budapestconvention/1680972d07 (Last access 12.12.2022).

Protection of 2014: the so-called Malabo Convention) prove the lack of possibility of imposing a single regulation at the level of international law.

Secondly, states are extremely reluctant to be bound by specific interpretations of controversial legal issues and, therefore, to express their opinion on cybernetic law. So, instead of developing or interpreting laws, state representatives seek refuge in the more ambiguous terms of "legal norms", or they simply find extrajudicial solutions: for example, bilateral extradition agreements or in the preventive stages, various types of cyber commands. The reluctance of states to participate in drawing up international regulations has left a power vacuum, corroborating affirmations that international law fails when it attempts to deal with the modern challenges posed by the rapid development of technology. In response to this tendency, various non-state regulations promoted by sector multinationals have attempted to fill the void, including Microsoft's proposed cybernetic rules (cf. Barlow 1996) and the Tallinn Manual Project (Tallinn Manual on the International Law Applicable to Cyber Warfare 2013). But the inclusion of non-state actors with huge actual power must be very closely examined and modulated at a decision-making level within political arenas, due to the clear conflict of interests that emerges when private tools are used for the purposes of regulation.

Hence, the role of the European Union and the European area (including, therefore, the Council of Europe and the European Court of Human Rights) is crucial to convey and maximise the contribution of multinationals. Comparative law not only deals with the analysis of rules, but with the way in which rules are adopted, which tends towards normative harmonisation. It is important to study the process of adopting, for example, regulations on cybersecurity that are currently being forged with the participation of institutions representing different interests and parties as well corporations of stakeholders. A brief comparative study clearly shows a powerful move towards harmonisation in spaces of EU regulation.

With regard to the regulatory factor, the EU's pursuit of cybersecurity by respecting the fundamental rights of its citizens is particularly relevant (contained within articles 7 and 8 of the EU's Charter of Fundamental

Rights), pursued not only through the adoption of regulations and directives, but also through Action Plans promoted by the European Commission and the case law of the European Court of Justice and the Court of Human Rights with regard to cybernetic identity and cyberspace itself as a place for the protection of virtual and non-virtual individuals. Battles over laws and rights in the 21st century will almost certainly be waged over the protection and circulation of sensitive data.

Given the complexity of cyberspace and the number of stakeholders involved in its management and use, the majority of controlling initiatives came from businesses and civil society, and the role played by states was limited to indirect influence. The models of governance promoted by the states are highly disparate. On the one hand, a number of non-European countries such as the US, Japan, Canada and Australia share the EU's vision of stakeholder governance. They feel that centralised models are ill-suited to decentralised, global, publicly shared communication networks which are largely developed in the private sector. However, they do not agree in their determination of stakeholders. Where the EU recommends the inclusion of all citizens and stakeholders, the US is moving towards a governmental model with strong business participation.

The stakeholder approach is very controversial, on the other hand, in countries such as Russia, China, Iran, Vietnam and India, which defend a centralised and intergovernmental approach. Arguing that Western countries – in particular the US – opt for a dangerous potential regarding management of the internet, they advocate far more governmental participation in cyberspace, such as the International Telecommunication Union (ITU), a UN body. The problem, however, is far more complex than a binary option between private and public, freedom and control (cf. Van Puyvelde / Brantly 2019).

There is an element of transversality that is present not only in the *summa divisio* between the internal and the external, national and international, but also between the public and private, and between factors of military strategy and the protection of fundamental rights – in other words, between security understood as a factor in national defence and in terms of a fundamental right to the safeguarding of cybernetic identity.

V. Europe between Cyber Leviathans: Neo-Liberal and Neo-Marxist Criticism of Current Models of Governance

Two recent analytical proposals – liberal and neo-Marxist – have sifted through the empirical data reported above, with a view to stigmatising the tendency towards a new uncontrolled Leviathan or surveillance capitalism. Firstly, criticisms leveled against a post-modern mandarinate that roots its power in the Confucian belief that decision-making can only be left to the intelligentsia, or a return to illiberal Russian Tsarist sovereignty, should not make us forget that the US has radicalised and intensified the Californian countercultural dynamic. The spirit of Silicon Valley has disdained European tradition and is leading a digital soft-totalitarianism that seeks, in the long term, to eradicate all democratic life in favour of an algorithmic and definitive administration (cf. Buchanan 2017: 5ff.).

Secondly, set against the communist dictatorship that has evolved to create the conditions to establish a perfect digital dictatorship, a new model of voracious and burgeoning capitalism of disproportionate and unprecedented size is being proposed by America's Silicon Valley. Analysis of the Chinese and American cybersecurity acts shows, on the one hand, the emergence of cognitive capitalism of public platforms and a hierarchical institutional structure that governs, without political opposition, a community devoted to the mass consumption of applications (cf. Dunn Cavelty / Egloff 2019). On the other hand, an initial synergy is emerging, a convergence of economic interests between the major technology multinationals and a legislatively defenceless state.

1. Lassalle's Cyber Leviathan

The first neo-liberal thesis has been put forward by Lassalle, who argues that the only alternative to the Cyber Leviathan is a liberal uprising which promotes an agreement between technology and humanity. Lassalle (2019: 24) reasons in terms of Cyber Leviathans and sees the US and China as two examples of them:

> Ambos países lideran los modelos que, desde las corporaciones privadas o el Estado, tratan de fomentar la instauración de una dictadura tecnológica que garantice dos objetivos globales. Por un lado, la maximización de la prosperidad que impulsa la economía cognitiva o del conocimiento y, por otro, la eficiencia del orden que necesita la organización automatizada de nuestras sociedades y el control pacifico de los cambios sociales que están generando las aplicaciones desarrolladas por las tecnologías exponenciales.[22]

The term Cyber Leviathan designates a new concentration of power that, precisely for the sake of security and cybernetic order, encompasses a controlling power that is unprecedented in the history of humanity, obliterating, or depleting at any rate, the modern idea of freedom. Kant's understanding of freedom, visualised in terms of reaching maturity through the exercising of freedom, is powerfully altered by the bewildering data overdose, together with the impossibility of deciphering virtual and actual reality. There is a practical disconnect between democracy and rationality that populism exploits to justify the repudiation of liberalism (cf. Lassalle 2019: 75).

The facilities provided by a new digital world, often liberating us from the heavy burden of having to decide for ourselves, undermine the anthropological basis of post-modern humankind. The fear of losing this technological comfort zone through cyber-attacks lays the foundations for an unprecedented totalitarian experience justifying our relinquishment of emancipation in defence of our own well-being. As Fogel argues, "it is a sovereign whose power is not the sum of men but the formidable network of screens connected by the Internet" (Fogel 2007: 4).

---

[22] Author's translation: Both countries lead the models that, from private corporations or the State, attempt to promote the establishment of a technological dictatorship that has two global aims. On the one hand, the maximisation of prosperity that drives the cognitive or knowledge economy and, on the other, the efficiency of the order that the automated organisation of our societies needs and the peaceful control of the social changes that generate the applications developed by exponential technologies.

Hence, a situation of clear factual and legal disparity is generated between the citizen and the new Cyber Leviathan. We are witnessing a programming scenario that recreates human nature without any legal controls, making it more dependent on an algorithmic mechanism guarded jealously by the technicians "*y que hacen inaccesible dentro de una relación absolutamente desequilibrada entre la plataforma y el usuario*" (Lassalle 2019: 93).[23] We can draw an initial conclusion that is extremely far-reaching.

The problem raised by cyber-attacks is not merely a technical question with regard to technological security; it also relates to the response given in normative and strategic terms to such incursions. "Este escenario abre el camino hacia formas de concentración de la información que podrían instaurar un despotismo algorítmico que canalizara las decisiones humanas hacia la aclamación de un poder irresistible que ofrezca orden y seguridad" (Lassalle 2019: 104). For the protection of our cybernetic identity, as Hobbes theorised in the 17th century, Cyber Leviathans are created in order to manage the deepest recourses of the digital revolution without democratic control or legal interference. In fact, the Leviathan was conceived within the chaos of the Civil War as a biblical sea monster that guarantees the reciprocal relationship between protection and obedience. A crucial point in a new foundational agreement will be how to define or delimit the disproportionate power of the Cyber Leviathan, how to reinterpret the liberal – or even Marxist – idea of cybernetic freedom.

> Vivimos bajo el poder de una tecnología que es el soporte estructural de un capitalismo cognitivo que carece de una gobernanza que gestione los cambios sociales y defina las responsabilidades éticas dentro del proceso. Además, favorece la concentración monolítica del poder al alinear la técnica y la economía y amparar una permanente desregulación de los datos, así como una

---

[23] AT: "[…] and that make it inaccessible within an absolutely imbalanced relationship between the platform and the user."

> ausencia de derechos individuales en la red que impida a las plataformas seguir cartelizando sus servicios y monopolizando la captación de datos sin contraprestación ni control sobre la privacidad. (Lassalle 2019: 117f.)[24]

> Ya sea en su versión china o norteamericana, la preservación futura del orden y la prosperidad solo podría darse bajo la arquitectura de vigilancia y control que el Ciberleviatán promueve a partir de la comunidad electrónica que ha desarrollado dentro de Internet. (Lassalle 2019: 131)[25]

Lassalle's thesis coincides with the analyses put forward by Soshana Zuboff in her study about surveillance capitalism and the top-down bloodless *coup d'état* the technological patriarchy would have staged by denying democracy the right to legally control digital transformation.

2. Zuboff's criticism of surveillance capitalism

Taking the view of a recent Neo-Marxist vision, the term surveillance capitalism describes:

> 1. A new economic order that claims human experience as free raw material for hidden commercial practices of extraction, prediction, and sales; 2. A parasitic economic logic in which the production of goods and services is subordinated to a new global architecture of behavioral modification; 3. A rogue mutation of capitalism marked by concentrations of wealth, knowledge, and power unprecedented in human history; 4. The foundational framework of a surveillance economy; 5. As significant a threat to human nature in the twenty-first century as industrial capitalism was to the natural world in the nineteenth and twentieth; 6. The origin of a new instrumentarian power that asserts dominance over society and presents startling challenges to market democracy; 7. A movement that aims to impose a new collective order based on total certainty; 8. An expropriation of critical human rights that is best

---

[24] AT: "We live under the power of a technology that is the structural support of a cognitive capitalism lacking a governance that manages social changes and defines ethical responsibilities within the process. In addition, it favors the monolithic concentration of power by aligning technology and the economy and protecting a permanent deregulation of data, as well as an absence of individual rights in the network that prevents platforms from continuing to cartelise their services and monopolise the collection of data without consideration or control over privacy."

[25] AT: "Whether in its Chinese or American version, the future preservation of order and prosperity could only occur under the architecture of surveillance and control that Cyber Leviathan promotes from the electronic community it has developed within the Internet."

> understood as a coup from above: an overthrow of the people's sovereignty. (Zuboff 2019: 23)

Zuboff agrees *mutatis mutandis* with Lassalle that:

> Today these rights to privacy, knowledge, and application have been usurped by a bold market venture powered by unilateral claims to others' experience and the knowledge that flows from it. [..] It is about the darkening of the digital dream and its rapid mutation into a voracious and utterly novel commercial project that I call surveillance capitalism. (Zuboff 2019: 43)

Surveillance capitalism unilaterally reworks human experience as a raw material in its purest state to be transformed into behavioural data. Although some of those data are applied to improve products and services, the remainder are processed like a patented "over-behavior", feeding into advanced manufacturing processes known as "machine intelligence" and manufactured into prediction products. Eventually, those prediction products are commercialised in a new type of market for behavioural predictions that are defined as behavioral future markets. Social media have allowed for a subsequent step forward in the translation and consolidation of this intangible (cf. Quintarelli 2019) or surveillance capitalism (cf. Richards 2013).

> Just as industrial capitalism was driven to the continuous intensification of the means of production, so surveillance capitalists and their market players are now locked into the continuous intensification of the means of behavioral modification and the gathering might of instrumentarian power. (Zuboff 2019: 44)

The conclusions drawn by Zuboff are not that different, in spite of a different historical context and discordant ideology, from the control exerted in Chinese or Russian society. They are Neo or Cyber Leviathans which place the yoke of multinationals or totalitarian states around individual autonomy, also in the name of order and security.

> The evidence and reasoning employed here suggest that surveillance capitalism is a rogue force driven by novel economic imperatives that disregard social norms and nullify the elemental rights associated with individual autonomy that are essential to the very possibility of a democratic society. (Zuboff 2019: 67)

The mobilisation and resistance which the thinkers and jurists quoted here are calling for will take place and define a key battlefield on which the possibility of mankind's future will be fought on the new frontier of power. These invasive operations were powerfully nurtured not only by corporate voraciousness but also by the absence of national and supranational laws that might prevent their advance because of the initial alignment of interests between incipient surveillance capitalists and state intelligence agencies.

VI. The European Deal

The European Union offers the possibility of being an alternative of resistance and change in the face of the technological dystopia that the United States and China project for the future. The main aim is to develop digital governance based on a resignification of human dignity through the generation of fundamental rights that protect people and give meaning to their connection with AI and robotics (cf. Dunn Cavelty / Egloff 2019). The European Union and the European legal domain will not only bring forth a project forged around the law, as Zuboff claims, but a regulation that is closely and firmly anchored in fundamental rights. The Court of Justice will play a vital role in this strategic operation, since, from a broad perspective, it has outlined the essence of the fundamental right to privacy and the protection of personal data.[26]

It is a model of limits and responsibility with regard to the role of technology which is inscribed within the very identity of European culture (cf. Lassalle 2019: 141), an agreement that is also grounded in Locke's idea of freedom, not only Hobbesian obedience; a liberal idea such as that defended by Locke, which, in the 21st century, develops in accordance to a technological ethic based on a new idea of responsibility. This, as argued by Jonas, should be inspired by an imperative that safeguards the right to an authentic life in human terms (cf. Jonas 1984: 24).

---

[26] Extremely illuminating is the work of Brkan (2019).

VII. EU regulations

The European cybersecurity strategy was presented in February 2013 by the European Commission and the EU's high commissioner: it was the first attempt to establish a global approach to cybersecurity in the EU. It includes and coordinates policies in previously separate areas, in particular civil aspects of cybersecurity and cyber defence for the common policy of security and defence. The strategy begins with three basic principles of cybersecurity:

i. The same fundamental values, laws and rules that apply in the physical world also apply in the cybernetic domain. In particular, any exchange of information for the purposes of cybersecurity when personal data are at stake must comply with the EU data protection law and take full account of people's rights.
ii. The internet is a public and collective good that must be available and accessible to all.
iii. The model of internet governance must be democratic, and cybersecurity policy must also imply a responsibility on the part of stakeholders.

An additional aim of this strategy is to strengthen cooperation between public and private sectors. The overarching cybersecurity strategy was accompanied by a European Directive on the security of network and information systems (Directive (EU) 2016/1148 of the Parliament and Council of Europe, of 6 July 2016, regarding the measures aimed at guaranteeing a high common level of security of network and information systems in the Union). This directive has provoked a clear centripetal movement in national legislations and has imposed obligations for member states (resilience) and for operators of critical infrastructures and information society service providers (including social media, services in the cloud, and search engines). Hence, the EU has moved beyond a voluntary approach and is opting for a more prescriptive focus that requires private operators to adopt security measures and to share information with authorities about incidents detected. This prescriptive approach is new and may guide national strategies globally with regard to cybersecurity.

1. Features of the legislative formant[27]

Now is not the moment to examine the set of directives and regulations implemented within the EU. Instead, I shall attempt to briefly analyse some of the characteristics of EU legislation. The hallmark of EU legislation, apart from its capacity for harmonisation as discussed previously, principally lies in the pursuit of the rights guaranteed by the Charter of Fundamental Rights and in the approval of rules in a process that involves possible stakeholders, without giving them the last word in that regard.

Froomkin (1997: 129) designates the Internet as the "modern Hydra". Every time the heads of the mythical beast are cut off, new ones are grown. The same thing occurs when regulators attempt to interfere with the online environment (by cutting off one of the Hydra's heads) and users easily bypass the new rules (the growth of new heads). This metaphor illustrates not only the trade-off that governments faced at the end of the last century between innovation and the protection of constitutional rights, but also why (democratic) states adopted a free-market approach in relation to the digital environment (i.e. digital liberalism). This liberal framework characterised the EU legislative formant at the beginning of this century, mainly in the e-Commerce Directive 2000/31/EC of the European Parliament and the Council of 8 June 2000.

Another example of the first period is the Data Protection Directive 95/46/EC of the European Parliament and of the Council of 24 October 1995. In the disjunctive "regulation versus absolute freedom", or to put it in strategic-political terms of international governance, Chinese or Vietnamese regulation against US law, only after decades and thanks to the judicial formant, the European Union and the Council of Europe have established an intermediate milestone based on the defence of fundamental rights (cf. Guiora 2017; Gallego / Garrido / Velázquez / Munoz 2017;

[27] Legal formant is a comparative law feature, coined by Rodolfo Sacco (1991) using linguistic terminology, applied to known national systems by the decomposition of a national model into its components.

López 2019: 16ff.). And in the next disjunctive "self-regulation versus hetero-regulation", they have taken a clearly favourable stance towards the consultation of all stakeholders and political decision making, incorporating case law from the Court of Justice and the European Court of Human Rights as it sets out to safeguard citizens' fundamental rights.

2. European Governance

The EU's objective of developing soft cybernetic power which privileges defence, resilience and civil society contrasts harshly with the national cybersecurity policies that are developed both in and outside of Europe. In Europe, where governments tend to capitalise on emotional reactions to terrorist threats to support traditional approaches to national security, there is still tremendous uncertainty surrounding the affiliation of the member states to a common approach. In the rest of the world, the major cyber players (particularly the US, Russia, and China) have different concepts, cultures and logics in such matters, especially with regard to cybersecurity rules of conduct.

The approaches taken by the EU and the US regarding cybersecurity, for example – even though they present certain common features – also embody major differences, since the war on terror launched by the Bush administration gave rise not only to doctrines of war and prevented policy guided by technology but also helped to shape a legal framework which, today, is accused of having laid the foundation for mass surveillance programmes (cf. Bradford 2015: 107). Two examples of EU governance can be found with regard to foreign policy in the approval of legislation governing exports of dual use products and in the approval of the Cybersecurity Regulation.

3. Examples of European Governance

3.1. The new cybersecurity regulation

Regulation 2019/881[28] which entered into effect on 27 June 2019 seeks to take a substantial leap in the matter of improving protection from cybernetic vulnerability. The Cybersecurity Regulation was proposed as part of a raft of far-reaching measures aimed at tackling cyber-attacks and reinforcing cybersecurity in the EU. I would like to highlight two points. The first pertains to a public element of cybersecurity. The ENISA will act as an independent centre for specialist knowledge helping to promote a high degree of awareness among citizens and businesses as well as to assist institutions and member states of the EU in drafting and applying policies. The second element refers to and affects the private sector, creating a framework of European cybersecurity certificates for products, processes and services that will be valid throughout the whole of the EU. This is the first legislative act within the EU market tackling the challenge of improving and strengthening the cybersecurity of connected products by means of a broad consultation of stakeholders.

3.2. Proposed Regulation on the Exportation of Dual Use Products

In the proposed regulation on the exportation of dual use products,[29] the EU's intervention is justified by the Charter of Fundamental Rights since various human rights can be affected by the circulation of certain goods, in particular cyber surveillance technology. In recent years, there have been numerous reports about the exportation of cyber surveillance technologies to repressive regimes and their improper use that violates human rights

---

[28] Regulation (EU) 2019/881 of the European Parliament and of the Council of 17 April 2019 on ENISA (European Union Agency for Cybersecurity) and on cybersecurity certification of information and communication technologies and repealing Regulation (EU) No. 526/2013 ('Cybersecurity Regulation').

[29] Proposal for a regulation of the European parliament and of the Council setting up a Union regime for the control of exports, brokering, technical assistance, transit and transfer of dual-use items (recast) 2016/0295(COD).

throughout the entire MENA zone. It sets out more restrictive authorisations for cybersecurity technologies which have been used improperly for internal repression by authoritarian governments for the purpose of infiltrating the computer systems of dissidents and human rights activists.

4. Features of judicial formant

In addition to the legislative action analysed now, the case law of the European Courts also plays a part of which I will only extrapolate a few rulings that pursue the protection of fundamental rights on the issue of cybersecurity. Within the European conceptual legal perimeter, the judicial formant is the most prominent component.

> In 2011, the CJEU shifted its approach from a merely economic perspective to a fundamental rights-based approach. It is not by accident that this turning point occurred in the wake of the Lisbon Treaty recognizing that the EU Charter has the same legal value as EU primary law. (De Gregorio 2021: 52)

The first constitutionalist judicial approach is consumed within the regulatory framework of the Union, annulling for the first time a Community directive, i.e. 2006/24/EC. In Digital Rights Ireland (Cases C-293/12 and C-594/12, Digital Rights Ireland Ltd v. Minister for Communications, Marine and Natural Resources and Others and Kärntner Landesregierung and Others, ECLI:EU:C:2014:238), the Court considers that effects of this normative on fundamental rights are disproportionate by considering, as a constitutional court, injustified the interference of the Directive on the rights to privacy and data protection of Union citizens protected by the Charter of the European Union. The CJEU has been aware of the risks of new technologies for the protection of the fundamental rights of EU citizens. In fact, the retention of all traffic data "applies to all means of electronic communication. […] It therefore entails interference with the fundamental rights of virtually the entire European population" (Cases C-293/12 & C-594/12, *Digital Rights Ireland*, ECLI:EU:C:2014:238, at 56).

> First, as in Digital Rights Ireland and Schrems, the Court granted a high level of protection to privacy and data to ensure the effective protection of these fundamental rights by virtue of a (constitutional) interpretation. Second, the

> Google Spain case demonstrates a first judicial attempt to face the power of online platforms and address the legislative inertia of the EU, thereby laying a foundation for European digital constitutionalism. (De Gregorio 2021: 55)

With those decisions, the CJEU judicially constructs certain important elements of European governance with regard to cybersecurity and articles 7 and 8 of the EU's Charter of Fundamental Rights.

The block of rulings discussed here (8 April 2014, Digital Rights Ireland Ltd v. Minister for Communications, Marine and Natural Resources and others, and Kärntner Landesregierung and others; C- 362/14, Maximiliam Schrems vs. Data Protection Commissioner of 6 October 2015; Patrick Breyer vs. Bundesrepublik Deutschland, C-582/14 of 19 October 2016; Tele2 Sverige AB / Post-och telestyrelseny, C-203/15; Secretary of State for the Home Department/Tom Watson and others C-698/15; Fiscal Ministry, C-207/16 of 2 October 2018) represents, in effect, the essence of the fundamental right to digital identity.

> In the constitutional shaping of the concept of essence of fundamental rights, the case law of the Court of Justice of the EU ('CJEU' or 'the Court') in the field of privacy and data protection plays a crucial role. (Brkan 2019: 864)

This case law interacts with legislative action and subsequent legislative transplants. It is often the judicial formant that promotes the guidelines to which European co-legislators have subsequently adapted, as in the case of the "Directiva NIS" and the General Data Protection Regulation (GDPR). Its implementation in mid-2018 has given rise to various transplant initiatives on the topic of security and privacy in countries outside the European Union. Canada and Brazil have passed legislation similar to the GDPR, which will enter into effect in 2020. Australia and Singapore have regulated reporting within 72 hours, inspired by this regulation. India is considering similar legislation to the GDPR, and California passed a similar privacy law, considered to be the strictest in the US to date.

5. Judicial dialogue inside and outside the European judicial area

Another correlate of the case law of the European Court of Justice is the dialogue it establishes with the European Court of Human Rights which began with the Ruling of 3 April 2007 in the "Caso Copland". The recent ruling on Benedik v. Slovenia of 24 July 2018 continues the dialogue with the European Court of Justice on the construction of a European judicial area from a distance (Schwartz 2019: 773), affirming the primacy of the right to a private and family life over cybernetic interventions. The protection of privacy is a crucial goal in European political and legal culture, not least because it was formed against the backdrop of the horrors of the Nazi and Communist regimes. In the long run, privacy will be a fundamental right only as long as it is defended by society, and will disappear if society ceases to see it as an essential value.

It is essential to provide a constitutionally enshrined guarantee of protection against cyber-attacks as indicated some time ago by Stefano Rodotà, striking a balance between the principles human beings continue to acknowledge and a wider world thanks to a reality that has been exponentially augmented by computer technologies (cf. Rodotà 2012: 238). The famous Italian jurist focuses on a foundational element of the new *uomo macchina* in the ruling of 27 February 2008, issued by Germany's constitutional court, holding that an amendment to the security services act of North Rhine-Westphalia (cf. Judgment of the German Constitutional Court 2008: 317ff.) was contrary to the *Grundgesetz.* This ruling ushered in a new vision of the extension of constitutional rights to cyberspace which revolves around "a new fundamental right to privacy and the integrity of technology information systems" (cf. Judgment of the German Constitutional Court 2008: 388) as part of the general right of personality recognised by the German Constitution. A new form of guarantee is evidenced which surpasses the dichotomy between *habeas corpus*, associated with the physical body, and *habeas data*, understood as an extension of that same historical protection to the electronic body. The aim, in greater depth, is to construct and oversee a digital identity (cf. Lasica 2009: 1) by means of case law elaborations of article 8 of the Charter of Fundamental Rights of the European Union.

On the other hand, the territorial scope of the EU General Data Protection Regulation in its article 13 seeks to promote European values, projecting them outside its territorial horizon. While the regulation received international attention, it remains questionable whether provisions with extraterritorial effect support a power-based approach or a value-driven strategy. Developments around the enforceability of a 'right to be forgotten', or the difficulties in regulating transatlantic data flows, raise doubts as to whether unilateral standard setting does justice to the plurality and complexity of the digital sphere. Extraterritorial application of EU data protection law currently can promote European values sustainably only if the judicial dialogue within the Union described above is projected in the international arena. Otherwise, the universality of individual rights could transform itself into a form of European judicial neo-colonialism (Gstrein / Zwitter 2021: 29).

VIII. Epilogue

Algorithmic processes must be placed in the service of a transnational citizenship which enjoys a broad catalogue of fundamental rights within the digital sphere. Unless fundamental rights are guarded, protection against cyber-attacks and the freedom we enjoy would become a mutilated or assisted freedom, undermined by the direction of biometric algorithms that even shape up our sensitivity and determine our behavior. This means that digital security and order have to go hand in hand with legal governance that establishes a series of fundamental rights to ensure, paraphrasing Habermas, that the technological challenge is not only met through technology but also, and mainly, through digital rights (cf. Habermas 2013). The heralded 'digital tsunami', therefore, is the result not only of the opportunities provided by technology but also of the fact that personal data are drawn into the omnivorous orbit of security companies and organisations. A new space has been constituted which is hard to define according to the traditional frames of public / private reference.

This is not a question of the traditional individual aspects of personal privacy. As we have seen in this study, it covers a further, wider social and political spectrum concerning democratic life (Nemitz 2018: 84). For these reasons, the future of the values of the European Union is closely linked to the defense of digital fundamental rights. And for this reason, the European Union defends these rights far beyond its borders. This extraterritoriality has to be well understood: it should not be interpreted as a new attempt to impose new universal rights, but as a spur to transactional judicial dialogue. Ultimately, the new giant repositories of information increase social vulnerability, not merely in the manner that is frequently flagged, as tools to control people. The concentration of growing databases of information organised by various public and private entities offers the opportunity to utilise this information for purposes other than which they were created for.

> Questo è prova evidente della nuova vulnerabilità sociale, che capovolge in specie la funzione assegnata alle banche dati, che, concepite per meglio garantire la sicurezza, si trasformano in strumenti che rendono invece possibili aggressioni proprio alla sicurezza delle persone.[30] (Rodotà 2012: 238)

Consequently, the primordial questions which emerge when studying cyber-attacks and cybersecurity ("Two questions always hang in the air either explicitly or implicitly: Security of what? And security from whom?") must be approached in a complex and axiological way. We conclude by stressing that cybersecurity refers to the public good and private properties and that the organisations and bodies designated to protect them must be subject to the scrutiny of constitutionally relevant rules (produced by judicial transnational dialogue), lest they become genuine Cyber Leviathans

IX. References

Barlow, John Perry. 1996. *A Declaration of the Independence of Cyberspace.* https://www.eff.org/cyberspace-independence. Last access 12.12. 2022.

---

[30] AT: "This is clear evidence of the new social vulnerability, which overturns in particular the function assigned to databases, which, designed to better guarantee security, are transformed into tools that make possible aggressions precisely to the safety of people".

Blume, Joshua D. 2018. Reading the Trade Tealeaves. A Comparative Analysis of Potential United States Wto-Gats Claims against Privacy, Localization, and Cybersecurity Laws. *Georgetown Journal of International Law* 49 (2), 801-843.

Bradford, Anu. 2015. The Brussel Effect. *Northwestern University Law Review* 107 (1), 1-64.

Brkan, Maja. 2019. The Essence of the Fundamental Rights to Privacy and Data Protection. Finding the Way Through the Maze of the CJEU's Constitutional Reasoning. *German Law Journal* 20, 864-883.

Buchanan, Bonnie G. 2017. *Securitization and the Global Economy. History and Prospects for the Future*. New York: Palgrave Macmillan.

Bygrave, Lee. 2014. *Data Privacy Law. An International Perspective*. Oxford: Oxford University Press.

Chi, Josh / Eva Dou. 2016. China's New Cybersecurity Law Rattles Foreign Tech Firms. *The Wall Street Journal*. https://www.wsj.com/articles/china-approves-cybersecurity-law-1478491064. Last access 12. 12.2022.

Daskal, Jennifer. 2016. Law Enforcement Access to Data Across Borders. The Evolving Security and Rights Issues. *Journal of National Security Law & Policy* 8, 473-501.

De Gregorio, Giovanni. 2021. The Rise of Digital Constitutionalism in the European Union. *International Journal of Constitutional Law* 19 (1), 41-70.

Dunn Cavelty, Myriam / Florian J. Egloff. 2019. The Politics of Cybersecurity. Balancing Different Roles of the State. *St Antony's International Review* 15 (1), 37-57.

Finnemore, Martha / Duncan B. Hollis. 2016. Constructing Norms for Global Cybersecurity. *American Journal of International Law* 110 (3), 425-479.

Fogel, Jean Françoise. 2007. Veinte apuntes sobre el ciber-Leviatán. *Letras Libres* (103), 8-12.

Froomkin, A. Michael. 1997. The Internet as a Source of Regulatory Arbitrage. In: Brian Kahin / Charles Nesson (Eds.), *Borders in Cyberspace.*

Cambridge, MA: MIT Press, 129-163. https://letraslibres.com/revista-espana/veinte-apuntes-sobre-el-ciberleviatan/. Last access 12.12.2022.

Gstrein, Oscar J. / Andrej J. Zwitter. 2021. Extraterritorial Application of the GDPR. Promoting European Values or Power? *Internet Policy Review* 10 (3), 2-30.

Guiora, Amos N. 2017. *Cybersecurity Geopolitics, Law, and Policy*, Routledge: New York.

Jonas, Hans. 1984. *The Imperative of Responsibility. In Search of an Ethics for the Technological Age*. Chicago: University of Chicago Press.

Kausch, Kristina. 2017. Cheap Havoc. How Cyber-Geopolitics Will Destabilize the Middle East. *Policy Brief German Marshall Fund*, 24.11.2017. https://www.gmfus.org/news/cheap-havoc-how-cyber-geopolitics-will-destabilize-middle-east. Last access 12.12.2022.

Kokas, Aynne. 2019. *Cloud Control. China's 2017 Cybersecurity Law and its Role in US Data Standardization.* https://ssrn.com/abstract=3427832 or http://dx.doi.org/10.2139/ssrn.3427832. Last access 12.12.2022.

Lasica, Joseph D. 2009. *Identity in the Age of Cloud Computing. The Next-Generation Internet's Impact on Business, Governance and Social Interaction.* Washington: The Aspen Institute.

Lassalle, José María. 2019. *Ciberleviatán*. Barcelona: Arpa.

Lee, Kai-Fu. 2019. *AI Superpowers. China, Silicon Valley and the New World Order.* Boston: Houghton Mifflin Harcourt.

Mishra, Neha. 2019. Privacy, Cybersecurity, and GATS Article XIV. A New Frontier for Trade and Internet Regulation? *Word Trade Review* 19 (3), 1-24.

Nemitz, Paul. 2018. Constitutional Democracy and Technology in the Age of Artificial Intelligence. *Philosophical Transactions of the Royal Society* A 376 (2133), 1-14.

Parasol, Max. 2018. The Impact of China's 2016 Cyber Security Law in Foreign Technology Firms, and on China's Big Data and Smart City Dreams. *Computer Law and Security Review* 34 (1), 67-98.

Quintarelli, Stefano. 2019. *Capitalismo immateriale*. Torino: Bollati Boringhieri.

Richards, Neil M. 2013. The Dangers of Surveillance. *Harvard Law Review* 16, 455-477.

Rodotà, Stefano. 2012. *Il diritto di avere diritti.* Bari: Laterza.

Sacco, Rodolfo. 1991. Legal Formants. A Dynamic Approach to Comparative Law (Installment I of II). *The American Journal of Comparative Law* 39 (1), 1-34.

Schwartz, Paul M. 2019. Global Data Privacy. The EU Way. *New York University Law Review* 94, 771-818.

Tallinn Manual on the International Law Applicable to Cyber Warfare. Prepared by the International Group of Experts at the Invitation of the NATO Cooperative Cyber Defence Centre of Excellence Cambridge. 2013. New York: Cambridge University Press.

Tiezzi, Shannon. 2014. Xi Jinping Leads China's New Internet Security Group. *The Diplomat*. http://thediplomat.com/2014/02/xi-jinping-leads-chinas-new-internet-security-group/. Last access 12.12.2022.

Van Puyvelde, Damian / Aaron F. Brantly. 2019. *Cybersecurity. Politics, Governance and Conflict in Cyberspace.* Cambridge: Polity Press.

Von Finckenstein, Valentina. 2019. *Cybersecurity in the Middle East and North Africa*. Beirut: Konrad Adenauer Foundation Lebanon Office.

Wagner, Daniel. 2019. What China's Cybersecurity Law says about the Future. *Sunday Guardian*. https://www.sundayguardianlive.com/news/chinas-cybersecurity-law-says-future/. Last access 12.12.2022.

Zuboff, Shoshana. 2019. *The Age of Surveillance Capitalism. The Fight for a Human Future at the New Frontier of Power.* New York: Public Affairs.

Section II

Digitalisierung im nationalen Kontext /

Digitisation in National Contexts

Chiara Preite

"Vos amis notaires vous répondent" – Popularising Legal Knowledge for Citizens on the *Notaires.fr* Website

Abstract

The present contribution aims at analysing the communication that the French Notaries' Association sets up to popularise notarial knowledge for citizens' legal needs. The study will focus on the simplification of notarial concepts and procedures, as constructed in *notaires.fr* webpages through three channels: different reformulating and defining strategies of specialised terms; a *Lexique* gathering some terminology considered as fundamental for textual developments; videos summarising news about a specific institution or offering expert answers to specific questions.

I. Introduction

This contribution aims at analysing the communication that the *Association des Notaires de France* (French Notaries' Association) sets up to communicate notarial knowledge and to satisfy citizens' needs in this field. Attention will be focused in particular, on the one hand, on the cognitive support that the official website *www.notaires.fr* offers to citizens in their effort to understand notarial law, as formulated in "informative and explanatory" discourse (Candel 1995; see section III). On the other hand, we will consider a number of videos that, in our opinion, share the function of mitigating the feeling of strangeness and the lack of confidence that citizens generally hold towards the law, lawyers and their language, which is perceived as strongly corporative and initiatory. This is particularly true for notaries, since they exercise their functions in a liberal framework.

Therefore, the website shows an informative and popularising tendency as it is structured in such a way as to guide laypeople into the world of notaryship. In Engberg's (2020a: 58) view "popularization is more than just disseminating expert knowledge" to the layperson: it also works in a way "to create a link to the popular culture of the receiver", and this is what we attempt to discuss in this study. Notarial professionals open up to laypeople (thereby to potential clients) by transmitting part of their knowledge to the outside world in order to make one of the less understandable specialised discourses more transparent (mainly because of its highly specialised and culture-bound terminology). The popularisation of legal knowledge via the website is intended to create a place in which laypeople needing notaries' services may have a first encounter with the specialised knowledge of this legal branch.

This involves the recontextualisation (cf. Calsamiglia / van Dijk 2004: 371) for a wide audience of legal knowledge, originally produced in specialised contexts, in order to adapt to the new communicative event in which it appears. The "simplification" moves used "to manipulate input to bring it close to the reader's level of linguistic competence and thus to help his intake" (Bathia 1983: 45) essentially involve the reformulation of contents (including technical terminology and concepts) but also the clarification of textual developments by providing different kinds of definitions, exemplifications and explanations. So, these strategies adapt the information to the assumed knowledge of laypeople and share the aim of enabling them to understand, internalise, and cognitively structure a body of knowledge as well as overcoming distrust.

First, we will briefly describe the popularising aim and the multimodal (cf. Kress 2009; Kress / van Leeuwen 2001) or pluri-semiotic (cf. Rabatel 2010) architecture of the *notaires.fr* section devoted to the thematic developments specifically designed for citizens (section II). Then, we will address the simplification of notarial concepts and procedures as constructed in the web pages under investigation where information is delivered through three channels: (1) Different reformulating and defining strategies of specialised terms come into play in what Candel (1995: 24) calls "discours définitoires et informatifs" (section III). These "informative and explanatory discourses" provide a useful basis for the non-expert's understanding of texts, in that they make it possible to approach knowledge of fundamental notions, underlying explanations, and information delivery;

(2) a *Lexique* gathers terminology considered as fundamental for the development of the topics dealt with by the website; (3) videos (section IV) either specifically recorded for *notaires.fr* by a notary who summarises news about a specific institution, or recorded for the TV program "Le club du droit". Videos and the TV features explain legal institutions and often offer expert answers to specific questions asked by lay-people about personal cases.[1] Videos are generally conceived to provide an entertaining way to convey contents, and this complies with the central aim of popularisation in law, which is, in Engberg's (2020b: 180) words, to "make institutions part of the popular culture and thus to turn it into an accessible, accepted and liked entity."

II. The website *www.notaires.fr*

The website under investigation serves different purposes: it offers useful information to clear doubts about legal institutions related to the world of the notary's office, about the services that citizens can enjoy, and importantly, it offers instructions to follow in order to enjoy them. With regard to its organisation, the thematic section can be found in a horizontal, grey banner at the top of the homepage:

[1] By writing to *leclubdudroit@bfmbusinness.fr*.

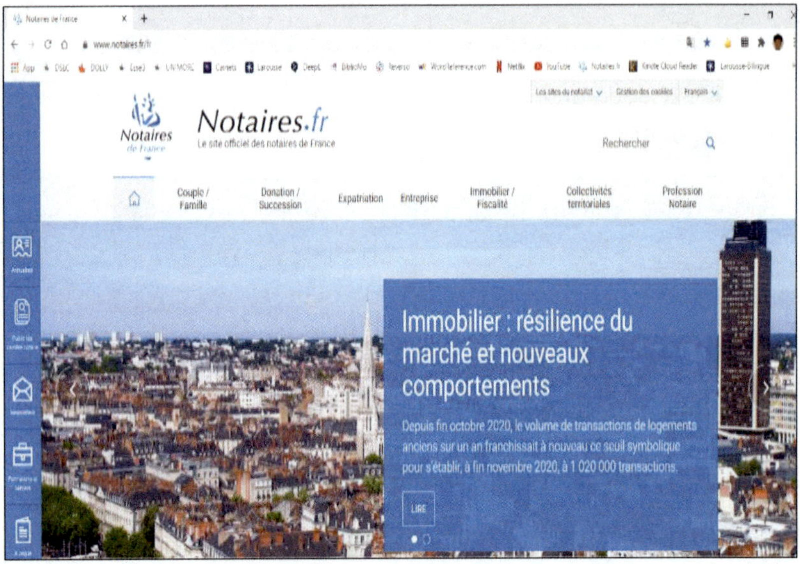

Fig. 1: Homepage (https://www.notaires.fr/fr)

The thematic section is divided into several topics dealing with legal institutions widely affecting general life and requiring a notary's intervention: 'Couple / Famille'; 'Donation / Succession'; 'Expatriation'; 'Entreprise'; 'Immobilier / Fiscalité'; 'Collectivités territoriales'; 'Profession notaire'.[2] Clicking on the selected button opens a menu that displays the correlated sub-topics (see Fig. 2) which, in turn, lead to pages where contents are expanded.

[2] Translated by the author: Couple / Family; Donation / Succession; Expatriation; Enterprises; Real estate / Revenues; Territorial community; Profession of notary.

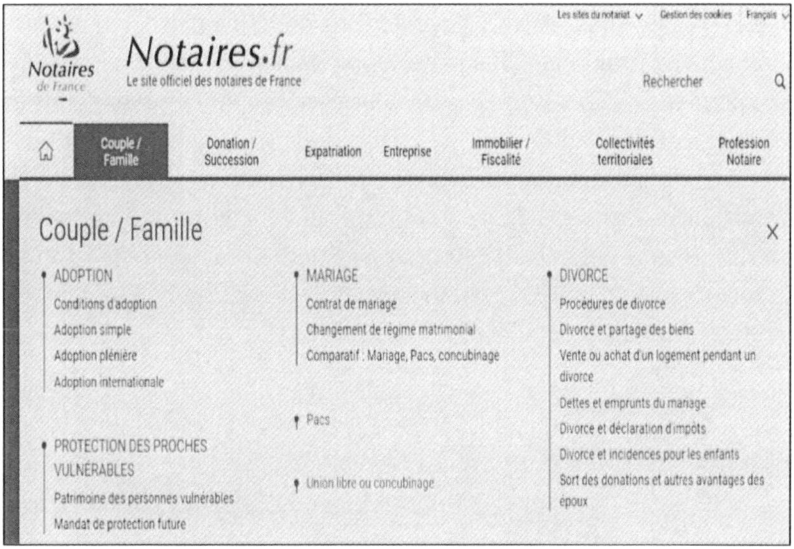

Fig. 2: Couple / Family sub-topics (https://www.notaires.fr/fr)

The pages devoted to the explanation of each topic contain hypertextual links leading to other online texts hosted by the same website or to further pages of a different nature (either internal or external to the website)[3] enabling the users to broaden their knowledge. In a multimodal architecture, it is also possible, for example, to watch explanatory videos, listen to MP3 recordings, read data charts, look up information in guides, search for a notary, etc. The texts on the website are not only informative, they also emphasise instructional or procedural (cf. Werlich 1975) steps to be taken to assert one's rights. In this way, popularisation is not limited to theoretical disciplinary knowledge, but it offers a service that conveys practical knowledge (cf. Preite 2016), and it is most often structured according to the question / answer pattern that could be seen as a strategy of "easyfication" (Bathia 1983).

[3] The hypertext structure of websites makes reading potentially limitless. For this reason, we are not taking into account the pages connected via hyperlinks, limiting our study to the main pages of the central site.

This strategy builds links between paragraphs and enhances engagement with the readers by promising an answer (in written or video form) expanding their knowledge: This may concern either a simple understanding of the information or the highlighting of instructions and advice that citizens must follow to obtain a result. As shown, for example in Figure 3, every topic is introduced by a heading, a subhead and a picture related to the topic itself. The integration between linguistic and visual signs[4] is a multimodal popularisation feature. Then, the question / answer development begins and texts alternate with videos.

Fig. 3: Images and questions[5]

We will now turn to the reformulation and definitional strategies used in *notaires.fr* website's texts and in the related *Lexique* to offer a sample of their interaction.

---

4 According to Jacobi (1987), visual signs play a prominent role in popularisation even in books and the press. This happens all the more in contemporary digital icono-textual productions (cf. Sagnier 2018): Linguistic texts always come with iconographic elements in a multimodal intertwinement. On the relationship between texts and visual signs, see among others Martinec / Salway (2005); and particularly on this relationship as developed in institutional online popularisation discourse, see Silletti (2018) and Engberg (2020a).

5 https://www.notaires.fr/fr/couple-famille/protection-des-proches-vuln%C3%A9rables/le-patrimoine-des-personnes-vuln%C3%A9rables) (Last access 12.12.2022).

III. Informative and explanatory discourse: definitional reformulations

We start with the assumption that the texts under investigation represent what Candel (1995) calls informative and explanatory discourse,[6] e.g., texts containing different reformulating and defining strategies of specialised terminology, aiming at content and concept simplification. Candel (1995: 35) claims that intra-textual definitions assume the role of *reformulation définitoires* (definitional reformulations). They develop information by establishing temporary conceptual equivalences with specialised terms in order to clarify their meaning and to facilitate the reconstruction of underlying concepts and objects (cf. Engberg 2010, 2013) as well as of the semantic-conceptual links between related notions. Several elements are therefore intended to foster the cognitive process of reconstruction and learning of legal knowledge by laypeople, and it is precisely these strategies that we shall now turn our attention to.

We shall explore the categories proposed for French scientific discourse[7] by Candel (1995) herself and by Loffler-Laurian (1983) who distinguishes *dénomination*, *fonction*, *équivalence*, *analyse* and *caractérisation* (denomination, purpose, equivalence, analysis and characterisation), often co-working in the same explanation. We shall, thus, show a representative sample of definitional reformulations of specialised terms and, if present, their link to the *Lexique*'s definitions. In fact, terms appearing in the explanatory texts are sometimes (but not systematically) hyperlinked to their definitions in the lexicon, which are also shown in pop-ups, thus avoiding

---

[6] Candel (1995: 34): "Ce que nous appelons discours définitoire et informatif est constitué de l'ensemble des énoncés dans lesquels transparaît une activité définitoire ou, plus généralement, une réflexion sur les mots permettant de mieux appréhender leur sens." Translated by the author: "What we call informative and explanatory discourse is made up of all the statements in which a defining activity or, more generally, a reflection on the words allows for better understanding of their meaning."

[7] Candel's (1995) and Loffler-Laurian's (1983) classifications mostly overlap. Their point of view combines "definition / description" and "reformulation or paraphrase" (Calsamiglia / van Dijk 2004) into definitional reformulations which include "denomination" (Calsamiglia / van Dijk 2004) as a type of definition with "purpose", "equivalence", "analysis", and "characterization" (Loffler-Laurian 1983).

changing the page for their retrieval. This connection fosters the progression of understanding and, in consequence, the mediation of knowledge: in such a view, terms play the role of units of understanding, of cognition and therefore of knowledge.

1. Denomination

Thanks to this strategy, a link between old and new knowledge, known and unknown words is established. *Associative denomination* puts the reformulation in apposition and is often marked by parentheses (see example 1), inverted commas, and the junction *ou* (see example 2). Reformulations generally occur after the term; see example 1: "eaux de vannes (eaux provenant des WC)" and "eaux grises (eaux issues des lavabos, de la cuisine, du lave-linge [...])":

(1) *Les propriétaires d'habitations non desservies par un réseau public ont l'obligation de s'équiper d'un système autonome (dit individuel) d'assainissement tant des eaux de vannes (eaux provenant des WC) que des eaux grises (eaux issues des lavabos, de la cuisine, du lave-linge [...]) avant de les rejeter dans le milieu naturel. (Traitement des eaux usées: assainissement collectif et non-collectif)*[8]

But they can also be placed before it (see example 2), generally when the term is considered particularly unfamiliar: "this way, the reader will not be confused or slowed down by the obscure term, but instead ready for it" (Darian 2003: 55) and therefore will understand it.

(2) *[...] Et si le paiement ne se fait pas comptant, une garantie est prise pour protéger le vendeur ("privilège de vendeur" ou "privilège de nantissement"). (Le fonds de commerce)*[9]

---

[8] Translated by the author: Owners of dwellings that are not served by a public network are obliged to equip themselves with an *autonomous (so-called individual)* sanitation system for both *black water* (water from toilets) and *grey water* (water from washbasins, the kitchen, the washing machine, etc.) before discharging it into the natural environment. (*Wastewater treatment: collective and non-collective sanitation*) The emphasis in the examples is ours, while – where present – underlining refers to authentic hyperlinks.

[9] Translated by the author: And if payment is not made in cash, security is taken to protect the seller ("seller's lien" or "pledge lien"). (*The business*)

Metalinguistic denomination exploits some expressions (see example 1: "dit", example 3: "c'est-à-dire", example 4: "appelé aussi", "nommé", etc.) joining the definitional reformulation of a concept to the term naming it in both directions:

(3) *Si le conjoint survivant est locataire de ce logement les loyers sont à la charge de la succession, c'est-à-dire des héritiers. (Succession entre époux: les droits du conjoint survivant)*[10]

(4) *Le compromis de vente et la promesse de vente sont deux contrats aux conséquences différentes pour l'acheteur et le vendeur. […] Dans la promesse de vente (appelée aussi "promesse unilatérale de vente"), le propriétaire s'engage auprès du candidat acheteur (nommé bénéficiaire) à lui vendre son bien à un prix déterminé. […] Dans le compromis de vente (ou "promesse synallagmatique de vente"), vendeur et acheteur s'engagent l'un comme l'autre à conclure la vente à un prix déterminé en commun. (La promesse de vente et le compromis de vente)*[11]

Example 4 shows multiple metalinguistic denominations highlighted by typography (parenthesis and inverted commas) and also an equivalence (see section 2) between two terms (*compromis de vente* and *promesse de vente*) and their legal hypernym (*contrats*). In the same way, *substitutive denomination* retrieves a term by different forms of lexical anaphora (e.g., by a synonym or by a hypernym), as in the following example 5:

(5) *Le* divorce par consentement mutuel. Cette procédure amiable *suppose que le couple s'accorde non seulement sur le principe même du divorce, mais aussi sur l'ensemble de ses effets […]. La loi […] a instauré le divorce par*

---

[10] Translated by the author: If the surviving spouse is the tenant of this dwelling, the rent is payable by the estate, i.e. the heirs. *(Inheritance between spouses: the rights of the surviving spouse)*

[11] Translated by the author: Are you about to sign a preliminary sales agreement? This is called a "preliminary contract". The preliminary sales agreement and the promise to sell are two contracts with different consequences for the buyer and the seller. […] In the promise to sell (also known as a "unilateral promise to sell"), the owner undertakes to the prospective buyer (named beneficiary) to sell his property to him at a set price. […] In the preliminary sales agreement (or bilateral promise to sell), both the seller and the buyer undertake to conclude the sale at a jointly determined price. (*The promise to sell and the preliminary sales agreement*)

consentement mutuel sans procédure judiciaire (parfois appelé "divorce sans juge"*). (Quelle procédure en cas de divorce?)*[12]

We discover here that the "divorce par consentement mutuel" is a "procédure" by which people find an 'amicable settlement' out of court.

2. Equivalence

Equivalence generally resorts to the verb 'to be' followed by a hypernym (see example 4: "Le compromis de vente et la promesse de vente sont deux *contrats*"), or a few other verbs (see example 6: 'consist') linking the definitional reformulation (cf. Loffler-Laurian 1983).

(6) *La donation-partage consiste à transmettre et à repartir, de son vivant, tout ou partie, de ses biens. (Donation-partage et donation transgénérationnelle)*[13]

The verb 'consister' appears in several headings in the form of questions. This prepares for the following definitional reformulation, even if it is not reused in the answer, which mainly takes the form of a characterisation (see section 5), for example:

(7) *En quoi* consiste *le régime de la communauté universelle? [...] Dans le régime de la communauté universelle, tous les biens, présents et à venir, possédés par les époux sont mis en commun [...]. (Choisir la communauté universelle)*[14]

The definitional reformulation by equivalence, in combination with purpose (see section 4) or other strategies, can also be exploited to simplify

---

[12] Translated by the author: Divorce by mutual consent. This amicable procedure presupposes that the couple agrees not only on the very principle of divorce but also on all its effects [...]. The law [...] has introduced divorce by mutual consent without judicial procedure (sometimes called "divorce without a judge"). (*What is the procedure in the event of a divorce?*)

[13] Translated by the author: A shared donation consists of the mediation and distribution of all or part of one's assets during one's lifetime [...]. (*Shared gifts and transgenerational gifts*)

[14] Translated by the author: What is the regime of the universal community? [...] In the regime of a universal community, all the goods, present and future, owned by the spouses are pooled, [...]. (*Choosing the universal community*)

cognition by creating encyclopaedic competencies. Example 8 explains the functions of a "will" and informs the reader that it must take a written form:

(8) *Le testament est un écrit par lequel une personne majeure prend des décisions et précise ses volontés pour la période qui suivra son décès. (Testament: pourquoi et comment?)*[15]

(9) *Testament. Acte par lequel une personne décide de la manière dont sa succession doit être réglée. (Lexique)*[16]

The pop-up window linked to the lexicon (see example 9) defines the *testament* as an *acte* which must therefore be "written". In both cases, the reformulation grafts the specialised term onto prior linguistic knowledge (the general hypernym *écrit* and the specialised one *acte*), which also informs the reader about the extralinguistic need to produce a document in written form. We can also consider that the definitions by inclusion offered by the *Lexique* generally replace a term by its hypernym, thus filling it in this category. These definitions are more technical than definitional reformulations, and resort to legal institutions working as hypernyms: *acte* ('deed'), *pacte* ('pact'), *convention* ('agreement') and *procedure* ('procedure'), etc. Making relationships among concepts explicit, which otherwise would remain unknown, helps the lay-user to build up legal knowledge, as can be seen not only in examples 8 and 9 but also in the *Lexique's* definition of *compromis de vente* in example 10 as against example 4 (where it is defined by the general term "contract"):

(10) *Compromis de vente. Avant-contrat, acte synallagmatique par lequel les parties, vendeur et acquéreur, constatent leur accord sur les conditions d'une vente en attendant la réalisation des conditions suspensives. (Lexique)*[17]

---

[15] Translated by the author: A will is a written document in which a person of full age makes decisions and specifies his or her wishes for the period following his or her death. (*Will: why and how?*)

[16] Translated by the author: Will. The deed by which a person decides how his or her estate is to be settled. (*Lexicon*)

[17] Translated by the author: Sales agreement. Preliminary contract, a synallagmatic act by which the parties, seller and buyer, note their agreement on the terms of a sale pending the fulfilment of the conditions precedent. (*Lexicon*) None of the specialised terms used

The lexicon chooses two specific hypernyms to define *compromis de vente*: *avant-contrat* and *acte synallagmatique*. Moreover, both examples 4 and 10 create conceptual networks by linking more terms to the central notion in order to facilitate their acquisition. We discover that the two 'parties' in this contract are the 'seller' (*vendeur*), who is also called the 'owner' (*propriétaire*, see example 4), and the 'buyer' (*acquéreur*), who is also called the 'beneficiary' (*bénéficiaire*, see example 4), and that they have to fulfill some conditions (*conditions suspensives*) to sign the contract.

3. Analysis

The definitional reformulation by *analysis* (cf. Loffler-Laurian 1983) consists in listing the composition of a legal object, concept, or institution:

(11) *L'adoption simple [...] peut être révoquée par le juge à la demande de l'adoptant ou de l'adopté, mais uniquement pour des motifs graves (alcoolisme grave, inconduite scandaleuse, extorsion de fonds, ingratitude [...]). (L'adoption simple)*[18]

This strategy can be used to reconstruct the conceptual framework of concepts divided by law into several elements or considered as parts of an ordered whole. As the subdivision is non-natural, laypeople cannot recognise the relationship among the elements without the intervention of a legal practitioner. Cornu (1990: 184) calls such terms "opposants de classification" as they are opposed by the specific difference highlighted by their approximation within a "purely legal" classification.

---

by *Lexique* is defined in turn, except *condition suspensive*: "La condition suspensive est un évènement futur et incertain dont on fait dépendre la naissance du contrat." Translated by the author: "The suspensive condition is a future and uncertain event on which the realisation of the contract depends." (*Lexicon*) This means a gap in the reader's chance to fully understand.

[18] Translated by the author: A simple adoption [...] may be revoked by the judge at the request of the adopter or adoptee, but only for *serious reasons* (*serious alcoholism, disgraceful misconduct, extortion, ingratitude* [...]). (*The simple adoption*)

4. Purpose or function

As we have already mentioned, different definitional reformulations are often mixed within the same explanation: In fact, the *purpose* or *function* of the concept, institution or object – e.g., their usefulness for citizens – often enriches an equivalence (see section 2 and example 12) or an analysis (see section 3 and example 13) and relies on deontic modality:

(12) *La convention de concubinage est un contrat dont le contenu libre a pour finalité principale d'organiser la vie commune. [...] Elle permet essentiellement de faire l'inventaire des biens [...]. En revanche, elle ne permet en aucun cas d'organiser de manière générale la propriété des biens qui seront acquis en cours de concubinage [...]. (Vie maritale: union libre ou concubinage?)*[19]

(13) *L'acte de notoriété liste les personnes appelées à recueillir la succession, ainsi que leurs droits respectifs. Pour cela, il a besoin que les proches du défunt lui fournissent les documents permettant d'identifier les membres de la famille concernés par la succession (livret de famille, contrat de mariage, jugement de divorce, etc.). (Règlement des successions)*[20]

In this particular kind of informative and explanatory discourse, the frequency of this strategy results from the effort to offer instructions about procedures merging with popularising legal knowledge.

5. Characterisation

A *characterisation* consists of a description of the characteristics attributed to an object. This strategy is very frequent in scientific popularisation, but the legal domain focuses more on *denomination* and on the consequences

[19] Translated by the author: The cohabitation agreement is a contract whose free content has the main purpose of organising life together. [...] It essentially *allows* making an inventory of property, [...]. On the other hand, it *does not* in any case *allow* organising in a general way the ownership of property acquired during the cohabitation [...]. (*Marital life: free union or cohabitation?*)

[20] Translated by the author: The deed of notoriety lists the persons called upon to collect the inheritance, as well as their respective rights. To do this, it requires the deceased's relatives to provide it with the documents enabling it to identify the family members affected by the inheritance (family record, marriage contract, divorce decree, etc.). (*Inheritance settlement*)

that a legal concept or institution can produce. In consequence, characterisation often comes with other kinds of definitions (as in example 7). A specific strategy is presented in example 14:

(14) *Le partage [...]. Les héritiers peuvent décider de ne pas partager: ils restent alors en "indivision". (Le règlement d'une succession)*[21]

Here, characterisation is introduced by mere punctuation, with the specialised term in inverted commas.

6. Exemplification and generalisation

As we already mentioned, Candel's (1995) and Loffler-Laurian's (1983) classifications combine into definitional reformulations the categories of "definition / description"[22] and "reformulation or paraphrase", also proposed for scientific discourse by Calsamiglia / van Dijk (2004). In addition, definitional reformulations include "denomination" as a type of definition. However, Calsamiglia / van Dijk (2004) also consider "exemplification", e.g., providing specific examples of general phenomena, and "generalisation", e.g., drawing general conclusions from specific examples or cases. In our (non-scientific) informative explanatory corpus, we only find one example:

(15) Zoé et Yohan ont décidé de vivre ensemble. *Leur objectif est de faire coïncider le cadre juridique de leur union avec leur situation actuelle et à venir.* Le notaire leur explique les conséquences juridiques, financières et fiscales de chaque statut.
Si Yohan et Zoé se marient.
Ils concluent un acte à la fois juridique et solennel [...].
Si Yohan et Zoé optent pour le PACS.
Ils signent un contrat au terme duquel [...].
Si Yohan et Zoé optent pour le concubinage.

---

[21] Translated by the author: Sharing [...]. The heirs can decide not to share: they then remain in "indivision". (*The settlement of a succession*)

[22] Calsamiglia / van Dijk (2004: 379) state that even if a definition is used to explain unknown words, and description is used to explain unknown things, it is often hard to distinguish between them.

Le concubinage est une situation de fait [...]. (Mariage, Pacs, concubinage: avantages et inconvénients)[23]

Even if we easily imagine that Zoé and Yohan are real people whose situation is used as an example, the informative and explanatory discourse is framed as a generalisation that could be useful for everyone. Exemplification and generalisation seem to be more frequent in videos thanks to the TV program where professional answers are offered to laypeople's questions.

IV. Videos

In the age of digitalisation and multimodality, institutional communication with citizens also includes videos.[24] We shall now focus on their added value, on the extra function performed by the videos embedded in the website under investigation in terms of simplification of concepts and popularisation, and on the comparison with the informative and explanatory texts. In our opinion, videos contribute not only to the popularisation of notarial knowledge by moves such as exemplification and generalisation, but also to image building and promotion. They are tools to construct an appealing appearance of the notary for the audience – or potential clients – who are more and more accustomed to multimodal communication.

---

[23] Translated by the author: Zoé and Yohan have decided to live together. Their aim is to make the legal framework of their union coincide with their current and future situation. The notary explains to them the legal, financial and fiscal consequences of each status. If Yohan and Zoé marry, they conclude an act which is both legal and solemn [...]. If Yohan and Zoé opt for PACS, they sign a contract at the end of which [...]. If Yohan and Zoé opt for cohabitation, cohabitation is a de facto situation [...]. (*Marriage, Pacs, cohabitation: advantages and disadvantages*)

[24] This in not only true for disseminating research (see among others Engberg / Maier 2019; Luzón 2019) but also for the popularisation of legal knowledge.

1. Exemplification and generalisation in videos

As we mentioned before, videos[25] (which might also be cartoons; see Fig. 4) are either specifically recorded for the website by a guest notary in order to explain news about a specific institution, or recorded for the TV program “Le club du droit” (see Fig. 5) to offer both explanations on legal institutions and expert answers to specific questions asked by laypeople about personal cases through the feature *Vos questions* (‘Your questions’).

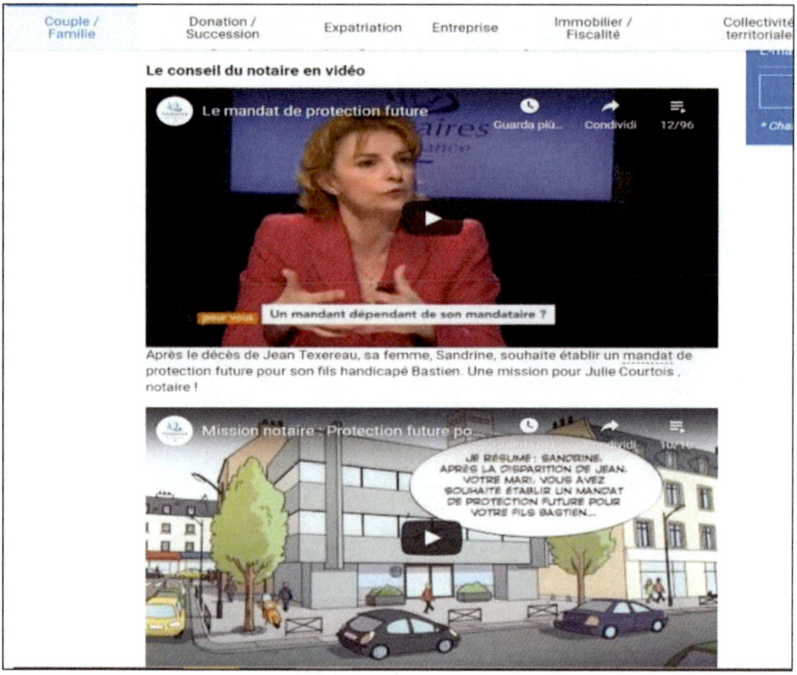

Fig. 4: “Le conseil du notaire en video” (The notary’s advice in the video) and the Cartoon “Mission notaire” (Notary mission)[26]

---

[25] All videos are also available on the YouTube channel “Notaires de France – Conseil supérieur du notariat”. https://www.youtube.com/user/NotairesdeFrance1 (Last access 12.12.2022).

[26] Brackets translated by the author. https://www.notaires.fr/fr/couple-famille/protection-des-proches-vuln%C3%A9rables/le-patrimoine-des-personnesvuln%C3%A9rables (Last access 12.12.2022).

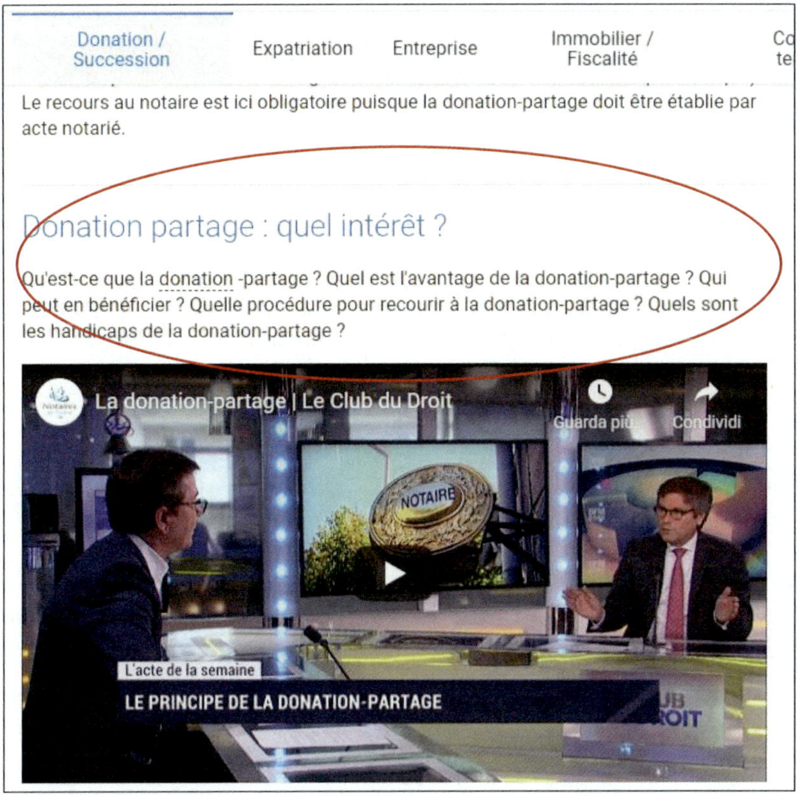

Fig. 5: The TV program "Le club du droit"[27]

All videos assume the same informative and explanatory form as the written texts: They mostly define (by definitional reformulations) the legal institutions ruled by notarial deeds, and make their functions explicit, as well as the procedures that citizens may exploit to protect themselves or to enjoy their rights. Cartoons, in particular, point out and stress part of the content in speech bubbles, read out by a voice-over in a multimodal (or pluri-semiotic) structure contributing to transmitting specific knowledge to users. Even though language still plays a prominent role in videos, images, non-

[27] https://www.notaires.fr/fr/donation-succession/donation/succession-donation-partage-et-et-donation-transg%C3%A9n%C3%A9rationnelle (Last access 12.12.2022).

verbal sounds, spoken language and sometimes written language are mixed in order to reach a common goal in notarial knowledge popularisation.

Let us state that the contents retrieved in videos generally focus on *L'acte de la semaine* ('the weekly deed') and mostly overlap with the informative and explanatory texts which can be read along on the web pages. Both in videos from *Le club du droit* and in videos recorded by a notary for the website, after a general introduction about a deed or institution, the presenter shifts to the feature *Passez-moi le notaire* ('pass me the notary') and reads the specific questions asked via e-mail to the editorial staff by a citizen. Hence, the invited notary speaker dwells on a particular case and, through his / her answer, offers further generalisations on a topic.

2. Engaging the audience

We must add that, unlike written texts where terms are immediately reformulated or linked by pop-ups to their definitions in the *Lexique*, obviously videos cannot take advantage of these possibilities but might need prior reading to reach a full understanding. Therefore, we believe that even if videos repeat and widen what the user could have already learnt by reading the web pages, they hold a major function related to the audience. Their particular purpose lies in the attempt to engage[28] lay-users and put them in a favourable mood by the promise of easy and clear explanations, as stated, for example in the video in Figure 5:

(16) *Le plus simplement et le plus clairement possible [...] ce sont vos amis notaires qui vous répondent [...] dans un esprit pédagogique. (Lexique)*[29]

Two important strategies that merge in this attempt are the use of questions and of pronouns, both belonging to the notion of *dialogisation intérieure*[30] ('internal dialogism'; cf. Bres / Nowakowska 2005: 139). Figure 5 above

[28] In Hyland's (2010: 295) view "engagement [is; CP] an alignment dimension of interaction where writers acknowledge and connect to others."

[29] Translated by the author: As simply and as clearly as possible [...] it is your notary friends who answer you [...] in a pedagogical spirit]. (*Lexicon*)

[30] For a detailed analysis of different strategies of internal dialogism in the popularisation of legal knowledge, see Preite (2018).

shows how videos are generally introduced by sub-headings in form of questions, aiming at arousing users' curiosity and attention by the enhancement of a *dialogisme intralocutif*[31] ('intralocutive' or 'autodialogism') between the video and the text on the webpage. The questions actually recall the general questions that the presenter will ask the guest notary about the institution they are talking about. Instead, pronouns like *vous / vos* ('you / your', see example 16) or *moi* ('me'; in the title of the feature *Passez-moi le notaire*) build a *dialogisme interlocutif*[32] ('interlocutive dialogism') that addresses and solicits the audience, therefore orientating the discourse towards it.

We should, though, recognise that the real pedagogical attempt (*esprit pédagogique*, see example 16), as far as the simplification of legal language is concerned, is made on the written webpages, while videos are more interested in engaging users after they have looked up the topic they are interested in. This strategy helps to overcome distrust and accomplishes the goal to turn the notary office into an accessible and liked (or at least not disliked) institution.

V. Concluding remarks

It was the aim of this contribution to highlight how the *notaires.fr* website is structured in order to reach citizens with popularisation of legal knowledge. According to Engberg (2020b: 180), this particular kind of popularisation has three main features: "influencing behavior", "rendering information", and "reducing alienation of citizens from legal institutions". "Influencing behavior" is achieved by offering instructions about the procedures that citizens can follow in order to enjoy their rights, generally

[31] Bres / Nowakowska (2005: 139): "Le locuteur est son premier interlocuteur dans le processus de l'autorécéption." Translated by the author: "The speaker is the first interlocutor in the process of self-reception."

[32] Bres / Nowakowska (2005: 139): "Le locuteur s'adresse à un interlocuteur sur la compréhension-réponse duquel il ne cesse d'anticiper." Translated by the author: "The speaker addresses an interlocutor whose comprehension-response he / she constantly anticipates."

developed in a question / answer pattern and made explicit through definitional reformulations by purpose or function (cf. Preite 2016). "Rendering information" is mainly fulfilled through definitional reformulations by denomination, equivalence, analysis, characterisation, exemplification, and generalisation.

These are accomplished both in written informative and explanatory discourses and in videos as well as in the lexicon's definitions and are meant to build a path planned to lead laypeople to reconstructing and understanding new knowledge about legal institutions and objects. Specialised terms are defined and related in a conceptual network that is based on weaving their semantic relationships. In this way, the website texts allow readers to graft terms that denote specialised concepts, previously unknown, onto a core of encyclopædic and linguistic knowledge that has been either previously acquired or constructed at the same time. This creates a useful exchange between widely shared general knowledge and specific legal knowledge and terminology which citizens can seize and structure cognitively. It also proves a strong "explanatory ambition" (Engberg 2020a: 50).

As far as "reducing alienation" is concerned, the multimodal architecture of the website and different forms of scripto-visual relationships (e.g., images and videos) play a prominent role in mitigating the feeling of strangeness (cf. Preite 2013) that citizens generally hold towards several aspects of the legal world. In particular, every topic covered by written informative and explanatory discourses is enhanced by videos. In terms of contents and knowledge mediation, those videos would not be necessary because they are a partial repetition of written presentations, but they cater to users accustomed to multimodal communication, and they engage with the audience (in particular "Le club du droit"). Therefore, we join Cavalieri's (2018: 267) claim that in legal popularisation videos tend prominently to focus on "liaising with the audience". They are exploited to bring the notary office closer to citizens, making it accessible and acceptable, if not appreciated.

VI. References

Association des Notaires de France / Notaires.fr: https://www.notaires.fr/fr. Last accessed 12.12.2022.

Bhatia, Vijay K. 1983. Simplification vs. Easyfication. The Case of Legal Texts. *Applied Linguistics* 4 (1), 42-54.

Bres, Jacques / Alexandra Nowakowska. 2005. Dis-moi avec qui tu 'dialogues', je te dirai qui tu es … De la pertinence de la notion de dialogisme pour l'analyse du discours. *Marges linguistiques* 9, 137-153.

Calsamiglia, Helena / Teun A. van Dijk. 2004. Popularization Discourse and Knowledge about the Genome. *Discourse & Society* 15 (4), 369-389.

Candel, Danielle. 1995. Le discours définitoire. Variations discursives chez les scientifiques. In: Sophie Moirand / Abdelmadjid Ali Bouacha / Jean-Claude Beacco / André Collinot (Eds.), *Parcours linguistiques de discours spécialisés*. Bern: Peter Lang, 33-44.

Cavalieri, Silvia. 2018. Broadcasting Legal Discourse. The Popularization of Family Law through YouTube. In: Jan Engberg / Karin Lutterman / Silvia Cacchiani / Chiara Preite (Eds.), *Popularization and Knowledge Mediation in the Law / Popularisierung und Wissensvermittlung im Recht*. Wien: Lit, 251-270.

Cornu, Gérard. 1990. *Linguistique juridique*. Paris: Montchrestien.

Darian, Steven G. 2003. *Understanding the Language of Science*. Austin: University of Texas Press.

Engberg, Jan. 2010. Knowledge Construction and Legal Discourse. *Journal of Pragmatics* 42, 48-63.

Engberg, Jan. 2013. Legal Terminology. On Intelligibility and Strategies for Dissemination. *Synaps* 29, 18-30.

Engberg, Jan. 2020a. Multimodal Institutional Knowledge Dissemination and Popularization in an EU Context. Explanatory Ambition in Focus. In: Girolamo Tessuto / Vijay K. Bhatia / Ruth Breeze / Nicholas Brownlees / Martin Solly (Eds.), *The Context and Media of Legal Discourse*. Newcastle upon Tyne: Cambridge Scholars, 50-76.

Engberg, Jan. 2020b. Institutional Dissemination of Legal Knowledge. An Instance of Knowledge Communication. In: Maurizio Gotti / Stefania Maci / Michele Sala (Eds.), *Scholarly Pathways. Knowledge Transfer and Knowledge Exchange in Academia*. Frankfurt am Main: Peter Lang, 175-205.

Engberg, Jan / Carmen D. Maier. 2019. Researchers' Move from Page to Screen. Addressing the Effects of the Video Article Format upon Academic User Engagement and Knowledge-Building Processes. In: Carmen Sancho Guinda (Ed.), *Engagement in Professional Genres*. Amsterdam: John Benjamins, 179-195.

Hyland, Ken. 2010. Constructing Proximity. Relating to Readers in Popular and Professional Science. *Journal of English for Academic Purposes* 9, 116-127.

Jacobi, Daniel. 1987. *Textes et images de la vulgarisation scientifique*. Bern: Peter Lang.

Kress, Gunther. 2009. *Multimodality. A Social Semiotic Approach to Contemporary Communication*. London: Routledge.

Kress, Gunther / Theo van Leeuwen. 2001. *Multimodal Discourse. The Modes and Media of Contemporary Communication*. London: Hachette UK.

Loffler-Laurian, Anne-Marie. 1983. Typologie des discours scientifiques: deux approches. *Études de linguistique appliquée* 51, 8-20.

Luzón, María-José. 2019. Bridging the Gap between Experts and Public. The Role of Multimodality in Disseminating Research in Online Videos. *Ibérica* 37, 167-192.

Martinec, Radan / Andrew Salway. 2005. A System of Text-Image Relations in New (and Old) Media. *Visual Communication* 4 (3), 339-374.

Preite, Chiara. 2013. Comunicare il diritto. Strategie di divulgazione del discorso giuridico. In: Cristina Bosisio / Stefania Cavagnoli (Eds.): *Comunicare le discipline attraverso le lingue*. Perugia: Guerra Edizioni, 245-262.

Preite, Chiara. 2016. La vulgarisation des termes juridiques et la construction d'un savoir ("que") faire chez le grand public. In: Danio Maldussi

(Ed.), *Le terme. Un produit social?, Repères DoRiF* 10. http://www.dorif.it/ezine/ezine_articles.php?dorif_ezine=f10d525e5f4b23fe1994a7237638e6a7&art_id=316. Last accessed 12.12.2022.

Preite, Chiara. 2018. Stratégies dialogiques et transmission du savoir juridique dans le site du Ministère de la Justice français. In: Jan Engberg / Karin Lutterman / Silvia Cacchiani / Chiara Preite (Eds.), *Popularization and Knowledge Mediation in the Law / Popularisierung und Wissensvermittlung im Recht*. Wien: Lit, 149-167.

Rabatel, Alain. 2010. *Les reformulations pluri-sémiotiques en contexte de formation*. Besançon: Presses Universitaires de Franche-Comté.

Sagnier, Christine. 2018. *Des images et des mots ... au XXIe siècle. Nouvelles perspectives sur la multimodalité, la communication visuelle et les multilittératies*. Brussels: Peter Lang.

Silletti, Alida M. 2018. Analyse des publications de l'Union européenne à visée vulgarisatrice. Le cas des illustrations. In: Jan Engberg / Karin Lutterman / Silvia Cacchiani / Chiara Preite (Eds.), *Popularization and Knowledge Mediation in the Law / Popularisierung und Wissensvermittlung im Recht*. Wien: Lit, 223-248.

Werlich, Egon. 1975. *Typologie der Texte. Entwurf eines textlinguistischen Modells zur Grundlegung einer Textgrammatik*. Heidelberg: Quelle & Meyer.

Karin Luttermann / Jan Engberg

„Justiz verstehen!" – Kulturkontrastive Analysen digitaler Rechtskommunikation auf ministeriellen Webseiten in Deutschland und Dänemark

Abstract

Der Beitrag befasst sich mit der digitalen Rechtskommunikation des deutschen Bundesjustizministeriums und des Justizministeriums in Dänemark im Internet. Ein zentrales Merkmal des Kommunikationskanals ist seine hohe Zugänglichkeit, wodurch Bürger relativ einen direkten Zugang zu Rechtsinformationen haben. Aufgrund dieser Zugänglichkeit eignet sich der Kanal besonders für Popularisierung, d.h. für die Kommunikation der juristischen Institution, mit der sowohl eine Vermittlungsfunktion als auch eine vertrauensfördernde Funktion angestrebt wird. Die Analysen leiten Fragen zum Vertrauensaufbau, zur Multimodalität und Interaktivität sowie zur Bürgernähe. Im Ergebnis kann gezeigt werden, dass die Vertrauensförderung durch Personalisierung und das Eingehen auf die Denkweisen und Bedürfnisse der angesprochenen Bürger in der Kommunikation des deutschen Justizministeriums deutlich stärker ausgeprägt sind als in der Kommunikation des dänischen Ministeriums. Die Kommunikation des deutschen Ministeriums ist damit stärker auf die Popularisierung der Institution in Bezug auf seine Bürger ausgerichtet, während das dänische Ministerium eher Wissen vermittelt, dessen Bürger-Zugänglichkeit für die Arbeit des Ministeriums selbst relevant ist.

This contribution deals with the digital legal communication of the German Federal Ministry of Justice and the Ministry of Justice in Denmark via the Internet. A central feature of this communication channel is its high level of accessibility, which gives citizens relatively direct access to legal information. Due to this accessibility, the channel is particularly suitable for popularisation, i.e. for institutional legal communication aiming both at a mediating function and a trust-promoting function. The analyses are guided by questions concerning trust building, application of multimodality and interactivity, and whether the institution is brought closer to the citizens. The study shows that the promotion of trust through personalisation and responding to the mindsets and needs of the citizens addressed is much more pronounced in the communication of the German Ministry of Justice than in the communication of the Danish Ministry. The German Ministry's communication is thus more strongly geared towards popularising the institution among citizens; for the Danish Ministry it instead seems to be important to convey knowledge to citizens in fields where it is important for the work of the Ministry itself that citizens possess this knowledge.

I. Einleitung

Rechtslinguistik bewegt sich an der Schnittstelle zwischen Sprache und Recht. Es handelt sich um eine Teildisziplin der modernen Linguistik, die primär in der Fachkommunikation verortet ist. Die Entwicklungslinien verlaufen im Großen und Ganzen nahezu deckungsgleich. An die Stelle der zunächst sprachsystematischen, d.h. lexikalisch-terminologischen und stilistisch-syntaktischen Beschäftigungsphase mit Fachsprachen im Recht sind verstärkt die handlungs-pragmalinguistische Phase und die kognitiv-kommunikative Phase getreten (vgl. im Überblick z.B. Roelcke 2020: 13ff.; Schubert 2007: 141ff.). Die Perspektivenerweiterung reicht also von Fachsprachen als Zeichensysteme über Fachsprachen als Textäußerungen bis hin zu den (intellektuellen) Voraussetzungen von Produzenten und Rezipienten beim Kommunizieren im Fach.[1]

Mit der Hinwendung zum Sprachgebrauch und zu kognitiven Aspekten rücken die Darbietung und Vermittlung von Wissen in der fachspezifischen Experten-Laien-Interaktion in den Fokus. Dabei spielen Popularisierung von Rechtswissen und Digitalisierung eine zunehmend wichtige Rolle (vgl. im Überblick z.B. Engberg / Luttermann / Cacchiani / Preite 2018; Luttermann / Engberg 2023a; Anesa / Engberg 2023). Das gilt vor allem,

---

[1] Umfasst sind alle natürlichen Geschlechter.

wenn es darum geht, Kommunikationsprozesse zu optimieren oder Verständlichkeit und Vertrauen in die staatlichen Institutionen zu generieren (vgl. z.B. Luttermann 2010, 2021; Luttermann / Engberg 2024), um Bürger auch emotional zu erreichen.

Der vorliegende Beitrag widmet sich der digitalen rechtlichen Fachkommunikation. Mit wachsender Bedeutung des Internets als Kommunikationsmedium steigt auch die Anzahl an linguistischen Veröffentlichungen im Bereich des Rechts. Ein zentrales Merkmal des Internets als Kommunikationskanal ist sein hoher Grad an Zugänglichkeit: Wer über eine Internetverbindung verfügt, hat im Prinzip – setzt man die technische Handhabung voraus – Zugang zu allen Seiten, die von den Verfassern nicht dezidiert verschlossen sind. Das bedeutet, dass dieser Kommunikationskanal für den Kontakt zwischen Fachexperten und Behörden auf der einen Seite und Nicht-Fachleuten und Bürgern auf der anderen Seite ein gut geeignetes und probates Mittel ist (vgl. Bondi / Cacchiani 2021).

So nutzen zum Beispiel Rechtsanwälte das Internet, um Mandanten oder Personal zu akquirieren sowie ihre Expertise und professionellen Dienstleistungen anzubieten und zu bewerben. In dem Zuge entstehen – wie textlinguistische Forschung zeigt – neue digital vermittelte Subgenres der biographischen Selbstdarstellung (vgl. Lombardi / Luttermann 2023; Luttermann / Lombardi 2025), die auch Rückschlüsse auf berufliche Wertvorstellungen der Anwaltschaft erlauben (vgl. Lombardi 2024; Luttermann 2024). Ein häufiger Untersuchungsgegenstand in dem Zusammenhang sind überdies juristische Internet-Foren und sogenannte Blawgs, d.h. typisch Blogs von Rechtsanwälten, in denen sie als Ratgeber für juristische Laien fungieren (vgl. Anesa 2016; Diani 2023; Garzone 2014; Tessuto 2015; Turnbull 2023).

In diesem Beitrag konzentrieren wir uns auf einen anderen Typ digitaler Experten-Vermittlung, und zwar die offiziellen Seiten der Justizministerien in Deutschland und Dänemark. Der Beitrag reiht sich somit in einer Gruppe von Arbeiten ein, in der die offizielle Kommunikation zwischen Behörden und Bürgern untersucht wird (vgl. z.B. Cacchiani 2018; Engberg / Luttermann 2014; Preite 2018; Wiesmann 2023). Wir analysieren konkret die kommunikative Gestaltung der Webseite des deutschen Bundesministeriums der Justiz, Berlin, und vergleichen diese mit dem Webauftritt des Justizministeriums in Dänemark, Kopenhagen. Dabei interessieren vor allem die Fragen:

i. Wie präsentiert sich jeweils die Justiz gegenüber den Bürgern, um Vertrauen in sich als Behörde aufzubauen?
ii. Inwieweit sind fachliche Informationen multimodal dargeboten und interaktiv zugänglich?
iii. Welchen Raum nehmen Verständlichkeit und Bürgernähe ein bzw. welche Bedeutung misst die Justiz selbst dem zu?

Darauf konzentrieren wir uns in diesem Beitrag und gehen wie folgt vor: Zunächst werden die Kriterien der Popularisierung (Ziffer II) und Elemente der Multimodalität (Ziffer III) als handlungstheoretische Grundlagen für die – kulturkontrastiven – Analysen der Webseiten behandelt. Vor diesem Hintergrund wird danach die Webseite des deutschen Bundesjustizministeriums hinsichtlich der Art und Weise der Darbietung der Informationen, der fokussierten Themen und der Maßnahmen, verständlich mit den Bürgern zu kommunizieren, analysiert (Ziffer IV). Im Anschluss daran geht es um die Analyse der Webseite des dänischen Ministeriums der Justiz entlang der Leitfragen (Ziffer V). Dann werden die beiden Webseiten auf Gemeinsamkeiten und Unterschiede sowie unter dem Aspekt der Verständlichkeit miteinander verglichen (Ziffer VI). Abschließend werden die Ergebnisse zu „Justiz verstehen“[2] zusammengefasst, reflektiert und in den Forschungskontext eingeordnet (Ziffer VII).

II. Was ist Popularisierung – und wie geht Popularisierung als Methode über Vermittlung hinaus?

Wesentlich für die Beschäftigung mit Vermittlung und Popularisierung im Rechtswesen ist es, das Merkmal juristischer Kommunikation mit in die

---

[2] Bürgerkommunikation, Systemstabilisierung, Demokratie.

theoretisch-methodischen Überlegungen einzubauen.[3] So muss die juristische Fachlichkeit immer auch Normvorstellungen der Gesellschaft spiegeln. Mit Blick auf die Wahrung der Rechtssicherheit und die Vertrauensbildung in das Funktionieren der Institutionen ist es wichtig, dass der Sprachgebrauch der Juristen sich nicht allzu weit von dem der Bevölkerung (Empfängerhorizont) entkoppelt (vgl. Luttermann 2010: 150). Die Begriffe müssen im Wesentlichen semantisch dasselbe Konzept ausdrücken. Wo zum Beispiel Astronomie in der Entwicklung ihrer Begrifflichkeit nur von der eigenen Fachlichkeit gesteuert wird, liegt es in der Natur der juristischen Fachlichkeit, dass sie jedenfalls zu einem gewissen Grad in Einklang mit den Haltungen der Bevölkerung zu sein hat (vgl. Engberg 2017). Dies setzt – schon aus rein demokratischen Gedanken (vgl. Luttermann 1999, 2021) – ein Rechtsverstehen auf Seiten der Bürger voraus:

> Trotz der Pluralität der fachwissenschaftlichen Perspektiven besteht Konsens über die Grundannahme, dass in einem demokratischen Staat eine prinzipielle Verständlichkeit von Gesetzen gewährleistet sein muss. Denn: Mangelndes Verständnis des herrschenden Normensystems und daraus resultierendes Misstrauen in RechtspraktikerInnen (Stichworte ‚Juristenschelte', Sprache als ‚Herrschaftsmittel') können langfristig das notwendige Vertrauen der BürgerInnen in den Rechtsstaat untergraben. (Vogel / Deus / Luth / Schmallenbach / Felder 2022: 18)

Wir werden uns später mit der Konkretisierung des Begriffs *Verständlichkeit* im Recht befassen (siehe Ziffern VI.2 und VI.3). Es ist aber schon hier darauf hinzuweisen, dass sich die Aufgabe nicht in einer Vermittlung des Inhalts juristischen Denkens erschöpft. Es ist auch notwendig, dass eine Relation zwischen Experten-Vermittler und Bürger entwickelt wird (vgl. Myers 2003). Um diese Notwendigkeit genauer auszuleuchten, haben wir in unterschiedlichen Arbeiten vorgeschlagen, Vermittlung und Popularisierung begrifflich zu trennen (vgl. Luttermann / Engberg 2018, 2023b). *Popularisierung* sehen wir dabei als eine Informationshandlung, die zusätzliche Kriterien zu erfüllen hat, die sie von der Vermittlung unterscheiden (vgl. z.B. Engberg 2020: 182; Luttermann / Engberg 2023b: 104ff.):

---

[3] Juristische Kommunikation wird dadurch getragen, dass Recht für die Menschen da ist; vgl. Ziffer VII.

- Es existiert eine Wissensasymmetrie zwischen den Teilnehmenden an der Kommunikationssituation (Experten-Laien-Relation).
- Experten beabsichtigen, den Laien Rechtswissen vorzustellen (Reformulierungs- und Vermittlungsintention).
- Rechtswissen wird außerhalb des institutionellen Kontexts verortet, in dem es normalerweise Verwendung findet (Rekontextualisierungsintention).
- Experten beabsichtigen, Rechtwissen in einer Weise vorzustellen, die zur Etablierung einer Verbindung zur Kultur der Laienempfänger beiträgt (Popularisierungsintention).

Damit von Popularisierung und nicht lediglich von Vermittlung gesprochen werden kann, muss über die Wissensasymmetrie, Reformulierungs-, Vermittlungs- und Rekontextualisierungsintention hinaus ein Wunsch da sein, eine Relation zur nicht-juristischen Kultur und Alltagswelt der Empfänger zu schaffen, wodurch auch an der Popularität im Sinne des Gemocht-Werdens (Akzeptanz) und Vertrauen-Schaffens gearbeitet wird. Ein Ziel angemessener Kommunikation ist dabei, dass eine gegenseitige Relation der Empathie zwischen Behörde und Bürger entsteht. Eine solche Relation ist auch relevant, da die Sprachlichkeit des Rechts eine inhärente Vagheit in sich birgt, die eine positive Haltung bei den Bürgern voraussetzt, die dazu führt, dass diese aktiv versuchen und sich bemühen, die tatsächliche Intention (Willen) des Gesetzgebers zu ermitteln (vgl. Luttermann 2010, 2021; Engberg 2014; Felder 2023; Felder / Deutsch / Vogel / Höfler / Hörth / Gleichmann / Luth / Pick / Kudlich / Bülow 2020). Dieser Punkt wird im Folgenden eine zentrale Rolle in unseren Analysen spielen.

III. Elemente der multimodalen Beschreibung

Als theoretisch-methodische Grundlage für die Beantwortung der ersten und dritten Forschungsfrage – also den Fragen nach der Darstellung der Informationen durch die Justiz und nach verständlicher Kommunikation (siehe Ziffer I) – funktioniert der vorstehend erörterte Begriff der *Popularisierung* in seiner Abgrenzung zur weniger auf den Aufbau persönlicher und popularitätsbezogener (empathischer) Relationen ausgerichteten Vermittlung (siehe Ziffer II). Dagegen möchten wir uns für die Beantwortung der zweiten Forschungsfrage, wie es sich mit der Nutzung der Potentiale von Multimodalität und Interaktivität auf den Seiten der beiden Ministerien verhält (siehe Ziffer I), eines Ansatzes bedienen, der sich weniger stark auf den verbal vermittelten Inhalt des Webauftritts bezieht, sondern dagegen die Relation zwischen unterschiedlichen Zeichenmodalitäten bei der Vermittlung ins Visier nimmt. Unter dem Begriff der *Zeichenmodalität* verstehen wir mit Wildfeuer / Bateman (2018: 19) die Art des kommunikativ eingesetzten Materials, das nach bestimmten kompositionellen und diskurssemantisch-konventionalisierten Regelmäßigkeiten für das Schaffen bedeutungstragender Zeichen verwendet werden kann.

Die hier über die verbalen Zeichen in Form der Sprache hinausgehenden und für unsere Zwecke besonders relevanten Zeichenmodalitäten sind die non-verbalen Zeichen in Form von Fotos und die paraverbalen Zeichen in Form von (Hintergrund-)Farben. Die Verortung der untersuchten Texte in dem Webauftritt der beiden Justizministerien bedeutet, dass sie als Internet-Hypertexte wegen ihrer notwendigen Verwaltung über das Medium des Computers eine inhärente potenzielle Multimodalität aufweisen (vgl. Storrer 2019: 318, 320f.; Engberg / Luttermann 2014: 70ff.). Nach Bucher / Boy / Christ (2022: 4) eröffnet gerade diese Internetverortung und damit die Digitalisierung der Kommunikation eine „fortschreitende Multimodalisierung" wissensbezogener Kommunikation.

Diese Multimodalisierung kann in unterschiedlicher Weise realisiert werden. Wir sind in erster Linie daran interessiert, welche Rolle die unterschiedlichen vorgefundenen Zeichenmodalitäten für die Vermittlung des rechtlichen Wissens spielen, insbesondere inwiefern den unterschiedlichen Zeichenmodaltitäten eine eigene Rolle in der Vermittlung und darüber hinaus bei der Popularisierung verliehen wird. Dabei beziehen wir uns auf einen Analyseansatz, nach dem die Interaktion zwischen Zeichenmodalitäten und ihrer jeweiligen Rolle erfasst wird (vgl. Engberg / Maier 2015 für einen Überblick). Der Schwerpunkt des Ansatzes liegt darauf, wie die Interaktion unterschiedlicher Modi eine komplexe Repräsentation von wissenschaftlichem Wissen schafft und welche Relationen zwischen den Modi bestehen. Im Kern fragen wir also danach, ob die unterschiedlichen Zeichenmodalitäten eine selbstständige Rolle bei der Darbietung des Wissens einnehmen oder ob sie primär eine unterstützende Rolle haben.

In dem zugrundeliegenden Analyseansatz wird zwischen zwei wesentlichen intendierten Prozesstypen bei der Darbietung von Wissen unterschieden: der Wissenserweiterung und Wissensvertiefung (vgl. Engberg / Maier 2015: 231f.). Wir befassen uns hier in der Analyse nicht mit dem Prozess der Wissenserweiterung, bei dem es um die Darbietung neuer Bedeutungsdimensionen geht, sondern ausschließlich mit dem Prozess der Wissensvertiefung, da dieser auf den untersuchten Seiten die größte Rolle spielt. Die Wissensvertiefung ist dadurch gekennzeichnet, dass durch die Kombination mehrerer Zeichenmodalitäten ein Aspekt des Beschriebenen, der durch eine Zeichenmodalität eingeführt wird, durch weitere Modalitäten ausdifferenziert und vertieft wird. Als Beispiel kann eine Analyse in einer unserer früheren Arbeit dienen. In Luttermann / Engberg (2023b: 117ff.) haben wir eine Informationsbroschüre des Bayerischen Staatsministeriums der Justiz zum Erbrecht untersucht und gesehen, dass hier Figuren und Farben für die Gestaltung einzelner Bestandteile zur Verdeutlichung und Vertiefung von verbal eingeführten Aussagen verwendet werden.

Bei dem semiotischen Prozess der Wissensvertiefung kann man unterscheiden zwischen tatsächlicher und repetitiver Wissensvertiefung (vgl. Jaki / Engberg 2024: 243f.). Bei der tatsächlichen Vertiefung leistet jeder Zeichenmodus einen selbstständigen Beitrag zur Wissensdarbietung, sodass etwa wie im oben angeführten Analysebeispiel durch die Kombination von verbalem Text und dem visuellen Element der Figur unterschiedliche Details dargeboten werden. Wenn dagegen ein Foto lediglich eine schmückende Funktion übernimmt, ohne dass durch das Foto neue Details über das Besprochene präsentiert werden, ist die Wissensvertiefung lediglich repetitiv. Im Analyseteil werden wir einige Beispiele dieser Art der Wissensvertiefung geben (siehe Ziffern IV und V). Ausgehend von den theoretischen Annahmen werden wir im Folgenden die Gestaltung der Webseiten – zunächst des bundesdeutschen und dann des dänischen Ministeriums der Justiz – analysieren.

IV. Gestaltung der BMJ-Webseite

1. Aufbau

Die Webseite des Bundesministeriums der Justiz (BMJ) will Bürger über das Recht informieren. Dieser kommunikative Zweck prägt die Gestaltung der Navigationsleiste. Die Navigationsleiste hat fünf Reiter (*Rechtsstaat kompakt*, *Themen*, *Ministerium*, *Presse*, *Service*) und eine Lupe (siehe Abb. 1). Klickt man auf die Lupe, erscheint ein Suchfeld mit der an Bürger adressierten Frage „Wie können wir Ihnen helfen?". Zugleich erscheinen fünf Suchvorschläge (*Digitales*, *Krieg in der Ukraine*, *Bürokratieabbau*, *Rechtsstaat kompakt*, *Gesetzgebungsverfahren*), die mit Teilen der Unter-Webseiten verlinkt sind. Mit der Fragehandlung richtet sich das Justizministerium direkt an seine Nutzer und fordert sie auf, ihr jeweiliges Rechtsanliegen zu kommunizieren. Oben links neben den Reitern befindet sich das Logo des Bundesministeriums mit dem Bundesadler und den Farben der Flagge der Bundesrepublik Deutschland. Daneben steht in Majuskeln und in weißer Schrift „WIR FEIERN / 75 JAHRE / GRUNDGESETZ", nacheinander farblich unterlegt in Schwarz, Rot, Gold. Die Farbgebung der Bundesflagge (Artikel 22 Absatz 2 Grundgesetz / GG) gilt als Sinnbild für Einheit, Freiheit und Demokratie.

Abb. 1: Startseite BMJ (Letzter Zugriff 25.8.2024)

Über der Navigationsleiste gibt es vier Hilfsfunktionen: *Inhaltsverzeichnis*, *Kontakt*, *Gebärdensprache* (davor Ikon: zwei Hände) und *Leichte Sprache* (davor Ikon: Gesicht und Buch). Der Reiter *Inhaltsverzeichnis* gibt einen Überblick über den gesamten Inhalt, der Gegenstand der Bürgerkommunikation ist, und schafft Verbindungen zu den Unterseiten. Die *Kontakt*-Seite begrüßt alle Interessierten („Willkommen beim Bürgerdialog") und bietet diverse Kontaktmöglichkeiten an nebst einem Kontaktformular mit Pflichtangaben für „Bürgeranfragen". Dagegen wenden sich die beiden Reiter *Gebärdensprache* und *Leichte Sprache* (siehe Ziffer IV.5) an einen eingeschränkten Adressatenkreis und stellen für Menschen mit Beeinträchtigungen speziell aufbereitete Rechtsinformationen (z.B. Angebote zur Vorsorgevollmacht in Gebärdensprache, Informationsbroschüren in Leichter Sprache) bereit.

Die Eingangsseite besteht aus mehreren großen und farbigen Rechtecken, die Informationen rund um das Recht – einschließlich des Bereichs Verbraucherschutz[4] (wofür das deutsche Justizministerium ebenfalls zuständig ist) – enthalten und die Bevölkerung zum Dialog einladen. So insinuiert gleich das erste, in verschiedenen Blautönen gestaltete Rechteck einen Dienstleistungscharakter des Justizministeriums gegenüber Verbrauchern („SERVICE.JUSTIZ.DE/FLUGGASTRECHTE"). Das zweite Rechteck mit einem Foto vom amtierenden Bundesjustizminister „Dr. Marco Buschmann" demonstriert mit den Links *Zum Minister*, *Interviews*, *Reden*, *JETZT ERST RECHT* Nahbarkeit und Handlungsstärke. Das gilt auch für das dritte Rechteck mit weiteren Fotos vom Minister und mit den Verlinkungen *Interview*, *Gesetzentwurf* und *Pressemitteilung*. Der *JETZT ERST RECHT*-Link führt zum vierten Rechteck. Hier behandelt der Minister in einem Clip („Buschmanns 60 Sekunden") jeweils aktuelle Themen von gesellschaftlicher Relevanz (z.B. „Einfaches Bauen").

Das fünfte Rechteck fordert Bürger dazu auf, sich mit dem Grundgesetz zu befassen („Entdecke das Grundgesetz in deinem Alltag!"). Begründet wird das damit, dass „unse[r] demokratische[r] Rechtsstaa[t]" ohne Wenn und Aber „an Recht und Gesetz" gebunden ist. Daran schließt das sechste Rechteck mit den Links *Rechtsstaat kompakt*, *Unser Grundgesetz*, *Unser Rechtsstaat* an, die inhaltlich einen direkten Bezug zu den Reitern der Navigationsseite (Menüliste) haben und auf Unterseiten verweisen. Dass die Webkommunikation vernetzt ist, ist auch am „Bürokratieabbau" zu sehen. Der „Bürokratieabbau" ist Gegenstand des siebten Rechtecks, aber auch an dritter Stelle als Subthema des Reiters *Themen* zu finden. Das achte Rechteck dient der Selbstdefinition und dem Selbstverständnis des Justizministe-

---

4 Hier geht es um die Stärkung der Position der Verbraucher gegenüber der Wirtschaft.

riums („Wir sind das Haus für Recht und Freiheit!“), das mehrere Gesetzgebungsverfahren ausgestalten und versinnbildlichen.

Das neunte Rechteck „Justiz und Fragen? Just Ask!“ ist ein Videoformat. Die Justiz in Gestalt des Bundesjustizministers beantwortet Rechts- und Verbraucherfragen (z.B. zum Namensrecht), zu denen das Ministerium zum Teil auch Informationsbroschüren (u.a. Patientenverfügung) herausgibt, die man als PDF-Datei herunterladen und / oder bestellen kann. Zudem gibt es zu bestimmten Themen (z.B. zum Grundgesetz) abrufbare Erklärfilme. Die Webseite vermittelt im Ganzen den Eindruck, dass Bürgerkommunikation wichtig ist. Dementsprechend stellt das Justizministerium diverse Kommunikationsformate (Instagram, X / Twitter, Youtube, LinkedIn, Facebook) bereit und fordert Bürger auf, diese zu nutzen („Folgen Sie uns“). Das zehnte Rechteck „Services“ umfasst die Links *Veranstaltungen*, *Formulare*, *Gesetzgebung* und *Publikationen*. Wer zum Beispiel *Publikationen* anklickt, kann kostenlos Informationsmaterialien bestellen und frei Haus beziehen. Auf der Seite werden die Bestellungsmodalitäten und Kontaktdaten (Telefonnummer, E-Mail-Adresse) benannt.

2. Die Hauptbereiche

Die Navigationsleiste besteht aus den fünf beschrifteten Links, die auf Hauptbereiche des Webauftritts verweisen: Hier haben die Reiter *Rechtsstaat kompakt*, *Themen*, *Ministerium*, *Presse* und *Service* in erster Linie informierende Funktion. Es fällt auf, dass es nicht nur zwischen bestimmten Reitern und Rechtecken – wie oben ausgeführt (siehe Ziffer IV.1) – inhaltliche Überschneidungen gibt, sondern auch zwischen den Reitern selbst. Das ist zum Beispiel bei *Rechtsstaat kompakt* und *Themen* der Fall, wo mehrere Verlinkungen die Judikative behandeln. Unter *Rechtsstaat kompakt* öffnet der Link *Die Rechtsprechung* neue Felder, die u.a. über die Funktion der Gerichte im Allgemeinen und die Bundesgerichte und das Bundesverfassungsgericht im Besonderen Auskünfte geben. Die jeweils passend zum Text erscheinenden Farbfotos (wie die Justitia mit Augenbinde oder die Fassade des Gerichtsgebäudes) haben dabei illustrierenden Charakter.

Über den Reiter *Themen* und den Unterlink *Wege zum Recht* findet der Nutzer weiterführende Informationen bezüglich Rechtsprechung und Gerichtsverfahren mit Downloads und Schaubildern. Der Nutzer soll auf verschiedenen Wegen Rechtsinformationen finden und abrufen können. Dafür müssen die verbalen und visuellen Elemente sinnstiftend interagieren und in seine Wahrnehmungsreichweite kommen.[5] Mit anderen Worten: Die Webseite des Bundesjustizministeriums ist ein Hypertext. Dafür ist charakteristisch, dass der Textproduzent die vielen Informationen auf mehrere Hyperlinks und Module verteilt, die durch Computertechnik miteinander verknüpft sind. Der einzelne Nutzer entscheidet – je nach Interesse – selbst, in welcher Reihenfolge er auf welchen Reiter und welchen Link zugreifen möchte und ob er die Seiten, die Bestandteil der Navigationsleiste sind, vollständig durchscrollt oder nicht.

Möglich ist auch ein direkter Zugriff auf das *Inhaltsverzeichnis*, das sich in der Menüleiste mit den Hilfsfunktionen oberhalb der Reiter befindet. Hier liegt es ebenso im alleinigen Interesse des Nutzers, entweder ausgewählte Seiten aufzurufen oder sich der Reihe nach mit den Links und den dahinter liegenden Texten und Bildern zu befassen. Interessant ist zudem, dass das Inhaltsverzeichnis auf wissenschaftliches juristisches Arbeiten rückschließen lässt. Gewissermaßen in lehrbuchartiger Weise sind die Hauptbereiche dezidiert und die Unterbereiche kleinschrittig gegliedert. Die Hauptbereiche sind fünf an der Zahl. *Rechtsstaat kompakt* hat vier Unterbereiche mit noch einmal 21 Unterunterbereichen. Der Hauptbereich *Themen* ist am komplexesten, bestehend aus 13 Unterbereichen, 58 Unterunterbereichen und 93 Unterunterunterbereichen. Das *Ministerium* hat acht Unterbereiche, 26 Unterunterbereiche und einen einzigen Unterunterunterbereich.

Der Hauptbereich *Presse* hat die wenigsten Gliederungseinheiten mit drei Unterbereichen und weiteren drei Unterunterbereichen. Der Hauptbereich *Service* umfasst schließlich sieben Unterbereiche und zwölf Unterunterbereiche. Summa summarum ist die ministerielle Webseite – wie das Inhalts-

---

[5] Verfahren zur Wahrnehmung wie das Eye-Tracking können individuelle Lesepfade nachzeichnen.

verzeichnis zusammenhängend zeigt – in fünf Hauptbereiche, 35 Unterbereiche, 120 Unterunterbereiche sowie 94 Unterunterunterbereiche gegliedert. Wenn auch der verbale Anteil in allen Bereichen klar dominiert, so sind gleichwohl die bildlichen Elemente ein häufig vorkommender, integraler Teil der Webkommunikation mit den Bürgern und tragen mit zum Wissens- und Beziehungsaufbau bei. Es gibt also eine Fülle an Informationen, die mehrfach miteinander vernetzt sind und auf die der Nutzer durch Anklicken beschrifteter Links kommt, die er nach eigenem Ermessen (Motivation, Interesse, Vorkenntnissen u.a.) auswählt.

Das zeigen wir im Folgenden am Beispiel des Reiters *Rechtsstaat kompakt* (siehe Ziffer IV.3), den wir aufgrund seiner Vernetzung mit den Reitern *Themen* und *Ministerium* (siehe Ziffer IV.4) analysieren.[6] Die Hilfsfunktion *Leichte Sprache* (siehe Ziffer IV.5) wird ebenfalls in die Analyse einbezogen, um zu ermitteln, welche Informationen das Bundesjustizministerium der Zielgruppe Menschen mit Beeinträchtigungen (nicht: den Durchschnittsbürgern) darbietet und wie es mit ihnen kommuniziert.

3. Hauptbereich *Rechtsstaat kompakt*

Der erste Reiter der Navigationsleiste ist der Hauptbereich *Rechtsstaat kompakt*. Klickt man darauf, so erscheinen die Links *Unser Rechtsstaat*, *Unser Grundgesetz*, *Wie entsteht ein Gesetz?* und *Die Rechtsprechung*. Es werden also zentrale Begriffe des Rechtstaates und der Gewaltenteilung (Legislative und Judikative) eingeführt. Direkt im ersten Satz des sechszeiligen Textes präsentiert das Bundesjustizministerium Deutschland als Rechtsstaat („In Deutschland leben wir in einem Rechtsstaat“) und liefert das semantische Konzept gleich mit. Das bedeutet, dass die staatliche Gewalt laut „Art. 20 Abs. 3 GG“ an das Gesetz gebunden ist und das „Rechtsstaatsprinzip“ unserer freiheitlichen Demokratie im Grundgesetz verankert ist. Über dem kurzen Text befindet sich erneut ein Bild der Justitia mit Waage und Schwert, aber ohne Augenbinde. Justitia gilt als römische Göttin der Gerechtigkeit. Interessant ist, dass im direkten Anschluss an den

[6] Informationsdarbietung durch die Justiz, Multimodalität und Interaktivität, Verständlichkeit und Vertrauen.

Kurztext ein einminütiges Video des Bundesministers „Dr. Marco Buschmann“ mit Untertiteln folgt (siehe Abb. 2). In dem Format JETZT ERST RECHT erklärt er kurz und bündig, was *Demokratie* bedeutet („Buschmanns 60 Sekunden: Demokratie“, Folge 9) und fordert zudem die Nutzer zum Mitmachen auf („Demokratie ist kein Geschenk, das man bekommt und einfach behalten kann, sondern eine Aufgabe, an der wir alle immer wieder mitwirken müssen“).

Der Minister spricht die Bürger direkt an und bezieht sich ausdrücklich in den Appell, für die Demokratie einzustehen und Haltung zu zeigen, mit ein, indem er beispielsweise die Possessiv- und Personalpronomen „unser“ und „wir“ verwendet. Durch diese Form des Sprachgebrauchs erzeugt er eine Gemeinschaft zwischen dem Justizministerium, dem Staat und seinen Bürgern. Das schafft kommunikative Nähe. Ebenso die Tatsache, dass nicht das Gebäude der Justiz abgelichtet wird, sondern der Mensch als Minister im Videoclip auftritt, der zusätzlich durch Gestik, Mimik und Intonation nahbar erscheint und seine Botschaft akzentuiert: „Aber das Wichtigste ist, dass wir als Bürgerinnen und Bürger in breiter Mehrheit hinter unserer Verfassung stehen“ (00:52-00:58 Minuten).[7]

Abb. 2: Dr. Marco Buschmann

[7] https://www.youtube.com/shorts/vDm7RD1ggbY?app=desktop&cbrd=1 (Letzter Zugriff 25. 8.2024).

An die Videobotschaft schließen sechs gleich große gelbe Quadrate (jeweils drei in einer Reihe) mit schwarzer Schrift an. Jedes Quadrat hat eine Überschrift und einen kurzen Text im Umfang von maximal zwei Sätzen. Es geht dabei um rechtsstaatliche Prinzipien wie Gewaltenteilung; Bindung an Verfassung, Recht und Gesetz; Rechtssicherheit; Verhältnismäßigkeit; effektiven Rechtsschutz gegen staatliche Maßnahmen; richterliche Unabhängigkeit. Wer die Überschriften anklickt, gelangt zu den Unterseiten und erhält weitere detaillierte Informationen. Zudem gibt es teils Fotos von roten Gesetzbüchern (z.B. „Deutsche Gesetze. Textsammlung") oder von Richtern in schwarzen Roben, die illustrierende Funktion haben. Die Webseite *Rechtsstaat kompakt / Unser Rechtsstaat* endet mit drei dunkelblauen Quadraten, die in einer Reihe angeordnet und deren Überschriften und Kurztexte weiß beschriftet sind. Das sind übrigens die Links des Unterbereichs der Hauptseite. Hier kann der Nutzer „[m]ehr zum Thema Rechtsstaat" erfahren, indem er auf die beschrifteten Links *Unser Grundgesetz*, *Wie entsteht ein Gesetz?* und / oder *Rechtsprechung* zugreift.

Das mittlere Quadrat mit der Fragehandlung *Wie entsteht ein Gesetz?* ist für unser Untersuchungsziel der verständlichen Rechtskommunikation insofern besonders interessant, als die Gesetzesqualität unmittelbar in den Rahmen der Rechtsstaatlichkeit und des Gesetzgebungsprozesses eingebunden wird. Auf der Unterseite stehen horizontal angeordnet in zwei Reihen je drei weiße Rechtecke, die schwarz beschriftet sind. Gleich das erste Rechteck über *Die Gesetzgebung* ist zentral. Zur Beantwortung kann man dem bewährten Frage-Antwort-Muster und dem als Link unterlegten Lokaladverb *hier* folgen. In wenigen Schritten gelangt man zu dem vom Bundesministerium der Justiz herausgegebenen *Handbuch der Rechtsförmlichkeit* (HdR), wovon es aber kein Cover-Foto gibt (siehe Ziffer IV.4). Vielmehr ist es in der amtlichen Bekanntmachung vom 22. September 2008 im Bundesanzeiger als PDF-Datei verfügbar. Legisten sollen sich daran bei der rechtsförmlichen Gestaltung von Gesetzesentwürfen „nach § 42 Absatz 4 der Gemeinsamen Geschäftsordnung der Bundesministerien" (GGO) orientieren. Das Handbuch adressiert zwar nicht unmittelbar die Bürger. Gleichwohl sendet das Ministerium damit in dem Handlungskontext die

Botschaft aus, dass die Gesetzesarbeit zum Nutzen der Bevölkerung rechtsstaatlich und kommunikativ fundiert abläuft. Obwohl das HdR auch auf Unterseiten des Reiters *Themen* und *Ministerium* mehr oder weniger direkt eine Rolle spielt, wird darauf nicht verwiesen.

4. Hauptbereiche *Themen* und *Ministerium*

Der Hauptbereich *Themen* gibt Informationen über 13 Unterbereiche. Diese sind: *Digitales*; *Gesellschaft und Familie*; *Bürokratieabbau und Rechtsetzung*; *Vorsorge und Betreuungsrecht*; *Völkerstrafrecht*; *Wege zum Recht*; *Patientenrechte*; *Kaufen, Reisen, Wohnen*; *Wirtschaft und Finanzen*; *Terrorismus, Extremismus, Prävention und Opferhilfe*; *Rehabilitierung und Resozialisierung*; *Menschenrechte*; *Für Recht und Freiheit: Unsere Schwerpunkte*. Der Weg zum Handbuch der Rechtsförmlichkeit (BMJ 2008) führt über den dritten Unterbereich *Bürokratieabbau und Rechtsetzung*. Es erscheinen vier gleich große weiße Rechtecke mit schwarzer Beschriftung: hintereinander horizontal *Bürokratieabbau*, *Bessere Rechtsetzung* und *Nationaler Normenkontrollrat* sowie untereinander auf vertikaler Ebene *Bürokratieabbau* und *Zentrum für Legistik*. Erklärtes Ziel ist, dass auch Bürger Rechtsvorschriften verstehen sollen.

Unter *Bessere Rechtsetzung* sind vier Unterunterunterbereiche subsumiert, darunter derjenige der *Rechtsprüfung und Gesetzesredaktion*, worauf wir gleich noch näher eingehen werden (siehe Ziffer VI.2). Über die Justitia als Wahrzeichen des Rechtswesens gelangt man zu drei hellblau hinterlegten Rechtecken mit schwarzer Schrift. Das mittlere Kästchen („Systemisch und formal richtiges Recht: Rechtsprüfung“) enthält Informationen über rechtssystematische und rechtsförmliche Fragen – sowie farblich in dem Goldton der Bundesflagge in einem Rechteck hervorgehoben – zum Handbuch der Rechtsförmlichkeit (siehe Abb. 3). Der Hyperlink bringt eine statische Version (Inhaltsübersicht) der dritten Auflage des HdR und eine PDF-Version zum Download zum Vorschein. Es erfolgt aber kein Verweis auf den Reiter *Rechtsstaat kompakt*, über den der Nutzer – wie ausgeführt (siehe Ziffer IV.3) – ebenso einen Zugang erhält.

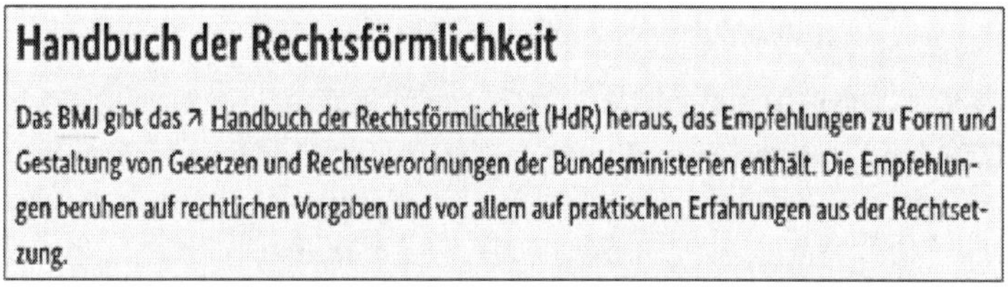

Handbuch der Rechtsförmlichkeit

Das BMJ gibt das ↗ Handbuch der Rechtsförmlichkeit (HdR) heraus, das Empfehlungen zu Form und Gestaltung von Gesetzen und Rechtsverordnungen der Bundesministerien enthält. Die Empfehlungen beruhen auf rechtlichen Vorgaben und vor allem auf praktischen Erfahrungen aus der Rechtsetzung.

Abb. 3: Handbuch der Rechtsförmlichkeit des BMJ (2008)

Eine andere Zugangsmöglichkeit besteht außerdem darin, dass der Nutzer den Reiter *Ministerium* aufruft und versucht, sich anhand des Organigramms über Maßnahmen bzw. Zuständigkeiten zu informieren, die zu besserer Rechtsetzung beitragen können. Das Organigramm kann heruntergeladen werden und ist im Unterbereich *Aufgaben und Organisation* und hier wiederum im Unterunterbereich *Abteilungen und Referate* als „Organisationsplan" hinterlegt. Man findet es, wenn man die Seite ganz herunterscrollt. Das Foto am Anfang der Seite zeigt Flure von Abteilungen im BMJ und hat für die Gesetzgebungspraxis keinen Informationswert. Das Organigramm ist dagegen von Belang, da es Zuständigkeiten namentlich ausweist und den Text kohärent mit Details ergänzt. Der Bereich „Bessere Rechtsetzung" liegt in der Verantwortung der Abteilung D, die Herr Meyer-Cabri leitet, respektive der Unterabteilung D A 1 „Rechtsprüfung: Gesetzesredaktion" unter der Leitung von Frau Gerds. Für den Nutzer geht damit im Ganzen die Botschaft einher, dass im BMJ Kompetenz waltet und auf mehrere Schultern verteilt ist, um Recht verständlich, d.h. „praxistauglicher, wirksamer und nutzungsorientierter zu machen."

5. Hilfsfunktion *Leichte Sprache*

Bei der Leichten Sprache (siehe Abb. 1) handelt es ich um eine Sprachvarietät, die für Menschen mit Beeinträchtigungen zum Zwecke der Selbstbestimmung und gesellschaftlichen Teilhabe geschaffen wurde (vgl. im Überblick Luttermann 2017). Charakteristisch dafür sind die aus der Praxis entstandenen universellen Regeln. So werden Informationen für Texte jedweder Art mittels reduzierter Lexik und reduktionistischer Syntax aufbereitet, um die Zielgruppe zu erreichen (vgl. Maaß 2015). Die Komplexitätsreduzierung hat Auswirkungen auf den Textinhalt, der zuweilen stark gegenüber dem Ausgangstext abgewandelt ist. Linguistische Forschung etwa zur Praktikabilität der Universalregeln oder zum Textverstehen übt Kritik an dieser Sprachvarietät und sucht nach alternativen Lösungswegen (vgl. z.B. im Überblick Bock / Fix / Lange 2017). Behörden des Bundes sind – trotzdem – verpflichtet, in Leichter Sprache zu kommunizieren und die Hilfsfunktion auf ihren Webseiten vorzuhalten. Dem Auftrag kommt das Justizministerium in Berlin nach.

Die Art und Weise der Ausgestaltung der Webkommunikation liegt allerdings im Ermessen eines jeden Ministeriums. Zwar informiert das Bundesministerium der Justiz über sich in der Leichten Sprache, aber weniger umfangreich als es das bei den fünf Hauptbereichen auf der Startseite und den Unterseiten für die Durchschnittsbürger macht (siehe Ziffer IV.2). Der Fokus liegt auf dem Ministerium selbst, d.h. konkret auf den Aufgaben, der Leitung und den Abteilungen. Überdies unterscheidet sich die Informationsdarbietung auch darin, dass der Nutzer seinen persönlichen Lesepfad nicht individuell bestimmen (navigieren), sondern nur die Seite herunterscrollen kann. Zu diesem begrenzten Ausschnitt („zur Arbeit und den Aufgaben des Ministeriums") gibt es vier Fragen, die als Spiegelpunkte und unterhalb eines Farbfotos aufgelistet sind.

Das Foto präsentiert das Eingangsportal des Justizgebäudes und fungiert als schmückendes Beiwerk zum Text (siehe Abb. 4). Es hätte stattdessen der Bundesjustizminister Dr. Marco Buschmann fotografiert sein können, um zu den Adressaten eine Beziehung aufzubauen und um die Fragen, was das BMJ ist, welche Aufgaben es hat, wer es leitet und wie es unterteilt ist, zu stellen (siehe Ziffer IV.3).[8] Die dritte Frage nach der Leitung des BMJ wäre damit anschaulich beantwortet. Die Antworten sind insgesamt sehr allgemein gehalten. So wird die Frage nach der Unterteilung dahingehend beantwortet, dass das BMJ „viele Abteilungen" und jede Abteilung „eine Leitung" hat. Es gibt hier kein Organigramm.

---

[8] Auf der Eingangsseite erfolgt zwar eine Begrüßung („Willkommen auf der Internet-Seite vom BMJ"), aber nicht durch den Minister selbst.

Abb. 4: BMJ in Berlin

Im Gegensatz dazu ist der Webauftritt des Hauptbereichs *Ministerium* interaktiver und vielseitiger gestaltet und lässt dem Nutzer erheblichen Raum für interessengeleitete Klicks (siehe Ziffern IV.2 und IV.4). Über das Ministerium wird detailliert informiert. Die Informationen reichen vom Unterbereich *Hausleitung* über *Veranstaltungen* und *Forschung & Förderung* bis hin zu den Unterbereichen *Gesellschaftliches Engagement* und *Ausschreibungen* mit 26 verlinkten Unterunterbereichen. Am Anfang steht die *Hausleitung*, die aktuell der Bundesminister innehat, und das Community-Video-Format „Just Ask“. Es folgen Angaben zu *Aufgaben und Organisation*. Von den vier Unterunterbereichen haben für die Informationsvermittlung in Leichter Sprache – wie oben ausgeführt – nur „Aufgaben des BMJ“ und „Abteilungen und Referate“ Relevanz, nicht aber „Geschäftsbereich“ und „Gremien“. Obwohl der Unterbereich *Gesellschaftliches Engagement* mit den Unterunterbereichen „Beruf und Familie“, „Charta der Vielfalt“ und „Menschen mit Behinderungen“ explizit die Zielgruppe der Leichten Sprache in Bezug nimmt, gibt es keine Verlinkung zwischen dem Navigationsmenü und der Hilfsfunktion. Zum Informationsportfolio gehören zudem die *Geschichte* des BMJ und des Gebäudes wie auch die *Karriere* mit Stellenangeboten (u.a. Referendarstation, Studentenpraktikum).

Vor diesem Hintergrund vergleichen wir die Webkommunikation des deutschen Bundesjustizministeriums, dessen kommunikative Analyse keinen Anspruch auf Vollständigkeit erhebt, aber die angeführten Tendenzen und Strategien in Bezug auf Vermittlung und Popularisierung zeigt, mit der Webkommunikation des dänischen Justizministeriums.

V. Gestaltung der dänischen JM-Webseite im Vergleich

1. Aufbau

Auch der Webauftritt des dänischen Justizministeriums (JM) hat Teile, die auf Informationen über rechtliche Inhalte ausgerichtet sind. Insbesondere anhand der Eingangsseite und des generellen Aufbaus des Webauftritts entsteht aber der Eindruck, dass hier die Eigenperspektive des Ministeriums äußerst prägend gewesen ist: Es wird über das Ministerium und seine Arbeit mehr denn über das Recht an sich informiert. Im Vergleich zum deutschen Ministerium kommt hinzu, dass der bürgernahe Bereich des Verbraucherschutzes und der Verbraucherinformation in der dänischen Aufgabenverteilung nicht beim Justizministerium, sondern beim Industrie-, Banken- und Unternehmensministerium (*Erhvervsministeriet*) angesiedelt ist.[9]

Abb. 5: Startseite JM (Letzter Zugriff 1.10.2024)

Anders als beim deutschen Ministerium gibt es hier nur eine Reihe von Links oben auf der Seite, die der Navigation auf der Seite dienen (siehe Abb. 5). Es kommen keine Links vor, die sich direkt an einen fragenden Bürger wenden. Auch werden die Nutzer auf der Vorderseite nur in Einzelfällen direkt angesprochen. Zum Beispiel gibt es zwei beschriftete Links, die zum Lesen der Pressemitteilungen auffordern. Die Navigationsleiste enthält die folgenden Überschriften, die zu Teilen der Webseite weiterführen: *Kontakt* (‚Kontakt'), *Ministeriet* (‚Ministerium'), *Presse* (‚Presse'), *Forskning* (‚Forschung'), *Temaer* (‚Themen'), *Karriere* (‚Karriere') sowie ein unspezifisches Suchfeld, markiert durch eine Lupe.

---

[9] https://www.forbrug.dk/. Dieses Verbraucherportal wird von einem Teil des *Erhvervsministeriet* betrieben.

Links zu Informationen in Leichter Sprache oder Gebärdensprache sind nicht vorhanden. Oben auf der Seite gibt es aber eine Leiste, mit der man die Lesbarkeit der Seite durch Änderung von Schrifttyp und Schriftgröße sowie Kontrast verbessern kann. Ein anderes Ministerium, das Digitalisierungsministerium, stellt kostenlos eine App zur Verfügung, die Menschen mit Leseschwierigkeiten installieren können, um Teile einer Webseite vorgelesen zu bekommen, die sie markieren. Auf der Seite wird aber nicht auf diese App verwiesen. Die App bietet zudem lediglich einen Wechsel in die mündliche Modalität an, keine inhaltliche Komplexitätsreduktion.

Die Eingangsseite besteht primär aus Auszügen aus Pressemitteilungen des Ministeriums über seine Initiativen. Weiter unten auf der Seite (Herunterscrollen notwendig) gibt es eine Sektion mit Links zu den Behörden des Justizwesens, eine Sektion mit wenigen Informationen zum Minister und ein Link zu einer gesonderten Präsentationswebseite sowie eine Sektion, die durch die direkt anredende Überschrift *Vil du være en del af holdet?* (‚Möchtest Du Teil des Teams werden?') zur Aufnahme einer Karriere im Ministerium auffordert. Hier gibt es auch ein weiteres Beispiel eines beschrifteten Links, der den Leser direkt anspricht und zum Start einer Karriere auffordert (*Start din karriere her* – ‚Beginne hier deine Karriere'). Die Themenauswahl (Pressemitteilung, Behördenlinks, Minister, Karriere) zeigt den Fokus der Seite eher auf Informationen über das Ministerium denn über das Recht.

Über die genannten, auf der Eingangsseite hervorgehobenen Elemente gibt es also sechs beschriftete Links in einer Leiste (siehe Abb. 5), die auf Hauptbereiche des Webauftritts verweisen und als Grundstruktur für unsere Analyse dienen. Da wir hier nicht an einer kompletten Analyse der enthaltenen Informationen interessiert sind (siehe Ziffer I zu den Forschungsfragen), werden wir uns beim Durchgehen der jeweiligen Bereiche hinter den Links darauf fokussieren, das multimodale Profil und den Anteil zu beschreiben, der einer verständlichen Vermittlung juristischer Themen gewidmet ist, um dadurch erfassen zu können, wie sich das Ministerium den Bürgern gegenüber präsentiert.

2. Hauptbereich *Kontakt* (‚Kontakt‘)

Durch das Anklicken dieses Links kommt man auf eine Seite, auf der Kontaktmöglichkeiten zum Ministerium (u.a. Anschrift, Mail, Telefon) und zu den Justizbehörden, die auch auf der Eingangsseite auftreten (Links zu ihren Webseiten), angeführt sind. Die Angaben zum Ministerium und zu den Behörden sind durch unterschiedliche Farbhinterlegung voneinander abgegrenzt. Darüber hinaus gibt es einen wiederum farblich unterschiedenen Teil der Seite mit einem Link zur Presseabteilung des Ministeriums, der nach seiner Beschriftung für „Mitglieder der Presse“ gedacht ist. Über die Markierung der unterschiedlichen Teile der Seite durch Farbhinterlegung gibt es auf der Seite ein Foto von einem alten Gebäudehof, der durch die sichtbaren Türme als in Kopenhagen nahe dem Parlament gelegen erkennbar ist.

Abb. 6: Illustration auf der Seite *Kontakt*

Wahrscheinlich handelt es sich um ein Bild des Hofes des Ministerialgebäudes. Das Bild hat primär eine schmückende Funktion.

3. Hauptbereich *Ministeriet* (‚Ministerium‘)

Wie im vorhergehenden Hauptbereich des Internetauftritts sehen wir auf der Seite, zu der man durch Anklicken des Links kommt, oben links ein Bild, das wahrscheinlich das Ministerialgebäude betrifft. Darüber hinaus werden hier auch Farbhinterlegungen zur Unterscheidung von drei Bereichen verwendet: Aufgaben des Ministeriums, Mission des Ministeriums und Vision des Ministeriums. In prominenter Position oben rechts wird in großer Schriftgröße und farblich hervorgehoben (weiße Buchstaben auf schwarzem Grund) angeführt, dass „das Justizministerium Aufgaben für das gesamte Justizwesen ausführt.“ Darunter gibt es einen Link mit der Beschriftung „Læs her“ (‚*Hier lesen*‘), der zu einer Überblicksseite über die Behörden des Justizwesens führt. Die Information auf dieser Unter-Eingangsseite bezieht sich auf das Ministerium und dessen Aufgaben, jedoch ohne vertiefende Erklärungen. Die Seite entspricht den „Wir über uns“-Seiten, die man auf Unternehmenswebseiten findet.

Wenn man die Maus über den Link *Ministeriet* hält, wird eine Liste von Unterseiten zu diesem Hauptbereich sichtbar:

- *Ministeren* (‚der Minister‘): Der Minister wird vorgestellt, u.a. durch ein Foto. Es handelt sich um die Seite, auf die auch von der Eingangsseite verlinkt wird.
- *Justitsvæsenet* (‚das Justizwesen‘): Es wird zu der oben erwähnten Überblicksseite über die Behörden des Justizwesens mit Links zu Beschreibungen der Behörden verlinkt und von dort aus zu deren Webseiten. Es gibt auch einen Link zu dem Organisationsdiagramm. Bildlich gibt es auf der Seite ein Illustrationselement mit stilisierter Ministerialkrone.
- *Departementet* (‚die Ministerialbehörde‘): Hier wird der ständige Staatssekretär (*departementschef*) mit Foto und früherer Anstellung sowie ein Foto seiner direkten Mitarbeiter vorgestellt. Es gibt Links zu Beschreibungen der Abteilungen mit Angabe der jeweiligen Abteilungsleiter (mit Foto) sowie der jeweiligen Büros und deren Aufgaben.
- *Råd nævn og udvalg* (‚unterschiedliche Arten der Ausschüsse‘): Hier wird eine Liste über unterschiedliche Ausschüsse, die zum Justizministerium gehören, mit Link zu einer kurzen Beschreibung und dort mit Link zur Webseite des Ausschusses dargeboten. Weiter gibt es Links zur Publikationsseite des Webauftritts und als Ausschmückung ein künstlerisches Foto eines Sitzungszimmers auf der Eingangsseite (siehe Abb. 7).

- *Aktindsigt* (‚Akteneinsicht‘): Es wird beschrieben, wie gut das Ministerium die Zielvorgaben zur Gewährung der Akteneinsicht an Journalisten zwischen Dezember 2019 und Juni 2024 erreicht hat. Zudem wird ein Foto mit Akten gezeigt.
- *Lovprogram* (‚Gesetzesprogramm‘): Hier erfolgt ein Überblick über Gesetzesvorlagen im Parlament durch das Ministerium. Außerdem ist ein Foto des Parlamentsgebäudes sichtbar.
- *Whistleblowerordning* (‚Whistleblower-Regelung‘): Hier erscheinen Überblicksseiten mit einem Link zu Beschreibungen der Whistleblower-Regelung der Ministerialbehörde und der untergeordneten Behörde des polizeilichen Nachrichtendienstes sowie zu einer Statistik über die Arbeit der Whistleblower-Regelung der Ministerialbehörde. Die Beschreibungen der Regelungen enthalten Informationen, die primär für Angestellte der Behörde relevant sind. Darüber hinaus liegen Fotos der Ministerial- und Nachrichtenbehörde vor.

Abb. 7: Künstlerisches Foto eines Sitzungssaals

Zusammenfassend handelt es sich um einen Überblick über das Ministerium und die Behörden, die zu ihm gehören, über ihre Strukturen und ihre Aufgaben. Das Ministerium wird mit seiner Aufteilung in Abteilungen und Referate und mit der Angabe der Leiter der jeweiligen Abteilungen recht detailliert dargestellt. Es wird viel Wert auf Strukturbeschreibungen mit Personenangaben sowie auf Listen von Aufgabenlösungen und auf die Erfüllung von Zielvorgaben gelegt. Darüber hinaus ist die Beschreibung der Whistleblower-Regelung eindeutig eher an Mitarbeiter gerichtet. Alle

Seiten zeigen Fotos, die zwar thematisch zu den Seiten passen, aber eine rein schmückende Funktion haben.

4. Hauptbereich *Presse* (‚Presse')

Hier gibt es Links zu der Kontaktseite mit der Presse, zu der Seite mit den Pressemitteilungen und zu der Seite mit den Newslettern. Zu allen Seiten wird auch von der Kontaktseite (siehe Ziffer V.2) oder von der Eingangsseite des Webauftritts (siehe Ziffer V.1) verlinkt. Auf der Presse-Seite werden diese drei Themen ebenfalls behandelt, unterschieden durch unterschiedliche Farbhinterlegung. Ganz unten gibt es ein Formular, mit dem man sich für die Zusendung von Pressemitteilungen und Newsletter anmelden kann, sowie Verweise auf Publikationen des Ministeriums. Oben rechts befindet sich ein Foto aus dem dänischen Parlamentssaal mit schmückender Funktion. Interessant ist hier insbesondere, dass es einen gesonderten Eingang für die Presse gibt, von der aus primär auf Seiten verlinkt wird, die auch von anderen Seiten und Hauptbereichen zugänglich sind. Dies zeugt von besonderer Aufmerksamkeit des Ministeriums gegenüber der Presse als Nutzer des Webauftritts.

5. Hauptbereich *Forskning* (‚Forschung')

Durch den Link zu diesem Hauptbereich gelangt man zu der Seite des Forschungsbüros des Ministeriums. Diese Seite enthält erstens einen Abschnitt mit einer kurzen Beschreibung des Forschungsbüros und seiner Aufgaben; zweitens einen Abschnitt mit Links zu einer nach Erscheinungsjahr sortierten Liste aller Forschungsberichte des Büros, zu von dem Ministerium geförderten Berichten externer Forscher und zu prämierten Preisaufgaben von Studierenden; drittens gibt es einen Abschnitt mit Links zu Forschungsberichten zu drei ausgewählten Themen (Kinder- und Jugendkriminalität, Opferuntersuchungen, kriminelle Gruppierungen). Die Abschnitte sind durch farbliche Unterlegung unterschieden. Zu jedem Link gehört ein künstlerisch-illustrierendes Foto.

Wenn man auf die Seiten der thematisch hervorgehobenen Berichte geht, findet man außer den Berichten auch eine Liste über Sammlungen von

Berichten zu weiteren Themen. Insgesamt gibt es zehn solcher Sammlungen. Über den Zugang von jeder Sammlungsseite über eine Link-Liste hinaus hat man auch Zugang zu den thematischen Sammlungen über Links, die sichtbar werden, wenn man die Maus über den Link des Hauptabschnitts hält. Interessant ist hier insbesondere, dass die Berichte durch unterschiedliche Links zugänglich sind und dass sie sowohl chronologisch als auch thematisch geordnet präsentiert werden. Eine Vermittlung der Inhalte der Berichte kommt nicht vor. Sie werden lediglich in ihrer ursprünglichen fachlichen Form zugänglich gemacht. Hier spiegelt sich wahrscheinlich eine Ausrichtung auf den eigenen fachlichen Fokus des Ministeriums und auf die fachlichen Bedürfnisse von Juristen wider.

6. Hauptbereich *Temaer* (‚Themen')

Dieser Hauptbereich ist von den Untersuchten der heterogenste aller Hauptbereiche im Webauftritt. Vom Link in der Navigationsleiste wird man nicht auf eine gesonderte Seite des Hauptbereichs geleitet. Stattdessen wird eine Liste der enthaltenen Themen sichtbar, wenn man die Maus über den Link hält. Es werden die folgenden Themen behandelt:

- *Flagning* (‚Verwendung der dänischen Fahne'): Beschrieben werden die Regeln zur Verwendung der dänischen Flagge mit Links auf spezifischere Regelungen. Typisch werden auf jeder Seite die Regeln kurz zusammengefasst und dann wird auf die offiziellen Regelungsdokumente verlinkt.
- *Indstillinger fra Epidemikommissionen* (‚Empfehlungen der Epidemiekommission'): Ohne Darstellung dessen, was die *Epidemikommissionen* ist (die Kommission, die zwischen März und Juni 2021 über Maßnahmen in Verbindung mit der Covid-19-Epidemie entschieden hat), werden die Empfehlungen in der Form von Links für die offiziellen Dokumente – bestehend aus der Wiedergabe des offiziellen Inhalts der Empfehlungen – veröffentlicht.
- *Vejledning om lovkvalitet* (‚Richtlinie über Gesetzesqualität'): Es handelt sich hier um eine Sammlung von Links zu Richtlinien und Schablonen, die als Hilfe bei der Gesetzesformulierung durch Ministerial-

beamte eingesetzt werden. Es gibt keine vermittelnden Informationen zu den Links.

- *Våben og krigsmateriel* (‚Waffen und Kriegsmaterial‘): Hier werden kurz die Grundregeln zum Waffenbesitz sowie zu der Herstellung und dem Import von Kriegsmaterial dargestellt. Bezüglich der Waffen wird weiter auf die Polizei als Zulassungsbehörde verwiesen. Bezüglich des Kriegsmaterials wird direkt auf die Gesetzesgrundlage und auf die für Zulassungen durch das Ministerium relevanten Seiten verlinkt.
- *Sådan klager du til FN og Den Europæiske Menneskerettighedsdomstol* (‚So reichst Du Klage bei der UNO und beim Europäischen Gerichtshof für Menschenrechte ein‘): Es gibt einen Leitfaden für Bürger, die beim Europäischen Gerichtshof für Menschenrechte oder bei einem der Komitees, die für die Einhaltung der sechs UNO-Konventionen zu den Menschenrechten zuständig sind, Klage einreichen möchten, sowie Links zu relevanten Formularen und weiteren Informationsseiten.
- *Offentligt ansattes ytringsfrihed* (‚Äußerungsfreiheit von öffentlich Angestellten‘): Auf dieser Seite existieren Links zu einem Leitfaden für öffentlich Angestellte und zu einem Online-Kurs für solche Mitarbeiter. Es werden aber auf der Seite keine Informationen zu den Prinzipien der Äußerungsfreiheit, zu ihrem genaueren Inhalt oder Ähnliches gegeben.
- *Afrapportering fra Den uafhængige kontrol- og styregruppe i teledatasagen* (‚Bericht von Der unabhängigen Kontroll- und Lenkungsgruppe im Teledaten-Fall‘): Auf dieser Seite wird kurz der dänische Teledaten-Fall (= Fehler bei der Verwendung von Mobilfunk-Daten in Strafverfahren) dargestellt und ein Link auf den offiziellen Bericht der genannten Gruppe geschaltet.
- *Energieffektiviseringsplan* (‚Energieeffizienzplan‘): Auf dieser Seite besteht ein Link zum Plan des Ministeriums zur Energieeffizienz der Gebäude für den Zeitraum 2022 bis 2024.

- *Whistleblowing* (‚Whistleblower-Regelung‘): Hier finden wir Links zu drei Publikationen des Ministeriums: dem generellen Leitfaden zu Whistleblower-Regelungen, dem Leitfaden für Whistleblower-Regelungen bei privaten Arbeitsplätzen und dem Leitfaden für Whistleblower-Regelungen bei Behörden. Zusätzlich gibt es einen Link zur Seite der übergeordneten Behörde, die für die generelle dänische Whistleblower-Regelung zuständig ist.
- *Justitsministeriet 175 år* (‚175 Jahre Justizministerium‘): Auf dieser Seite liegt eine Online-Publikation mit Beiträgen zur Geschichte des Ministeriums vor.

Auf allen Seiten sind künstlerisch-illustrierende Fotos ohne selbständige Informationsfunktion vorhanden. Bei dem Hauptteil *Temaer* (‚Themen‘) springt ins Auge, dass die Themen sehr unterschiedlich sind, sowohl was ihren Inhalt (Verwendung der dänischen Fahne parallel mit Gesetzesregeln über Waffen und Ausschussberichte) als auch den Grad der Detaillierung und das vorausgesetzte Wissen angeht.

Zudem wenden sich die jeweiligen Themen-Seiten an unterschiedliche Adressaten (u.a. Bürger, Produzenten von Waffen, Ministerialbeamte, öffentlich Angestellte) und haben entweder eher informativen Charakter (z.B. Energieeffizienzplan) oder eher verwaltungsbezogenen Charakter (z.B. Leitfaden zu Menschenrechtsklagen). Der Eindruck ist, dass dieser Hauptbereich primär zur Erfüllung einer Reihe von Verpflichtungen verwendet wird, die das Ministerium hat, die aber nicht als ausreichend wichtig erachtet worden sind, um eigene Hauptbereiche zu erhalten. Dies ist insofern vermittlungsmäßig problematisch, als es für die Adressaten schwierig ist, durch die Überschrift des Hauptbereichs zu erschließen, dass sie hier Informationen zum Beispiel über die Verwendung der dänischen Fahne sowie über Zulassungen zum Import von Waffen finden können.

VI. Vergleich der ministeriellen Webkommunikation

1. Multimodalität und die Stellung der Bürger

Als Zwischenfazit kann festgehalten werden, dass die dänische Webseite weitaus stärker als die deutsche Webseite eine Intention abbildet, über sich selbst Informationen herauszusenden, die für die Einschätzung des Ministeriums als effizient erachtet werden und die für eine zügige Sachbearbeitung relevant sind. Es wird viel weniger an der Etablierung von Relationen mit den Bürgern gearbeitet. Vielmehr scheint das dänische Justizministerium besonders auf die Bedürfnisse der Kommunikation mit der Presse ausgerichtet zu sein. Darüber hinaus enthält die Seite Informationen, die primär für die unternehmensinterne Kommunikation relevant sind, sowie Informationen, die für das Verhältnis zwischen Behörde und Staatsverwaltung im Rahmen von New Public Management eine Rolle spielen. Die Dominanz des verbalen Textes und die rein schmückende Funktion der Fotos unterstützen die Einschätzung, dass es sich hier um eine Seite handelt, die alle Stereotypen über die Kommunikation juristischer Behörden wie zum Beispiel inhaltliche Hermetik, Bevorzugung des verbalen Modus für Informationen sowie Behördenfokus bestätigt. Die Webseite des Bundesministeriums der Justiz wählt hier einen anderen Weg, wie wir in den folgenden beiden Absätzen genauer ausführen werden.

2. Verständlichkeit und Sprachprüfung im BMJ

Dem Bundesministerium der Justiz obliegt die Rechtsprüfung von Gesetz- und Verordnungsentwürfen und die Gesetzesredaktion. Es hat die Aufgabe, die eigenen Entwurfstexte und diejenigen der anderen Bundesministerien rechtlich und sprachlich zu prüfen (Rechtsförmlichkeitsprüfung) und ist „für eine verständliche Gesetzessprache“, d.h. für die Redaktionsarbeit an und mit Gesetzen verantwortlich. Diese Informationen lassen sich über den Hauptbereich *Themen* und durch die Verlinkungen *Bürokratieabbau und Rechtsetzung / Bessere Rechtsetzung / Rechtsprüfung und Gesetzesredaktion* oder dem Organigramm abrufen (siehe Ziffer IV.4). In der ministeriellen Phase des Rechtsetzungsverfahrens ist die Gesetzesredaktion des

BMJ nunmehr allein für die Sprach- und Verständlichkeitsprüfung zuständig.[10] Das veranschaulicht ein Schaubild auf der Seite und vertieft dabei noch einzelne Aspekte. Die Informationsvermittlung steht letztlich anders als auf den entsprechenden Seiten des dänischen Ministeriums ausdrücklich auch im Dienst der Bürger. Sie sollen wissen, dass das BMJ alles dafür tut, dass die Gesetze so verständlich wie möglich sind und sie davon profitieren.

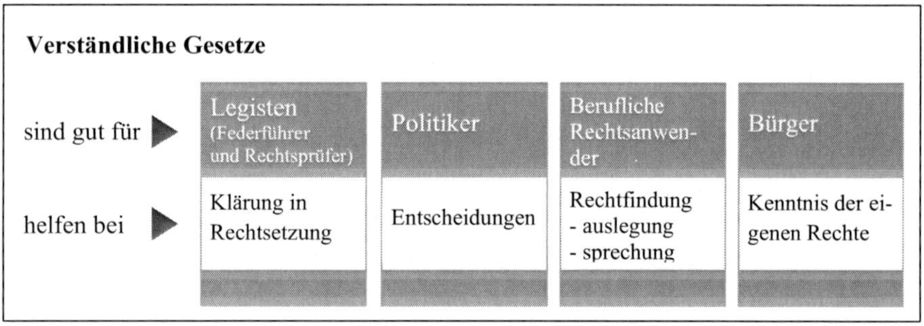

Abb. 8: Adressaten und Funktionen verständlicher Gesetze

Worauf fokussiert das BMJ? – Das Ministerium will eine „bessere Rechtsetzung“, „gutes Recht“ und „sprachlich richtig[e] und möglichst verständlich[e]“ Gesetze schaffen, damit Rechtsanwender wie Gerichte und Behörden besser damit arbeiten können und Unternehmer und Bürger leichter Zugang dazu finden und die „eigenen Rechte“ kennen. Mit der Etablierung der Gesetzesredaktion beim BMJ und dem Handbuch der Rechtsförmlichkeit (BMJ 2008), das es in mehreren Sprachen gibt (Arabisch, Chinesisch, Englisch, Polnisch, Rumänisch, Russisch, Serbisch, Türkisch), sollen die Ziele erreicht werden. Darüber hinaus gibt das BMJ zur Unterstützung seiner Arbeit auch Forschungsprojekte und Evaluationen an Universitäten und unabhängige Sachverständige in Auftrag. Im Ganzen wird den Bürgern auf den Webseiten vermittelt, dass das BMJ viele Maßnahmen ergreift

[10] Zuvor hat der Redaktionsstab Rechtssprache der Lex Lingua die bundesministeriellen Entwürfe, das BMJ ausgenommen, geprüft; vgl. Thieme / Parádi (2021). Für die parlamentarische Phase ist nach wie vor der Redaktionsstab der Gesellschaft für deutsche Sprache beim Deutschen Bundestag zuständig; vgl. Hallik (2021).

und umsetzt, um die Gesetzesqualität nachhaltig für alle Menschen zu verbessern.[11]

3. Bedeutung der Verständlichkeit für das dänische JM im Vergleich

Auch das dänische Ministerium hat die Aufgabe, die Qualität von Gesetzesvorschlägen zu prüfen, bevor sie zur endgültigen Verabschiedung vorgelegt werden. Dabei liegt das absolute Hauptgewicht auf einer Prüfung der Gesetzestechnik und der Vereinbarkeit des Vorschlags mit dem Grundgesetz und mit anderen Gesetzen. Die Prüfung der Verständlichkeit stellt keinen gesonderten Punkt in der Richtlinie dar, die oben unter *Temaer* (‚Themen') behandelt wird (siehe Ziffer V.6). Es gibt aber einen Bereich zur Sprache, wo relativ übergeordnete Aspekte wie Kürze, Prägnanz und Vermeidung von Fach- und Fremdwörtern und deren mögliche Beeinflussung der Verständlichkeit erwähnt werden, aber ohne eine detaillierte Operationalisierung vorzunehmen. Jedoch ist der Leiter der Abteilung für Gesetzesqualität auch Mitglied des Beirats des dänischen Sprachenamts, das sich generell mit Sprachfragen und Rechtschreibung in Dänemark befasst. Als Fazit kann gesagt werden, dass Verständlichkeit als Thema nicht völlig vernachlässigt wird, allerdings keine hervorgehobene Stellung im dänischen System einnimmt, weder in der Struktur noch in der Kommunikation auf der Webseite.

VII. Resümee und Ausblick

Für das Recht ist Vertrauen der Bürger elementar, um Gesetze zu befolgen und letztlich die Demokratie und das Funktionieren der Rechtsinstitutionen zu gewährleisten. Effektives Arbeiten an der Sprache des Rechts (z.B. Gesetze, Webseiten) kann zum Aufbau von Vertrauen beitragen. In Analogie zur Unternehmenskommunikation kann man auch der Webkommunikation von Behörden menschliche Eigenschaften wie ‚kompetent', ‚verständlich'

---

[11] Beispiele geben auch Norwegen und Schweden, wo man auf wissenschaftliche Expertise zur Förderung der Klarheit von Normtexten zurückgreift; vgl. z.B. Nordrum / Reksten / Schaller-Bøyum (2021); Nordrum / Reksten / Schaller-Bøyum / Våge (2025); Mertzlufft (2021).

oder ‚sympathisch' zuordnen. Diese Merkmale fungieren in linguistischen Arbeiten als „Symptome" (Keller 2009: 39) für Vertrauenswürdigkeit. Die Strategie des deutschen und des dänischen Justizministeriums besteht darin, Vertrauen primär durch Kompetenz zu generieren (vgl. zum Kompetenz-Merkmal Reinmuth 2009: 135, 137f.).

Allerdings fällt auf, dass das dänische Ministerium der Justiz sich mehr wie eine Behörde benimmt und auf der Grundlage seiner eigenen Interessen und Denkweisen kommuniziert, wogegen das deutsche Justizministerium in einem höheren Maße auf Dialog und Vermittlung ausgerichtet ist. Für Bürger besteht in diesem Zusammenhang die Möglichkeit, soziale Medien wie Instagram, Facebook, Youtube oder Twitter zu nutzen und bestimmte Informationen auch in anderen als der deutschen Sprache abzurufen (siehe Ziffer VI.2).

Die Kommunikation zu personalisieren, ist ebenfalls ein bedeutsamer, handlungsstrategischer Indikator, Vertrauen aufzubauen. Auf den Webseiten des BMJ ist mehrfach der amtierende Bundesjustizminister abgebildet oder er erscheint in Videoclips (z.B. JETZT ERST RECHT, „Just Ask"). Damit gibt er dem anonymen Ministerium quasi ein Gesicht und rückt die unpersönliche Institution (Justizministerium, Justizgebäude) in den Hintergrund (siehe Abb. 2). Es wird die Botschaft transportiert: Im „Haus für Recht und Freiheit" agieren Menschen und reden mit bzw. zu den Menschen außerhalb des Hauses.[12] Auch auf der Eingangsseite des dänischen Ministeriums ist der amtierende Minister abgebildet, aber erst am unteren Ende der Seite, und man muss recht lange scrollen, bis man dahin kommt. Oben auf der Eingangsseite wird stattdessen ein Bild des Amtsgerichts Kopenhagen, das im klassischen Stil mit Säulen gebaut ist, dargestellt.

Im dänischen Fall ist die Personalisierungsintention folglich nicht besonders prominent. Zusätzlich erzeugen im deutschen Fall bestimmte Prono-

---

[12] Dr. Katarina Barley, Ministerin a.D. des Bundesministeriums der Justiz und für Verbraucherschutz (BMJV), hat während ihrer Amtszeit den Stellenwert des Menschen betont: „[…] Freiheit und Selbstbestimmung sind die zentralen Werte unserer Verfassung. Das letzte Wort bei wichtigen Entscheidungen muss immer der Mensch haben." Die Webseite des BMJV ist deaktiviert (Letzter Zugriff 24.5.2019).

men („wir“, „unser“ u.a.) eine persönliche Beziehung zwischen Sender und Empfänger und ein Wir-Gefühl. Zudem adressiert das BMJ explizit Informationen für „Menschen mit Behinderungen“ und trägt ihren erschwerten Rezeptionsbedingungen Rechnung, indem es Gebärdensprache und Leichte Sprache verwendet. Sie werden begrüßt und eingeladen, die Informationsangebote anzunehmen (siehe Ziffer IV.5). Beim dänischen Ministerium fehlt diese Zielgruppe gänzlich.

Zusammengefasst zielt das dänische Justizministerium darauf, sich selbst als Behörde vorzustellen und somit Kontaktmöglichkeiten zu den Hauptbereichen zu schaffen. Viel Wert scheint dabei auf die Presse (z.B. durch einen eigenen Zugangslink), auf Mitarbeiter der Behörde (z.B. durch kommentierte Links zu Richtlinien mit Relevanz für die Arbeit in der Behörde und durch die prominente Platzierung von Links zu Karriereseiten schon auf der Eingangsseite, einschließlich eines von wenigen Beispielen direkter Anrede) und auf Juristen (z.B. dadurch, dass Forschungsarbeiten nach unterschiedlichen Kriterien mehrfach gelistet werden) als Zielgruppen gelegt zu werden. Auf dieser Grundlage ist deutlich, dass der Webauftritt des dänischen Justizministeriums durch eine Vermittlungsintention charakterisiert werden kann.

Dagegen ist der Webauftritt des BMJ stärker durch eine Popularisierungsintention geprägt. Das BMJ zielt darauf, die Menschen zu erreichen und verständlich über Recht und Gesetz zu informieren, sodass sie gewappnet sind, ihre Rechte und Pflichten entsprechend wahrzunehmen.[13] Sie sollen wissen, dass sie in einem „Rechtsstaat statt Überwachungsstaat“, in einer „Demokratie“ und in „Freiheit“ leben sowie mündig und selbstbestimmt handeln können. Zugleich fordert das Ministerium die Bevölkerung dazu auf, „Tag für Tag aufs Neue“ die rechtsstaatlichen Werte „gemeinsam“ zu verteidigen. Inwieweit die Strategien der Vermittlung und Popularisierung

---

[13] Unter der Leitung der Ministerin a.D. Dr. Katarina Barley hat das BMJV Erklärvideos zum Verbraucherschutz mit dem Slogan „Wissen wappnet“ publiziert; vgl. https://www.youtube.com/playlist?list=PLFL8UotHiBrZE1c_M2Ds-za-5Tf3L-lyZ (Letzter Zugriff 25.8.2024). Der Slogan hat einen hohen Wiedererkennungswert und sendet die Botschaft aus, dass man sich ‚präparieren‘, ‚rüsten‘, ‚schlau machen‘ kann, um keine Rechtsnachteile zu erleiden.

und der teilweise fachliche Sprachgebrauch die Bürger tatsächlich erreichen und wie die Webkommunikation auf sie wirkt, kann man anhand der hier vorgestellten Analysen nicht entscheiden.

Diese Ergebnisse können aber als Eingangshypothesen für die empirische Erfassung der tatsächlichen Aufnahme der Informationen und ihrer emotionalen Effekte fungieren. Als Beispiel können empirische Verständlichkeitstests (Probandenbefragungen) nach Maßgabe des Rechtslinguistischen Verständlichkeitsmodells (vgl. z.B. Luttermann 2010, 2021) eingesetzt werden, um solche Einsichten zu schaffen. Das ist eine Aufgabe für die Zukunft. Darüber hinaus wären die Verwendung multimodaler Mittel, die Auswahl fachlicher Informationen über Wesen und Funktion der Justiz sowie ungenutzte handlungsstrategische Vermittlungs- und Popularisierungspotentiale für den Dialog mit Bürgern und zum Aufbau von Vertrauen aus rechtslinguistischer Sicht vertiefend zu behandeln und zu bewerten.

VIII. Literatur

Anesa, Patrizia. 2016. The Deconstruction and Reconstruction of Legal Information in Expert-Lay Online Interaction. *ESP today,* 4 (1), 69-86.

Anesa, Patrizia / Jan Engberg (Hrsg.). 2023. *The Digital (R)Evolution of Legal Discourse*. Berlin: de Gruyter Mouton.

Bock, Bettina M. / Ulla Fix / Daisy Lange (Hrsg.). 2017. *"Leichte Sprache" im Spiegel theoretischer und angewandter Forschung*. Berlin: Frank & Timme.

Bondi, Marina / Silvia Cacchiani. 2021. Knowledge Communication and Knowledge Dissemination in a Digital World. *Journal of Pragmatics* 186, 117-123.

Bucher, Hans-Jürgen / Bettina Boy / Katharina Christ. 2022. *Audiovisuelle Wissenschaftskommunikation auf Youtube. Eine Rezeptionsstudie zur Vermittlungsleistung von Wissenschaftsvideos*. Wiesbaden: Springer VS.

Bundesministerium der Justiz (BMJ). 2008. *Handbuch der Rechtsförmlichkeit*. 3. Auflage. Köln: Bundesanzeiger.

Cacchiani, Silvia. 2018. The Voice of the Law on Gov.uk and Justice.gouv.fr. Good Value to Citizens and Institutions? In: Jan Engberg / Karin Luttermann / Silvia Cacchiani / Chiara Preite (Hrsg.), *Popularization and Knowledge Mediation in the Law / Popularisierung und Wissensvermittlung im Recht*. Wien: Lit, 117-148.

Diani, Giuliana. 2023. Disseminating Legal Information on Online Law Forums in English and Italian. *Ibérica* (46), 299-320.

Engberg, Jan. 2014. General and Specific Perspectives on Vagueness in Law. Impact upon the Feasibility of Legal Translation. In: Barbara Pasa / Lucia Morra (Hrsg.), *Translating the DCFR and Drafting the CESL. A Pragmatic Perspective*. München: Sellier European Law Publisher, 147-159.

Engberg, Jan. 2017. Fachkommunikation und fachexterne Kommunikation. In: Ekkehard Felder / Friedemann Vogel (Hrsg.), *Handbuch Sprache im Recht*. Berlin: de Gruyter, 118-137.

Engberg, Jan. 2020. Institutional Dissemination of Legal Knowledge. An Instance of Knowledge Communication. In: Maurizio Gotti / Stefania Maci / Michele Sala (Hrsg.), *Scholarly Pathways. Knowledge Transfer and Knowledge Exchange in Academia*. Frankfurt am Main: Lang, 175-205.

Engberg, Jan / Karin Luttermann. 2014. Informationen auf Jugend-Webseiten als Input für Wissenskonstruktion über Recht. *Zeitschrift für Angewandte Linguistik* 60 (1), 67-91.

Engberg, Jan / Karin Luttermann / Silvia Cacchiani / Chiara Preite (Hrsg.). 2018. *Popularization and Knowledge Mediation in the Law / Popularisierung und Wissensvermittlung im Recht*. Wien: Lit.

Engberg, Jan / Carmen Daniela Maier. 2015. Challenges in the New Multimodal Environment of Research Genres. What Future do Articles of the Future Promise us? In: Natascha Artemeva / Aveva Freedmann (Hrsg.), *Genre Studies around the Globe. Beyond the Three Traditions*. Edmonton: Inkshed Publications, 225-250.

Felder, Ekkehard. 2023. Empathie und Vagheit in der Rechtssprache. In: Karin Luttermann / Jan Engberg (Hrsg.), *Popularisierung als Methode der Wissensvermittlung in der Rechtslinguistik / Popularisation as a*

Method of Knowledge Mediation in Legal Linguistics. Berlin: Lit, 83-98.

Felder, Ekkehard / Andreas Deutsch / Friedemann Vogel / Stefan Höfler / Christina Hörth / Aza Gleichmann / Janine Luth / Ina Pick / Hans Kudlich / Lars Bülow. 2020. Empathie im Recht. In: Katharina Jacob / Klaus-Peter Konerding / Wolf-Andreas Liebert (Hrsg.), *Sprache und Empathie. Beiträge zur Grundlegung eines linguistischen Forschungsprogramms*. Berlin: de Gruyter, 333-376.

Garzone, Giuliana. 2014. Investigating Blawgs through Corpus Linguistics. Issues of Generic Integrity. In: Maurizio Gotti / Davide S. Giannoni (Hrsg.), *Corpus Analysis for Descriptive and Pedagogical Purposes. ESP Perspectives*. Frankfurt am Main: Lang, 167-188.

Hallik, Sibylle. 2021. Der Redaktionsstab der GfdS beim Deutschen Bundestag. Sprachberatung für die Legislative. In: Karin Luttermann / Albert Busch (Hrsg.), *Sprache und Recht. Konstitutions- und Transferprozesse in nationaler und europäischer Dimension*. Berlin: Lit, 301-320.

Jaki, Sylvia / Jan Engberg. 2024. Forenkommunikation als kooperative Wissenskonstruktion? Eine Analyse multimodaler Elemente des Heimwerkerforums bastler-treffpunkt.de. In: Sylvia Jaki / Matthias Meiler / Jana Pflaeging / Janina Wildfeuer (Hrsg.), *Multimodalität in Wissensformaten. Analytische und anwendungsorientierte Perspektiven*. Bern: Lang, 225-258.

Keller, Rudi. 2009. Die Sprache der Geschäftsberichte. Was das Kommunikationsverhalten eines Unternehmens über dessen Geist aussagt. In: Christoph Moss (Hrsg.), *Die Sprache der Wirtschaft*. Wiesbaden: Springer, 19-44.

Lombardi, Alessandra. 2024. Stellenanzeigen im Sprach- und Kulturkontrast. Zur fachkommunikativen Komplexität juristischer Stellenangebote als kulturbedinge Handlungspraktiken. In: Albert Busch / Karin Luttermann (Hrsg.), *Professionskommunikation*. Hildesheim: Universitätsverlag, 149-170.

Lombardi, Alessandra / Karin Luttermann. 2023. Legal Specialists Telling their Stories on the Internet. A Comparative Analysis of Professional

Self-Portrayals on German and Italian Law Firm Websites. In: Patrizia Anesa / Jan Engberg (Hrsg.), *The Digital (R)evolution of Legal Discourse. New Genres, Media, and Linguistic Practices*. Berlin: de Gruyter Mouton, 53-66.

Luttermann, Karin. 1999. Gesetzesverständlichkeit als interdisziplinäre Aufgabe. Gedanken am Beispiel von § 211 I StGB. *Zeitschrift für Rechtspolitik* 32 (8), 334-339.

Luttermann, Karin. 2010. Verständliche Semantik in schriftlichen Kommunikationsformen. *Fachsprache* 32 (3-4), 145-162.

Luttermann, Karin. 2017. Klare Sprache als Mittel für Fachkommunikation und Wissenstransfer. *Information. Wissenschaft & Praxis* 68 (4), 217-226.

Luttermann, Karin. 2018. Kommunikativ-funktionale Analyse von werbenden Gebrauchstexten in der Wirtschaft. In: Kerstin Kazzazi / Karin Luttermann / Sabine Wahl / Thomas Fritz (Hrsg.), *Worte über Wörter*. Tübingen: Stauffenburg, 301-318.

Luttermann, Karin. 2021. Klare Sprache für eine verständliche Kommunikation im Rechtsbereich. Ein handlungspragmatischer Ansatz. In: Karin Luttermann / Albert Busch (Hrsg.), *Sprache und Recht. Konstitutions- und Transferprozsesse in nationaler und europäischer Dimension*. Berlin: Lit, 101-132.

Luttermann, Karin. 2023. Museumskommunikation in Klarer Sprache. Theorie, Praxis und Perspektiven. *Linguistik Online* 124 (6), 63-84.

Luttermann, Karin. 2024. Personalwerbung in Stellenanzeigen. Ein textpragmatischer Zugang. In: Albert Busch / Karin Luttermann (Hrsg.), *Professionskommunikation*. Hildesheim: Universitätsverlag, 121-148.

Luttermann, Karin / Jan Engberg. 2018. Vermittlung rechtlichen Wissens an Kinder und Jugendliche im Internet und in Broschüren. In: Jan Engberg / Karin Luttermann / Silvia Cacchiani / Chiara Preite (Hrsg.), *Popularization and Knowledge Mediation in the Law / Popularisierung und Wissensvermittlung im Recht*. Wien: Lit, 85-115.

Luttermann, Karin / Jan Engberg (Hrsg.). 2023a. *Popularisierung als Methode der Wissensvermittlung in der Rechtslinguistik / Popularisation as a Method of Knowledge Mediation in Legal Linguistics*. Berlin: Lit.

Luttermann, Karin / Jan Engberg. 2023b. Erklärvideos und Broschüren als Information und Mittel zum Aufbau von Verständlichkeit und Vertrauen – eine Fallstudie. In: Karin Luttermann / Jan Engberg (Hrsg.), *Popularisierung als Methode der Wissensvermittlung in der Rechtslinguistik / Popularisation as a Method of Knowledge Mediation in Legal Linguistics*. Berlin: Lit, 99-130.

Luttermann, Karin / Jan Engberg. 2024. Verständlichkeit und Vertrauen durch Popularisierung am Beispiel des Erbrechts. In: Pavla Schäfer / Milena Beloševič (Hrsg.), *Sprache und Vertrauen. Facetten der linguistischen und interdisziplinären Vertrauensforschung*. Berlin: de Gruyter, 165-183.

Luttermann, Karin / Alessandra Lombardi. 2025. Anwälte adressieren Klienten. Eine vergleichende Analyse von Berufsbiographien auf deutschen und italienischen Kanzlei-Webseiten. In: Karin Luttermann / Jan Engberg (Hrsg.), *Digitalisierung und multimodale Ressourcen in diskursiven juristischen Prozessen / Digitalisation and Multimodal Resources in Discursive Legal Processes*. Berlin: Lit (in diesem Band).

Maaß, Christiane. 2015. *Leichte Sprache. Das Regelbuch.* Berlin: Lit.

Mertzlufft, Christine. 2021. Der schwedische Weg zu einer klaren und verständlichen Behördensprache. In: Karin Luttermann / Albert Busch (Hrsg.), *Sprache und Recht. Konstitutions- und Transferprozsesse in nationaler und europäischer Dimension*. Berlin: Lit, 349-378.

Myers, Greg. 2003. Discourse Studies of Scientific Popularization: Questioning the Boundaries. *Discourse Studies,* 5 (2), 265-279.

Nordrum, Jon Christian F. / Torunn Reksten / Janine Schaller-Bøyum. 2021. Der Weg zu mehr sprachlicher Klarheit in der norwegischen Gesetzgebung. In: Karin Luttermann / Albert Busch (Hrsg.), *Sprache und Recht. Konstitutions- und Transferprozsesse in nationaler und europäischer Dimension*. Berlin: Lit, 321-348.

Nordrum, Jon Christian F. / Torunn Reksten / Janine Schaller-Bøyum / Ole Våge. 2025. In: Karin Luttermann / Jan Engberg (Hrsg.), *Digitalisierung und multimodale Ressourcen in diskursiven juristischen Prozessen / Digitalisation and Multimodal Resources in Discursive Legal Processes*. Berlin: Lit (in diesem Band).

Preite, Chiara. 2018. Stratégies dialogiques et transmission du savoir juridique dans le site du Ministère de la Justice française. In: Jan Engberg / Karin Luttermann / Silvia Cacchiani / Chiara Preite (Hrsg.), *Popularization and Knowledge Mediation in the Law / Popularisierung und Wissensvermittlung im Recht*. Wien: Lit, 149-168.

Reinmuth, Marcus. 2009. Vertrauen und Wirtschaftssprache. Glaubwürdigkeit als Schlüssel für erfolgreiche Unternehmenskommunikation. In: Christoph Moss (Hrsg.), *Die Sprache der Wirtschaft*. Wiesbaden: VS, 127-145.

Roelcke, Thorsten. 2020. *Fachsprachen*. 4. Auflage. Berlin: Schmidt.

Schubert, Klaus. 2007. *Wissen, Sprache, Medium, Arbeit*. Tübingen: Narr.

Storrer, Angelika. 2019. Hypertextlinguistik. In: Nina Janich (Hrsg.), *Textlinguistik. 15 Einführungen*. Tübingen: Narr, 315-331.

Tessuto, Gerolamo. 2015. Posted by…: Scholarly Legal Blogs as part of Academic Discourse and Site for Stance and Engagement. *Textus,* 15 (2), 85-106.

Thieme, Stephanie / Zsuzsa Parádi. 2021. Die Sprache, mit der Recht gemacht wird. In: Karin Luttermann / Albert Busch (Hrsg.), *Sprache und Recht. Konstitutions- und Transferprozsesse in nationaler und europäischer Dimension*. Berlin: Lit, 275-300.

Turnbull, Judith. 2023. "Where do I stand?". Online Legal Information for Children and Adolescents. In: Karin Luttermann / Jan Engberg (Hrsg.), *Popularisierung als Methode der Wissensvermittlung in der Rechtslinguistik / Popularisation as a Method of Knowledge Mediation in Legal Linguistics*. Berlin: Lit, 313-338.

Vogel, Friedemann / Fabian Deus / Janine Luth / Joline Schmallenbach / Ekkehard Felder. 2022. *Gesetzesverständlichkeit aus rechtslinguistischer Perspektive. Evaluation der gesetzesredaktorischen Arbeit zur Optimierung von Rechtsvorschriften im Bundesministerium der Justiz und für Verbraucherschutz*. Berlin: Duncker & Humblot.

Wiesmann, Eva. 2023. Klimawandel und Klimaschutzmaßnahmen. Eine kontrastive Untersuchung der Webkommunikation des deutschen und des italienischen Umweltministeriums. In: Karin Luttermann / Jan

Engberg (Hrsg.), *Popularisierung als Methode der Wissensvermittlung in der Rechtslinguistik / Popularisation as a Method of Knowledge Mediation in Legal Linguistics.* Berlin: Lit, 157-193.

Wildfeuer, Janina / John A. Bateman. 2018. Theoretische und methodologische Perspektiven des Multimodalitätskonzepts aus linguistischer Sicht. *Image. Zeitschrift für interdisziplinäre Bildwissenschaft* (28), 5-46.

Untersuchte Webseiten

https://www.bmj.de/DE/Startseite/Startseite_node.html (Letzter Zugriff 25.8.2024).

https://www.justitsministeriet.dk/ (Letzter Zugriff 1.10.2024).

Patricia Rawinsky

Multimodalität und Popularisierung – eine Beispielanalyse von Erklärvideos zur Erstellung der Steuererklärung

Abstract

Auf welche Weise werden multimodale Elemente bei der Vermittlung von rechtsbezogenen Fachinhalten im Rahmen der Popularisierung eingesetzt? Hinsichtlich der Angemessenheit des anvisierten Adressatenkreises sind nicht allein schriftsprachliche Vermittlungsmethoden relevant, sondern auch visuelle und auditive Elemente können den Vermittlungsprozess unterstützen. Der vorliegende Beitrag zeigt anhand von Erklärvideos zu dem Erstellen von Steuererklärungen auf, welche multimodalen Mittel hierbei eingesetzt werden können. Ziel der Analysen ist es, die Verschränkung der Popularisierung mit der Multimodalität mit Rückgriff auf deren Nutzbarkeitsmachung für Vermittlungszwecke aufzuzeigen.

In which way are multimodal elements used for the knowledge mediation of specialised content (in this present case: legal content) in the context of popularisation? While the main goal of communication is to maintain adequacy with regard to the group of addresses, the methods of communications are not limited exclusively to the means of written language. In addition, visual and auditory elements can provide support within the communication process. This contribution uses explanatory videos on how to draw tax returns in order to display which kind of multimodal elements can be used for the purpose of popularisation. The aim of the analysis is to show the interconnection of popularisation and multimodality by considering the utilisation for mediation purposes.

I. Einleitung

Das Vermitteln von Fachinhalten unterliegt in einem fachlichen Kontext besonderen Rahmenbedingungen und muss sich mit besonderen Herausforderungen konfrontiert sehen: Neben unterschiedlichen Formen der Vermittlung (Popularisierung) von fachrelevanten Inhalten an einen heterogenen Adressatenkreis (Experten bis Laien)[1] gehören auch immer neue Kommunikationsmedien zum Analysegegenstand der Linguistik: Inhalte werden nicht mehr alleine mittels Texte an eine bestimmte Rezipientengruppe weitergegeben, sondern auch Hypertexte und Videos dienen als Informationsträger. Zu der Ebene des Textes kommen somit auch auditive und visuelle Vermittlungsmöglichkeiten.

Die damit einhergehende Multimodalität zeichnet sich durch den Einsatz verschiedener Zeichen aus, die jedoch eine Gemeinsamkeit besitzen: Ohne Kenntnis der Zeichen und ihrer Verwendung, d.h. einer gemeinsamen Wissensbasis, werden sowohl auf der Produzenten- als auch auf der Rezipientenseite entsprechende kommunikative Ziele für gelingende Verständigung nicht erreicht. Im Rahmen der Popularisierung bedeutet dies vor allem die Vermittlung von fachrelevanten Informationen an ein Laienpublikum etwa mittels Emotionalisierung und Abbau von Ängsten (vgl. Luttermann / Engberg 2023). Es ergibt sich ein doppelter Wissenshorizont: Die multimodal kodierten Zeichen müssen hinsichtlich ihrer Verwendung den Rezipienten bekannt sein und gleichzeitig müssen auch die Fachinhalte angemessen wiedergegeben werden. Es ist eine gegenseitige Bedingtheit festzustellen. Die Angemessenheit kann derweil nur unter Fach- und Sachkonstanz (Konzept der *Klaren Sprache*; Luttermann 2021) erzielt werden, die Klarheit und Handlungsanweisungen bestimmen. Untersuchungen zu der daraus resultierenden Verständlichkeit haben gezeigt, dass sich Rezipienten genau dies wünschen (vgl. Rawinsky 2024: Kapitel 16.2).

Besonders relevant ist dies in institutionell geprägten Fachkontexten, da hier die Kommunikation zwischen Staat und Bürger in den Fokus rückt. Diese Kommunikation unterliegt besonderen Anforderungen, da sie mit

---

[1] Die Bezeichnung von Personen(gruppen) schließt alle natürlichen Geschlechter mit ein.

rechtsrelevanten Inhalten verbunden ist. Dabei gilt es, Vertrauen herzustellen, um eine Vermittlung von rechtsrelevanten Inhalten auf einem rezipientenorientierten Niveau zu ermöglichen. Eine inzwischen auch im Rechts- und Verwaltungsbereich beliebte Form der Informationsdarlegung sind sogenannte Erklärvideos, mithilfe derer sich Laien selbständig fachrelevantes Wissen aneignen können. Auf der Videoplattform *Youtube* sind unzählige solcher Videos publik – auch zu dem Thema: Wie wird eine Steuererklärung erstellt? Die Notwendigkeit, eigenständig Informationen einzuholen, ergibt sich für (juristische) Laien aus der in der Verwaltungskommunikation deutlich empfundenen Unverständlichkeit, zu der auch der Kommunikationsbereich Steuern zählt (vgl. Efing 2020). Mittels Erklärvideos wird fachinternes Wissen an ein breites Publikum kommuniziert und popularisiert. Welche Strategien der Popularisierung in Verschränkung mit einer multimodalen Darstellung hierzu verwendet werden und wie diese die Zielsetzungen der Popularisierung fördern, fokussiert der vorliegende Beitrag.

Zu diesem Zweck wird die Popularisierung unter dem zentralen Aspekt der Wissensvermittlung vorgestellt (Ziffer II). Für den Untersuchungskontext ist vornehmlich die Vermittlung von rechtsrelevantem Wissen entscheidend (Ziffer II). Die Modellierung der Multimodalität (Ziffer III) schafft schließlich die Ausgangslage für die Untersuchung der Erklärvideos zu dem Themenkomplex *Steuererklärung erstellen* (Ziffer IV). Besonderes Augenmerk wird hier auf die thematische Entfaltung sowie den Umgang mit Fachwörtern gelegt, da diese zentrale Wissensträger sind und Aushandlungsprozesse von Bedeutung gestalten können (vgl. Felder 2006).

II. Popularisierung als Wissensvermittlung

Die Weitergabe von Wissen, insbesondere von Wissen, das innerhalb von Institutionen generiert wird, unterliegt speziellen Zielsetzungen. Diese sind mit den Institutionen als Produzenten und ihrem zugrundeliegenden Zweck verbunden: Institutionen als Regelsysteme verfolgen den Zweck, eine soziale Ordnung herzustellen. Die Kommunikation von institutionellen Inhalten unterstützt diese Intention, wenngleich das Erreichen mit einer für die Bürger angemessenen Kommunikation verbunden sein muss.

Relevant ist in diesem Zusammenhang die Auswahl der Informationen und die Darstellungsweise dieser für die Rezipienten. Die Popularisierung als Methode stellt nun Kriterien zur Wissensvermittlung zur Verfügung. Sie versucht, den popularisierten Gegenstand einer Allgemeinheit näher zu bringen, „damit es nicht den Personen mit spezifischen institutionellen Merkmalen reserviert bleibt“ (Engberg 2021: 33). Im Folgenden geht es um den Begriff des Wissens, der für Popularisierung durch die Skalierung von Experten und Laien als Produzenten und Rezipienten eine zentrale, jedoch nicht final determinierende Rolle spielt. Im Anschluss daran werden die Grundlagen sowie Besonderheiten der Popularisierung bei institutionell-rechtsrelevanten Inhalten erörtert.

1. Wissensbegriff

Bei der Frage nach verstehensrelevantem Wissen unter Rückgriff auf eine semiotische Betrachtung ist konstituierend, dass Wissen keine inhärente Eigenschaft von Zeichen ist, sondern vielmehr das Produkt eines aktiven Prozesses der Anbindung von bestimmten Inhalten an eine Zeichenform (vgl. Klug 2016: 165). Damit steht nicht mehr allein die Form der Zeichen im Vordergrund, sondern auch der Aspekt, ob und wie die Zeichennutzer einen gemeinsamen Zugang zu diesen besitzen bzw. erlangen (vgl. Klug 2016: 166). Im vorliegenden Kontext soll dies mittels der Popularisierungsstrategie unterstützt werden.

Grundsätzlich kann zwischen Faktenwissen als *Wissen* und Handlungswissen als *Können* unterschieden werden (vgl. Janich 2009: 31). Weiter ist *Wissen* von dem Begriff der *Information* zu differenzieren: *Wissen* entspricht Informationen, die bereits eine höhere Stufe der Reflexivität erreicht haben (vgl. Antos 2020: 58). *Wissen* entsteht bei der qualitativen Bewertung einer Information, wobei diese Bewertung in Hinblick auf die Semantik zu sehen ist. Während Informationen den inhaltlichen Anteil am Wissensbegriff und damit sowohl eine Geltungswahrscheinlichkeit als auch den Möglichkeitsausschluss in einem Wissensraum abbilden, der durch den Ausschluss von für die Fragestellung nichtkonformer Sachlagen Grenzen zieht (vgl. Spinner 2002: 44), ist Wissen weiter ratifiziert und damit in bestehende Wissensbestände integriert worden. Für die Einordnung als Wissen bedarf es weiterer Verarbeitungsprozesse wie beispielsweise die Einordnung als richtig oder wichtig. Die *Kenntnis* entsteht schließlich auf Grundlage einer ausgewählten, aktiven Information und stellt damit den pragmatischen Gebrauchsbegriff dar (vgl. Spinner 2002: 45).

Eine Unterscheidung in kollektives und individuelles Wissen legt ferner nahe, dass kollektives Wissen das Resultat und Sediment kommunikativer Prozesse ist, während individuelles Wissen die Gesamtheit der gedächtnismäßigen Repräsentationen eines Individuums umfasst (vgl. Antos 2020: 58). Damit wird deutlich, dass Wissen – analog zu den Individuen – nicht homogen ist. Wissen bildet sich stets in Bezug auf individuell kognitive Strukturen aus und ist aufgrund dessen an die einzelnen Personen, in denen es sich manifestiert, gebunden (vgl. Weber 2009: 14).

Fachwissen setzt sich aus verschiedenen Arten des Wissens zusammensetzt und ist somit komplex; es ist nicht rein durch Fakten zu erlernendes Wissen, sondern auch praktisches Wissen und speist sich auch durch Erfahrungen. Mit anderen Worten: Fachwissen stellt nunmehr jenes Wissen dar, das im Laufe des Lebens auf unterschiedliche Weise erworben wird. Es fundiert auf persönlich aufgebautem Erfahrungs-, Alltags- oder Weltwissen und wurzelt meist nur implizit in fachlichen Zusammenhängen (vgl. Kalverkämper 1998: 14). Das sich daraus ergebende Handlungswissen kann sich durch eine Fachausbildung vertiefen und lässt sich zudem segmentieren: Auf der einen Seite entsteht Faktenwissen und relationales bzw. funktionales Wissen, auf der anderen Seite fachsprachliches Wissen, das als terminologisch, argumentativ, fachtextstrukturell, stilistisch etc. charakterisiert werden kann (vgl. Kalverkämper 1998: 14).

Für die Beziehung zwischen Produzenten und Rezipienten bedeutet dies, dass der Produzent möglichst die Wissensvoraussetzungen des Rezipienten kennen muss (vgl. Kalverkämper 1998: 18). Als Repräsentationsformen können hierfür Wissensbestände in Hinblick auf lexikalische Einheiten, textuelle Formen[2] sowie semiotische Mittel gefordert sein (vgl. Kalverkämper 1998: 18). Wissen erscheint auf diese Weise als individuelle Größe, die jedoch auf überindividueller Kodiertheit beruht. Die Möglichkeit zum Ausschluss bestimmten Wissens innerhalb eines Wissensbereichs bringt die Notwendigkeit der Informationenauswahl zum Ausdruck, die bei der Gestaltung der popularisierten Inhalte zentral ist:

> Furthermore, the discretion that is granted to specialists in selecting materials to be simplified in a popularization even though not always a tool for 'influencing downstream audiences' […] or generating distortions, can be seen to enact forms of power […]. (Polese / D'Avanzo 2014: 200)

Wissensvermittlung bedeutet in der Konsequenz auch Machtausübung. So zeigt sich beispielsweise bei dem Einsatz von unterschiedlichen Modalverben, denen eine rechtssprachliche Bedeutung inne ist, das Beibehalten des fachlichen Kontextes als Ausüben und Aufrechterhalten einer Machtbeziehung (vgl. Polese / D'Avanzo 2014: 203; Dietrich 1992: 62ff.). In dem Kontext der Popularisierung von institutionellen Inhalten ist hier umso sorgfältiger auf die Angemessenheit in der Darstellung der Kommunikation zu achten (vgl. Luttermann 2021: 118f.).

2. Grundlagen der Popularisierung

Popularisierung ist als (emotionalsierte) Vermittlung von spezialisiertem Wissen in verständlicher Form zu definieren und weist so darauf hin, dass nicht allein das spezialisierte Wissen, sondern die Art und Weise des Weitergebens im Fokus steht. Damit ist Popularisierung mehr als reine Vermittlung und Didaktisierung. Die Sprache erhält hier einen zentralen Stellenwert (vgl. Bongo 2014: 224). Die Vermittlung kann als eine an den Rezipienten (Laien) ausgerichtete Transformation von Wissensbeständen aus der wissenschaftlichen Welt in die Alltagswelt hinein angesehen werden (vgl. Felder 2003: 96). Damit stehen Texte oder Inhalte als Ausgangspunkt, die innerhalb der fachinternen Kommunikation zu verorten sind

---

[2] Insbesondere in (Fach-)Texten kommt das Informationsverhältnis zwischen Autor und Adressaten zum Ausdruck; vgl. Kalverkämper (1998: 18).

(vgl. Niederhauer 1999: 101) und nun fachextern kommuniziert werden sollen. Hierbei werden (fachliche) Inhalte in einen neuen, möglicherweise nicht fachlichen Argumentationszusammenhang (Rekontextualisierung) gestellt, sodass es zu einer anderweitig akzentuierten Gewichtung der (fachlichen) Inhalte kommen kann (vgl. Niederhauser 1999: 197).

Der dadurch geschaffene öffentliche, allgemein gültige Charakter stellt eine neue Wissensvermittlung an Laien dar, die sich von den herkömmlichen Formen des Bekanntmachens von Wissen sowie dessen Weitergabe unterscheidet: Es geht nicht mehr um einen hierarchischen Wissenstransfer, dessen Vermittlungsgeschehen sich weiterhin an einem Expertenkreis orientiert,[3] sondern um Wissensproduktion und Wissensdistribution als Kontinuum (vgl. Kretschmann 2003: 9). Damit einher geht auch ein „Aspekt der Sympathie- und Beliebtheitsgewinnung" (Engberg 2021: 33). Ein weiteres Charakteristikum der Popularisierung ist die ebenso in der Experten-Laien-Kommunikation erfasste Wissensasymmetrie zwischen Produzenten und Rezipienten (vgl. Engberg 2017: 119), die Beziehungsarbeit bei den beiden Kommunikationspartnern erfordert.

Wissen steht daher in einem unmittelbaren Zusammenhang mit dem sprachlichen Konstitutions- und Rekonstitutionsprozess (vgl. Bongo 2014: 241) und soll vor allem auf angemessene Weise dargestellt werden. Das Konzept der *Klaren Sprache* (Luttermann 2021) kann als zentrale Kommunikationsgrundlage gesetzt werden, da hier die Voraussetzungen der Rezipienten miteinbezogen werden. Umso relevanter wird dies bei institutionellen Inhalten, die aufgrund ihrer Rechtsrelevanz für die heterogene Gesamtheit der Bürger zugänglich gemacht werden müssen. Der ausdifferenzierte Laienbegriff (vgl. Luttermann 2017: 218f.; Luttermann / Rawinsky 2020: 147f.) bringt schließlich die Notwendigkeit zum Ausdruck,

---

[3] Wie im Rahmen des Begriffs der Expertokratie richtig für den Bereich des Rechts erfasst ist, ist „[d]ie Einbeziehung von Expertenwissen in die demokratisch legitimierte Entscheidungsfindung […] einem dauerhaften Konflikt ausgesetzt: Sich einerseits verfügbaren Erkenntnissen nicht verschließen, sich andererseits aber auch nicht auf nur vermeintlich objektives Wissen zu stützen und deshalb verfrüht andere mögliche Entscheidungsalternativen zurückzuweisen" (Münkler 2020: 12f.).

bei der Vermittlung von Fachinhalten unterschiedliche Wissensvoraussetzungen zu berücksichtigen.

Bei der Popularisierung können unterschiedliche Zielsetzungen verfolgt werden: Neben der informationsorientierten Vermittlung kann auch eine gewisse Verhaltensbeeinflussung angestrebt werden. Die Ziele der Popularisierung wie ‚zum Treffen politischer Entscheidungen befähigen', Kontrolle über die Ausübung des eigenen Rechts erhalten' sowie ‚Erweiterung des Horizonts' sind unter dem Bereich der Verhaltensbeeinflussung subsummierbar (vgl. Engberg 2017: 120). Gleich der informationsbasierten Vermittlung, die Ziele wie ‚Nutzen haben', ‚Gefahr erkennen', ‚Horizont erweitern' oder ‚dem Sender Legitimation geben' miteinschließt, findet auch hier eine Rekontextualisierung statt (vgl. Engberg 2017: 120). Zuletzt kann auf den Abbau von Verfremdung und dem Aufbau von Vertrauen gegenüber dem Recht und den Institutionen verwiesen werden (vgl. Preite 2013: 247; Luttermann / Engberg 2004: 177ff.).

3. Besonderheiten der Popularisierung von institutionell-rechtsrelevanten Inhalten

Die Popularisierung von institutionellen Inhalten schließt zum größten Teil Rechtswissen und verwaltungskulturelles Wissen mit ein. Der Fokus des vorliegenden Beitrags liegt auf der – popularisierenden – Vermittlung von rechtsrelevantem Wissen.Grundsätzlich kann institutionelles Handeln als sprachliches Handeln angesehen werden (vgl. Becker-Mrotzek / Scherner 2000: 632). Die damit verbundenen sprachlichen Besonderheiten sind durch die Fächer des Rechts und der Verwaltung bedingt. Sowohl sprachlich als auch inhaltlich ist die Weitergabe von Rechtswissen vor allem von der Wissensasymmetrie geprägt, die im Rahmen der Experten-Laien-Kommunikation beschrieben wird und innerhalb der Popularisierung weitere Relevanz erhält. Damit können folgende Charakteristika für die Vermittlung und Popularisierung von rechtsrelevantem Wissen festgestellt werden (vgl. Engberg / Luttermann / Cacchiani / Preite 2018: XII):

- Die Beziehung der Gesprächspartner basiert auf der Opposition Experte-Laie (Experten-Laien-Beziehung)

- Rechtswissen wird aus dem institutionellen Kontext in ein neues kommunikatives Umfeld gebracht (Rekontextualisierung)
- Der Experte möchte dem Laien dieses rechtsrelevante Wissen näherbringen (Wissensverbreitung)
- Der Experte wendet die Experten-Laien-Kommunikation überschreitenden Strategien zur Wissensvermittlung an (Popularisierung)

Auch wenn die innersprachlichen Beziehungen damit durch Kontraste geprägt sind, müssen Möglichkeiten für einen Abbau dieser Kontraste gefunden werden, da diese sonst in Kommunikationsbarrieren (dazu weiterführend Schubert 2016) enden können. Durch die Strategien der Popularisierung und deren Zielsetzungen, in Verbindung mit denen des jeweiligen Fachs, wird dies möglich gemacht.

Im Hinblick auf eine multimodale Darstellung kann nun festgehalten werden, dass sich bei der Konkretisierung von Rechtsinhalten durch nichtsprachliche Mittel Möglichkeiten ergeben, Sachverhalte hierarchisch oder chronologisch zu präsentieren (vgl. Engberg 2017: 133f.): Weiter können Begrifflichkeiten und deren Verbindungen in Form von Netzwerken abgebildet werden. Filmmedien sind darüber hinaus besonders für eine persuasive Darstellung von Inhalten geeignet; ebenso aber auch für eine rein informative Vermittlung. Der entscheidende Vorteil von Filmmedien besteht darin, dass der emotionale Hürdenabbau deutlich leichter bewerkstelligt werden kann (vgl. Engberg 2017: 134). Ein wesentlicher Teil des zu vermittelnden Wissens liegt dabei in Form von Fachwörtern vor. Wie der Umgang mit diesen in einem durch die Popularisierung geprägten Kontext aussehen kann, zeigen die anschließenden Ausführungen.

4. Umgang mit rechtsrelevanten Termini

Fachwörter oder auch Termini bilden das fachliche Wissen ab. Daher muss ihnen besondere Aufmerksamkeit gezollt werden, denn deren Dekonstruktion und Rekontexualisierung entscheidet für Laien über das Verstehen der Inhalte. Die häufige Verwendung von Fachwörtern und deren Bedeutung für Fachtexte stellt bei der Popularisierung eine wesentliche Grundfrage im Umgang mit diesen dar. Die Wissensumfänge von Fachwörtern (sowie damit verbundene Wissensrahmen, die nicht mit Begriffsdefinitionen gleichzusetzen sind) weisen vor allem auf Expertenwissen hin und sind daher nicht immer oder nur in einem gewissen Umfang bei Laien anzunehmen. Es handelt sich um vernetztes Wissen, sodass die Aufgabe der Experten (Vermittlungsinstanzen) darin besteht, Wissenszusammenhänge explizit darzustellen.

Für den Umgang mit Fachwörtern in populärwissenschaftlichen Texten stehen verschiedene Techniken zur Verfügung. Zum einen können Fachwörter mit Hilfe von Definitionen[4] ausgedrückt werden (vgl. Niederhauser 1999: 143). Dies geschieht durch die Nennung des entsprechenden Fachworts und einer angeschlossenen definitorischen Beschreibung des zugehörigen fachlichen Gehalts (vgl. Niederhauser 1999: 143). Es wird versucht, mit den popularisierten Bestimmungen der Fachwörter an Alltagswissen anzuknüpfen und damit einen Erklärungskontext zu bieten, an den Laien anschließen können (vgl. Niederhauser 1999: 143). Außerdem können Fachwörter auch mittels Kurzdefinitionen[5] und Kurzerläuterungen zugänglicher gemacht werden. Der Anspruch besteht nicht in der Vollständigkeit, sondern darin, ausführlich genug zu sein, um einem Nicht-Fachkundigen einen ungefähren fachlichen Hintergrund zu vermitteln (vgl. Niederhauser 1999: 147f.).

Zugleich können Fachwörter mittels impliziter Fachworterklärungen durch entfaltende Definitionen abgebildet werden. Hierbei werden Fachworterklärungen über mehrere Stellen im Text verteilt, indem das Fachwort genannt und dann mehrfach aufgegriffen wird (vgl. Niederhauser

---

4 Dies kann innerhalb des Fließtextes wie auch in Form einer ausführlicheren Definition erfolgen, die nicht in den Text integriert, sondern in einem eigenen Bereich angeordnet ist; vgl. Niederhauser (1999: 144f.).

5 Kurzdefinitionen sind sprachlich durch Parenthesen und Ellipsen gekennzeichnet und meist nicht länger als zwei bis drei Sätze in hypotaktischer Gliederung; vgl. Niederhauser (1999: 148f.). Die Problematik bei dieser Form der Darstellung von Fachwörtern ist durch ein Spannungsverhältnis charakterisiert, das sich aus der Gegenüberstellung von notwendiger Vereinfachung und unzulässigen Simplifizierungen ergibt. Einmal mehr kommen Bedeutung und Notwendigkeit der Ausrichtung eines Textes an entsprechende Rezipienten und deren Bedürfnisse zum Ausdruck.

1999: 150). Mit den Wiederaufnahmen können auf diese Weise verschiedene Facetten aufgezeigt werden (vgl. Niederhauser 1999: 152). Problematisch ist, dass hierdurch der Status der Fachwörter nicht erkennbar wird. Zudem muss der Umgang mit vernetzt dargestellten Informationen dem Leser vertraut sein. Nur so können verteilte Informationskomponenten dem Text entnommen werden (vgl. Niederhauser 1999: 151). Es ist davon auszugehen, dass für diese Art der Erläuterung mehr (fachliches) Vorwissen notwendig ist.

Abschließend sei noch auf die Option verwiesen, Fachwörter unerklärt zu lassen. Dies ist nur in spezialisierten Formen der Popularisierung anzutreffen wie zum Beispiel in Fachjournalen (vgl. Niederhauser 1999: 155). Ob ein Fachwort erklärt werden muss oder nicht, wird damit durch den Adressatenkreis festgelegt. Durch den Einsatz von Multimodalität ergeben sich abschließend Möglichkeiten, vernetzte Inhalte, die durch Fachwörter abgebildet werden, anschaulich darzustellen. Die Grundlagen der Multimodalität und die damit verbundenen textlinguistischen Modelle werden im Folgenden dargelegt.

III. Multimedialität als Multimodalität – Wissen in vielfältiger Form

Multimodalität beschreibt zunächst den Rückgriff auf verschiedene Zeichenmodalitäten im Rahmen der Kommunikation (vgl. Klug 2016: 167). Wissen, das sich erst kollektiv als Wissensstrukturen etablieren kann und damit zu gesellschaftlichem Wissen wird, aktualisiert sich, indem „Menschen ganz usuell auch auf andere Zeichenmodalitäten als Sprache zurück[greifen] […]“ (Klug 2016: 167). Dazu zählen beispielsweise Bild, Musik und Geräusche, wobei die Abgrenzbarkeit und Typologisierung von Zeichenmodalitäten in einem kommunikativen Gebrauch nicht als strikt angesehen werden können (vgl. Stöckl 2016: 5ff.). Die Zeichenmodalitäten begründen sich durch die jeweilige Sinnesmodalität bzw. den Wahrnehmungskanal (vgl. Stöckl 2016: 6). Aus semiotischer Sicht bedingt dies vor allem die Zugehörigkeit zu einem Kode oder einem Zeichensystem (vgl. Stöckl 2016: 8). Die Kodiertheit drückt dabei das Vorhandensein eines kulturell etablierten und konventionell verwendeten Zeichensystems aus, das für eine absichtsvolle Kommunikation genutzt wird.

Es stellt sich die Frage nach der Unterteilung der Modalitäten. Germanistische Medien(text-)linguistik führt eine Einteilung nach Kommunikationsformen durch, sodass die medial-materiellen, zeitlich-räumlichen und situativen Aspekte der Kommunikation erfasst und typisiert werden können (vgl. Stöckl 2016: 8). Im Kern geht es darum, ob Sprache, die durch zwei Modi – gesprochen und geschrieben – realisiert wird, sogleich als multimodal zu bezeichnen ist. Sicher ist, dass eine medial unterschiedliche Realisierung vorliegt und mediale Aspekte einen konstituierenden Einfluss auf die Struktur und den Gebrauch von Zeichenmodalitäten besitzen (vgl. Stöckl 2016: 8). Multimedialität konstituiert ergo durchaus Multimodalität. Eine multimodale Textanalyse kann nun folgende Schritte miteinbeziehen (vgl. Stöckl 2016: 23ff.):

i. Gliederung und Abgrenzung: Binnenstruktur (Anordnung der Handlungen und Themen)
ii. Handlungsstruktur: Pragmatische Leistung der einzelnen Modalitäten (Beitrag zu dem übergeordneten Ziel (hier: Popularisierung))
iii. Themenstruktur: Organisation der abzubildenden Wissensrahmen und die damit verbundene mediale bzw. modale Darstellung
iv. Multimodale Verknüpfung: Bezüge der Modalitäten zueinander
v. Intertextualität: Explizite Verweise auf benachbarte Texte

Ausschlaggebend für die Multimodalität ist, wie auch für die Popularisierung, eine gemeinsame Wissensbasis. In einer multimodalen Ausarbeitung trägt jede gebrauchte Zeichenressource einen Anteil zu der Bedeutungsbildung (vgl. Klug 2016: 169). Die Art und Weise der Verknüpfung der Zeichen durch unterschiedliche Modalitäten zu einem kommunikativen Ganzen geschieht demnach vor dem Hintergrund des semiotischen Potenzials der einzelnen Zeichenressourcen (vgl. Klug 2016: 172). Die Zeichenmodalitäten können sich so im Rahmen der Bedeutungsbildung gegenseitig unterstützen, bestätigen oder zu einer Fokussetzung beitragen (vgl. Klug 2016: 174). Die eingesetzten kommunikativen Strukturen müssen ebenso

Bezüge zu dem Vorwissen und auch den Kompetenzen der Adressaten aufweisen, wenn Verständlichkeit und damit Verstehen erzielt werden soll. Eine multimodale Darstellung der semantischen Relationen innerhalb eines Fachgebiets bietet deshalb einen Zugewinn an Möglichkeiten für die Popularisierung von Inhalten. Die anschließende Analyse von zwei Erklärvideos zentriert die Frage, in welcher Form Multimodalität der Popularisierung von rechtsrelevanten Inhalten in der Praxis von Nutzen sein kann.

IV. Praxis

Die beiden zur Analyse herangezogenen Erklärvideos sind in den thematischen Rahmen *Steuererklärung erstellen* einzuordnen. Während das erste Erklärvideo eine ganze Anlage der Steuererklärung erläutert (Anlage KAP), wird in dem zweiten Erklärvideo ein dieser Anlage zugrundeliegendes fachliches Konzept erläutert: der Freistellungsauftrag. Beide Videos haben zum Zweck, ihren Zuschauern Informationen für das Erstellen einer Steuererklärung zu geben und ihnen die Scheu vor dem Themengebiet *Steuern* zu nehmen. Der Analyse liegen nun zwei zentrale Fragestellungen zugrunde:

- Wie erfolgt die Popularisierung der rechts- und verwaltungsrelevanten Inhalte?
- Inwieweit kann von einer multimedialen bzw. multimodalen Präsentation der popularisierten Inhalte gesprochen werden?

In Hinblick auf die Popularisierung der Fachinhalte ist vor allem relevant, in welchem Ausmaß über die Experten-Laien-Kommunikation hinausgehende Strategien zur Wissensvermittlung angewendet werden und wie diese sich – in Hinblick auf die Multimodalität – auf die Handlungs- und Themenstruktur wie auch auf die multimodale Verknüpfung niederschlagen. Damit werden Methoden der Korpus- und Bildlinguistik miteinander verknüpft sowie Fachinhalte mittels der Kriterien der Popularisierung bewertet.

1. Untersuchungsgegenstand

Die beiden Erklärvideos sind öffentlich auf *Youtube* zugänglich. Die Auswahl der beiden Videos gründet sich vor allem auf dem fachlichen Hintergrund der Videoersteller. *FinanzNerd*[6] (Erklärvideo 1 [EV 1]) hat bis dato ein Buch zu Steuertipps veröffentlicht und bietet zudem auf seiner Homepage verschiedene Services an, wie etwa einen Depot- oder Girokontovergleich. Neben Steuern werden so auch die Themenbereiche Finanzen und Versicherungen abgedeckt. Der Homepage weiter zu entnehmen ist, dass der ‚FinanzNerd' Simon Neumann selbst eine Versicherungsausbildung und eine Zusatzausbildung Bankbetriebslehre der IHK und somit ein gewisses Expertenwissen besitzt. Mit ihm ist noch ein Kameramann Teil der OHG FinanzNerd.

Evergreen[7] (Erklärvideo 2 [EV 2]) vertreibt ebenfalls Vermögensberatung. Darüber hinaus existiert eine App und ist das Unternehmen auf allen gängigen Social Media Plattformen vertreten. Der Geschäftsführer Iven Kurz, der auch in dem Erklärvideo zu sehen ist, tritt auf der Homepage mit dem Leiter Asset Management und dem Manager, der die operativen Geschäfte leitet, auf. Alle drei verfügen über Ausbildungs- und Arbeitserfahrung im Bereich Finanzen. Die *Evergreen* GmbH ist ferner als Finanzdienstleistungsunternehmen eingetragen.

2. Erklärvideo 1

Bei dem ersten Erklärvideo[8] (EV 1) handelt es sich um das Video von FinanzNerd. Es trägt den Titel *Zinsen, Gewinne & CO: Anlage KAP 2022 ausfüllen Steuererklärung 2022 in Elster ☑ (Anlage KAP 2022)*. Insgesamt hat das Video 11.165 Aufrufe, ist seit März 2023 online und besitzt eine Gesamtlänge von 12:14 Minuten.

---

6 Alle Informationen zu *FinanzNerd* wurden der Homepage entnommen: https://www.finanznerd.de (Letzter Zugriff 17.5.2023).

7 Alle Informationen zu *Evergreen* wurden der Homepage entnommen: https://www.evergreen.de/ (Letzter Zugriff 17.5.2023).

8 https://www.youtube.com/watch?v=kuFyU1_V_qM (Letzter Zugriff 17.5.2023).

Bei der Vorstellung der Person, die durch das Erklärvideo führen wird, erscheint Simon, der FinanzNerd, vor einem dunkelblauen Hintergrund, auf welchem Geldscheine zu sehen sind. Er selbst trägt ein weißes Oberteil, eine Jeans und wirkt dadurch sehr leger und nahbar. Durch die Alltäglichkeit dieses Auftretens ist zu erwarten, dass sich die Zuschauer mit ihm identifizieren können. Im Weiteren begleitet Simon das Video teils als kleine Figur am Rande, die über die fachlichen Inhalte spricht und diese erläutert (siehe Abb. 1). Die Zuschauer werden stets persönlich angesprochen. Dadurch wird eine persönliche Bindung zu ihnen aufgebaut.

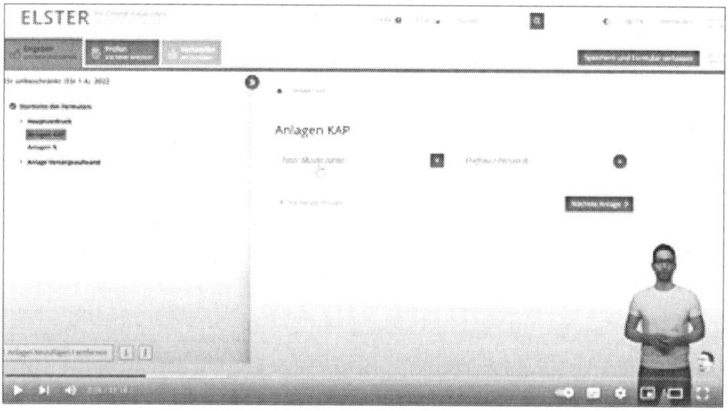

Abb. 1: Beziehungsaufbau zwischen Videoersteller und Zuschauer durch Präsenz des Sprechers (EV 1 – 2:26 Minute)

Zum Hinweis, der am Ende des Erklärvideos angebracht wird, sei angemerkt: Laut diesem wurden in Hinblick auf die Verständlichkeit nur wichtige Felder der Elsterformulare kommentiert (11:42 Minute). Die Gesamtauswahl der popularisierten Informationen beruht konsequenterweise auf der Einschätzung der Wichtigkeit, die von Seiten des Videoerstellers geschieht. Eine Reihe von Fachkonzepten der von dem Videoersteller betitelten ‚Sonderfälle' werden dabei ausgelassen. Dazu zählt zum Beispiel die fiktive ausländische Quellensteuer (10:24-10:36 Minuten).

2.1. Inhaltliche Struktur

In diesem Abschnitt wird eine Beschreibung der Binnenstruktur vorgenommen. Methodisch entspricht dies dem ersten Schritt des multimodalen Textanalysemodells (siehe Ziffer III). Zu Beginn des Erklärvideos stellt sich Simon, der FinanzNerd, selbst vor und beginnt das Erklärvideo mit dem Hinweis, dass nun gezeigt wird, wie die Anlage KAP[9] in der Steuererklärung ausgefüllt werden kann. Daran anschließend macht er Werbung für das von ihm veröffentlichte Buch *100 Steuertipps und Tricks 2022/23. Einfach Steuern sparen.*

Das Video wird durch die Leitfrage: „Wie verhält es sich mit der Versteuerung und Angabe von Kapitalerträgen?“ (1:01-1:16 Minuten) gegliedert. Davon ausgehend wird erläutert, dass die Kapitalerträge einer Abgeltungssteuer unterliegen, genauer der Kapitalertragssteuer. Weiter wird angeführt, dass diese Steuer meist schon durch die Anbieter, beispielsweise einer Bank, direkt abgeführt wird und daher von Seiten der Steuerzahler keine weiteren Handlungen notwendig sind. Dann erfolgt jedoch der Hinweis, dass es sich in manchen Fällen lohnen kann, eine Eintragung in der Steuererklärung vorzunehmen und diese Fälle werden dann anhand des Steuerprogramms Elster gezeigt. Der Zuschauer wird hierbei durch Elster geführt, indem der Videoersteller sich durch das Programm klickt. Demgemäß ist die Ansicht gleich eines tatsächlichen Benutzers bzw. Erstellers einer Steuererklärung in Elster.[10]

So startet das Video auch in der Anlagenauswahl, die in Elster bei der Erstellung der Steuererklärung getroffen werden muss. Es wird darauf verwiesen, dass unterschiedliche Anlagen KAP vorhanden sind (Anlage KAP, Anlage KAP-BET, Anlage KAP-INV). Die Anlage KAP bildet unterdies

9 Die Anlage KAP dient der Erklärung von Einkünften aus Kapitalvermögen. Durch die Abgeltungssteuer ist sichergestellt, dass die Steuern bereits abgeführt wurden. In manchen Fällen, z.B. bei Kapitalerträgen, die nicht dem Steuerabzug unterlagen, muss die Anlage KAP dennoch abgegeben werden; vgl. Anleitung zur Anlage KAP 2022.

10 Sie zum Vergleich die Selbstversuche von Holly (2020) mit Elster-online.

immer die Grundlage für die weiteren Anlagen KAP. Diese werden als „gewisse Sonderfälle“ bezeichnet.[11]

Im Anschluss daran wird der Zuschauer chronologisch durch die Anlage KAP geführt. Diese ist in Unterkapitel unterteilt (z.B. „1 Anträge“ oder „2 Erklärung zur Kirchensteuerpflicht“). Gut gelungen ist meines Erachtens, dass an den jeweiligen Stellen auf die Steuerbescheinigung verwiesen wird (z.B. 3:31 Minute) und darauf, von welchen Zeilen dieser Bescheinigung welche Angaben in das Steuererklärungsformular übertragen werden können. Hier kann ein deutlicher Handlungsbezug festgestellt werden, da die Zuschauer klare Anweisungen erhalten.

Die für die Popularisierung ausgewählten Inhalte beschränken sich somit überwiegend darauf, wie das Steuerprogramm Elster auszufüllen ist. Die Dichte der Informationen und die Schnelligkeit des Gesprochenen erscheinen eher hinderlich: Erst nach mehrfachen Zurückklicken und erneutem Anhören können die gesprochenen Inhalte den gezeigten Formularstellen zugeordnet werden.

2.2. Umgang mit Fachwörtern

Bei dem Umgang mit Fachwörtern steht die Themenstruktur des multimodalen Textanalysemodells im Vordergrund. Dies entspricht dem dritten Schritt des multimodalen Textanalysemodells (siehe Ziffer III). Grundsätzlich ist anzumerken, dass das Erklärvideo 1 äußerst fachsprachlich erscheint, was nicht zuletzt darauf zurückzuführen ist, dass die in dem Steuerprogramm Elster enthaltenen Inhalte mehrheitlich den Zuschauern wortwörtlich vorgelesen werden (vgl. beispielhaft 3:31-3:38 Minuten).[12] Dies ist mehrfach und für eine Vielzahl von fachsprachlichen Konzepten, die in

---

[11] Es wird angeführt, dass es sich um die Anlage KAP Beteiligungen und die Anlage KAP für Kapitalerträge aus Investments handelt, diese werden aber nicht weiter kommentiert.

[12] Hier geht es um die Eintragung von Kapitalerträgen, bei denen auch korrigierte Beitrage eingetragen werden können. Welcher Unterschied hierbei besteht, bleibt aber unerklärt. Vermutlich ist dies darauf zurückzuführen, dass – wie an dieser Stelle im Erklärvideo erwähnt wird – der Regelfall darin besteht, dass Kapitaleträge erzielt werden und den Bescheinigungen zu entnehmen sind wie auch zu übertragen sind.

Elster angeführt werden, der Fall. Damit kann für den Umgang mit Fachwörtern vor allem konstatiert werden, dass diese weithin unerläutert bleiben. Daneben werden auch zusätzliche Fachwörter eingeführt, wie beispielsweise *p-to-p-Kredite* (7:40 Minute), die ebenfalls keine Erläuterung erhalten. Zu denjenigen Fachwörtern, die einer genaueren Analyse unterzogen wurden und zudem zentral für das Gesamtverständnis der Anlage KAP sind, zählen *Günstigerprüfung* und *Sparer-Pauschbetrag*. Inwiefern es sich hier um eine popularisierte Darstellung handelt, wird nachfolgend aufgezeigt.

2.2.1. Günstigerprüfung

Ein zentrales Fachwort für die Verwendung der Anlage KAP ist *Günstigerprüfung*. Dieses wird gleich zu Beginn des Videos (2:28 Minute) genannt und auch der Videoersteller weist auf die Bedeutung des Konzepts hin: „Denn wie erwähnt, fallen ja sonst pauschal 25% plus Soli und teilweise auch Kirchensteuer an, was zusammen durchaus mal 28,375% ausmacht.“ Unklar bleibt, wie sich dieser Steuersatz zu diesem Prozentsatz zusammensetzt. Ist der persönliche *Einkommensteuersatz*[13] nun niedriger als 28,375%, weil man in einem Jahr weniger verdient oder nicht durchgehend gearbeitet hat, dann kann das Finanzamt durch die Auswahl der Günstigerprüfung verpflichtet werden, zu prüfen, was „günstiger“ ist – die Anwendung der Kapitalertragssteuer oder die Anwendung des persönlichen Einkommensteuersatzes (2:45-2:51 Minuten). So zumindest wird *Günstigerprüfung* in dem Erklärvideo dargelegt. Sprachlich handelt es sich demnach um eine Paranthese. Kritisch anzuführen ist dabei die Verwendung des Lexems *günstig*. Ein Fachwort unter Verwendung eines Teils desjenigen Fachworts, das eine Erläuterung bedarf, erscheint wenig zielführend. Die Bedeutung von *günstiger* im Sinne von ‚besser‘ für den Steuerpflichtigen wird hier nur indirekt zum Ausdruck gebracht. Ein Anknüpfen an alltagssprachliches Wissen kann nicht festgestellt werden.

---

[13] Das Fachwort wird ebensowenig erläutert.

Letztlich wird darauf verwiesen, „dass es nichts kostet“, diese Prüfung durchführen zu lassen. Die genauen Voraussetzungen oder Bedingungen, unter denen die Anwendung des einen oder des anderen Steuersatzes geschehen, werden hier nicht dargelegt bzw. bleiben unbestimmt. Unter Einbezug von Fachliteratur kann festgestellt werden, dass das Erklärvideo das grundsätzliche Verfahren der Günstigerprüfung fachlich korrekt wiedergibt:

> Auf Antrag des Steuerpflichtigen werden die nach § 20 EStG ermittelten Kapitaleinkünfte der Summe der Einkünfte hinzugerechnet und der tariflichen Einkommensteuer unterworfen, wenn dies zu einer niedrigeren Einkommensteuer als bei Anwendung des Steuersatzes von 25% führt (Günstigerprüfung). (Ronig o.J.)

In dem Erklärvideo bleibt dies aber zu unbestimmt (2:45-2:51 Minuten) und führt im Folgenden zu einer fachlich zu vagen Aussage, die von Laien falsch aufgefasst werden kann: Es wird behauptet, dass, wenn eine gewisse Einkommensgrenze nicht erreicht wurde, die Günstigerprüfung zur Ermittlung des persönlichen Steuersatzes vom Finanzamt gefordert werden kann. Die Günstigerprüfung kann jedoch unabhängig vom Verdienst verlangt werden; der konkrete Steuersatz steht hingegen tatsächlich in Abhängigkeit von dem persönlichen Einkommen. Bereits ab ca. 17.400€ (oder Zusammenveranlagung 34.800€) muss der einkommensteuerliche (Grenz-) Steuersatz von 25% angewendet werden (vgl. Ronig o.J.); ebenso gilt dies für Kapitalerträge im Allgemeinen. Zwar spricht der Verfasser des Videos zuvor von einem „persönlichen Steuersatz“, der sich bei geringen Einkünften ergeben kann, aber nicht ergeben muss. Diesen statt der 25% Steuer auf Kapitalerträge in der Günstigerprüfung anwenden zu lassen, ist jedoch mit der Bedingung des Finanzamts verknüpft, alle Daten offenzulegen, was häufig von Steuerzahlern als unangenehm empfunden wird und in dem Video zudem nicht aufgegriffen wird. Die konkreten Einkommensgrenzen für einen möglicherweise niedrigeren Steuersatz, der zu einer Anpassung des Steuersatzes für Kapitalerträge führen könnte, werden ebenfalls nicht angeführt.

Grundsätzlich bleibt das doch komplexere Verfahren der Günstigerprüfung bei der Anlage KAP viel zu allgemein und kann insbesondere bei Laien aufgrund der fehlenden fachlichen Hintergrundinformationen zu Missverstehen führen. Auch wenn das Auswählen der Günstigerprüfung für den Ersteller des Steuerbescheids keinen Mehraufwand bedeutet, so werden doch falsche Hoffnungen auf Steuerermäßigung geweckt und wird ein Arbeitsmehraufwand für die Behörden durch die Notwendigkeit zur Prüfung generiert.

2.2.2. Sparer-Pauschbetrag

Der *Sparer-Pauschbetrag* stellt ein weiteres wesentliches Konzept für die gesamte Anlage KAP dar. Dieser lässt Kapitalerträge bis 801€ abgeltungssteuerfrei – sofern der Freistellungsauftrag gestellt wurde (vgl. Kutschera o.J.). Das heißt: Der Sparer-Pauschbetrag muss durch den Freistellungsauftrag beantragt werden, sonst werden auch Kapitalerträge unter der Grenze von 801€ besteuert. Erst wenn der Freistellungauftrag nicht gestellt wurde oder Kapitalerträge über 801€ erzielt wurden, ergeben entsprechende Angaben in der Anlage KAP Sinn. Dies geht aus dem Erklärvideo 1 jedoch nicht in dieser Form hervor. Erst in der Mitte des Erklärvideos (6:47-6:54 Minuten) wird dieses zentrale und für die ganze Anlage wesentliche Konzept in einem kurzen Satz angeführt.

Zuvor wird die Höhe des Sparer-Pauschbetrags genannt (ab 6:00 Minute). Außerdem wird darauf hingewiesen, dass Eintragungen an der vorgesehenen Stelle im Elsterformular nur vorgenommen werden können, wenn der Sparer-Pauschbetrag auch in Anspruch genommen wurde (6:24-6:43 Minuten). Die eben geschilderten Zusammenhänge von *Sparer-Pauschbetrag* und *Freistellungsauftrag* bleiben implizit. Der Freistellungsauftrag wird als „das ist ja dieses Geltend-Machen des Sparer-Pauschbetrags vorab“ bezeichnet. Schließlich heißt es: „[…] dann kann es sein, dass, wenn du einen neuen Anbieter hattest oder den gar nicht hinterlegt hattest, Steuern bezahlt wurden, obwohl du eigentlich noch unter diesen 801€ gelegen hast“ (6:37-6:45 Minuten). *Den* kann dabei auf zwei wesentliche Konzepte referieren, die durch die Unbestimmtheit gleichgesetzt werden: der *Sparer-Pauschbetrag* oder der *Freistellungsauftrag*. Gerade weil fachsprachliche Begrifflichkeiten häufig aufgrund ihres für Laien unbekannten Bedeutungsumfangs ungenau erscheinen und besonders alltagssprachlich undifferenziert verwendet werden,[14] ist dies nicht hinzunehmen.

Die Implizitheit von lexikalischen Verknüpfungen stellt bei der Auseinandersetzung mit Fachinhalten eine Hauptschwierigkeit für Laien dar (vgl. Niederhauser 1999: 153). Die semantische Verbindung des inhaltlichen Gehalts von *Sparer-Pauschbetrag* und *Freistellungsauftrag* muss ebenfalls von Seiten der Rezipienten erfolgen. Ohne das jeweilige Vorwissen evoziert diese Art der Präsentation mehr Fragen bezüglich des fachlichen Zusammenhangs als dass sie Unklarheiten beseitigt.

2.3. Multimodalität der popularisierten Inhalte

Die Multimodalität des Erklärvideos 1 stützt sich vor allem auf das Leiten der Zuschauer durch das Steuerprogramm Elster (vierter Schritt des multimodalen Textanalysemodells; siehe Ziffer III). Theoretisch könnte der Aufbau des Elster-Programms auch verbal erfolgen. Dies würde aber zu einer Überladung der verbalen Modalität führen und von den eigentlichen Inhalten, die vermittelt werden sollen, ablenken: das Anwenden der Fachkonzepte auf das Steuerprogramm Elster. Praktisch wird also mit einer zweiten, visuellen Modalität in diesem Video gearbeitet. Das Programm selbst kann ferner als Hypertext eingeordnet werden. Teils kommen in Elster hinterlegte hypertextuelle Elemente nicht zum Einsatz (z.B. Fachworterklärungen). Jedoch werden die unterschiedlichen Anlagen angeklickt; dies weist sehr wohl Hypertextualität auf, da unterschiedliche Textebenen aufgerufen werden.

Hinsichtlich der pragmatischen Leistung (zweiter Schritt des multimodalen Textanalysemodells; siehe Ziffer III) ist jedoch festzuhalten, dass sich die verbalen und visuellen Darbietungen kaum hinsichtlich ihres Inhalts

---

[14] Siehe HdR (2008: Rn. 57) zur alltagssprachlich synonymen Verwendung von *Eigentum* und *Besitz* sowie Luttermann (2015: 281f.).

unterscheiden: Das, was in dem Elster-Programm zu lesen ist, wird in der Mehrheit der Fälle schlichtweg vorgelesen, sodass durch die Verbalität der gesprochenen Sprache keine Ergänzungen an Informationen erfolgt. Die Modalität wird zwar geändert, es werden aber keine zusätzlichen Wissenselemente eingeführt. Die Kommunikation geschieht somit über unterschiedliche Sinneskanäle und hat einen vornehmlich handlungsgeleiteten Zweck: Es geht vor allem um die Veranschaulichung, was an welcher Stelle in das Steuerprogramm einzutragen ist (visuell), und nur selten um die tatsächliche Darlegung von Fachwissen (verbal). Die Wissensverbreitung beschränkt sich vornehmlich auf Handlungswissen.

Da die Zuschauer als Laien durch das Video die Möglichkeit besitzen, dem Ausfüllen der Anlageformulare beizuwohnen, wird eine reine Experten-Laien-Kommunikation insofern überschritten, als multimodale Aspekte des Vorgangs *Steuererklärung ausfüllen* überwiegen. Es können Elemente der Informationsbeeinflussung (wie ‚Kontrolle über das Ausüben des eigenen Rechts durch Bereitstellen von Fachinhalten in modifzierter Form') und der Verhaltensbeeinflussung (z.B. ‚Sender Legitimation geben, indem den Rezipienten das Fachkonzept nachvollziehbar gemacht wird') ausgemacht werden. Die Multimodalität wird demgemäß durch das Veranschaulichen des Handlungswissens in Elster bedingt. Die Rekontextualisierung als zentrales Merkmal der Popularisierung kann lediglich in der Multimodalität, nicht aber im Inhalt selbst identifiziert werden.

3. Erklärvideo 2

Das Erklärvideo 2[15] (EV 2) mit dem Titel *Freistellungsauftrag: So sparst Du Steuern bei der Geldanlage* von *Evergreen* ist seit September 2020 online, hat 1.234 Aufrufe und ist mit einer Länge von 5:05 Minuten deutlich kürzer als das Erklärvideo 1. In dem Video tritt der CEO von *Evergreen* selbst auf. Er erscheint sitzend in dem Bild und befindet sich in einem weiß gestrichenen Raum, der sanft von einer Stehlampe beleuchtet wird. Am linken Sichtrand befindet sich eine Grünpflanze. Auf diese Weise wird ein

---

[15] https://www.youtube.com/watch?v=agYPAdSuRPg (Letzter Zugriff 15.5.2023).

alltagsnaher Raum geschaffen, der den Zuschauern den Eindruck vermittelt, sich in einem Wohnzimmer zu befinden. Neben den verbalen Erläuterungen gibt es in dem Video von Anfang an eingeblendete Untertitel.

Zu Beginn des Erklärvideos wird weitere Nähe zu den Zuschauern aufgebaut, indem ausgesagt wird, dass „der Begriff Freistellungsautrag […] schon nach jeder Menge Bürokratie [klingt]“ (0:01 Minute), sich die Auseinandersetzung aber lohnt, da steuerliche Vorteile generiert werden können. So wird signalisiert, dass die Ersteller des Videos sich in die Rolle der Laien hineinversetzen und verstehen, dass die Beschäftigung mit dem Thema als unangenehm empfunden werden kann. Gleichzeitig werden direkt Steuervorteile adressiert, sodass Verfremdung abgebaut und Motivation zur Beschäftigung mit der Thematik geschaffen wird.

Wie auch in Erklärvideo 1 werden die Zuschauer geduzt. Dies kann als weitere Strategie, eine vertraute Beziehung zu den Rezipienten aufzubauen, gewertet werden. Auch wenn durch das Erklärvideo hindurch weiterhin fachsprachliche Begriffe und Wendungen verwendet werden („Steuer abführen“, 2:37 Minute), ergibt sich somit ein eher informeller Rahmen.

3.1. Inhaltliche Struktur

Die Darlegung der inhaltlichen Struktur des Erklärvideos entspricht methodisch dem ersten Schritt des multimodalen Textanalysemodells (siehe Ziffer III). Das Video startet direkt mit dem in das Konzept *Freistellungsauftrag*. Die Leitidee des Videos besteht darin, die steuerlichen Vorteile eines Freistellungsauftrags und darüber hinaus dessen Funktionsweise darzulegen (0:10-0:17 Minuten). Im Anschluss daran wird der Sprechende im Video vorgestellt. Es handelt sich dabei um den CEO von *Evergreen*, was aus einer kurzen Einblendung (ab 0:26 Minute) ersichtlich wird.

Grundsätzlich geht das Video in seiner inhaltlichen Struktur vom Allgemeinen zum Speziellen und erweist sich als äußerst strukturiert und übersichtlich. Die Ausgangsposition ist, dass Kapitalerträge besteuert werden müssen (ab 0:28 Minute). Zuerst wird daher erläutert, was *Kapitalerträge* überhaupt sind (ab 0:57 Minute), dann wie diese besteuert werden (ab 1:47

Minute) und zudem, wie sich der Steuersatz zusammensetzt (ab 2:08 Minute). Wesentliche Konzepte wie beispielsweise die Zusammensetzung des Steuersatzes werden stets durch eingeblendete Erklärkästchen visuell unterstützt (siehe Abb. 2). Schließlich gehen die Erläuterungen über zu der Darstellung, was ein *Freistellungsauftrag* ist (ab 2:16 Minute). Besonders positiv ist hervorzuheben, dass mittels einer Beispielrechnung gezeigt wird, wie sich das Stellen oder auch Nicht-Stellen eines Freistellungsauftrags steuerlich auswirkt (ab 2:54 Minute). Zuletzt wird erläutert, was passiert, wenn vergessen wurde, einen Freistellungsauftrag zu stellen (ab 3:48 Minute).

Die Auswahl der popularisierten Inhalte ist für die Leitfrage „Kapitalerträge müssen besteuert werden – was bedeutet das?“ als äußerst zielführend zu bewerten. Insbesondere die Unterteilung in kleine thematische Abschnitte führt zu der Behandlung der für den *Freistellungsauftrag* zentralen Konzepte wie dem damit verbundenen Steuersatz und dessen Anwendung.

3.2. Umgang mit Fachwörtern

Die thematischen Abschnitte des Erklärvideos greifen fachliche Konzepte – und damit verbundene Fachwörter – auf, die für das Verständnis des *Freistellungsauftrags* leitend sind. Dies ist der dritte Schritt des multimodalen Textanalysemodells (siehe Ziffer III). Im Folgenden wird die Handhabung bestimmter Fachwörter behandelt.

3.2.1. Abgeltungssteuer

Das Erklärvideo startet mit dem Grundlegenden: Wenn mit Geldanlagen „Gewinne erzielt [werden], also ein [..] Ertrag generier[t] [wird], dann müsst ihr darauf Steuern zahlen“ (0:28-0:39 Minuten). Dann wird Bezug auf die konkrete Steuer genommen, die für die Besteuerung von Kapitalerträgen relevant ist, und zwar die *Abgeltungssteuer* (0:44-0:52 Minuten). An dieser Stelle wird zudem kurz erläutert, wie hoch diese Steuer ist. Die Darlegung der Zusammensetzung der Abgeltungssteuer wird an thematisch passender späterer Stelle weitergeführt (ab 1:47 Minute). Die Informationen werden somit in dem Erklärvideo verteilt. Mit teilexpliziten Wiederaufnahmestrukturen wird sichergestellt, dass die Zuschauer die Orientierung im Geschehen beibehalten: So wird bei dem ersten Erwähnen der Abgeltungssteuer gesagt, dass diese 25% beträgt und „[d]ort kommt meist noch der Solidaritätszuschlag und gegebenenfalls Kirchensteuer hinzu, aber dazu später mehr“ (0:50-0:56 Minuten).

Auf diese Weise wird eine thematische Weiterführung signalisiert. Zur Grundlagenschaffung erfolgt eine Erläuterung, was *Kapitalerträge* überhaupt sind. Für die Rezipienten wird deutlich, worauf diese Abgeltungssteuer entfallen könnte. Die Wiederaufnahme zur Darlegung dessen, woraus sich die Abgeltungssteuer zusammensetzt, beginnt wie folgt:

> Wie hoch ist diese Steuer auf Kapitalerträge [...]? Diese Abgeltungssteuer, wie sie genannt wird, beträgt 25% zuzüglich des Solidaritätszuschlags. Dieser beträgt 5,5% [...] je nachdem, ob ihr Kirchensteuer zahlen müsst, kommt dieser Betrag dann auch nochmal oben drauf. (EV 2 – 1:49-2:13 Minuten)

Die zu Beginn des Erklärvideos gegebenen Zahlenwerte der Abgeltungssteuer und des Solidaritätszuschlags werden wiederholt. Zudem wird die Berechnung des Prozentsatzes ausgeführt und der Hinweis auf eine eventuell zuzüglich zu berechnende Kirchensteuer gegeben. Die Verben *betragen* und *darauf-* bzw. *hinzukommen* sowie die deiktische Verwendung von *diese*, die auf die Abgeltungssteuer verweist, welche gleichermaßen angeführt wird, tragen zu einem kohärenten Ganzen der Erläuterung bei.

Zu Klarheit soll auch beitragen, dass die einzelnen Bestandteile der Steuer (Steuersatz von 25%, Solidaritätszuschlag von 5,5%) zudem visuell verdeutlicht werden, indem in einem Erklärkästchen die Berechnung des Abgeltungssteuersatzes vorgestellt wird.[16] Es handelt sich also um eine entfaltende Definition (siehe Abb. 2):

---

[16] Bei dem zu Beginn des Videos gegebenen Verweis auf die Abgeltungssteuer (0:44-0:52 Minuten) wird ebenso mit einem Erklärkästchen gearbeitet. Es enthält jedoch nur den Schriftsatz „Abgeltungssteuer 25%”, wobei „Abgeltungssteuer” und „25%” untereinander geschrieben sind. Des Weiteren findet sich ein Stapel Geldmünzen neben den geschriebenen Inhalten, der wohl visualisieren soll, dass hier Geld gezahlt werden muss.

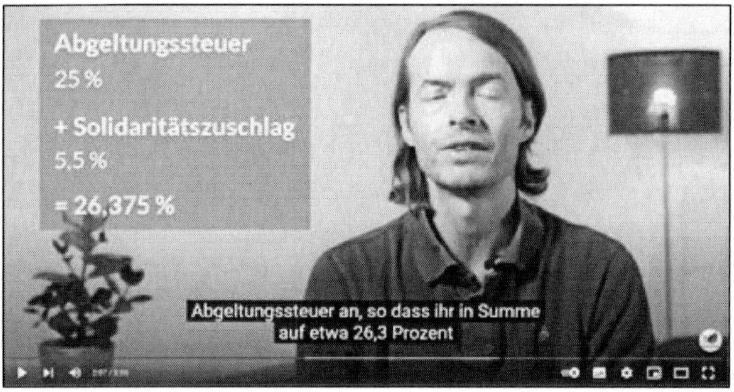

Abb. 2: Darstellung der Zusammensetzung der Abgeltungssteuer durch ein Erklärkästchen (EV 2 – 2:07 Minute)

Für die Rezipienten ist folglich klar ersichtlich, was besteuert wird („Kapitalerträge"), zu welcher Höhe dies geschieht („26,375%", 2:08 Minute) und wie sich diese Höhe rechnerisch zusammensetzt. Kritisch ist lediglich anzufügen, dass die gegebenenfalls anfallende Kirchensteuer in der Berechnung nur auditiv, nicht aber visuell berücksichtigt wird.

3.2.2. Kapitalerträge

Bei der Beschreibung *Kapitalerträge* ist nun auffällig, dass eine Menge weiterer Fachwörter verwendet werden, wozu zum Beispiel *Dividenden* oder auch *Gewinne durch Kursänderungen* gehören. Diese bleiben jedoch unerklärt. Positiv ist anzumerken, dass auch diese, parallel zu allen weiteren thematischen Einheiten, in einem inhaltlich aufbereiteten Erklärkästchen visualisiert werden (siehe Abb. 3):

Die Multimedialität dieser Darstellung ist fragwürdig, da bei der Erläuterung des Sparerfreibetrags in dem Erklärkästchen ebenfalls Geldscheine und Geldmünzen abgebildet werden (2:21 Minute). Es soll wohl den entsprechenden Geldbetrag ausdrücken, der steuerfrei ist. Die Verwendung der Zeichen ist mithin uneinheitlich.

Abb. 3: Wissensbestandteile des Fachworts *Kapitalerträge* (EV 2 – 1:43 Minute)

Alle dort angeführten Fachbegriffe bleiben aber ohne weitere Spezifizierung. Die Erläuterung des Fachworts *Kapitalerträge* wird demzufolge unter Darlegung seiner mit ihm verbundenen Wissensteile[17] realisiert. Da Fachwörter oftmals keine rein lexikalische Bedeutung besitzen, sondern ihnen vielmehr eine fachliche Konzeption zugrunde liegt, ist diese Form der Erläuterung zunächst als sinnvoll zu erachten. Dennoch ist fraglich, inwieweit die angeführten Bestandteile in Form von Beispielen den Rezipienten tatsächlich bekannt sind.

Hier werden Grenzen der Popularisierung sichtbar: Wie weit müssen Fachinhalte erläutert werden? Wissen Anleger, ob sie derartige Kapitalerträge erwirtschaftet haben, da sie die Anlage ja durchgeführt haben? Oder können sie sich gegebenenfalls an einen Bankberater wenden, der dies für sie vorgenommen hat, und sie benötigen diese Informationen überhaupt nicht? Die genaue Kenntnis der Zieladressaten und deren Vorkenntnisse erweist sich einmal mehr als weisend für die angemessene Auswahl an Informationen.

[17] Die angeführten Beispiele für die Arten der Kapitalerträge können unter Zuhilfenahme von Fachliteratur als fachlich korrekt eingeordnet werden; vgl. Hüsing (2020).

3.2.3. Freistellungsauftrag

Ab Minute 2:16 wird erläutert, was ein *Freistellungsauftrag* ist. Zu diesem Zweck wird zunächst der *Sparer-Pauschbetrag*, auch Sparerfreibetrag, erklärt, da dieser dem Freistellungsauftrag zugrunde liegt. Dies ist hinsichtlich der Chronologie der Informationen als äußerst sinnvoll zu betrachten. Auch hier wird mit einem Erklärkästchen gearbeitet. Zunächst werden die Fachkonzepte nebeneinander dargestellt: *Sparer-Pauschbetrag* bedeutet, dass Gewinne bis 801€ steuerfrei sind; Steuern werden stets dort abgeführt, wo sie entstehen (z.B. Bank). Und damit Steuern nicht automatisch an das Finanzamt abgeführt werden, muss der Freistellungsauftrag beantragt werden. Dies sind die Kernaussagen zu dem Sparer-Pauschbetrag (2:18-2:53 Minuten). So werden die fachlichen Informationen nacheinander gegeben und in Bezug zueinander gesetzt.

Abb. 4: Rechenbeispiel für die Besteuerung mit und ohne Freistellungsauftrag (EV 2 – 2:54-3:47 Minuten)

Die ab Minute 2:54 angeführte Beispielrechnung verdeutlicht schließlich in der Praxis, was der Freistellungsauftrag bedeutet: „Vereinfachung der steuerlichen Behandlung […] [von] Kapitalerträgen" (siehe Abb. 4). Die Vernetzung der zuvor angeführten Fachinhalte wird von Seiten des Videoerstellers auf anschauliche Art und Weise vorgenommen, indem die Einzelposten der Beispielrechnung erläutert werden. Auf diese Weise werden fachliche Zusammenhänge (Freistellungsauftrag als steuerliche Entlastung) klar kontextualisiert und abgebildet. Die Visualisierung von Inhalten bringt die Vorteile einer multimedialen Darbietung von Fachinhalten zum Ausdruck: Die zu der Beispielrechnung erfolgten auditiven Erläuterungen ergänzen die schriftlichen Informationen. Für die Beispielrechnung wird als Zahlenbeispiel der Sparer-Pauschbetrag verwendet, sodass direkter inhaltlicher Bezug zu den zuvor gegebenen Inhalten besteht. Die dazu begleitenden Erklärungen können aufgrund der Einfachheit des gesamten Rechenbeispiels als alltagsnah eingeordnet werden.

3.3. Multimodalität der popularisierten Inhalte

Die Multimodalität des Erklärvideos 2 ergibt sich ebenfalls aus dem Gebrauch der zusätzlichen Erklärkästchen, die an thematisch passenden Stellen eingeblendet werden (vierter Schritt des multimodalen Textanalysemodells; siehe Ziffer III). Diese wiederholen die bereits verbal kommunizierten Informationen und unterstützen das Gesagte in einer weiteren Modalität, die sich aufgrund der verschiedenen Medialitäten (Schriftlichkeit durch Texte vs. Mündlichkeit durch Erklärungen) ergibt. Der Sinneskanal wechselt zwischen dem Auditiven und dem Visuellen. Es handelt sich hierbei um eine Ergänzung bzw. Unterstützung, wodurch die Inhalte der gesprochenen Sprache auf die wesentlichen Punkte fokussiert und verengt werden. Nöth (2016: 211) spricht hier von einer sogenannten „Verankerung", bei der die Aufmerksamkeit der Zuschauer auf relevante Einzelheiten geleitet wird. Die für sie relevanten popularisierten Inhalte werden in den Fokus gerückt. Die visuelle Darbietung des Auditiven wird teils durch den Einsatz von unterschiedlicher Farbe begleitet. Die Erklärkästchen sind in hellgrüner Farbe gehalten, die Schriftfarbe ist weiß. Die Erläuterungen bleiben so gut lesbar.

Besonders positiv hervorzuheben sind die Rechenbeispiele. Gleich den Erklärkästchen findet hier ein Wechsel zwischen der Modalität (auditiv zu visuell) statt. Das erste Rechenbeispiel ist die Zusammensetzung des Steuersatzes der Abgeltungssteuer. Dieses ist sehr einfach gehalten, da die einzelnen Steuersätze („Abgeltungssteuer 25%“, „Solidaritätszuschlag 5,5%“) gleich den übrigen Erklärkästchen in hellgrüner Farbe und weißer Schrift gehalten sind. Der Fokus ist noch deutlich auf dem Gesprochenen.

Die Beispielrechnung zum Freistellungsauftrag ist auf unterschiedliche Weise illustriert. Die Abbildung der Rechnung in einem Erklärkästchen ist nicht nur ein Teil des Videos, beispielsweise als eingeblendetes Bild am Rand, sondern bedeckt den gesamten Videoraum (siehe Abb. 4). Durch den Einsatz von unterschiedlichen Farben – blau für die Überschriften, weiß für die Rechnung selbst und rot für die Rechenergebnisse – werden Inhalte weiter zusätzlich visuell betont.[18] Der grüne Hintergrund lässt die Schrift noch gut lesbar erscheinen. Es ist zu überlegen, ob für diesen Teil des Videos der Sprechende ausgeblendet werden könnte, da dieser immer noch im Hintergrund zu sehen ist. Die Geordnetheit der Rechenbeträge und deren chronologische Präsentation untereinander bietet den Rezipienten zusätzliche Orientierung in den bereits verbal popularisierten Fachinhalten, die hier anhand des Beispiels spezifiziert werden, was dem zweiten Schritt des multimodalen Textanalysemodells gleichkommt; siehe Ziffer III). Damit führt der Wechsel der Modalität zu Multimodalität, begründet durch den diversen Gebrauch der Zeichen.

Abschließend sei noch darauf hingewiesen, dass die gesprochenen Inhalte stets durch Untertitel begleitet werden. Diese sind nicht automatisch von Youtube erstellt, wie sonst teils üblich, sondern sind fester Bestandteil des Videos. Auch dies soll das Nachvollziehen der gesprochenen Informationen vereinfachen. Durch die Verwendung eines schwarzen Kästchens für die Untertitel, in denen die Schrift in weißer Farbe erscheint, sind die Untertitel zudem deutlich vom restlichen Hintergrund abgehoben und dabei

---

[18] In Hinblick auf die unterschiedlichen Ansätze zur Einteilung der Modalitäten, die im Zusammenhang mit der medialen Darstellung stehen, ist auf Stöckl (2016: 168) hinzuweisen, der die Farbe eher als Bestandteil einer Modalität denn als einen eigenen Mode sieht.

gut lesbar. Falls die Untertitel als störend empfunden werden, können sie in den Einstellungen des Videos jedoch auch ausgestellt werden.

V. Schlussbemerkung

Wie die vorliegende Untersuchung der Erklärvideos zu dem Themenbereich *Steuererklärung erstellen* zeigen konnte, sind Merkmale der Popularisierung auffindbar und zudem mit multimodalen Elementen verschränkt:

i. Die Videoverfasser verfügen als Experten über mehr Wissen zu dem relevanten Themengebiet, sodass zwischen den Sprechenden und den Adressaten eine Experten-Laien-Beziehung ausgemacht werden kann.
ii. Im Rahmen der Erklärvideos wird das Ziel der Wissensvermittlung verfolgt, indem entweder Handlungswissen zu dem Steuerprogramm Elster oder Fachwissen (zentrale Fachwörter) erläutert werden.
iii. Insbesondere die Visualisierung der zu vermittelnden Inhalte über Elster, aber auch das Berechnen von Steuern geht über übliche Strategien der Wissensvermittlung hinaus. Durch das gemeinsame Folgen des Programms bzw. durch das gemeinsame Rechnen wird eine Art Gemeinschaft (wie auch ein gemeinsamer Wissensraum) zwischen dem Experten und den Laienadressaten aufgebaut. Dies trägt zum Verständnis der Experten-Laien-Relation als Kontinuum bei. Überdies findet hier die Multimodalität durch Multimedialität ihren Einzug.

Die Modalität der Sprache wird in ihrer üblichen Unterteilung in gesprochen und geschrieben durch visuell unterstützende Einheiten, wie die Leitung durch eine Software, erweitert. Dieser Wechsel der Medialität kann eine Führung der Aufmerksamkeit bezüglich der popularisierten Inhalte bewirken. Unterdies ist für Erklärvideo 1 eine deutlich stärkere Multimodalität zu erkennen, da zu den gesprochenen Inhalten die Visualisierung von weiterem relevanten Wissen – Aufbau und Handhabung von Elster – geschieht. Es kann von dem Aufbau einer Metaebene gesprochen werden, auf der Handlungen und weniger jedoch Inhalte erläutert werden. Nicht zuletzt wird durch Hinweise bei komplexeren Inhalten, diese durch Steuerberater klären zu lassen, und durch deren Betitelung als „Sonderfälle" den Laien klar signalisiert, dass ihr Wissen nicht ausreichen kann (EV 1 – 9:15-9:23, 10:29-10:36 Minuten). Im Fokus des Videos steht Handlungswissen und weniger Fachwissen. *Wissen* wird hier also als *Können* und damit als prozedurales Wissen distribuiert.

Dagegen könnten bei Erklärvideo 2 hinsichtlich der Darstellung von Fachkonzepten, welche zentral für das Verständnis sind, eindeutigere Popularisierungsstrategien eingesetzt werden. Hier steht Faktenwissen als *Wissen* im Zentrum, das in Hinblick auf dessen semantische Zusammensetzung erörtert wird. Fachinhalte werden den Rezipienten anhand von Beispielen und entfaltenden Definitionen nähergebracht. Durch einen gezielten Wechsel der Medialität unterstützen unterschiedliche Modalitäten das Gesprochene. Diese Strategie erscheint sinnvoll, da neben dem auditiven auch der visuelle Verarbeitungskanal angesprochen wird. Eine weitere Rekontextualisierung der Inhalte würde jedoch die Popularisierungsabsicht noch mehr unterstützen. Es ist anzunehmen, dass hierdurch eine noch höhere Verständlichkeit der Fachinhalte zu erzielen wäre. Zuletzt lässt sich festhalten, dass die unterschiedlichen Strategien zur Wissensvermittlung Kenntnisse über die Rezipienten und ihre kommunikativen Bedürfnisse voraussetzen. Liegen hierzu Kenntnisse vor, kann eine Beurteilung zur Angemessenheit der Art und Weise der Vermittlung des Wissens getroffen werden (vgl. Luttermann 2021).

VI. Literatur

Anleitung zur Anlage KAP. 2022. https://www.formulare-bfinv.de/ffw/resources/93FEC1F0C1DC9451DED6/form/Anltg_KAP_22.pdf. Letzter Zugriff 17.5.2023.

Antos, Gerd. 2020. Mythen, Metaphern. Modelle. Konzeptualisierungen von *Kommunikation* aus dem Blickwinkel der angewandten Diskursforschung. In: Gerd Antos (Hrsg.), *Wissenskommunikation. Ausgewählte Aufsätze*. Frank & Timme: Berlin, 9-15.

Becker-Mrotzek, Michael / Maximilian Scherner. 2000. Textsorten der Verwaltung. In: Klaus Brinker / Gerd Antos / Wolfgang Heinemann / Sven Sager (Hrsg.), *Text und Gesprächslinguistik / Linguistics of Text and Conversation. Ein internationales Handbuch zeitgenössischer Forschung / An International Handbook of Contamporary Research*. Halbband 1. Berlin: de Gruyter, 628-641.

Bongo, Giancarmine. 2014. Die Sprache der Popularisierung. Eine Standortbestimmung. In: Giancarmine Bongo / Giuditta Caliendo (Hrsg.), *The Language of Popularization. Theoretical and Descriptive Models / Die Sprache der Popularisierung. Theoretische und deskriptive Modelle*. Wien: Lang, 223-246.

Dietrich, Rainer. 1992. *Modalität im Deutschen. Zur Theorie der relativen Modalität*. Opladen: Westdeutscher Verlag.

Efing, Christian. 2020. Verwaltungssprache und Kommunikation mit Verwaltungsinstitutionen. In: Thomas Niehr / Jörg Kilian / Jürgen Schiewe (Hrsg.), *Handbuch Sprachkritik*. Berlin: Metzler, 287-294.

Engberg, Jan. 2017. Fachkommunikation und fachexterne Kommunikation. In: Ekkehard Felder / Andreas Gardt (Hrsg.), *Handbuch Sprache im Recht*. Berlin: de Gruyter, 118-140.

Engberg, Jan. 2021. Popularisierung einer rechtlichen Institution durch Vermittlung von Rechtswissen. Eine Fallstudie zum WIE und WARUM im dänischen Kontext. In: Karin Luttermann / Albert Busch (Hrsg.), *Sprache und Recht. Konstitutions- und Transferprozesse in nationaler und europäischer Dimension*. Berlin: Lit, 27-56.

Engberg, Jan / Karin Luttermann / Silvia Cacchiani / Chiara Preite (Hrsg.). 2018. Studying Popularization in Legal Communication. Introduction and Overview. In: Jan Engberg / Karin Luttermann / Silvia Cacchiani / Chiara Preite (Hrsg.), *Popularization and Knowledge Mediation in the Law / Popularisierung und Wissensvermittlung im Recht*. Wien: Lit, IX-XXV.

Felder, Ekkehardt. 2003. *Juristische Textarbeit im Spiegel der Öffentlichkeit*. Berlin: de Gruyter.

Felder, Ekkehard. 2006. *Semantische Kämpfe. Macht und Sprache in den Wissenschaften*. Berlin: de Gruyter.

HdR / Bundesministerium der Justiz. 2008. *Handbuch der Rechtsförmlichkeit. Empfehlungen des Bundesministeriums der Justiz für die rechtsförmliche Gestaltung von Gesetzen und Rechtsverordnungen nach § 42*

Absatz 4 und § 62 Absatz 2 der Gemeinsamen Geschäftsordnung der Bundesministerien. 3. Auflage. Köln: Bundesanzeiger.

Holly, Werner. 2020. Wie diebisch ist diese ELSTER? Ein medienlinguistischer Versuch mit dem Online-Steuerverfahren. In: Rudolf Fisch (Hrsg.), *Verständliche Verwaltungskommunikation in Zeiten der Digitalisierung. Konzepte – Lösungen – Fallbeispiele*. Baden-Baden: Nomos, 183-200.

Hüsing, Silke. 2020. Einkünfte aus Kapitalvermögen. In: Gabler Wirtschaftslexikon Online. https://www.gabler-banklexikon.de/definition/einkuenfte-aus-kapitalvermoegen-57400. Letzter Zugriff 15.5.2023.

Janich, Nina. 2009. Kommunikative Kompetenz und Sprachkultiviertheit – ein Modell von Können und Wollen. In: Gerd Antos / Tilo Weber (Hrsg.), *Typen von Wissen. Begriffliche Unterscheidung und Ausprägung in der Praxis des Wissenstransfers*. Frankfurt am Main: Lang, 31-49.

Kalverkämper, Hartwig. 1998. Fach und Fachwissen. In: Lothar Hoffmann / Hartwig Kalverkämper / Herbert Ernst Wiegand (Hrsg.), *Fachsprachen / Language for Special Purposes*. Halbband 1. Berlin: de Gruyter, 1-23.

Klug, Nina-Maria. 2016. Multimodale Text- und Diskurssemantik. In: Nina-Maria Klug / Hartmut Stöckl (Hrsg.), *Handbuch Sprache im multimodalen Kontext*. Berlin: de Gruyter, 165-189.

Kretschmann, Carsten. 2003. Einleitung. Wissenspopularisierung – ein altes, neues Forschungsfeld. In: Carsten Kretschmann (Hrsg.), *Wissenspopularisierung. Konzepte der Wissensverbreitung im Wandel*. Berlin: Akademie Verlag, 7-22.

Kutschera, Andrea. o.J. Sparer-Pauschbetrag. *Haufe Steuer Office Excellence (Steuerrechtsdatenbank)*. https://www.haufe.de/steuern/haufe-steuer-office-excellence/sparer-pauschbetrag_idesk_PI25844_HI1637591.html. Letzter Zugriff 16.5.2023.

Luttermann, Karin. 2015. Linguistisch-pragmatische Zugänge zur Rechtssemantik. Was gesagt, was gemeint und was verstanden wird. In: Friedemann Vogel (Hrsg.), *Zugänge zur Rechtssemantik. Interdisziplinäre Ansätze im Zeitalter der Mediatisierung*. Berlin: de Gruyter, 275-292.

Luttermann, Karin. 2017. Klare Sprache als Mittel für Fachkommunikation und Wissenstransfer. *Information. Wissenschaft & Praxis* 68 (4), 217-226.

Luttermann, Karin. 2021. Klare Sprache für eine verständliche Kommunikation im Rechtsbereich. Ein handlungspragmatischer Ansatz. In: Karin Luttermann / Albert Busch (Hrsg.), *Sprache und Recht. Konstitutions- und Transferprozesse in nationaler und europäischer Dimension.* Berlin: Lit, 101-132.

Luttermann, Karin / Jan Engberg. 2018. Vermittlung rechtlichen Wissens an Kinder und Jugendliche im Internet und in Broschüren. In: Jan Engberg / Karin Luttermann / Silvia Cacchiani / Chiara Preite (Hrsg.), *Popularization and Knowledge Mediation in the Law / Popularisierung und Wissensvermittlung im Recht*. Wien: Lit, 85-115.

Luttermann, Karin / Jan Engberg. 2024. Verständlichkeit und Vertrauen durch Popularisierung am Beispiel des Erbrechts. In: Pavla Schäfer / Milena Belosevic (Hrsg.), *Sprache und Vertrauen. Facetten der linguistischen und interdisziplinären Vertrauensforschung.* Berlin: de Gruyter, 165-183.

Luttermann, Karin / Patricia Rawinsky. 2020. Fachtexte verstehen in *Klarer Sprache.* In: Franziska Heidrich / Klaus Schubert (Hrsg.), *Fachkommunikation – gelenkt, geregelt, optimiert*. Hildesheim: Universitätsverlag Hildesheim, 145-170.

Münkler, Laura. 2020. *Expertokratie. Zwischen Herrschaft kraft Wissens und politischem Dezisionismus*. Tübingen: Mohr Siebeck.

Niederhauser, Jürg. 1999. *Wissenschaftssprache und populärwissenschaftliche Vermittlung*. Tübingen: Narr.

Nöth, Winfried. 2016. Verbal-visuelle Semiotik. In: Nina-Maria Klug / Hartmut Stöckl (Hrsg.), *Handbuch Sprache im multimodalen Kontext.* Berlin: de Gruyter, 190-216.

Polese, Vanda / Stefania D'Avanzo. 2014. Popularization and Dissemination of Legal Knowdledge in EU Summaries of Directives on Immigration and Asylum. In: Giancarmine Bongo / Giuditta Caliendo (Hrsg.), *The Language of Popularization. Theoretical and Descriptive Models /*

Die Sprache der Popularisierung. Theoretische und deskriptive Modelle. Wien: Lang, 191-220.

Preite, Chiara. 2013. Communicare il diritto. Strategie di divulgazione del discorso giuridico. In: Cristina Bosisio / Stefania Cavagnoli (Hrsg.), *Communicare le discipline attraverso le lingue. Prospettive traduttiva, didattica, socioculturale*. Perugia: Guerra Edizioni, 245-262.

Rawinsky, Patricia. 2024. *Textlinguistik und Verständlichkeit. Die Bedeutung des Wissens für eine angemessene Verwaltungskommunikation*. Unveröffentlichte Dissertation. Katholische Universität Eichstätt-Ingolstadt.

Ronig, Roland. o.J. Kapitalvermögen. https://www.haufe.de/finance/haufe-finance-office-premium/kapitalvermoegen_idesk_PI20354_HI2208213.html. Letzter Zugriff 16.5.2023.

Schubert. Klaus. 2016. Barriereabbau durch optimierte Kommunikationsmittel. Versuch einer Systematisierung. In: Nathalie Mälzer (Hrsg.), *Barrierefreie Kommunikation – Perspektiven aus Theorie und Praxis*. Frank & Timme: Berlin, 15-34.

Spinner, Helmut. 2002. Das modulare Wissenskonzept des Karlsruher Ansatzes der integrierten Wissensforschung. Zur Grundlegung der allgemeinen Wissenstheorie für *Wissen aller Arten, in jeder Menge und Güte*. In: Karsten Weber / Michael Nagenborg / Helmut Spinner (Hrsg.), *Wissensarten, Wissensordnungen, Wissensregime. Beiträge zum Karlsruher Ansatz der integrierten Wissensforschung*. Wiesbaden: Springer, 13-46.

Stöckl, Hartmut. 2016. Mulitmodalität. Semiotische und textlinguistische Grundlagen. In: Nina-Maria Klug / Hartmut Stöckl (Hrsg.), *Handbuch Sprache im multimodalen Kontext*. Berlin: de Gruyter, 3-35.

Weber, Tilo. 2009. Explizit vs. implizit, propositional vs. prozedural, isoliert vs. kontextualisiert, individuell vs. kollektiv. Arten von Wissen aus der Perspektive der Transferwissenschaften. In: Gerd Antos / Tilo Weber (Hrsg.), *Typen von Wissen. Begriffliche Unterscheidung und Ausprägung in der Praxis des Wissenstransfers*. Frankfurt am Main: Lang, 13-22.

Jon Christian Fløysvik Nordrum / Torunn Reksten / Janine Schaller-Bøyum / Ole Våge

Klare und digitalisierungsfreundliche Gesetze in Norwegen – Möglichkeiten und Grenzen der Begriffsarbeit

Abstract

Dieser Beitrag diskutiert eine grundlegende Voraussetzung für viele Digitalisierungsprozesse in der öffentlichen Verwaltung, nämlich die Anpassung der Gesetzes- und Verwaltungssprache, insbesondere durch die Koordinierung von Begriffen. Vor allem in der Massenverwaltung steht man an einem Scheideweg, denn die Möglichkeiten, um unter anderem Daten sammeln, lagern, austauschen und analysieren zu können, haben sich innerhalb weniger Jahrzehnte radikal verändert. Nur eine gute Begriffsarbeit kann die Qualität dieser Daten gewährleisten. Wir zeigen auf, wie Begriffe und Benennungen in Norwegen mithilfe eines Verwaltungsstandards koordiniert werden. Es ist notwendig, diese Arbeit im Rechtssystem zu verankern und ihre Grenzen anzuerkennen, denn es gibt gute Gründe dafür, dass die Arbeit mit der Begriffskoordinierung im Juristischen auf Probleme stößt. Mitunter kann sie mit rechtsstaatlichen Prinzipien und demokratischen Idealen in Konflikt geraten.

This contribution discusses a basic requirement for many digitisation processes in public administration, namely the adaptation of legal and administrative language, in particular through concept coordination. In particular, large-scale public administration stands at a crossroads, due, among other things, to the radically changed possibilities for collecting, storing, exchanging and analysing data that we have witnessed in the last few decades. Only sound terminology can guarantee the quality of this data. We show how terms and concepts in Norway are coordinated with the help of an administrative standard. Still, it is necessary to anchor this work in the legal system and to recognise its limits, because there are good reasons why working with conceptual coordination in the legal field runs into problems. Sometimes it can even come into conflict with the rule of law and democratic ideals.

I. Einführung

Die Zahl der Nutzer digitaler öffentlicher Dienstleistungen sowie ihre Erwartungen an diese in Norwegen sind hoch. Und wie viele andere Länder hat auch Norwegen eine ambitiöse digitale Agenda. Eines der Hauptziele ist eine bürger- und unternehmerfreundliche sowie effektive öffentliche Verwaltung, die in der Bevölkerung ein hohes Maß an Vertrauen genießt. Um dieses Ziel zu erreichen, ist sowohl eine umfassende digitale Transformation der öffentlichen Verwaltung notwendig als auch das Schaffen guter Voraussetzungen dafür, dass diese auch in anderen Bereichen geschieht.

1. Digitale Verwaltung und klare Gesetzes- / Verwaltungssprache

Die digitale Agenda ist in Norwegen in einer Digitalisierungsstrategie für die öffentliche Verwaltung konkretisiert worden. Diese gilt sowohl für die staatliche als auch die kommunale Verwaltung. Eine Voraussetzung für nahtlos miteinander verknüpfte Dienstleistungen, die bürger- und unternehmerfreundlich sind und den Datenaustausch steigern, ist eine klare und digitalisierungsfreundliche Gesetzgebung.

Daher ist die digitale Transformation der öffentlichen Verwaltung eng mit der Verbesserung der Gesetzes- und Verwaltungssprache verbunden. Diese Arbeit hat ihre Wurzeln in der staatlichen Kommunikationspolitik mit dem Ziel, dass Bürger korrekte und klare Information über ihre Rechte, Pflichten und Möglichkeiten bekommen, mit der öffentlichen Verwaltung in Dialog treten können und ihre Bedürfnisse und Ideen, zum Beispiel bei der Entwicklung von Dienstleistungen, Gehör finden.

In den letzten Jahren ist die Arbeit mit klarer Gesetzes- und Verwaltungssprache in Norwegen gestärkt worden (vgl. Nordrum / Reksten / Schaller-

Bøyum 2021). Eine öffentliche Gesetzeskommission hat vorgeschlagen, eine generell formulierte Anforderung an klare Sprache in das geplante neue Verwaltungsgesetz aufzunehmen (vgl. NOU 2019). Auch das Sprachgesetz, das am 1.1.2022 in Kraft getreten ist, beinhaltet einen Paragraphen zu klarer Verwaltungssprache. Gemäß Paragraph 9 des Sprachgesetzes muss die öffentliche Verwaltung zielgruppengerecht in klarer und korrekter Sprache kommunizieren.

2. Digitalisierung der Massenverwaltung

Die Digitalisierung bietet umfassende Möglichkeiten, die öffentliche Verwaltung zu verbessern, vor allem in der Massenverwaltung. Mit Massenverwaltung ist hier der Teil der Verwaltung gemeint, in der sehr viele Entscheidungen, häufig innerhalb kurzer Zeit, bei ähnlicher Sachlage getroffen werden, von der sehr viele Bürger betroffen sind und für die eine auf eindeutigen Routinen beruhende Bearbeitung möglich ist. Solche Verwaltungsakte sind typisch in der Steuer-, Sozial-, Polizei-, Gesundheits- und Ausländerverwaltung. Steuer- und Sozialbehörden verwalten einen großen Anteil des norwegischen Staatshaushaltes, sowohl auf der Einnahmen- als auch auf der Ausgabenseite.

Die Massenverwaltung steht nun an einem Scheideweg, denn die Möglichkeiten, um Daten sammeln, lagern, austauschen, analysieren und auf andere Weise nutzen zu können, um Aufgaben der öffentlichen Verwaltung zu lösen, haben sich innerhalb weniger Jahrzehnte radikal verändert. Die Verwaltung kann nun in viel größerem Umfang als früher automatisieren, vorhersehen, identifizieren, abklären, überwachen, enthüllen, zielgerichtet handeln und sanktionieren. Es ist offensichtlich, dass die Digitalisierung zu einer effektiveren Massenverwaltung führen kann. Sie kann aber auch zu einer besseren Rechtssicherheit führen, unter anderem durch verbesserte Anleitung, Zurechtlegung, universelles Design und Transparenz.

Gleichzeitig stellt die Digitalisierung die öffentliche Verwaltung vor neue und ernst zu nehmende Herausforderungen. Diese werden in mehreren internationalen, europäischen und norwegischen Erklärungen und Publikationen benannt. So können beispielsweise Menschenrechte bei der Nutzung künstlicher Intelligenz in der öffentlichen Verwaltung unter Druck geraten.[1] Oder es kann mehr Wert auf Kosteneinsparung gelegt werden als auf eine Verbesserung des Lebensstandards sozial Benachteiligter.[2]

Der vorliegende Beitrag diskutiert eine grundlegende Voraussetzung für viele Digitalisierungsprozesse, nämlich die Anpassung der Gesetzes- und Verwaltungssprache, insbesondere durch die Koordinierung von Begriffen. Dementsprechend werden in Ziffer II die neuesten Maßnahmen in der systematischen Begriffsarbeit in Norwegen sowie die Entwicklung eines Verwaltungsstandards präsentiert. In Ziffer III werden einige der Herausforderungen erörtert, um das Ziel klarer und digitalisierungsfreundlicher Gesetzestexte zu erreichen. Abschließend wird diskutiert, wie eine systematische Begriffsarbeit innerhalb der geltenden Bedingungen zu einer Koordinierung beitragen kann (Ziffer IV).

II. Begriffskoordinierung

Der Wunsch, Begriffe in Gesetzestexten und in der Verwaltungssprache zu koordinieren, ist nicht neu. Jedoch hat die Digitalisierung diesem Bestreben Vorschub geleistet, da es für Maschinen leichter wird, Regeln anzuwenden, wenn Begriffe und Benennungen in Gesetzestexten harmonisiert sind und die Regeln keinen Ermessensspielraum zulassen.

In Norwegen begann man Anfang der 1970er Jahre, bei der Ausformung nationalen Rechts eine mögliche Automatisierung ernsthaft zu berücksichtigen. Eine öffentliche Kommission diskutierte in ihrem Abschlussbe-

---

1 https://www.coe.int/en/web/cepej/cepej-european-ethical-charter-on-the-use-of-artifici al-intelligence-ai-in-judicial-systems-and-their-environment (Letzter Zugriff 5.6.2024).

2 https://documents.un.org/doc/undoc/gen/n19/312/13/pdf/n1931213.pdf?token=uJD50iI BrvM1CDVz38&fe=true (Letzter Zugriff 5.6.2024).

richt die Bedingungen für eine Automatisierung in der öffentlichen Verwaltung und betonte besonders den Bedarf an Standardisierung von Begriffen (vgl. NOU 1973). Mit Blick auf die Sozialverwaltung schrieb Jon Bing, Pionier der norwegischen Rechtsinformatik, in seinem 1977 erschienenen Fachartikel *Automatisierungsfreundliche Gesetzgebung* über den Bedarf an Begriffskoordinierung als eines der Hauptthemen. Heute stehen wir vor den gleichen Herausforderungen, aber die digitale Transformation ist eine vollkommen andere und die Veränderung durch diese ist viel umfassender.

1. Warum Begriffskoordinierung?

Um ganzheitliche und gemeinsame Informationstechnik-Systeme entwickeln zu können, die Bürgern und der Wirtschaft den Alltag erleichtern, müssen wir dafür Sorge tragen, dass die Begriffe, die in den technischen Lösungen angewendet werden, eindeutig definiert sind, sodass diese richtig ausgelegt werden können, und zwar sowohl von Maschinen als auch von Menschen. Zudem sollten die Begriffe so einheitlich wie möglich verstanden werden, sowohl in Behörden als auch in Gesetzestexten. Digitalisierungsfreundliche Gesetze müssen auf einer konsequenten Anwendung von Benennungen und präzisen Definitionen von Begriffen beruhen.

Der automatische Datenaustausch zwischen Behörden erfährt besondere Aufmerksamkeit. Informationen, die Bürger und Unternehmen bereits an eine Behörde gemeldet haben, sollen in anderen Situationen wiederverwendet werden können. Diese in der Europäischen Union (EU) als ‚Once-only'-Prinzip bezeichnete Form der digitalen Informationsverwaltung ist jedoch schwierig in der Umsetzung. Dies liegt darin begründet, dass Rechtsregeln nicht einheitlich sind und dass Behörden Begriffe unterschiedlich anwenden. Daher haben zurzeit mehrere norwegische Behörden eine intensive Koordinierung von Begriffen und ihren Benennungen in Gang gesetzt, denen verschiedene Gesetzestexte zugrunde liegen.

Dieses Vorhaben ist ambitiös und nicht problemfrei. Eine Herausforderung ist, dass man nicht ohne weiteres wissen kann, welche Bedeutung Informationen, die von einer anderen Behörde stammen, tatsächlich haben. Die bisherigen Erfahrungen haben gezeigt, dass beispielsweise Informationen über ‚Einkommen' und ‚Lebensgefährte' unterschiedlich von Behörden verstanden werden oder wurden, teilweise sogar behördenintern (vgl. Våge 2018).

Begriffe wirken inhaltsgleich, da dieselbe Benennung genutzt wird. Eine gründliche Analyse zeigt allerdings auf, dass sich der Bedeutungsinhalt unterscheidet. In solchen Analysen ist es daher wichtig, zwischen *Begriff* und *Benennung* zu unterscheiden. Ein Begriff ist die abstrakte Darstellung eines Phänomens, während die Benennung (oder der Terminus) das Wort ist, das wir nutzen, um über den Bedeutungsinhalt zu sprechen oder zu schreiben (vgl. Riksrevisjonen 2023).

2. Was ist Begriffskoordinierung?

In Norwegen ist *Begriffskoordinierung* ein Überbegriff, unter dem sowohl *Begriffsharmonisierung* als auch *Begriffsdifferenzierung* verstanden wird. Bei der *Begriffsharmonisierung* werden eine gemeinsame Definition und eine gemeinsame Benennung erarbeitet, wo es zuvor mehrere verschiedene Definitionen oder Benennungen gab. Ein grundlegendes Prinzip bei jeglicher Begriffsarbeit ist, dass eine Bezeichnung (z.B. *Einkommen*) nur auf einen Begriff verweisen kann, niemals auf mehrere, um eine präzise Kommunikation zu gewährleisten (Monosemie). Wenn Behörden einen Begriff harmonisieren, führt dies zu einer gemeinsamen Definition, die einige oder alle bisher gebräuchlichen Definitionen ersetzt.

Unter gewissen Umständen ist es nicht möglich oder erstrebenswert, Begriffe in verschiedenen Gesetzen miteinander zu harmonisieren. Dann kann es sinnvoll sein, die Unterschiede zwischen sich ähnelnden oder überschneidenden Begriffen zu verdeutlichen, um Missverständnissen und Verwechslungen zu umgehen. Diese Art der *Begriffskoordinierung* wird in Norwegen *Begriffsdifferenzierung* genannt. Sollte es nicht möglich sein, den Inhalt eines Begriffes zu harmonisieren, können die Behörden besser deutlich machen, was unterschiedlich ist. Die Behörden können ihre Definitionen justieren, um noch deutlicher zu machen, was sich in den Gesetzestexten im Verständnis der Begriffe unterscheidet. Sie können auch einige der Benennungen ändern, sodass jede Definition eine eigene Bezeichnung erhält.

3. Wer koordiniert Begriffe?

Alle Behörden, die Informationen auf einem Sachgebiet verwalten, sind verantwortlich dafür, die zugehörigen Begriffe zu definieren. Zudem sollen die Begriffsdefinitionen bewusst so angelegt werden, dass sie einen Datenaustausch im Sinne des ‚Once-only'-Prinzips ermöglichen (vgl. Norwegian Ministry of Local Government and Modernisation 2016). Unterstützt werden die Behörden vom Sprachrat, Norwegens offiziellem staatlichen Fachinstitut für sprachliche Belange, der die Sprachpolitik der Regierung umsetzt. Zu seinen zentralen Aufgabenbereichen gehören klare Sprache und Terminologie. Der Sprachrat ist nationaler Koordinator für Terminologie und sorgt dafür, dass die verschiedenen Sektoren und Behörden effektiv mit ihrer Fachterminologie arbeiten können. Der Sprachrat bietet Kurse und andere Aktivitäten an, um die Kompetenz in der Gesellschaft auf dem Gebiet der Terminologie zu stärken, besonders in Behörden, die Begriffe koordinieren.

Außerdem arbeitet der Sprachrat im Bereich der Begriffskoordinierung von Verwaltungsstandards und bei der Entwicklung von Hilfsmitteln eng mit der Digitalisierungsbehörde zusammen. Der Sprachrat hat auch eine Schlüsselrolle bei der Arbeit mit klarer Sprache in der öffentlichen Verwaltung und arbeitet insbesondere mit klarer Sprache in Gesetzen und Vorschriften. Seit mehreren Jahren hat der Sprachrat Gesetzgebungskommissionen und Ministerien durch Qualitätssicherung der Sprache in ausgewählten Gesetzestexten beigestanden.

Terminologiearbeit und Begriffskoordinierung sind wichtige Bestandteile der Arbeit mit klarer Sprache, denn gute und konsequente Anwendung von Benennungen und Begriffen erleichtern das Finden, Verstehen und Nutzen von Information. Wenn ein Absender beispielsweise verschiedene Benennungen für einen Begriff in verschiedenen Texten nutzt, kann dies zu Verwirrungen und Unsicherheit beim Empfänger führen. Dies kann beiden Seiten unnötig Zeit und Geld kosten. So hat die norwegische Straßenverkehrsbehörde errechnet, dass ihr neuer, bürgernah formulierter Bescheid durchschnittlich in 40 Prozent kürzerer Zeit verstanden wurde als der vorherige (vgl. The Norwegian Public Roads Administration 2016). Dort hatte man unter anderem die bürokratische Benennung *periodische Fahrzeugkontrolle* durch die im Alltag gebräuchliche *EU-Kontrolle* ersetzt.

Es gibt auch Beispiele dafür, dass Behörden Alltagssprache verwenden, damit Bürger, die Dienstleistungen in Anspruch nehmen wollen, die für sie notwendigen Informationen besser finden und verstehen. So hat die Sozialbehörde das nicht offizielle, aber weit verbreitete Wort *pappaperm* (‚Papazeit') in die Suchfunktion ihrer Internetseiten eingepflegt, sodass Bürger, die dieses Wort eingeben, automatisch auf relevante Seiten verwiesen werden, die *fedrekvote* (‚Väterquote') enthalten, entsprechend der Bezeichnung im Sozialgesetzbuch. In ihrer Begriffsarbeit sollten Behörden also Rücksicht darauf nehmen, welche Wörter und Ausdrücke bereits benutzt werden, wenn sie Benennungen festlegen.

4. Verwaltungsstandard für Begriffskoordinierung

Um dazu beizutragen, dass die öffentliche Verwaltung bei ihrer Begriffskoordinierung auf gleiche Weise verfährt, wurde 2020 der *Verwaltungsstandard zur Begriffsharmonisierung und Begriffsdifferenzierung*[3] beschlossen. Dieser neue Standard baut auf einem ersten Standard aus dem Jahr 2013 auf.

Insbesondere durch die Arbeit mit der sogenannten A-Ordnung hat die norwegische Verwaltung viel gelernt. Die A-Ordnung ist eine digitale Dienstleistung, ein gemeinsames Meldesystem, in dem Arbeitgeber Informationen zu Lohnzahlungen gleichzeitig an mehrere Behörden geben können,

---

[3] https://data.norge.no/specification/forvaltningsstandard-begrepskoordinering/ (Letzter Zugriff 5.6.2024).

zum Beispiel an die Sozialbehörde, die Steuerbehörde und das Statistikamt. Früher mussten Arbeitsgeber diese Angaben einzeln an jede Behörde schicken – mit Hilfe mehrerer gedruckter Formulare. Eine Voraussetzung für ein gemeinsames System für mehrere Behörden war ein koordinierter Begriffsapparat. Die Angaben mussten dieselbe Bedeutung für alle Behörden haben.

Durch die Begriffsarbeit wurde deutlich, dass die verschiedenen Behörden scheinbar dieselben Begriffe benutzten, dass diese aber nicht dieselbe Bedeutung hatten. Der zentrale Begriff *Lohn* wurde in den verschiedenen Behörden unterschiedlich mit Inhalt gefüllt. Zum Beispiel waren bei der Steuerbehörde Überstundenbezahlung und einige Boni Teil des Lohns, während diese bei der Sozialbehörde nicht dazu gehörten. Gemeinsam mit dem Statistikamt koordinierten die Behörden ihre Begriffe auf drei unterschiedliche Arten:

- **Harmonisierte Begriffe:** Die Behörden einigten sich auf ein gemeinsames Verständnis eines Begriffes. Beispiel: Die Definition *Einkünfte* haben alle von der Steuerbehörde übernommen.
- **Behördenspezifische Begriffe:** Die Behörden einigten sich nicht, klärten und verdeutlichten jedoch die Unterschiede. Beispiel: *Arbeitnehmer* erhielt unterschiedliche Definitionen.
- **Neue Begriffe:** Die Behörden einigten sich auf vollkommen neue gemeinsame Begriffe.[4] Beispiel: *auskunftspflichtig* und *Einkünfteempfänger*.

5. Der Inhalt des Verwaltungsstandards

Der Standard ist ein Prozessstandard, der einen Stufenplan für Behörden enthält, die ihre Begriffe und Bezeichnungen gemeinsam harmonisieren und differenzieren wollen. Der Standard berücksichtigt sowohl die Koordinierung von Einzelbegriffen als auch von ganzen Begriffssystemen. Der

---

[4] https://www.regjeringen.no/contentassets/c8101339368148caba88fc1b9b60d099/arbeidsgrupperapport_edag_swn.pdf. (Letzter Zugriff 11.6.2024).

Standard kann auch von Abteilungen innerhalb einer Behörde genutzt werden, wenn diese beispielsweise Bedarf haben, einander überlagernde Begriffe zu koordinieren.

Grundlegende Prinzipien des Standards sind Zusammenarbeit und Konsensus der teilnehmenden Behörden. Fachlich liegen dem Standard etablierte terminologische Methoden und Prinzipien zugrunde, wie sie auch in anderen Standards gebräuchlich sind. Die Anforderungen, die der Standard an die Entscheidungsgrundlage und den Entscheidungsprozess stellt, entsprechen denen der Richtlinien zur Vorbereitung staatlicher Maßnahmen, die Konsequenzanalysen und die öffentliche Konsultation staatlich geplanter Maßnahmen im Allgemeinen regeln.

Gemäß dem normativen Teil des Verwaltungsstandards sollen spezifische Schritte verfolgt werden, die wir hier in Form eines Schaubildes (siehe Abb. 1) zeigen. Der Standard enthält darüber hinaus auch einen deskriptiven, nicht obligatorischen Teil. Dieser enthält Leitlinien und konkrete Beispiele, wie die einzelnen Schritte in die Praxis umgesetzt werden können.

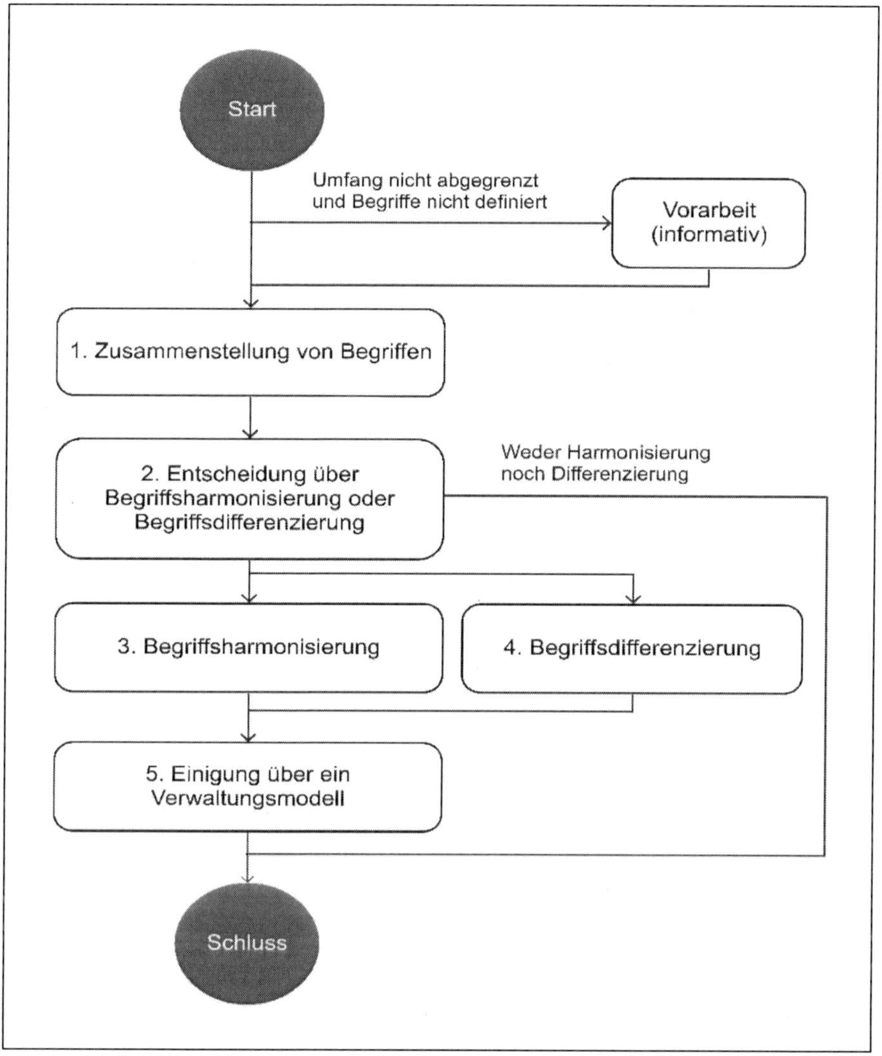

Abb. 1: Verwaltungsstandard zur Begriffsharmonisierung und Begriffsdifferenzierung; siehe dazu Digitaliseringsdirektoratet (2020)[5]

---

[5] https://data.norge.no/specification/forvaltningsstandard-begrepskoordinering (Letzter Zugriff 11.6.2024).

6. Voraussetzungen für das Funktionieren des Standards

Der Standard bietet einen gemeinsamen Bezugsrahmen für die Begriffsarbeit und das Nutzen von Benennungen (Termini) in der öffentlichen Verwaltung und trägt zu einem konsistenten Sprachgebrauch in der behördlichen Bürgerkommunikation bei. Eine Prozessbeschreibung allein ist allerdings nicht ausreichend. Damit der Standard zur Anwendung kommt und gut funktioniert, sind sowohl Kompetenz als auch allgemein zugängliche Hilfsmittel notwendig.

6.1. Gemeinsame Kompetenz und Fachkreis

Wer Begriffe koordinieren soll, muss selbstverständlich Kompetenz auf dem entsprechenden Sachgebiet haben. Zudem ist ausreichende Kompetenz im Bereich terminologischer Prinzipien und Methoden notwendig. Daher haben der Sprachrat und die Digitalisierungsbehörde zusammen relevante, allgemein zugängliche und kostenfreie Kurse (E-Learning) entwickelt.[6] Der Sprachrat hat sich zudem dafür eingesetzt, Terminologie als Fachgebiet an der Universität Bergen aufzubauen. Lehre und Forschung zu Terminologie werden die Kurse des Sprachrates ergänzen und wertvolle Einblicke in die Terminologiearbeit auf strategischer Ebene geben. Seit dem Jahr 2021 werden Terminologie als Fachgebiet sowie eine angeschlossene Terminologie-Datenbank mit ca. 400.000 € jährlich vom Staat unterstützt.

6.2. Gemeinsame Hilfsmittel

Eine Bedingung für Begriffskoordinierung ist eine Datenbank, in der Behörden ihre Benennungen und Begriffe einpflegen, sodass diese allgemein zugänglich sind. Dort können Behörden nachschlagen und einsehen, welche Begriffe und Definitionen andere Behörden anwenden und, noch wichtiger, ob andere Behörden Begriffe anders definieren als sie selbst. Eine

---

[6] https://laeringsplattformen.difi.no/kurs/971527404/begrip-begrepene-et-innforingskurs-i-terminologi-og-begrepsarbeid und https://laeringsplattformen.difi.no/kurs/991825827/den-gylne-pennen-et-e-laeringskurs-i-klarsprak/ (Letzter Zugriff 5.6.2024).

solche Datenbank (*felles begrepskatalog*[7]) ist in Norwegen 2018 etabliert worden. Verschiedene größere Behörden haben bereits mit mehreren tausend Begriffen und Benennungen beigetragen, aber es gibt nach wie vor Behörden, die sich noch nicht an dieser Arbeit beteiligt haben.

Was Terminologiearbeit in Norwegen im Allgemeinen angeht, so entwickelt die Universität Bergen zurzeit ein nationales Portal für Terminologie (*Termportalen*[8]), in dem Begriffe und Benennungen aller Fachgebiete eingehen sollen. Der Sprachrat und die Digitalisierungsbehörde haben zusammengearbeitet, um für das *Termportal* gemeinsame öffentliche Begriffe und Benennungen zu erarbeiten. Diese sind für verschiedene Behörden von zentraler Bedeutung und werden von mehreren Fachgebieten benutzt. Die Arbeit steht im Zusammenhang mit Datenmodellierung und der Beschreibung von Datensätzen.

III. Koordinierung von Begriffen in Rechtssystemen

Um die Ziele der ambitionierten Arbeit mit Begriffskoordinierung in der öffentlichen Verwaltung realisieren zu können, ist es notwendig, diese Arbeit in Rechtssystemen zu verankern. Das Ideal von und die Diskussion um Begriffsharmonisierung in Rechtssystemen ist nicht neu. So ist es bezüglich der Gewährleistung der Rechtssicherheit wichtig, dass die Rechtssprache sich nicht zu stark vom allgemeinen Sprachgebrauch unterscheidet. In gewisser Hinsicht kann auch das Auslegen von Begriffen zur Begriffsharmonisierung beitragen. Dementsprechend sollte auf das Ideal der Begriffsharmonisierung auch bei der Ausarbeitung von Gesetzestexten Wert gelegt werden. Unter anderem wird dieses Ideal in einer Darstellung von Gesetzesqualität ausgedrückt:

> Moreover, law must be drafted in a coherent manner, that is, the terms must be used to express the same concepts, and the law must hold no contradictions. (Ramos / Heydt 2017: 130)

---

[7] https://data.norge.no/concepts (Letzter Zugriff 5.6.2024).

[8] https://www.uib.no/ub/spesialsamlingene/160664/termportalen (Letzter Zugriff 5.6.2024).

Ähnliche Anforderungen finden sich auch in nationalen und europäischen Richtlinien zur Ausformung von Gesetzen. Ein Beispiel sind die 1998 vereinbarten *Gemeinsamen Leitlinien für die redaktionelle Qualität der gemeinschaftlichen Rechtsvorschriften* mit dem Ziel eines konsequenten Gebrauchs von Begriffen und Benennungen, gemäß Prinzip Nr. 6:

> Die verwendete Terminologie muß kohärent sein, und zwar ist auf Kohärenz sowohl zwischen den Bestimmungen ein und desselben Akts als auch zwischen diesem Akt und den bereits geltenden Akten, insbesondere denjenigen aus demselben Bereich, zu achten.
>
> Dieselben Begriffe sind mit denselben Worten auszudrücken und dürfen sich dabei möglichst nicht von der Bedeutung entfernen, die sie in der Umgangssprache, der Rechtssprache oder der Fachsprache haben.[9]

1. Herausforderungen der Begriffskoordinierung in Rechtssystemen

Die Empfehlungen zur Kohärenz sind dennoch wenig in der Praxis berücksichtigt worden, und die Arbeit mit Begriffskoordinierung ist im Juristischen auf mehrere Probleme gestoßen. Was sind die Gründe dafür?

Juristische Entscheidungssysteme sind zum einen nicht dahingehend ausgerichtet, Begriffskoordinierung zu fördern. Zum anderen haben sich Juristen zu wenig für den Bedarf, juristische Texte an eine digitale Verwaltung anzupassen, interessiert. Andererseits muss auch bedacht werden, dass die Ambitionen der Begriffskoordinierung nicht mit den reellen Grenzen einer solchen Koordinierung abgestimmt waren. Es ist nämlich nicht ohne weiteres möglich, für endgültig abgestimmte und einheitliche Begriffe und Benennungen zu sorgen. Die Empfehlungen sind damit nicht uneingeschränkt mit Erkenntnissen aus Rechtswissenschaft, Linguistik und Sprachphilosophie vereinbar.

Es wurde in der Rechtswissenschaft lange diskutiert, ob es möglich ist, das Rechtssystem um präzise und abgestimmte Begriffe zu organisieren. Der Wunsch nach Digitalisierung und Automatisierung hat zu einer Renais-

---

9 https://eur-lex.europa.eu/legal-content/EN/TXT/?uri=CELEX%3A31999Y0317%2801%29&qid=1723807242073 (Letzter Zugriff 5.6.2024).

sance dieser Ideen geführt (vgl. Timmermann 2020: 83). Besonders bekannt sind die Diskussionen im 19. Jahrhundert um das, was später von Rudolf von Jhering als Begriffsjurisprudenz (vgl. Timmermann 2020: 77ff.) charakterisiert wurde. In einem Rechtssystem, das um präzise definierte Begriffe herum konstruiert wird, könnte man erwarten, dass keine Widersprüche oder Unklarheiten entstehen. In solchen Systemen kann das Recht streng logisch angewendet werden, wie in statischen, auf Algorithmen aufbauenden Systemen (vgl. Timmermann 2020: 77). Die Rechts- und Sprachphilosophie hat dennoch gezeigt, dass es immer Bereiche geben wird, in denen rechtliche Begriffe unklar sein werden und in denen Begriffe nicht vollständig im Voraus, sondern erst auf Grundlage von Erfahrungen und Einzelfällen festgelegt werden können.

2. Die vage Regelsprache

Die Regelsprache ist vage, denn es ist schwierig, Begriffe – sowohl deskriptive als auch normative – sprachlich präzise widerzugeben. Diese grundlegende Tatsache ist eingehend in der Rechtsquellenlehre erörtert worden.[10] Die begrenzte Fähigkeit der Sprache, die Wirklichkeit zu beschreiben, ist Gegenstand des Diskurses verschiedener wissenschaftlicher Disziplinen, beispielsweise der Sprachphilosophie. Sprachliche Elastizität ist sowohl ein grundlegendes Merkmal von und eine Voraussetzung für Kommunikation. Diese Elastizität ermöglicht einen variierten Gebrauch von Begriffen und Benennungen, zum Beispiel indem verschiedene Wörter für denselben Begriff verwendet werden (Synonymie) oder indem ein und dasselbe Wort auf verschiedene Begriffe verweisen kann (Polysemie).

Dieses Phänomen ist typisch für juristische Texte. Und es ist charakteristisch für juristische Benennungen, dass diese polysem sind. Beispielsweise wird *Lebensgefährte* im Steuerrecht anders angewendet als im Familienrecht. Infolge Mattila (2016: 142) ist Polysemie in der Rechtssprache eher die Regel als eine Ausnahme, was darin begründet liegt, dass sich das Recht ständig ändert. Man kann sagen, Polysemie „allows the vocabulary

[10] Beispiel der norwegischen Rechtsquellenlehre Eckhoff / Helgesen (2001: 54ff., 62ff.).

of the language to transmit the infinitely varied ideas and feelings that arise in social life“ (Mattila 2016: 142).

Trotz dieser Begrenzungen gibt es auch im Rechtssystem mehrere Methoden und Arbeitstechniken, um Begriffe zu harmonisieren, beispielsweise die Berücksichtigung bereits bestehender Begriffe und Benennungen anderer relevanter Gesetze bei der Arbeit an neuen Rechtsnormen oder deren Auslegung in der Behandlung konkreter Fälle. Diese Methoden unterscheiden sich jedoch in vielerlei Hinsicht von denen, die in der systematischen Begriffsarbeit benutzt werden (siehe Ziffer II). Die zwei wichtigsten Unterschiede sind:

i. Die koordinierenden Mechanismen des Rechtssystems sind in der Regel nicht auf das System als Ganzes ausgerichtet, sondern konzentrieren sich auf Einzelfälle oder Teile des Systems.
ii. Das Ziel der Begriffsharmonisierung ist bedeutend weniger ambitioniert als das einer systematischen und ganzheitlichen Begriffsarbeit.

3. Begriffskoordinierung im Spannungsverhältnis zu demokratischen und rechtsstaatlichen Prinzipien

Eine Begrenzung ganz anderer Art ist, dass Begriffskoordinierung mit rechtsstaatlichen Prinzipien und demokratischen Idealen in Konflikt geraten kann. In demokratischen Rechtsstaaten werden Entscheidungen zeitlich und räumlich voneinander getrennt getroffen. Grundlegende Rechtsstaatsprinzipien bauen darauf auf, dass Entscheidungsbefugnisse und Machtausübung auf verschiedene Staatsorgane verteilt sind. Zentral dabei ist beispielsweise, dass der Gesetzgeber übergeordnete Rechtsregeln festlegt, während unabhängige Gerichte diese Regeln anhand von konkreten Fällen präzisieren.

Im norwegischen Rechtssystem werden Entscheidungsbefugnisse in großem Ausmaß an lokale Behörden und Fachleute delegiert. Diesem System liegt die Auffassung zugrunde, dass dies demokratischer ist und dass das Ermessen von Experten zu besseren Entscheidungen führt. In vielerlei Hinsicht steht die Vision einer Begriffsjurisprudenz im diametralen Gegensatz zu der zweckorientierten, pragmatischen und induktiven Form der Rechtsfindung im nordischen Rechtsystems. Gemäß der norwegischen Verfassung kann Gesetzgebungskompetenz weitestgehend delegiert werden, und in der Tat wird diese in großem Umfang an die staatliche Verwaltung und Kommunen delegiert. Dies führt dazu, dass ein großer Anteil norwegischer Rechtsnormen auf niedrigem Niveau in der Normenhierarchie produziert wird.

Begriffskoordinierung trägt im Gegensatz hierzu dazu bei, Entscheidungsbefugnisse zu zentralisieren, denn lokale Kompetenzen können unterschiedliche Begriffe hervorbringen. Ideale Voraussetzungen für Begriffskoordinierung wären in einem vollkommen zentralisierten Staat gegeben, mit weitreichenden Vollmachten und wenig rechtlicher Kontrolle. Zugespitzt gesagt: Je demokratischer, desto mehr dezentralisierte Machtausübung – je mehr Rechtsprechung, desto mehr Begriffschaos.

IV. Ausblick

Eine systematische und fachlich fundierte Begriffsarbeit kann eine gute Grundlage für gute Digitalisierung sein und für ein klareres und besser zugängliches Regelwerk sorgen. Norwegen hat eine ehrgeizige Arbeit gestartet, geeignete Methoden für Begriffskoordinierung zu entwickeln. Dabei ist entscheidend, dass die Begriffsarbeit die Grenzen der Koordinierung von Begriffen im Regelwerk berücksichtigt. Es kann gute Gründe dafür geben, die nordische und norwegische Herangehensweise mit vage formulierten und generellen Gesetzestexten beizubehalten, denn diese sind grundlegend in unserer Rechtskultur. Gleichzeitig gibt es gute Gründe dafür, sich zu fragen, ob es nicht auch innerhalb dieser Rechtskultur möglich ist, Methoden für die Begriffskoordinierung zu finden, die dazu geeignet sind, Digitalisierung zu fördern, beispielsweise auf einer niedrigeren Ebene in der Regelhierarchie als das zugrundeliegende Gesetz.

Unter Berücksichtigung der Möglichkeiten für gute Digitalisierung sollten wir sowohl bei der Ausformung als auch bei der Anwendung von Rechtsnormen größeren Wert darauf legen, wie Begriffe in angrenzenden Verwaltungsbereichen verstanden werden und wie Benennungen in der Praxis präzisiert wurden. Es kann zu größeren Konsequenzen in der Verwaltung führen, wenn ein gut eingearbeiteter Begriff, dessen Verständnis digitalisiert ist, in einer Einzelfallentscheidung verändert wird. Dies setzt jedoch voraus, dass in der Phase der Begriffsentwicklung besonders großer Wert auf Rechtssicherheit gelegt wird.

V. Literatur

Bing, Jon. 1977. Automatiseringsvennlig lovgivning. *Tidsskrift for rettsvitenskap* 90 (2-3), 195-229.

Eckhoff, Torstein / Jan Helgesen. 2001. *Rettskildelære*. Oslo: Universitetsforlaget.

Mattila, Heikki E. S. 2016. *Comparative Legal Linguistics. Language of Law, Latin and Modern Lingua Franca*. London: Routledge.

Nordrum, Jon Christian Fløysvik / Torunn Reksten / Janine Schaller-Bøyum. 2021. Der Weg zu mehr sprachlicher Klarheit in der norwegischen Gesetzgebung. In: Karin Luttermann / Albert Busch (Hrsg.), *Recht und Sprache. Konstitutions- und Transferprozesse in nationaler und europäischer Dimension*. Berlin: Lit, 321-348.

Norwegian Ministry of Local Government and Modernisation. 2016. *Digital Agenda for Norway in Brief – ICT for a Simpler Everyday Life and Increased Productivity*. Meld. St. 27 (2015-2016). Oslo. https://www.regjeringen.no/en/dokumenter/digital-agenda-for-norway-in-brief/id2499897/99897/. Letzter Zugriff 5.6.2024.

Norwegian Ministry of Local Government and Modernisation. 2019. *One Digital Public Sector – Digital Strategy for the Public Sector 2019-2025*. Oslo. https://www.regjeringen.no/en/dokumenter/one-digital-public-sector/id2653874/. Letzter Zugriff 5.6.2024.

NOU. 1973. 43 *Planlegging av databehandlingen i forvaltningen*. https://www.nb.no/items/URN:NBN:no-nb_digibok_2011053005046. Letzter Zugriff 11.6.2024.

NOU. 2019. 5 *Ny forvaltningslov*. Justis- og beredskapsdepartement. https://www.regjeringen.no/no/dokumenter/nou-2019-5/id2632006/. Letzter Zugriff 5.6.2024.

Ramos, Mario Hernández / Volker Heydt. 2017. Legislative Language and Style. In: Ulrich Karpen / Helen Xanthaki (Hrsg.), *Legislation in Europe. A Comprehensive Guide for Scholars and Practitioners*. London: Hart Publishing.

Riksrevisjonen. 2023. *Riksrevisjonens undersøkelse av myndighetenes tilrettelegging for deling og gjenbruk av data. Dokument 3:8 (2023-2024)*. https://kudos.dfo.no/documents/62686/files/34971.pdf. Letzter Zugriff 5.6.2024.

The Norwegian Public Roads Administration. 2016. Time, Money and Annoyances spared through Plain Language. In: Agency for Public Management and eGovernment (Hrsg.), *Good Results Using Plain Language. 10 Examples from the Norwegian State Administration and Municipalities*. Oslo: Agency for Public Management and eGovernment, 12-13. https://www.sprakradet.no/globalassets/klarsprak-ny/om-klarsprak/materiell/good-results-using-plain-language---10-examples-from-the-norwegian-state-administration-and-municipalities.pdf. Letzter Zugriff 5.6.2024.

Timmermann, Daniel. 2020. *Legal Tech-Anwendungen. Rechtswissenschaftliche Analyse und Entwicklung des Begriffs der algorithmischen Rechtsdienstleistung*. Baden-Baden: Nomos.

Våge, Ole. 2018. Språk under panseret. *Språknytt* 3, 10-12.

Section III

Digitalisierung im internationalen Kontext /

Digitisation in International Contexts

Karin Luttermann / Alessandra Lombardi

Anwälte adressieren Klienten. Eine vergleichende Analyse von Berufsbiographien deutscher und italienischer Anwaltsvideos auf Kanzlei-Webseiten

Abstract

Sprache und Kommunikation gelten im Alltags- wie im Geschäftsleben als Inbegriff menschlicher Beziehungen und Einflussnahmen. Der vorliegende Beitrag widmet sich biographischen Darstellungspraktiken von Rechtsanwälten, vorzugsweise in Boutique-Kanzleien, auf deutschen und italienischen Kanzlei-Webseiten. Berufsbiographien sind ein neu entstehendes digitales Subgenre der Selbstdarstellung gegenüber traditionelleren Formaten wie Lebensläufen. Im Mittelpunkt stehen Anwaltsvideos als ein audio-visuelles Format der Selbstpräsentation, um auf Adressaten einzuwirken. Welche Kommunikationsstrategien und multimodalen Mittel Anwälte für die Zielgruppenansprache, zum Imageaufbau wie auch zur Vermittlung beruflicher und persönlicher Werte verwenden, wird textpragmatisch und kulturvergleichend behandelt. Die Analyseergebnisse sind von Nutzen für die Rechtslinguistik, aber auch für die anwaltliche Praxis selbst.

In both everyday and business life, language and communication are regarded as the epitome of human relationships and influence. From this perspective, this contribution examines the biographical presentation practices of lawyers, particularly in boutique law firms, on German and Italian law firm websites. Professional biographies represent an emerging digital subgenre of self-presentation, distinct from traditional formats such as CVs. This study focuses on lawyer videos as an audiovisual format of self-presentation aimed at influencing clients. It analyses the communication strategies and multimodal techniques employed by lawyers to engage target audiences, establish their professional image, and convey personal and professional values. The analysis is conducted from a text-pragmatic and cross-cultural comparative perspective. The findings are valuable not only for the field of legal linguistics, but also for legal practice itself.

I. Einleitung

Kommunikation gilt im Privaten wie im Beruflichen als „das A und O einer jeden Beziehung – auch der Beziehung eines Unternehmens zu seiner Umgebung und seinen Anspruchsgruppen“ (Keller 2009: 20). Menschen können letztlich nur durch Kommunikation zueinander finden. Denn wenn wir in der Berufswelt „mit jemandem kommunizieren, versuchen wir, auf unseren Kommunikationspartner[1] in irgendeiner Form einzuwirken; wir wollen, dass er etwas erkennt, etwas Bestimmtes tut oder unterlässt, oder auch, dass er eine bestimmte Empfindung erlebt“ (Keller 2009: 20). Das trifft grundsätzlich auf sämtliche Bereiche der Professionskommunikation zu (vgl. im Überblick z.B. Busch / Luttermann 2024). Unser Untersuchungsgegenstand ist der Handlungsbereich des Rechts und speziell die Anwaltskommunikation in Videos, die aus pragmalinguistischer Perspektive behandelt wird. Rechtsanwälte stehen untereinander in einem scharfen Wettbewerb, um Adressaten als Mandanten zu gewinnen. Das erfordert über die fachliche Expertise hinaus eine sorgfältig geplante Kommunikation.

Für die Akquirierung neuer Kunden ist es nicht nur wichtig, was gesagt wird, sondern auch wie etwas gesagt wird und welches Medium genutzt wird. Das haben frühere kontrastive Studien über juristische Stellenanzeigen und anwaltliche Berufsbiographien ergeben (vgl. Lombardi 2024; Luttermann 2017, 2018, 2024; Luttermann / Engberg 2017). Danach haben moderne Stellenanzeigen nicht mehr nur die Funktion, eine vakante Stelle anzuzeigen, sondern sie sind kombinierte Werbetexte, die auf Adressaten einwirken und sie beeinflussen wollen. Mit anderen Worten: Die Texthybride sind nicht-bindende direktive Gebrauchstexte (vgl. Rolf 1993: 250, 261) und haben eine Doppelfunktion. Sie bezwecken, Juristen wie Mandanten von bestimmten Kanzleien zu überzeugen, indem sie sowohl appellieren als auch informieren. Dadurch wird die Grenze zwischen Employer

[1] Im Folgenden sind alle natürlichen Geschlechter mitgemeint.

Branding und Consumer Branding durchlässig (vgl. Stumpf 2017: 81ff.). Die Durchlässigkeit hat für die Selbstpräsentation von Anwälten in Videos auf Kanzlei-Webseiten ebenfalls erhebliche Relevanz. Rechtsanwälte erzählen ihren professionellen Werdegang, bestimmte Berufsspezifika und Berufswerte sowie ihre persönliche Geschichte und beabsichtigen so, die anvisierte Mandantschaft dazu zu bringen, die eigene Rechtsberatung und nicht die der Konkurrenz in Anspruch zu nehmen.

Im vorliegenden Beitrag geht es darum, wie Anwälte deutscher und italienischer Kanzleien ihre beruflichen Biographien im Internet zum Zwecke der Mandantengewinnung präsentieren. Damit knüpfen wir an unsere vorhergehende Studie an, in der wir unterschiedliche Ausprägungen der verbalen und bildlichen Selbstpräsentation ermittelt haben (vgl. Lombardi / Luttermann 2023). Dabei traten Berufsbiographien als neu entstehendes digitales Subgenre der fachlichen bzw. professionsspezifischen Selbstdarstellung gegenüber traditionellen Kommunikationsformaten wie dem Lebenslauf hervor. Hier stehen nunmehr biographische Darstellungspraktiken von Anwälten im Format der audio-visuellen Kommunikation im Mittelpunkt. Uns interessiert, ob und auf welche Art und Weise welche Alleinstellungsmerkmale in der digitalen Anwaltskommunikation versprachlicht werden und wie bestimmtes Fachwissen vermittelt wird. Es handelt sich um eine vergleichende Studie über epistemische Kulturen (vgl. Knorr-Cetina 1999; Liebert 2016), d.h. wir untersuchen Fachkommunikation und die Konstruktion von Fachwissen im Recht auf der Grundlage eines gemeinsamen begrifflichen und wertorientierten Hintergrunds.

Dabei gehen wir folgendermaßen vor: Zunächst ordnen wir unsere Studie in das Forschungsprojekt und in verwandte Arbeiten zum Employer Branding ein (Ziffer II). Dann definieren wir den Begriff der *Boutique-Kanzlei* und behandeln die Typen juristischer Berufsbiographien auf Boutique-Kanzlei-Webseiten (Ziffer III), die als Vergleichsfolie mit den Selbstpräsentationen im audio-visuellen Medium dienen. Darauf aufbauend wird die Korpusauswahl begründet und die Zielsetzung unseres Vorgehens spezifiziert (Ziffer IV). Danach folgen exemplarisch Analysen der deutschen und italienischen Anwaltsvideos sowie ein Vergleich der Ergebnisse (Ziffern

V bis VII). Abschließend werden weitere Forschungsschritte zur rechtslinguistischen Untersuchung der Professionskommunikation mit Anwälten im digitalen Umfeld umrissen (Ziffer VIII).

II. Funktionalität juristischer Stellenanzeigen

Unser Beitrag knüpft an vorausgehende kontrastive Arbeiten zu den textpragmatischen Merkmalen juristischer Stellenanzeigen an (vgl. Nielsen / Luttermann / Lévy-Tödter 2017; Luttermann 2017, 2018; Luttermann / Engberg 2017). Sie wurden im Sprach- und Kulturvergleich makro- und mikrostrukturell in Hinblick auf Schnittmengen und Abweichungen etwa von Handlungsmustern und Zielgruppenansprache untersucht. Der klassische Anzeigentext ist die konventionelle Kommunikationsform, um als Unternehmen potenzielle Mitarbeiter anzusprechen und als attraktiver Arbeitgeber wahrgenommen zu werden. Die Analysen der Mischformen haben gezeigt, dass die auf Kanzlei-Webseiten und in speziellen Fachzeitschriften platzierten Anzeigen bi-funktional sind. Die Selbstbeschreibung geht weit über das bloße Stellenangebot hinaus. Moderne Stellenanzeigen sind ein spezieller Fall der Beeinflussung. Es handelt sich um werbende Gebrauchstexte, deren Ziel darin besteht, durch funktionale Kombination – primär Informations- und Appellfunktion – die intendierte kommunikative Wirkung zu entfalten (vgl. Luttermann 2017: 58, im Ersch.).

Es geht darum, sich als Unternehmen in ein gutes Licht zu stellen und eine vakante Position mit einer hinreichend qualifizierten Person zu besetzen. Im Kern sind die Bereiche Marketing und Personalwesen betroffen. In diesem Sinne schreibt Marcus Stumpf (2017: 82) aus der Perspektive der Betriebswirtschaftslehre:

> Unternehmen verfolgen zwei Positionierungsstrategien am Markt – einerseits die Positionierung als Arbeitgebermarke und andererseits die Positionierung als Produktmarke. In diesem Zusammenhang wird zwischen der Unique Selling Proposition (USP) und der Unique Employment Proposition (UEP) eines Unternehmens differenziert. [...] Neben diesen beiden Positionierungsstrategien, die sich jeweils auf den Markt für Arbeitskräfte und den Markt für Produkte sowie Dienstleistungen beziehen, ist noch auf die Strategie zur Positionierung für das gesamte Unternehmen hinzuweisen, das in

> der Corporate Brand bzw. Unternehmensmarke als übergeordnetes Markenkonstrukt zum Ausdruck kommt […].

Vor diesem Hintergrund liegt es nahe und auf der Hand, den Arbeitsmarkt für Juristen auf einer breiteren Grundlage zu erforschen: also über Kommunikationsstrategien des Employer Branding hinaus den Fokus auch auf Strategien des Consumer Branding und auf Strategien der Corporate Brand sowie auf entsprechende kommunikative Formate zu richten. Hier besteht in der (Rechts-)Linguistik ein Forschungsdesiderat, das aufzuarbeiten ist, wozu wir mit unserer Untersuchung beitragen möchten. Die Idee des Employer Branding ist, Ansätze der Markenbildung auf die Mitarbeitergewinnung zu übertragen. Genutzt werden dafür Kategorien wie Retention (Bindung von Personal), Entwicklung (Unternehmen als solches) und Attraktion (Werben von Mitarbeitern). Die Eigenwerbung (Selbstdarstellung) ist Mittel zum Zweck, qualifizierte Mitarbeiter zu akquirieren. Die Attraktion als Handlung des Anwerbens ist auch für Berufsbiographien bedeutsam (siehe Ziffer III) und spielt bei den Video-Analysen von Anwälten, die in Kanzleien tätig sind und Umgang mit Klienten haben, eine essenzielle kommunikative Rolle (siehe Ziffern V und VI).

Rechtsanwälte stellen sich in der externen Kommunikation vor und geben eine Geschichte von sich preis, erzählen ihren spezifischen beruflichen Werdegang mit der kommunikativen Intention, neue Mandanten zu gewinnen. Sie wollen Zielgruppen dazu animieren, die eigene Kanzlei – anstelle der konkurrierenden Anwaltskanzleien – mit der rechtlichen Beratung zu betrauen. Eine Kanzlei muss dementsprechendes Wissen für Zielgruppen zur Verfügung stellen und begründen, warum ausgerechnet sie mandatiert werden soll und nicht die Konkurrenz. Die Analysen der Anwaltsvideos sind Teil des gemeinsamen Forschungsprojektes *Interkultureller Vergleich epistemischer Kulturen in der Wirtschaftskommunikation.*[2] Das Projekt befasst sich zum Beispiel mit Aspekten wie Interaktionsformen, Verständlichkeit oder Vertrauen, Vermittlungs- oder Popularisierungsstrategien und ungenutzten kommunikativen Potenzialen von Gebrauchstexten. Es

---

2 https://www.ku.de/fileadmin/130201/Homepage_Luttermann/Abstract_Epistemische_Kulturen_in_der_Wirtschaftskommunikation.pdf (Letzter Zugriff 1.8.2024).

will darüber hinaus auf praktische Herausforderungen im Beruf fundierte linguistisch-kulturelle Lösungen bereitstellen und den Nutzen der angewandten Linguistik vor allem für die wirtschafts- und rechtswissenschaftlichen Disziplinen aufzeigen.

III. Typisierung juristischer Berufsbiographien

Um einen ersten Einblick in die Art und Weise zu erhalten, wie sich Juristen im Internet präsentieren, haben wir in der ersten explorativen Phase ein Textkorpus aufgebaut, das 100 Anwaltsprofile aus 50 deutschen und 50 italienischen Boutique-Kanzlei-Webseiten umfasst. Als *Boutique-Kanzleien* gelten kleinere, hochspezialisierte Kanzleien, die eine Nischenstellung ausüben, wodurch eine besondere Qualität der Rechtsberatung für Mandanten angestrebt wird. Die durch Ausgründungen von Großkanzleien entstandenen Boutiquen sind in der Regel auf ein oder wenige Rechtsgebiete spezialisiert (vgl. Rossbach 2019: 69f.). Dementsprechend orientieren wir uns an die folgende Definition:

> **Boutiquen:** Dies sind spezialisierte Kanzleien, die auf ein oder mehrere Rechtsgebiete bzw. auf bestimmte Mandanten fokussiert sind. Boutiquen agieren in der Regel überregional und arbeiten für mittelständische und große Wirtschaftsunternehmen. Oftmals entstanden sie durch Ausgründungen, sogenannte ‚Spin-Offs', von Großkanzleien. (Schieblon 2019: 4; Fettdruck im Original)

Der Vergleich zwischen den deutschen und den italienischen Selbstdarstellungen lässt sowohl transkulturelle Gemeinsamkeiten als auch interkulturelle Differenzen hervortreten.[3] Die Konvergenzen betreffen in erster Linie die Wahl der Kommunikationsformate, die sich in beiden Teilkorpora grundsätzlich nach drei Kategorien richtet (vgl. Lombardi / Luttermann 2023: 60f.):

(1) Der *konventionelle Lebenslauf* (CV) bzw. die lebenslaufähnliche Darstellung mit der prototypischen Struktur eines tabellarischen Textes,

---

[3] Vgl. Zhao (2011: 134f.) zu den Begriffen *Inter-* und *Transkulturalität* von Textsorten.

der in thematische Abschnitte gegliedert ist, einen elliptischen Satzbau aufweist und eher neutral und entpersonalisiert wirkt.[4]

(2) Die *hybride Form*, die sowohl Merkmale des Lebenslaufs als auch ein ausformuliertes Profil in der dritten Person enthält, das die spezifischen Tätigkeitsbereiche und Kompetenzen des Anwalts in den Vordergrund stellt.[5]

(3) Die *Biographie* als Ich-Erzählung, die durch die Technik des autobiographischen Storytelling die wichtigsten Etappen im Werdegang des Anwalts narrativ rekonstruiert und dabei seine beruflichen Werte und fachlichen Qualifikationen in personalisierter Form darstellt.[6]

Aus der empirischen Analyse lassen sich auch Beispiele für die Integration der Typen (1) und (3) in ein und derselben Selbstdarstellung ermitteln.[7] Die Kombination von *Biographie* und *Lebenslauf* im selben Webauftritt ist insofern interessant, als sie zwei unterschiedliche, aber komplementäre Perspektiven auf das Anwaltsprofil bietet: eine eher konventionelle und formelle durch den CV und eine persönlichere und informellere durch die Biographie. Diese doppelte Perspektivierung wird manchmal durch eine gezielte visuelle Strategie verstärkt, d.h. durch ein speziell zugeschnittenes digitales Design, durch die unterschiedliche Farbgestaltung sowie durch die Kontrastierung zwischen der seriösen, professionellen und der ungezwungenen, gelassenen Abbildung des Anwalts in Zusammenhang mit der jeweiligen Präsentationsform (vgl. Lombardi / Luttermann 2023: 61).

Interkulturelle Divergenzen im deutsch-italienischen Vergleich betreffen zunächst den unterschiedlichen Einsatz von multimodalen Gestaltungsmitteln. Besonders die deutschen Kanzleien greifen auf digitale Multimedia-Tools zurück, um ihre jeweiligen kommunikativen Ziele zu erreichen. Digitale Animationen werden dabei funktional-strategisch eingesetzt, um bestimmte kommunikative Wirkungen auszulösen. Durch die Verwendung

---

[4] https://www.zitielloassociati.it/attorney/francesco-mocci/ (Letzter Zugriff 1.8.2024).

[5] https://honert.de/personen/irina-eppenstein/ (Letzter Zugriff 1.8.2024).

[6] https://www.wienbergs.com/ (Letzter Zugriff 1.8.2024).

[7] https://www.meruzzi.it/profilo-curriculum-vitae/ (Letzter Zugriff 1.8.2024).

von optischen Zoom-Effekten, bei denen der Anwalt oder die Anwältin aus einem unscharfen Hintergrund auftaucht und in den Fokus rückt, wird zum Beispiel eine besonders kundenfreundliche Haltung suggeriert.[8] Die Anwendung von Animationseffekten auf Miniaturporträts der einzelnen Mitarbeiter, die sich umschauen und einen wohlwollenden, lächelnden Blick auf denjenigen Kollegen richten, zu dem der Cursor bewegt wird, vermittelt hingegen eine team- bzw. partnerfreundliche Haltung.[9]

Der Einsatz dynamischer Anzeigen, die es ermöglichen, den Zugang zu den Informationen über die einzelnen Rechtsexperten je nach gewünschtem Detailgrad individuell zu gestalten, wirkt sich schließlich auf die interessierten Anwender als besonders nutzer- bzw. userfreundlich aus.[10] Überdies kommt den Feedbackstrategien auf den deutschen Kanzlei-Webseiten eine besondere Bedeutung zu. Interaktive Elemente sind oft in den Präsentationstext selbst integriert, meist in Form einer expliziten Aufforderung, Online-Plattformen mit Nutzerbewertungen zu den Kanzleileistungen direkt aufzurufen.[11]

Interkulturelle Unterschiede lassen sich auch inhaltlich feststellen, etwa in Bezug auf kulturspezifische Schwerpunktsetzungen bei der Selbstpräsentation. So gilt zum Beispiel der besondere Nachdruck, der auf Kompetenz und Reputation gelegt wird, als typisch deutsches Argument. Um hohe fachliche Standards zu kommunizieren, führen deutsche Anwälte sehr häufig Referenzen, Auszeichnungen und Bewertungen von externen Gutachtern an, welche ihre beruflichen Fähigkeiten als Top-Spezialisten im jeweiligen Rechtsbereich belegen und zertifizieren.[12]

Als typisch italienisch erscheint hingegen die besondere Betonung zwischenmenschlicher Werte und Beziehungskompetenzen (wie Freundlichkeit, Kontaktfreudigkeit, Geselligkeit), die unter anderem darauf abzielt, die sozial empfundene Distanz zwischen Rechtsberater und Mandant kom-

---

[8] https://www.glademichelwirtz.com/team/dr-felix-bangel/ (Letzter Zugriff 1.8.2024).
[9] https://www.kmlz.de/de/team (Letzter Zugriff 1.8.2024).
[10] https://lambrecht.eu/ (Letzter Zugriff 1.8.2024).
[11] https://zametzer-law.de/ (Letzter Zugriff 1.8.2024).
[12] https://www.lutzabel.com/anwaelte/dr-wolfgang-abel (Letzter Zugriff 1.8.2024).

munikativ zu überbrücken.[13] Für den italienischen Durchschnittsmandanten, der oft durch rechtliche Komplikationen eingeschüchtert ist, bietet sich die Aussicht auf eine enge, persönliche, vertrauensbasierte Beziehung sicherlich als zugkräftiges Argument an.[14]

Unsere Analyseergebnisse bestätigen grundsätzlich, dass juristische Biographien – als besondere Ausprägung des professionellen Storytelling – kulturübergreifend als Schlüsselelemente einer kundenorientierten Marketingstrategie (Consumer Branding) eingesetzt werden. Dies wird besonders deutlich, wenn deutsche und italienische Rechtsexperten ihr ‚Idealbild des Rechtsanwalts' beschreiben, traditionelle Berufsstereotypen hinterfragen oder die Beziehungspflege als grundlegende Aufgabe ihres beruflichen Handelns bezeichnen. Biographien können allerdings auch als Teil einer Employer-Branding-Strategie betrachtet werden. Zum Beispiel da, wo die Rekonstruktion des eigenen Werdegangs mit der Darstellung der Grundwerte und der beruflichen Standards der Anwaltskanzlei verbunden wird, sodass die biographische Profilierung neben potenziellen Kunden gleichzeitig auch potenzielle Bewerber anspricht, die in diesen professionellen Werterahmen passen könnten.[15]

IV. Anwaltsvideos als Untersuchungsgegenstand

1. Kriterien der Stichprobenauswahl

Die Erweiterung der Forschungsperspektive auf Anwaltsvideos – als neu entstehende Kommunikationsform – ermöglicht es, den spezifischen Einfluss von Multimodalität bzw. der Ressourcenintegration (vgl. Baldry / Thibault 2005) auf die professionelle Personalpräsentation im Recht näher zu beleuchten. Videoporträts auf juristischen Webseiten stellen ein anschauliches Beispiel für Remediatisierung dar (vgl. Erll / Rigney 2009;

[13] https://www.alfierizullino.it/relazioni/prendiamoci-un-caffe/ (Letzter Zugriff 1.8.2024).

[14] Zum Thema *Vertrauen* in der Mandatsbeziehung in Italien vgl. z.B. https://studiolegale-galizia.it/perche-e-nata-questa-rubrica-comprendere-il-mondo-e-le-regole-degli-avocati-per-imparare-a-fidarsi/ (Letzter Zugriff 1.8.2024).

[15] Siehe z.B. *Mein Weg zu Streck Mack Schwedhelm* unter https://steueranwalt.de/team/dr-rolf-schwedhelm (Letzter Zugriff 1.8.2024).

Bolter / Grusin 1999), durch deren Einsatz spezifische kommunikative Effekte erzeugt werden (siehe Ziffer IV.2). Besonders auffällig ist dabei das Aufkommen eines informelleren und persönlicheren Tons, der einen Kontrast zum eher unpersönlichen und nüchternen Stil der ausformulierten Selbstdarstellungen bildet, mit denen die einzelnen Videos auf der Webseite intertextuell bzw. intermodal verbunden werden. Videovorstellungen lassen sich zudem als Instrumente einer eher positiven Stereotypisierung interpretieren: wenn Anwälte beispielsweise ihr berufliches Selbstverständnis zum Ausdruck bringen oder wenn sie auf die Wahrnehmung des Anwaltsberufs durch Laien explizit eingehen.

Zum Zeitpunkt der Datenerhebung (im Frühjahr 2023) waren nur wenige Videos auf den Webseiten der in der ersten Phase der Studie untersuchten Boutique-Kanzleien verfügbar. Somit war keine hinreichende Datenbasis für eine Typologisierung der Videovorstellungen vorhanden. Zum Zweck der vorliegenden Fallbeispiel-Analysen wurden, um möglichst homogene Daten zu untersuchen, aus der damaligen Stichprobe (aus zehn deutschen und zehn italienischen Anwaltsvideos) jeweils zwei Videos pro Sprache ausgewählt, die Ähnlichkeiten in Bezug auf Größe und Spezialisierung der Kanzleien aufweisen. Im Folgenden wird anhand dieser Videoprofile exemplarisch aufgezeigt, wie die audio-visuellen Personalpräsentationen ins digitale Ökosystem der Kanzlei-Webseite eingebunden sind und zudem sozial und funktional-kommunikativ gestaltet werden.

Anzumerken bleibt: Das audio-visuelle Medium ist – wie kurz vor Drucklegung dieses Beitrags ersichtlich – mittlerweile (seit dem Herbst 2024) zum Bestandteil vieler Kanzlei-Webauftritte geworden. So gibt es inzwischen sowohl auf deutschen Kanzlei-Webseiten (wie in der Kanzlei Streck Mack Schwedelm)[16] als auch auf italienischen Kanzlei-Webseiten (z.B. die Anwaltskanzlei Lipani)[17] Videopräsentationen, die beim Aufrufen der Startseite direkt abgespielt werden können. Das zeigt, wie dynamisch und

---

[16] https://steueranwalt.de/en/ (Letzter Zugriff 1.8.2024).
[17] https://www.lipani.it/ (Letzter Zugriff 1.8.2024).

innovativ sich dieser Untersuchungsbereich insbesondere für die angewandte und kritische Rechtslinguistik entfaltet.

2. Leitfragen

Der traditionelle Lebenslauf hat zwar mit den typischen Merkmalen schriftlich, tabellarisch, entpersonalisiert – in verschiedenen Sprachen und Kulturen (vgl. Pöckel 1999) – einen hohen Standardisierungsgrad. Jedoch ist die Textsorte durch das Medium des Internets zunehmend im Wandel. Mittels Remediatisierung werden Inhalte immer neu und anders vernetzt und verfügbar gemacht und neue Textvarianten hervorgebracht, die sich wechselseitig ergänzen und darauf gerichtet sind, die Corporate Brand mitzuformen (siehe Ziffer II). Forschung, die sich der Kulturbedingtheit von Textsorten widmet, hat sich holistisch auszurichten und grundsätzlich jedwede Zeichenarten zu inkludieren, d.h. sprachliche, parasprachliche und außersprachliche Zeichen bzw. multimodale Elemente wie die geschriebene und gesprochene Sprache, das stehende oder bewegte Bild sowie Musik, Geräusche oder Töne. Im Prinzip umfasst ganzheitliches textanalytisches Vorgehen die:

> verbalen (lexikalischen, syntaktischen und rhetorisch-stilistischen Vertextungsmittel, Makrostrukturen, funktionalen und thematischen Elemente usw.), paraverbalen (Typographie, Satzanordnung, Spaltenanordnung, Interpunktion, Schriftart, Schriftgröße usw.), nonverbalen (Format, Papierqualität, Farbe, Layout, Bilder usw.) und extraverbalen (Zeit, Raum, soziale Variablen usw.) Merkmale. (Zhao 2011: 129)

Angenommen wird, dass für die Herstellung der „intermodale[n] Kohärenz“ (Stöckl 2012: 247) relevant ist, „welches distinkte Ausdruckspotenzial die verschiedenen ‚modes‘ haben, welcher Logik […] sie folgen und über welche semantisch-pragmatische Reichweite […] sie verfügen“ (Stöckl 2016: 4). Angesichts dieser theoretischen Grundannahmen und Prämissen liegt der Fokus der Video-Analysen auf der intermedialen Einbettung und auf Kommunikationsstrategien hinsichtlich Zielgruppenansprache, Imageaufbau, fachlicher Expertise und Berufsethos. Dafür werden verschiedene multimodale Ressourcen des digitalen Mediums in den Blick genommen. Unsere untersuchungsleitenden Fragen sind:

i. In welchem kontextuellen Zusammenhang steht die audio-visuelle Selbstpräsentation und was ist ihre spezifische kommunikative Leistung im gesamten Erscheinungsbild der Kanzlei?
ii. Welche kommunikativen Strategien verwenden Anwälte, um potenzielle Mandanten anzusprechen und Image aufzubauen?
iii. Welche multimodalen Mittel setzen Anwälte wie ein, um berufliche und persönliche Werte zu vermitteln, Fachwissen darzulegen und Glaubwürdigkeit auszustrahlen?
iv. Welche Gemeinsamkeiten und Unterschiede lassen sich im deutsch-italienischen Sprach- und Kulturvergleich ableiten?

Die Videos werden entlang der vier Fragen der Reihe nach anlaysiert. Das heißt: Zunächst werden zwei Anwaltsvideos, die auf deutschen Kanzlei-Webseiten eingebettet sind, untersucht (siehe Ziffer V) und anschließend zwei Anwaltsvideos auf italienischen Kanzlei-Webseiten (siehe Ziffer VI). Die Analyseergebnisse bilden die Basis für unsere kontrastiven Reflexionen oder – besser gesagt (angesichts der Korpusgröße) – für die Ermittlung von Tendenzen im Sprach- und Kulturvergleich (siehe Ziffer VII). Darauf lässt sich mit einer breiteren Datengrundlage im Projekt aufbauen mit dem Ziel, fundierte Erkenntnisse sowohl für die linguistische Disziplin (z.B. Textlinguistik, Angewandte Linguistik) als auch für die Rechtskommunikation, hier vor allem für die Anwalt-Klienten-Kommunikation, zu generieren.

V. Video-Analysen deutscher Anwaltsbiographien

1. Fallbeispiel (1) – Dr. Oliver Daum

1.1. Kontextuelle Einbettung

Der Aufbau der Kanzlei-Webseite[18] besteht aus den Reitern *Startseite*, *Über mich*, *Rechtsgebiete*, *Leistungen* und *Blog* in blauer Majuskelschreibung auf weißem Grund. Links davon stehen die miteinander verschränkten Initialen O (in Blau) und D (in Grau) sowie Dr. Oliver Daum (in Blau)

---

[18] https://www.anwalt-daum.de/ (Letzter Zugriff 1.8.2024).

und Rechtsanwalt (in Grau und Majuskeln). Die Berufsbezeichnung ist an bestimmte Bedingungen geknüpft. In Deutschland muss ein *Rechtsanwalt* das zweite Juristische Staatsexamen, eine Berufshaftpflichtversicherung und eine Anwaltszulassung haben und außerdem bei der Rechtsanwaltskammer angemeldet sein. Klickt man den Reiter *Über mich* an, kommt man zur Unterseite mit der Selbstpräsentation. Es fällt auf, dass auch hier die Farben Weiß, Blau und Grau dominieren und die Seite dreigeteilt ist. Im ersten Drittel befindet sich abermals die Überschrift *Über mich* (in Blau). Darunter steht der Satz (in Grau): „Als erfahrener Anwalt setze ich mich mit hohem Engagement für ihre rechtlichen Interessen ein und unterstütze Sie bei der Erreichung eines bestmöglichen Ergebnisses." Somit hebt der Rechtsanwalt eingangs schon seine Kompetenzen hervor: Erfahrung, Engagement, Erfolg.

Im Hauptteil geht es um den akademischen Werdegang von Dr. Oliver Daum. Der Teil ist nochmals mit *Über mich* (in grauen Majuskeln) und „Dr. Oliver Daum" (in Blau) betitelt. Auf der linken Seite befindet sich in grauer Schrift die ausformulierte Biographie in der ersten Person Singular (siehe Ziffer III). Es werden in der Ich-Erzählung markante berufliche Stationen dargelegt. So hat der Anwalt Rechtswissenschaften an der Universität in Kiel und zwei Semester an der Universität in Paris studiert. An der Universität Trier war er wissenschaftlicher Mitarbeiter und hat dort auch promoviert. Vor der Selbstständigkeit hat er in einer internationalen Wirtschaftskanzlei in Hamburg gearbeitet und erste Berufserfahrungen als Anwalt erworben. Über die Qualifikationen hinaus kommen – im Layout durch einen Absatz vom bisherigen Text abgesetzt – auch persönliche Werte und Wesenszüge zur Sprache. Danach ist der Rechtsanwalt ein Familienmensch („In meiner Freizeit verbringe ich viel Zeit mit meiner Familie"), dem die Ehefrau und die Kinder sowie die Freunde wichtig sind. Zu seinen Interessen gehört die deutsche und europäische Geschichte.

Abb. 1: Dr. Oliver Daum am Schreibtisch in seiner Kanzlei

Demgegenüber befindet sich auf der rechten Seite das Video, das nachstehend transkribiert, deskribiert und reflektiert wird (siehe Ziffern V.1.2 und V.1.3). Dr. Oliver Daum ist lächelnd und mit halb geöffnetem Mund abgebildet, um Klienten zu adressieren. Unterhalb des Videos erscheinen erneut Vor- und Nachname mit akademischem Titel in blauer Schrift. Darunter sind in grauer Schrift schlagwortartig der Berufstitel, das Spezialgebiet und spezielle Zuständigkeiten aufgelistet: „Rechtsanwalt, Fachanwalt für IT-Recht, IT-Sicherheitsbeauftragter (IHK), Datenschutzbeauftragter (IHK)." Als Ausweis seiner anwaltlichen Kompetenz gelten ferner die Veröffentlichungen, die mittels eines blauen Rechtecks und weißer Schrift („Aktuelle Publikationen") gut sichtbar sowie abrufbar sind. Scrollt man die Webseite bis ganz nach unten, so gelangt man im letzten Drittel zu einem auf blauem Grund hinterlegten Kontaktformular für die Vereinbarung eines Termins.

Die Entscheidungsfrage („HABEN SIE FRAGEN?") und die Ich-Botschaft („Ich freue mich auf Ihre Anfrage! Für Sie bin ich 5 Tage pro Woche da und antworte im Regelfall innerhalb von 48 Stunden auf Ihre Nachricht") – beide weiße Schrift auf blauem Hintergrund – dienen dem Beziehungsaufbau und der Kontaktherstellung. Auffällig ist, dass das Formular, obwohl es standardisiert ist (z.B. Name, Telefonnummer, E-Mail-Adresse), was Distanz schafft, auch mit der expressiven Äußerung „ICH FREUE MICH AUF SIE!" eine emotionale Befindlichkeit und soziale Nähe zum Ausdruck bringt. Das Satzzeichen hat die Funktion, die Freude noch einmal zu verstärken. Zusammenfassend ist zu sagen, dass die Art der Kommunikation und die Bilder im intermodalen Wechselspiel ein ganzheitliches Profilbild ergeben. Danach ist Dr. Oliver Daum kompetent und nahbar. Er kommuniziert durchgehend aus der Ich-Perspektive und erzählt im Video eine Geschichte, die eine ganz persönliche familiäre Note beinhaltet.

1.2. Inhalt

In dem Video,[19] das fünfzig Sekunden dauert, präsentiert sich der Rechtsanwalt den Adressaten mit folgendem Wortlaut: „Hallo, mein Name ist Dr. Oliver Daum. Ich bin Ihr Rechtsanwalt aus Kiel. Das Thema Gerechtigkeit beschäftigt mich schon seit Kindheitstagen. Als drittes von acht Kindern war ich zum Beispiel zuständig für die Verteilung der Süßigkeiten. Und man kennt es ja: Süßigkeiten stellen unter Geschwistern immer ein Streitthema dar. Mir fiel sozusagen die Rolle des Vermittlers und des gerechten Verteilers zu. Schon damals entwickelte sich also mein Gerechtigkeitsempfinden, das ich heute als Anwalt brauche. Dass ich also Anwalt werden würde, stand damals schon relativ früh fest. Wenn Sie also vor einer rechtlichen Herausforderung stehen oder anwaltlichen Beratungsbedarf zu Vertragsfragen haben beispielsweise, nehmen Sie gerne per Anruf oder per E-Mail Kontakt zu mir auf. Ich freue mich auf Sie. Ihr Oliver Daum."

1.3. Analyse

Der Rechtsanwalt adressiert die Zielgruppen (hier rot markiert) von seinem Anwaltsbüro aus mit „Hallo". Die Begrüßungsform „Hallo" ist weder eine förmliche Anrede (wie z.B. ‚Sehr geehrte Damen und Herren') noch eine

---

[19] https://www.anwalt-daum.de/zur-person/ (Letzter Zugriff 1.8.2024). Für die Verschriftlichung des Videos – wie auch der anderen Videos – wurden keine Transkriptionszeichen (z.B. für Pausen, Intonation) verwendet, da sie bei der Analyse keine Rolle spielen.

vertraute Anrede (wie z.B. ‚Liebe Mandantinnen und Mandanten'). Vielmehr liegt sie zwischen Distanz- und Nähesprache. Möglicherweise soll so für die telefonische („per Anruf") oder elektronische („per E-Mail") Kontaktaufnahme Distanz abgebaut und soziale Nähe aufgebaut werden. Im Weiteren verwendet der Anwalt, wie im deutschen Geschäftsverkehr üblich, die Höflichkeitsformen „Sie" (Personalpronomen dreimal) und „Ihr" (Possessivpronomen zweimal). Er begrüßt die potenzielle Mandantschaft mit der gesetzlich geschützten Berufsbezeichnung „Ihr Rechtsanwalt" und verabschiedet sich mit vollem Namen „Ihr Oliver Daum". Die formelhafte Wendung ist typisch für Briefe, also für die Schriftsprache, und lässt darauf zurückschließen, dass der Anwalt den Text zuvor schriftlich verfasst hat, bevor er ihn mündlich vorträgt. Mithin haben wir es hier mit konzeptioneller Schriftlichkeit und medialer Mündlichkeit zu tun (vgl. Koch / Oesterreicher 2008: 199ff.).

Was seine Wertvorstellungen betrifft, so stellt der Rechtsanwalt gleich nach der Begrüßung klar, dass „das Thema Gerechtigkeit" (hier grün markiert) sein berufliches Handeln bestimmt. Semantisch interessant ist für unsere Zwecke die Isotopiekette „Gerechtigkeit", wozu die Elemente „des gerechten Verteilers" und „mein Gerechtigkeitsempfinden" gehören. In *gerecht* steckt das Lexem ‚recht'. Das Adjektiv hatte ursprünglich die Bedeutung ‚gerade' bzw. ‚geradlinig' (vgl. Dudenredaktion 2014: 331). Im heutigen Sprachgebrauch hat sich daraus die Verwendung ‚richtig' im Sinne von ‚den Gesetzen und Geboten entsprechend', ‚sittlich gut', ‚redlich' ‚gesetzlich' und ‚dem Recht entsprechend' entwickelt (vgl. Dudenredaktion 2014: 682). Mit diesen Werten identifiziert er sich. Sie machen seine Persönlichkeit aus und prägen sein Berufsethos, was er an einem Alltagsbeispiel aus seiner Kindheit (hier braun markiert) veranschaulicht.

Dr. Oliver Daum hat bereits in „Kindheitstagen" einen Sinn für gerechtes Verhalten bei der „Verteilung der Süßigkeiten" entfaltet. Auffällig ist, dass er an dieser Stelle ein einziges Mal von der Ich-Perspektive in die verallgemeinernde Man-Perspektive wechselt: „Und man kennt es ja: Süßigkeiten stellen unter Geschwistern immer ein Streitthema dar." Mit dem Perspektivenwechsel knüpft er an eine konsensuelle Erfahrung an und generiert sich zugleich als idealen Konfliktlöser. Als „drittes von acht Kindern" ist ihm „die Rolle des Vermittlers und des gerechten Verteilers" zugefallen. Aus der menschlichen Tugend leitet er seine fachliche Expertise ab („Dass ich also Anwalt werden würde, stand damals schon relativ früh fest") und fordert dazu auf, ihn zu kontaktieren. Den Beziehungsaufbau konsolidieren der direkte Blickkontakt und die expressive Freude („Ich freue mich auf Sie").

Der Rechtsanwalt verfolgt im Wesentlichen zwei Kommunikationsstrategien, um gegenüber potenziellen Mandanten Vertrauen aufzubauen. Zum einen demonstriert er Kompetenz (hier blau markiert), indem er sich zum Beispiel mit seinem Doktortitel vorstellt („Mein Name ist Dr. Oliver Daum") sowie als Experte bei „einer rechtlichen Herausforderung" und als Berater in „Vertragsfragen" ausweist (vgl. z.B. Keller 2009: 39f.). Simultan unterschreibt er – sinnbildlich – mit der rechten Hand einen Vertrag. Sein Interesse am Völkerrecht und am internationalen Seerecht sowie die Bürogemeinschaft mit dem Anwalt Ralf Höfer zum Handels-, Gesellschafts-, Arbeits- und Insolvenzrecht kommt im Video dagegen nicht zur Sprache und lässt sich ausschließlich der Webseite entnehmen. Die Äußerung „Ihr Oliver Daum" und das mit untermalender Hintergrundmusik eingeblendete Kanzlei-Logo (mit den Initialen) am Ende des Videos sollen Expertise, Qualität und Glaubwürdigkeit im Sinne von ‚Dafür stehe ich mit meinem Namen'[20] zertifizieren.

Darüber hinaus spielen Seriosität und Authentizität für den Vertrauensaufbau eine wichtige Rolle. Der Anwalt erzählt eine Episode über ‚Rechtshandeln', als er noch ein Kind war, aus der Ich-Perspektive; dabei gebraucht er Personal- und Possessivpronomen wie „ich" oder „mein" (hier violett markiert) und setzt sich in Relation zu seinen sieben Geschwistern. Das Video ist ganz auf ihn zugeschnitten und zeigt (fast) nur ihn als Person. Er trägt einen dunkelblauen Anzug und ein weißes Hemd (siehe Abb. 1) und sitzt hinter einem Schreibtisch in einem schlichten Büro, das im Wesentlichen nur mit einem Computer und einem Telefon ausgestattet ist. Bei

[20] Siehe z.B. die Claus Hipp-Werbung (2012): https://www.youtube.com/watch?v=54p7Bd E6hys (Letzter Zugriff 1.8.2024).

der Vertragsunterzeichnung wird durch die Kameraeinstellung der Ehering fokussiert, der seinen Sinn für Familie symbolisiert (siehe Ziffer V.1.1). Er hat eine Frau und zwei Kinder.[21] Schon in seiner Kindheit und Jugend hat die Familie (haben seine sieben Geschwister) ihn geprägt. Das positiv konnotierte Privatleben wird hier unidirektional auf das Berufsleben projiziert. Der Anwalt erzählt aus seinem Leben, um eigene Werte glaubhaft zu kommunizieren. Das Tageslicht rückt ihn unterstützend in ein helles Licht.

2. Fallbeispiel (2) – Dr. Stefanie Kunz

2.1. Kontextuelle Einbettung

Auf das Anwaltsvideo kommt man, wenn man auf der Homepage[22] der Kanzlei „schulte.rechtsanwälte" von den insgesamt sechs Reitern (*Home*, *Aktuelles*, *Rechtsgebiete*, *Team*, *Downloads*, *Karriere*) den Reiter *Team* anklickt. Hier sind acht Rechtsanwälte gelistet, wovon drei einen akademischen Titel haben. Die Anwältin Dr. Stefanie Kunz befindet sich an vorletzter Stelle. Die weißgrundige Webseite besteht im Kern aus drei Teilen, die Informationen über die Vita der Anwältin enthalten. Im ersten Teil ist die Anwältin – dem Betrachter zugewandt – auf einem Farbfoto abgebildet, das Ähnlichkeit mit einem Passfoto hat. Daneben stehen in Spiegelpunkten bestimmte Angaben zur Person: der Vor- und Nachname mit dem akademischen Grad („Dr. Stefanie Kunz"), der Beruf bzw. Fachanwaltstitel („Fachanwältin für Strafrecht"), der Status („Partnerin in der Kanzlei") und das Rechtsgebiet, auf das sie spezialisiert ist, um Klienten rechtlich zu beraten und vor Gericht zu vertreten („Schwerpunkt: Wirtschaftsstrafrecht, Steuerstrafrecht und Selbstanzeige"). Die Bezeichnung *Fachanwalt* ist erlaubnispflichtig. In Deutschland darf ein Anwalt den Titel nur führen, wenn er in einem bestimmten Rechtsgebiet in einem förmlichen Prüfungsverfahren (über den Prüfungsstoff im Juristischen Staatsexamen hinausgehende) besondere fachliche Expertise erworben hat und außerdem regelmäßig an Fortbildungen teilnimmt.

---

[21] Das geht nicht aus dem Video hervor, sondern steht auf der Webseite.
[22] https://lawplus.de/kunz/ (Letzter Zugriff 1.8.2024).

Direkt darunter ist unter *Allgemeine Informationen* in blauer Schrift der „Persönlich[e] Werdegang" der Anwältin in der dritten Person Singular ausformuliert hinterlegt. Der Fließtext umfasst sechs Sätze. Der zweite Satz hebt – ebenfalls wieder spiegelpunktartig – die Gebiete, für die Dr. Stefanie Kunz in der Kanzlei speziell ausgewiesen ist und Verantwortung trägt, hervor: Steuer- und Medizinstrafrecht sowie Wirtschaftsrecht und Allgemeines Strafrecht. Allerdings irritiert in diesem Kontext das Rechtsgebiet „Wirtschaftsrecht", da sie „Fachanwältin für Strafrecht" ist. Es muss, so wie es sowohl im tabellarischen Lebenslauf als auch im Anwaltsvideo der Fall ist, richtigerweise „Wirtschaftsstrafrecht" heißen (siehe Ziffer V.2.3). Die beiden Kommunikationsformate übernehmen mithin die Aufgabe der Klarstellung und entpuppen sich als intertextuelles Korrektiv.

Zudem gehört neben der langjährigen Berufserfahrung als Strafverteidigerin (seit 1996) auch der Fachanwaltstitel für Strafrecht, den sie seit dem Jahr 2000 innehat, zum Profilbild. Die Anwältin wirbt vor allem mit den Argumenten Erfahrung, Kompetenz und Engagement um Mandanten. Dabei verwendet sie hochwertende Attribute wie etwa „viel Fachwissen", „höchstes Engagement", „ausführliche Beratung", „bundesweite Verteidigung" oder Rechtsvertretung durch „alle Instanzen", um sich vorteilhaft nach außen zu präsentieren und ihr berufliches Selbstverständnis zu exponieren.

Im dritten Teil stellt sich die Rechtsanwältin selbst in dem Video vor, um ihr profundes Fachwissen anzubieten und damit bei Klienten zu punkten. Es geht darum, durch das Medium eine größere Nähe zu den anvisierten Adressaten zu schaffen und letztendlich durch die Vergabe eines Mandates „als Strafverteidigerin" beauftragt zu werden. Dafür befinden sich neben der Videovorstellung in einem blauen Kasten die Kontaktdaten mit der Anschrift der Kanzlei in Düsseldorf-Oberkassel, Telefon, Fax und E-Mail. Die Angaben laden zur Kontaktaufnahme ein. Die Adressaten können frei wählen, ob sie der Aufforderung nachkommen wollen und in welcher Form sie gegebenenfalls den Kontakt aufnehmen möchten.

Abb. 2: Dr. Stefanie Kunz am Schreibtisch in ihrer Kanzlei

2.2. Inhalt

Zur Selbstdarstellung äußert sich die Rechtsanwältin in dem zweiminütigen Video[23] folgendermaßen: „Herzlich willkommen. Ich bin Frau Dr. Kunz, Fachanwältin für Strafrecht. Wir sind hier in meinen Kanzleiräumen am Kaiser-Wilhelm-Ring in Düsseldorf. Schwerpunkt meiner Strafverteidigung sind die Bereiche Wirtschaftsstrafrecht, Steuerstrafrecht, hier natürlich Selbstanzeigenberatung, Stichwort Steuer-CD, Medizinrecht, aber ich arbeite auch im Allgemeinen Strafrecht. Allgemeines Strafrecht, das kann sein, Verkehrsunfallflucht bis hin zum Tötungsdelikt. Die häufigste Frage, die mir als Strafverteidigerin gestellt wird, lautet: Wie kannst du diesen Beruf ausüben? Kommst du nicht ständig in Konflikt mit deinem Gewissen? Ganz klare Antwort: Nein, ich komme nicht in Konflikt mit meinem Gewissen. Denn das Recht auf Verteidigung ist ein Menschenrecht, das jedem zusteht. Ein Vorwurf kann schnell erhoben werden. Und deshalb kann ein Vorwurf auch sehr schnell falsch sein. Und hier ist es eben wichtig, kompetente Verteidigung zu haben.

---

[23] https://www.youtube.com/watch?v=tUcvv0NqjgA&t=3s (Letzter Zugriff 1.8.2024).

Wie kann das eigentlich sein, dass es zu unterschiedlichen rechtlichen Bewertungen kommt? Denn Staatsanwälte und Richter sind ja auch Juristen. Das liegt daran, dass wir eine Fülle von Gesetzesvorschriften haben und dass viele Begriffe ausgelegt werden müssen. Von daher gilt der bekannte Spruch: Zwei Juristen, drei Meinungen. Es kommt im Strafrecht also sehr häufig auf Wertungen an. Jeder kennt den bekannten Spruch: Ist das Glas halb leer oder ist es halb voll? Ganz konkret bedeutet das für meine Arbeit, dass ich Staatsanwälte und Richter davon überzeuge, dass der Tatvorwurf, der gegen meinen Mandanten erhoben wird, falsch ist oder zumindestens [sic!] nicht in der erhobenen Form richtig ist. Das erreiche ich durch eine sehr genaue Kenntnis der Sach- und Rechtslage und natürlich durch Argumentationsgeschick. Ich arbeite jetzt seit zwanzig Jahren als Strafverteidigerin und meine Erfolge beruhen darauf, dass ich einfach zäh bin. Das heißt, ich suche so lange nach Lösungen, bis ich das buchstäbliche Loch in der Betonwand gefunden habe.“

2.3. Analyse

Die Rechtsanwältin begrüßt die Adressaten mit „Herzlich willkommen“ und lächelt dabei freundlich in die Kamera (ebenso zum Schluss der Selbstpräsentation). Durch die Art der Begrüßung (im Text rot markiert) versucht sie, was die Wortwahl, die Intonation und das ganze Erscheinungsbild betrifft, eine nahbare Beziehung zu potenziellen Mandanten aufzubauen, zu denen grundsätzlich eine asymmetrische Kommunikationskonstellation und Distanz besteht (dazu weiter unten). Während der Dauer des Videos ist Dr. Stefanie Kunz überwiegend in der abgebildeten Pose zu sehen und zu hören (siehe Abb. 2). Primär handelt sie in der Ich-Perspektive, wodurch sie sich sprachlich von den auf der Webseite vorhandenen biographischen Texten abhebt (siehe Ziffer V.2.1). Der Wechsel von der dritten in die erste Person Singular ist eine kommunikative Strategie, die dem Beziehungs- und Vertrauensaufbau zwischen ihr und den Mandanten dient. Vereinzelt wird sie am Laptop arbeitend oder mit einem Buch in der Hand herangezoomt, trägt eine Brille oder steht an einem Bücherregal. In der Kulisse erscheint sie als eine belesene und pflichtbewusste Person.

Über die Begrüßung hinaus stellt sich die Anwältin mit dem akademischen Titel und der Fachanwaltschaft vor („Ich bin Dr. Kunz, Fachanwältin für Strafrecht") und bezieht ihr Gegenüber in die Vorstellungsrunde mit ein („Wir sind hier in meinen Kanzleiräumen"). Mit dem Gebrauch des kollektiven Personalpronomens *wir* lädt sie in erster Linie die potenzielle Mandantschaft dazu ein, nach Düsseldorf in den Kaiser-Wilhelm-Ring 43a zu kommen, der mit seinen alten weißen Villen herrschaftlich und mondän erstrahlt. Darüber hinaus können die szenischen Einblicke in das Kanzleileben (z.B. großer Besprechungstisch mit buntem Blumenstrauß, hohe Bücherwände mit Fachliteratur bestückt, d.h. mit braunen NJW-Jahresbänden und schwarzer BGHSt-Entscheidungssammlung)[24] ebenfalls interessierte Juristen anregen, für ein etwaiges Beschäftigungsverhältnis Kontakt zu der Gemeinschaftskanzlei und speziell zu Dr. Stefanie Kunz aufzunehmen.

Die Außen- und Innensicht, also der Außenbereich der Kanzlei und die Innenräume, in denen gearbeitet wird und Mandantengespräche stattfinden, sind kohärent aufeinander abgestimmt und erzeugen insgesamt eine positive Atmosphäre und ein glaubwürdiges Image. Mit anderen Worten: Durch die Text-Bild-Passungen und die verwendeten multimodalen Mittel (z.B. Stimme, Intonation, Gestik, Mimik, Farben, Musik im Hintergrund) entstehen Synergien, die vor allem Aspekte des beruflichen Ethos (z.B. Recht auf Verteidigung und anwaltlichen Rechtsbeistand) und Persönlichkeitsmerkmale der Anwältin wie Standhaftigkeit, Ausdauer oder Willensstärke versinnbildlichen: Dr. Stefanie Kunz ist – analog etwa zu der Außenfassade der Patrizierhäuser – hell gekleidet (altweißer Pullover, hellgrauer Hosenanzug), sitzt im Büro vor einer braunen Bücherwand (NJW) an ihrem Schreibtisch und blickt den Hörer direkt an, wenn sie ihn adressiert. Sie agiert sachlich und klar, indem sie unidirektional von den Kanzleiräumen auf ihre Fachexpertise zu sprechen kommt. Ihr Metier ist die Strafverteidigung.

Das Wirtschafts- und Steuerstrafrecht mit der Selbstanzeigenberatung („Stichwort Steuer-CD") bilden ihr Spezialgebiet, sie macht aber auch

---

[24] NJW = Neue Juristische Wochenschrift; BGHSt = Entscheidungen des Bundesgerichtshofes in Strafsachen.

Allgemeines Strafrecht (hier grün markiert). Die Anwältin erklärt das Rechtsgebiet stichpunktartig mit „Verkehrsunfallflucht bis hin zum Tötungsdelikt" und geht dabei nicht besonders in die Tiefe. Deutlicher tritt die Wissensasymmetrie zwischen der Anwältin (Rechtsexpertin) und den Zieladressaten (Laien) bei der Vermittlung bestimmter Fachbegriffe hervor, die zur Tätigkeit eines jeden Juristen gehören, wie *Verteidigung* und *Auslegung*. Der Hauptunterschied in der Explikation besteht darin, dass die Anwältin *Verteidigung* primär auf eine universelle Ebene hebt, während *Auslegung* eher personalisiert bzw. individuell auf ihre eigene Person zugeschnitten wird. Für sie steht fest, nur wer sein Handwerk beherrscht, kann Erfolge einfahren und Prozesse gewinnen.

Die Erklärung des Fachbegriffs *Verteidigung* (fünfmal im gesprochenen Text; braun markiert) hebt sich in Form und Detailgrad von der oberflächlichen Beschreibung des Begriffs *Allgemeines Strafrecht* ab. Die Rechtsanwältin gebraucht das Stilmittel der rhetorischen Frage, um den Adressaten unmissverständlich mitzuteilen, dass sie mit ihrem Gewissen im Reinen ist und keine Gewissensbisse hat, den Beruf auszuüben und als Rechtsbeistand zu fungieren („Wie kannst du diesen Beruf ausüben? Kommst du nicht ständig in Konflikt mit deinem Gewissen? Ganz klare Antwort: Nein, ich komme nicht in Konflikt mit meinem Gewissen"). Interessant ist an dieser Stelle, dass die Anwältin es nicht einfach bei dieser Feststellung bewenden lässt, sondern Gründe anführt. So wird die *Strafverteidigung* als ein universelles Recht, das für alle Menschen gültig und von Bedeutung ist, klassifiziert, d.h. als „ein Menschenrecht", auf das jedermann einen Anspruch hat („das jedem zusteht"). Die Begründung hat die kommunikative Funktion, nicht nur die Aussage als wahr zu gewichten, sondern auch argumentativ ins Detail zu gehen und Argumentationsstärke zu demonstrieren.

Im situativen Kontext ist das Lexem „Vorwurf" ein Schlüsselwort, das viel über die moralische Haltung und das Berufsethos der Anwältin offenbart. Dass ein Vorwurf „schnell erhoben werden", aber „deshalb […] auch sehr schnell falsch sein" kann, klingt in den Ohren juristischer Laien besorgniserregend und erzeugt Ängste. Dass die Justiz sich irren und fehlbar sein kann (Das Lexem *falsch* kommt zweimal vor), trägt nicht gerade zum Vertrauensaufbau in Rechtsinstitutionen bei. Doch anstatt zu erläutern, was „Vorwurf" im Strafverfahren – also im Rechtssinn – bedeutet (vgl. Luttermann 1996: 55ff., 293f.), nutzt die Anwältin die Strategie der Popularisierung dafür, zu emotionalisieren (vgl. Luttermann / Engberg 2023: 104ff.), indem sie auf das Gefühl der Angst mit einer konsensualen und vielversprechenden Lösung reagiert und zudem auf Kompetenz abstellt („Und hier ist es eben wichtig, kompetente Verteidigung zu haben"). Dadurch stellt sie sich und ihr individuelles Können rhetorisch geschickt in den Vordergrund und hebt sich von der juristischen Zunft, dem verlauteten *Wir* („dass wir eine Fülle von Gesetzesvorschriften haben"), zu der sie als Anwältin gehört, letztlich kämpferisch und willensstark ab (siehe dazu unten).

Darüber hinaus räumt Dr. Stefanie Kunz dem Begriff *Auslegung* (dreimal im Text und violett markiert) breiten Raum ein und vermittelt das Rechtskonzept wiederum anhand des Frage-Antwort-Musters sowie der Sprechhandlungen des Begründens und Argumentierens. Als Erstes verwendet sie wieder eine rhetorische Frage („Wie kann das eigentlich sein, dass es zu unterschiedlichen rechtlichen Bewertungen kommt?"), die keine Antwort verlangt, sondern der Bestätigung von rechtlichen Voraussetzungen dient. Sie erklärt *Auslegung* mit „Wertungen" und nutzt die beiden Begriffe synonym. Ein wesentlicher Teil der Erklärung stellt darauf ab, dass die institutionellen Rollenträger, wofür das exklusive (selbstreferenzielle) „Wir" steht – neben den Anwälten sind das die „Staatsanwälte und Richter" –, rechtliche Sachverhalte, die in vielen „Gesetzesvorschriften" geregelt sind, bewerten müssen. Dabei macht sie keinen Hehl daraus, dass die Begriffsauslegung juristisch diffizil ist und „Juristen" unterschiedliche Rechtsmeinungen haben. Zur Begründung greift sie auf den populären Spruch „Zwei Juristen, drei Meinungen" zu, der zwischen den Staatsanwälten und Richtern auf der einen Seite und den Rechtsanwälten auf der anderen Seite polarisiert und den besonderen Stellenwert von Anwälten im Rechtssystem bzw. im Strafverfahren zu erkennen gibt.

Die Popularisierungsstrategie, volksnahe Sprüche aus der fachlichen Sicht zu gebrauchen, dient aber nicht allein dazu, auf Auslegungsdivergenzen bzw. Bewertungsdiskrepanzen im Recht zwischen den Berufsgruppen zuzuspitzen. Vielmehr knüpft sie damit perspektivisch auch an die Alltagswelt und das Alltagswissen von Adressaten für die eigene Argumentation an („Jeder kennt den bekannten Spruch: Ist das Glas halb leer oder ist es halb voll?“) und bereitet dem Hörer eine Plattform, sich ihre persönlichen und berufsethischen Wertvorstellungen (hier blau markiert) zu Eigen zu machen und sich damit zu identifizieren. Außerdem sind die in der Bevölkerung weit verbreiteten Sprüche der Rechtsanwältin ein probates Mittel dafür, sich abermals in ein gutes Licht zu stellen und sich als äußerst kenntnisreich und qualifiziert zu präsentieren. Sie verfügt als Fachanwältin für Strafrecht über die nötigen Eigenschaften (wie langjährige Berufserfahrung, Akribie, Fachkenntnis), um erfolgreich zu sein und zufriedenstellende Lösungen zu finden.

Diese Botschaft wird im Sprachgebrauch manifest, und zwar sowohl explizit (z.B. „Argumentationsgeschick“, „meine Erfolge“ oder „sehr genaue Kenntnis der Sach- und Rechtslage“) als auch metaphorisch (z.B. „ich einfach zäh bin“, „bis ich buchstäblich das Loch in der Betonwand gefunden habe“). In dieser Klarheit macht sie also zugleich Werbung in eigener Sache und stellt sich als die fachkundige Verteidigerin dar, die engagiert und mit Eifer geflissentlich für ihre Klienten kämpft, um Richter und Staatsanwälte davon zu überzeugen, dass „der Tatvorwurf […] falsch“ oder „nicht in der erhobenen Form richtig ist.“ Die Selbstpräsentation ist somit ein Appell an die Zieladressaten, die Fachanwältin Dr. Stefanie Kunz aufgrund ihrer Expertise zu ermächtigen (autorisieren), ihnen im Strafverfahren als Rechtsgehilfin beizustehen (vgl. Luttermann 1996: 101).

VI. Video-Analysen italienischer Anwaltsbiographien

1. Fallbeispiel (3) – Dr. Mariapaola Marro

1.1. Kontextuelle Einbettung

Das Vorstellungsvideo der Kanzleigründerin, Dr. Mariapaola Marro, das über den Reiter *chi siamo* („Wer wir sind“) direkt von der Startseite abrufbar ist, ist unter einem Kurzporträt mit farbigem Foto der Anwältin platziert und trägt den Titel *I nostri punti di forza* („Unsere Stärken"). Im ausformulierten Kurzprofil (in der dritten Person) werden Höhepunkte und Erfolge ihrer beruflichen Laufbahn textlich stringent aufbereitet.

Abb. 3: Dr. Mariapaola Marro in ihrer Kanzlei

1.2. Inhalt

Im Video[25] (1:08 Minuten lang) stellt sich die Rechtsanwältin mit folgendem (aus dem Italienischen ins Deutsche übersetzten) Wortlaut vor: „Ich wollte schon immer Anwalt werden. Wähle eine Arbeit aus, die Dir gefällt, und Du wirst keinen einzigen Tag arbeiten, sagte Konfuzius. Nichts auf der Welt könnte wahrer sein. Anwalt zu sein, heißt für mich, verstehen wollen. Vor allem aber, den Leuten zuhören, die sich vertrauensvoll an meine Kanzlei wenden. Vertrauen ist alles, um eine gute Arbeit zu leisten, mehr ist nicht nötig. Vertrauen, dass jemand zuhört, versteht, Dich verteidigt. Und das ernsthafte Bemühen ist der erste Sieg. Denn Du weißt, dass alle ihr Bestes getan haben, um das Ziel zu erreichen. Es gibt kein Ziel ohne einen Weg, den man gehen muss, und letztendlich zählt, mit wem Du den Weg gegangen bist und wer dich an die Hand genommen hat. Niemand hat jemals einen Kampf allein gewonnen. In den Kampf geht man als

[25] https://www.legalmarro.com/chi-siamo (Letzter Zugriff 1.8.2024).

Gruppe und als Gruppe gewinnt man ihn. Und das sind wir: eine Gruppe von Kämpfern, die auch bei Mühen ihre Begeisterung nicht verliert. Und genau diese Kraft, Kompetenz und Begeisterung von uns allen sind unsere Besonderheit. Auch Du wirst als Teil dieser Gruppe begeistert sein [Pause] für den Teil des Weges, den Du mit uns hast gehen wollen oder müssen."

1.3. Analyse

Die extradiegetische Stimme der Anwältin kommentiert die filmischen Szenen aus dem Off und wechselt ständig zwischen der Du- und der Wir-Anredeform (hier rot markiert) hin und her. Bei der Du-Anrede lassen sich allerdings zwei verschiedene Varianten feststellen, die jeweils unterschiedliche interaktional-pragmatische Funktionen einnehmen. Als die Sprecherin eingangs das Konfuzius-Zitat und später die bewährte Maxime „Das ernsthafte Bemühen ist der erste Sieg" mit dem eigenen Berufsethos verbindet, verwendet sie das generische *Du* („Du wirst keinen einzigen Tag arbeiten. Denn Du weißt, dass alle ihr Bestes getan haben, um das Ziel zu erreichen"). Das generische *Du* wird hier funktional-äquivalent zum Indefinitpronomen *man* eingesetzt, denn neben dem selbstreferenziellen Bezug werden dadurch auch andere implizite, nicht näher bestimmte Referenten inkludiert. Im Gegensatz zu *man* wirkt aber das generische *Du* eher personalisierend, denn es ermöglicht, die potenziellen Adressaten „perspektivisch stärker in die Situation" (Stukenbrock / Bahr 2017: 150) einzubeziehen. Durch das generische *Du* und durch die Anspielung auf persönliche Wertvorstellungen, die als allgemein gültige Ansichten präsentiert werden, vermittelt die Rechtsanwältin nicht nur ihre subjektive Perspektive, sondern sie versucht, sie zustimmungsfähig zu machen. Auf diese Weise werden Konsens und Empathie mobilisiert (vgl. Stukenbrock / Bahr 2017: 171f.).

Das Personalpronomen *Du* wird zudem auch adressatendeiktisch verwendet, indem es am Ende des Videos auf die anvisierten Rezipienten (potenzielle Mandanten und künftige Mitarbeiter) bezogen wird („Auch Du wirst als Teil dieser Gruppe begeistert sein"). Hier signalisiert die vertrauliche Du-Anrede eher Informalität und kommunikative Nähe bzw. das Bestreben nach einer persönlichen Bindung sowie eine umfassende Einbeziehung der verschiedenen Anspruchsgruppen. Durch das kollektive *Wir* wird hingegen Bezug auf die Teamzugehörigkeit genommen. Die Kanzlei wird als eine sich als zusammengehörig begreifende Gruppe von Personen dargestellt, welche die Rechtsanwältin und ihre Partner und Mitarbeiter umfasst. Durch den Gebrauch des Personalpronomens *wir* kommen sowohl ein guter Teamgeist als auch ein besonderes Gemeinschaftsgefühl als professionelles Leitbild deutlich zum Ausdruck (vgl. Brewer / Gardner 1996: 87).

Berufsethos und persönliche Wertvorstellungen (hier grün markiert) werden gleich am Anfang programmatisch eingeführt. Das Video beginnt nämlich mit einer starken biographischen Note und die Rechtsanwältin legt sofort nahe, dass der Anwaltsberuf für sie eher eine Berufung als ein Beruf ist und mehr Freude als Frust bereitet. Fachliches Verstehen sowie aktives, einfühlendes Zuhören werden als notwendige Werkzeuge ihres beruflichen Handelns fokussiert und als Schlüssel zum professionellen Erfolg aufgefasst. Das wird auch visuell umgesetzt, und zwar durch die Szenen im hellen und modern ausgestatteten Kanzleibüro, wo sie mit konzentriertem Blick in das sorgfältige Lesen von Dokumenten vertieft ist und handschriftliche Notizen auf dem Whiteboard betrachtet oder lächelnd und aufmerksam ihren Mandanten zuhört oder sie berät.

Eine ganz zentrale Stellung nimmt beim Selbstporträt der Vertrauensbegriff ein (hier braun markiert). Das Lexem *Vertrauen* („fiducia") kommt im kurzen, gesprochenen Text viermal vor und wird als wertgeladenes Konzept sozusagen doppelt perspektiviert, indem es sowohl aus der Senderperspektive („Vertrauen ist alles, *um eine gute Arbeit zu leisten*, mehr ist nicht nötig") als auch aus der Empfängerperspektive aufgegriffen wird („Vertrauen, dass jemand zuhört, versteht, *dich verteidigt*").

Die Selbstprofilierung als zielstrebige und leistungsorientierte Anwältin wird mit Hilfe einer konzeptuellen Metapher, der Weg-Metapher (hier blau markiert), der das sogenannte Start-Weg-Ziel-Schema zugrunde liegt (vgl. Lakoff / Johnson 1980), veranschaulicht („Es gibt kein Ziel ohne einen Weg, den man gehen muss"). Die Weg-Metapher dient unter anderem dazu, das zweite bestimmende Thema der Videovorstellung einzuführen.

Es geht um die entscheidende Rolle der Gruppe als unterstützende und treibende Kraft für die Umsetzung eines effektiven Kanzleimanagements; das bildet ferner einen intertextuellen Verweis auf den vorgegebenen Video-Titel *Unsere Stärken* (siehe Ziffer VI.1.1).[26] Die besondere Expertise der Arbeitsgruppe wird im Video nicht explizit thematisiert. Nähere Informationen zu den spezifischen Tätigkeitsbereichen und fachlichen Kompetenzen der Rechstanwältin und ihrer Partner ist eher dem ausformulierten Text mit dem Titel *L'origine e la motivazione della collaborazione* („Ursprung und Motivation der Zusammenarbeit") zu entnehmen, der gleich unter dem Video angezeigt wird. Dadurch wird intermodale Kohärenz hergestellt und die Rezeption auf das gesamte Kommunikationsangebot gelenkt.

Ausgehend vom Leitgedanken der Gruppenstärke spannt die zweite konzeptuelle Metapher ‚der Anwaltsberuf ist ein Kampf' (im Text violett markiert) einen intratextuellen Bogen zwischen den eher subjektiv geprägten Äußerungen am Anfang („Ich wollte schon immer Anwalt werden") und den in der Kanzlei geteilten beruflichen Werten gegen Ende des Videos („Und das sind wir: eine Gruppe von Kämpfern"). Aufgrund der prinzipiellen Mehrfachadressierung können die hier ausgesprochenen professionellen Stärken, d.h. Kraft, Kompetenz und Begeisterung, sowohl als Unique Selling Proposition als auch als Unique Employment Proposition interpretiert werden (siehe Ziffer II). Die Beziehungsgestaltung, die anfangs eher implizit erfolgt, kommt in der finalen Pointe explizit zum Ausdruck und gipfelt sozusagen in einer emotionalen Klimax, und zwar in dem Versprechen, das an die potenziellen Empfänger gerichtet ist: „Auch du wirst als Teil dieser Gruppe begeistert sein [Pause] für den Teil des Weges, den du mit uns hast gehen wollen oder müssen."

Wie schon angedeutet, kommt *Vertrauen* als zentrales Hochwertwort eine besondere Bedeutung zu. Der Aufbau von Vertrauen gegenüber potenziellen Mandanten oder Mitarbeitern wird im Video nicht nur verbal, sondern vor allem multimodal realisiert, insbesondere durch das Zusammenspiel von akustischen und visuellen Gestaltungsmitteln, welche die verbale Ar-

[26] Für deutsche juristische Stellenanzeigen haben ebenfalls die Weg-Metaphorik und das Stärke-Argument hohe Relevanz; vgl. z.B. Luttermann (2017: 71ff. und 2024: 139ff.).

gumentation stützen. Die Selbstinszenierung der Rechtsanwältin als selbstbewusste und doch bescheidene Person lässt sich schon vom allerersten Auftritt an dem gepflegten und schlicht-eleganten Erscheinen (siehe Abb. 3) sowie am zielgerichteten und doch gelassenen Gehen ablesen (Im Video schreitet sie geradlinig den Weg zur Kanzlei entlang). Auch das Licht (als natürliches Sonnen- und Tageslicht bei den Außenaufnahmen und als helle Bürobeleuchtung bei den Innenaufnahmen) lässt sich als Gestaltungsmittel im Dienst der Vertrauensbildung interpretieren, indem es ermöglicht, eine Atmosphäre von Klarheit und Transparenz einerseits und von Wärme und Geborgenheit andererseits zu evozieren. Das alles entspricht den Erwartungen an eine umsichtige, ehrliche und zuvorkommende fachjuristische Vertretung.

Authentizität und Glaubwürdigkeit belegen insbesondere die Bildaufnahmen, welche die Rechtsanwältin jeweils im Freien und in den Innenräumen, allein und im Umgang mit Mitarbeitern und Mandanten bei der Ausübung ihrer Arbeit porträtieren. Denn dadurch kommen sowohl ihr Elan und Engagement im Berufsalltag als auch die analytische Sorgfalt und Einsatzbereitschaft bei der Mandantenbetreuung und Mandantenberatung zum Ausdruck. Durch die Darstellung eines positiven, partnerschaftlichen Klimas bzw. einer effizienten Zusammenarbeit bei der Ausführung von Mandantenaufträgen wird das Thema der Arbeitsgruppe bzw. der Gruppenstärke als Garantie für zufriedenstellende professionelle Leistungen und Ergebnisse somit auch visuell aufgegriffen.

Außerdem liefert die Analyse der akustisch-auditiven Ebene bedeutende Anhaltspunkte bei der Gesamtinterpretation. Analog zur Aufteilung der Bilder, die gleichzeitig Ruhe und Dynamik hervorruft, wirkt die Klaviermusik, die im Hintergrund mit atmosphärischer Funktion eingespielt wird, sanft und kraftvoll zugleich, genauso wie die Stimme der Rechtsanwältin, die angenehm tief und warm ist und daher sehr beruhigend klingt. Das vermittelt insgesamt ein Gefühl von Ruhe, Sicherheit und Verlässlichkeit, das sich ebenso vertrauensfördernd und authentisch auf die Wahrnehmung der anvisierten Adressaten auswirken soll.

2. Fallbeispiel (4) – Dr. Carlo Zaccagnini

2.1. Kontextuelle Einbettung

Das Videoportrait des italienischen Rechtsanwalts Dr. Carlo Zaccagnini stammt von der Webseite der gleichnamigen Kanzlei und ist über den Reiter *Professionisti* („Experten") abrufbar. Die dem Kanzleigründer gewidmete Unterseite zeigt oben links die Namen der Partner (mit Links zu den jeweiligen Vorstellungsseiten), in der Mitte ein Schwarz-Weiß-Brustfoto des Anwalts, das durch sein seriöses Erscheinungsbild zum visuellen Ersteindruck beiträgt, und rechts die jeweiligen Kontaktdaten und Tätigkeitsbereiche. Direkt unter dem Bild folgt ein kompakter Lebenslauf in der dritten Person Singular mit den wichtigsten Stationen der Ausbildung und des beruflichen Werdegangs. Ein Empfehlungstext (in Form eines rot markierten Zitats in Anführungszeichen – allerdings ohne Quellenangabe) rundet das ausformulierte Kurzprofil ab.[27]

Genau in der Mitte der Seite sind zwei Videos platziert: links die Selbstdarstellung des Anwalts (auf Italienisch) und rechts das Präsentationsvideo der Kanzlei (auf Englisch). In beiden kommt der Gründer und Namensgeber der Kanzlei direkt zu Wort. Im Kanzleiwerbefilm wendet sich Dr. Carlo Zaccagnini in englischer Sprache mit eingeblendeten Untertiteln an ein ausländisches Publikum. Dies soll einerseits auf die zunehmende internationale Ausrichtung der Kanzlei hinweisen und andererseits die Kompetenz des Anwalts (einschließlich seiner Englischkenntnisse) demonstrieren. Der gesprochene Text greift inhaltlich die gleichen Themen und Argumente auf, die auch im italienischen Video vorgebracht werden.

Durch verschiedene Kameraeinstellungen und Perspektivenwechsel wirkt die englische Version jedoch insgesamt wesentlich dynamischer als das eher statische italienische Video, in dem der am Schreibtisch sitzende Anwalt durchgehend nur auf Augenhöhe gefilmt wird (siehe Abb. 4). Im englischen Video wechselt die Bildsequenz ständig zwischen Außen- und Innenansichten des Kanzleisitzes und wird immer wieder das Gesprochene

---

[27] https://carlozaccagnini.it/it/professionisti/carlo-zaccagnini/ (Letzter Zugriff 1.8.2024).

durch Schnittbilder visuell unterstützt, die einzelne Momentaufnahmen aus der täglichen Teamarbeit und Mandantenbetreuung zeigen. Im unteren Bereich der Seite befindet sich eine Schaltfläche (Call-to-Action-Button) zur direkten Kontaktaufnahme mit der Kanzlei. Aufgrund der kontrastiven Zielsetzung des vorliegenden Beitrags – mit Schwerpunkt auf dem Sprachenpaar Deutsch-Italienisch (siehe Ziffer I) – soll im Folgenden nur das italienische Präsentationsvideo der Fallstudie sprachreflexiv unter die Lupe genommen werden.

Abb. 4: Dr. Carlo Zaccagnini am Schreibtisch in seiner Kanzlei

2.2. Inhalt

In der knapp zwei Minuten langen Videoaufzeichnung[28] stellt sich Dr. Carlo Zaccagnini den Adressaten mit folgendem (aus dem Italienischen ins Deutsche übersetzten) Wortlaut vor: „Guten Tag, ich bin Carlo Zaccagnini. Ich habe meine Kanzlei vor 20 Jahren gegründet. Wir beschäftigen uns ausschließlich mit Strafrecht. In ein Strafverfahren verwickelt zu werden, ist aller Wahrscheinlichkeit nach eine der schmerzlichsten Erfahrungen, die ein Mensch je erleben kann. Das Gleiche gilt, wenn man Opfer einer

[28] https://www.youtube.com/watch?v=ImCgrto7AvQ (Letzter Zugriff 1.8.2024).

Straftat wird. Unter diesen Umständen brauchen Sie einen Spezialisten mit zwei unverzichtbaren Eigenschaften. Erstens mit der Fähigkeit, jedes Dokument und jedes Ermittlungsergebnis zu deuten, das Ermittler und Polizei gegen Sie sammeln oder bereits gesammelt haben; zweitens soll der Strafverteidiger auch die Fähigkeit besitzen, zuzuhören. Er soll von Ihnen Ihre eigene und ehrliche Einschätzung des Sachverhalts hören, er soll hören, was Sie gesehen haben und was Sie direkt mit Ihren Sinnen wahrnehmen konnten. Dies ist der Punkt, an dem das Verteidigungsrecht eines jeden freien Bürgers entsteht. 90% der Justizirrtümer haben – wie die großen Autoren betonen – ihren Ursprung in der Phase der gerichtlichen Voruntersuchung. Aus diesem Grund ist es von diesem Moment an notwendig, einen Anwalt an Ihrer Seite zu haben, der sich mit dem Strafrecht befasst und nichts anderes im Auge hat als die Interessen seines Mandanten. Darum bemühen wir uns seit zwanzig Jahren, ich und meine vier Mitarbeiter. Wir werden versuchen, auch in Ihrem Fall Sie bestmöglich zu unterstützen."

2.3. Analyse

Der Rechtsanwalt, der in seinem Büro am Schreibtisch sitzt, stellt sich zunächst mit Vor- und Nachnamen vor und spricht seine Adressaten – eher höflich-distanziert – mit „Buongiorno" („Guten Tag") an. Er profiliert sich sofort – in der ersten Person Singular – als Kanzleigründer mit 20 Jahren Berufserfahrung. Wenn er dann auf die ausschließliche Spezialisierung seiner Boutique-Kanzlei hinweist, die im Strafrecht liegt, wechselt er von der Ich-Form in die Wir-Form und hebt damit implizit die Fachkompetenz im Team als besonderes Qualitätsmerkmal der Kanzlei hervor. Der Topos der ‚Arbeitsgruppe erfahrener Spezialisten' wird dann im Schlussteil – argumentativ unterstützend – wieder aufgegriffen (vgl. die violett markierten Stellen im Text).

Imagebildung und Kundenorientierung im Dienst der strategischen Positionierung erfolgen darüber hinaus meist emotionalisierend und erfahrungsbezogen. Auch hier wird die Zielgruppenansprache (im Text rot markiert) rhetorisch-argumentativ funktionalisiert. Vom eher unpersönlichen Verweis auf die erschütternde Erfahrung eines jeden, der in ein Strafverfahren verwickelt ist – sei es als Täter oder als Opfer einer Straftat –, leitet der Anwalt nahtlos zur Sie-Anrede über („eine der schmerzlichsten Erfahrungen, die ein Mensch je erleben kann [...]. Unter diesen Umständen brauchen Sie einen Spezialisten"). Damit wird der potenzielle Mandant nicht nur direkt angesprochen und in den Interaktionsraum einbezogen, sondern gleichzeitig auch als potenzieller Adressat einer einfühlsamen und persönlichen Rechtsberatung konturiert.

Sein professionelles Selbstverständnis (im Text blau markiert) kommt insbesondere im Mittelteil der Videoaufzeichnung zum Ausdruck. Hier geht der Anwalt auf die unverzichtbaren Eigenschaften ein, die seiner Meinung nach den Rechtsbeistand in einem Strafverfahren auszeichnen sollten: zum einen die fachliche Expertise zur rechtssicheren Auslegung aller Ermittlungsakten, zum anderen ein aufmerksames Zuhören bzw. ein offenes Ohr für die Sachverhaltsdarstellung des Mandanten und für seine individuellen Bedürfnisse und Anliegen („Fähigkeit, jedes Dokument und jedes Ermittlungsergebnis zu deuten [...]; zweitens soll der Strafverteidiger auch die Fähigkeit besitzen, zuzuhören"). Auch die Mandanten sollten sich ihrerseits, so Dr. Carlo Zaccagnini, der Wahrheit und Ehrlichkeit verpflichtet fühlen. Für den Anwalt ist dies die Voraussetzung für ein Vertrauensverhältnis, das weiterhin eine effiziente – und im besten Fall erfolgreiche – Strafverteidigung verspricht.

Die bisherige, primär auf Ethos und Pathos basierende Argumentation (vgl. Kreuzbauer / Gratzl / Hiebl 2007), die unter anderem von einer soliden Kenntnis der rhetorischen Mittel der forensischen Redekunst zeugt (wie etwa die kommunikative Perspektivierung vom Allgemeinen auf den Einzelfall; vgl. Mortara Garavelli 2001: 189ff.), wird im letzten Teil des Videos um ein Sachargument ergänzt, das die entscheidende Rolle einer spezialisierten Beratung im Ermittlungsverfahren konkret belegen soll (im Text braun markiert). Der Anwalt führt an, dass nach Ansicht führender Strafrechtler 90% aller Fehlurteile auf das Vorverfahren zurückzuführen seien. Dies mache die unverzügliche Beauftragung eines erfahrenen und engagierten Strafverteidigers nicht nur ratsam, sondern schlichtweg notwendig. Hier zielt die Strategie des „fachpersuasiven Kausalisierens"

(Busch 2024: 40) im Rahmen der Experten-Laien-Kommunikation offensichtlich darauf ab, Wissensasymmetrien zwischen Juristen und Laienadressaten argumentativ nutzbar zu machen. Obwohl der Anwalt keine genauen Quellen für die zitierte Prozentzahl angibt, genügt hier der bloße Hinweis auf „die großen Autoren" als Ausdruck strafrechtlicher Kompetenz und Gelehrsamkeit bzw. als argumentationsförderndes Alleinstellungsmerkmal zum Zweck des Personal Branding.

Im Video spricht Dr. Carlo Zaccagnini explizit die Wesensmerkmale des Strafverteidigerberufs an, die sein eigenes Berufsethos leiten und prägen. Damit verbunden ist das direkt ausgesprochene Versprechen, die Interessen der Mandanten in den Mittelpunkt seiner Berufspraxis zu stellen und sich um die bestmögliche Rechtsberatung im Einzelfall zu bemühen (grün markierte Stellen im Text). Die Selbstprofilierung als vertrauenswürdiger Strafrechtsexperte wird im Video mediengerecht aufbereitet und daher auch multimodal umgesetzt.

Intermodale Kohärenz lässt sich im gesamten Auftritt durch das sorgfältig abgestimmte Zusammenspiel von Körperhaltung, Mimik, Gestik, Intonation, Kleidung und Inszenierung erkennen. Der verbale Inhalt seiner Argumentation, der das Image eines seriösen und engagierten Fachjuristen vermitteln soll, spiegelt sich in der ernsten und entschlossenen Körperhaltung, dem selbstbewussten Tonfall und den energischen, ausdrucksstarken und leicht angespannten Gesten, welche die wichtigsten Passagen seiner Rede begleiten und unterstreichen, wider. Die massive und elegante Bauweise der im Video gezeigten antiken Möbel im klassischen Stil, die Teil der hochwertigen Büroeinrichtung sind (der hölzerne Schreibtisch und das Bücherregal mit zahlreichen Gesetzeskommentaren und einem umfangreichen Aktenarchiv), ist dabei nicht nur Ausdruck des sozioökonomischen Status und des guten Geschmacks. Sie soll auch die Vorstellung und die soliden Werte eines zuverlässigen und leistungsfähigen Spezialisten vermitteln, der bei der Fallbearbeitung gewissenhaft und sorgfältig arbeitet und sich der besonders anspruchsvollen Materie des Strafrechts sehr pflichtbewusst – auf der Grundlage einer langjährigen Tradition, Fachkompetenz und Erfahrung – nähert.

Auch die wenigen Objekte, die auf dem Schreibtisch hervorstechen, weisen – zumindest indirekt – auf die zentralen Aussagen des gesprochenen Textes hin und machen sie sozusagen bildlich greifbar. So ist die kleine Metallstatue eines antiken Soldaten mit Helm und Lanze nicht nur ein dekoratives Sammlerstück, das unter anderem auf die traditionsreiche Verbindung zum altrömischen Recht als Grundlage der europäischen Rechtskultur hindeutet, sondern sie illustriert auch recht plakativ die Metapher der Strafverteidigung „als Kampf um das Recht bzw. die Rechte des Beschuldigten" (Bernsmann 2013). Dadurch werden Einsatzfreude und Durchsetzungswille beim Verfolgen der Mandanteninteressen eindrücklich vermittelt. Einen impliziten Appell an den – eher aufmerksamen – Rezipienten stellen analog die vom Gebrauch etwas zerknitterten Bücher dar, die vorne auf dem Tisch liegen und bewusst so positioniert worden sind, dass sie dem Betrachter (und nicht etwa dem Anwalt zum täglichen berufsbedingten Nachschlagen) zugewandt sind. Der gut lesbare Titel des oben liegenden Bandes „Gli errori giudiziari" von Jaques Vergès, dem zeitweise international bekannten und umstrittenen französischen Anwalt, der viele aussichtslose Fälle mit Leidenschaft verteidigte (vgl. Hanimann 2013), wird hier als gezielte intermodale Anspielung auf das im gesprochenen Text vorgebrachte Sachargument, gegen „Justizirrtümer" anzukämpfen, verstanden (dazu weiter oben) und trägt somit auch entscheidend zur professionellen Imagebildung bei.

Sowohl auf visueller als auch auf sprachlicher Ebene lassen sich schließlich die Spuren einer berufsspezifischen Stereotypisierung erkennen. Die sehr elegante, formelle Kleidung des Anwalts (zweireihiger Tweed-Anzug mit passender Fliege) vermittelt nicht nur ein stilsicheres und gepflegtes professionelles Auftreten, sondern entspricht auch dem seriösen, formellen und konservativen – eher schwarz-weißen – Dresscode, der in italienischen Gerichtssälen konventionell erwartet und mit Professionalität und Ernsthaftigkeit assoziiert wird. Interessant ist in diesem Zusammenhang ebenfalls die Farbgestaltung der Webseite, die durch die ausschließliche Kombination von Schwarz-Weiß-Tönen zwar seriös und professionell wirkt, gleichzeitig aber auch einen gewissen Retro-Charme vermittelt, der ganz gezielt in das strafrechtliche Umfeld passt.

Den gesprochenen Text kennzeichnet insgesamt ein gehobenes Register. Auf der sprachlichen Mikroebene lassen sich lexikalische und syntaktische Besonderheiten (verbale Stereotype) identifizieren (wie z.B. „*essere attinti da* un procedimento penale“ oder „in questi *frangenti*“). Sie weisen auf einen tradierten, archaischen Ausdrucksvorrat hin, der sich im Laufe der Zeit in der italienischen Rechtskommunikation konventionalisiert hat und quasi zu einem Identitätszeichen des juristischen Sprachgebrauchs geworden ist. Die Verwendung dieser „Fossilien der Rechtssprache“ (Mortara Garavelli 2001: 154) zeichnet den Anwalt mithin als Mitglied der Fachgemeinschaft aus. Ob er sich aber bewusst ist, dass er dadurch die Kommunikation mit den anvisierten Laienadressaten möglicherweise erschwert, ist mittels gezielter Verstehens- und Wirkungsanalysen erst noch zu ergründen.

VII. Video-Berufsbiographien im Sprach- und Kulturvergleich

Aus der vergleichenden Analyse der hier vorgestellten Fallbeispiele lassen sich einige Tendenzen ableiten, die auf transkulturelle Gemeinsamkeiten und interkulturelle Unterschiede schließen lassen. Bei allen Selbstdarstellungen steht zunächst in den Anwaltsvideos die argumentative Vermittlung des eigenen Berufsethos im Vordergrund und weniger die Informationsvermittlung über die eigenen Tätigkeitsfelder, wie dies bei den ausformulierten Kurzprofilen auf den jeweiligen Webseiten eher der Fall ist. Als wesentlich transkulturell gilt zudem die Bezugnahme auf ein ähnliches Berufsverständnis durch die gezielte Hervorhebung bestimmter fachlicher Qualitäten (wie z.B. Kompetenz, fundierte bzw. anerkannte Fachexpertise, Erfahrung, Engagement) und persönlicher Eigenschaften (wie Pflichtbewusstsein, moralische Standfestigkeit, Ausdauer und Willensstärke), die in den untersuchten Videos als wesentliche Anforderungen an den juristischen Dienstleistungsberuf profiliert werden. Eine weitere Gemeinsamkeit bildet der Rückgriff auf tradierte Vorstellungen des Anwaltsberufs. Hier sticht vor allem die Metapher von der Rechtsverteidigung als *Kampf* bzw. vom Anwalt als *Kämpfer* ins Auge, der mit festem Durchsetzungswillen und hoher Einsatzbereitschaft versucht, die Interessen des Mandanten angemessen zu vertreten und effektiv durchzusetzen.

Der direkte Erfahrungsbezug sowie das Anknüpfen an allgemein geteilte Werte sind bewährte Argumentationsstrategien zur Konsens- und Vertrauensbildung, die alle analysierten Videoprofile kennzeichnen. Die Beziehungsgestaltung erfolgt dabei zumeist über die direkte Ansprache der Zielgruppen (vgl. Fallbeispiele 1, 2 und 4) und nur im Fallbeispiel 3 auch indirekt über die Andeutung gemeinsamer Werte- und Handlungshorizonte. Durch den Perspektivenwechsel von der dritten in die erste Person Singular oder Plural bzw. durch die Anknüpfung an eine konsensuelle Erfahrung (z.B. mit dem Indefinitpronomen *man*) wird nicht nur eine größere soziale Nähe zu den Adressaten angestrebt, sondern die Anwälte treten dadurch zugleich als verlässliche, vertrauenswürdige und gegebenenfalls mitfühlende Rechtsberater hervor.

Auch Licht und Musik bzw. die inszenierte Darstellung des Berufsalltags – einschließlich der Büroeinrichtung und Bürogegenstände sowie des äußeren Erscheinungsbildes (Kleidungsstil) der Anwälte – werden in den Videos kommunikationsstrategische Funktionen im Sinne des Personal Branding zugeschrieben. So gelten das digitale Logo und das Messingschild der Anwaltskanzlei in den Fallbeispielen 1 und 3 als Markenzeichen der beruflichen Identifizierung, Wiedererkennung und Imagebildung. Das schlichte, elegante und gepflegte Auftreten der beiden Strafjuristen in den Fallbeispielen 2 und 4 soll mithin den Eindruck von Seriosität und Professionalität vermitteln. Das wird im Bereich der Justiz von der Bevölkerung und von Mandanten besonders erwartet und vorausgesetzt. Nur im ersten deutschen Video (Fallbeispiel 1) wird das Verhältnis von Berufs- und Privatleben, das ein zentrales Anliegen im heutigen Arbeitsszenario darstellt, explizit sowohl verbal als auch visuell (z.B. durch das Zoomen auf den Ehering) thematisiert. Im ersten italienischen Video (Fallbeispiel 3) geschieht dies nur implizit visuell durch Einblicke in alltägliche Arbeitsabläufe sowie durch den Verweis auf persönliche Gegenstände auf dem offenen Büroregal. Interessanterweise wird das Thema in den Videovorstellungen der zwei Strafanwälte überhaupt nicht aufgenommen.

Zur kulturübergreifenden stereotypen Darstellung des Anwaltsberufs gehört auch der professionelle Umgang mit Akten, Gesetzesbüchern und Kommentaren, der in allen Videoaufzeichnungen gezielt in Szene gesetzt wird. Zumeist sitzen die Anwälte vor einer großen beeindruckenden Bücherwand, wenn sie in den Video-Berufsbiographien Klienten adressieren. Nur ausnahmsweise sind sie in einem eher kargen und sterilen Kanzleizimmer (wie in Fallbeispiel 1). Die Darstellung einer umfangreichen Fachbibliothek gilt in Deutschland wie in Italien als symbolischer Ausweis von Fachkompetenz und Leistungsbereitschaft. Dies entspricht nämlich der weit verbreiteten Vorstellung von der Jurisprudenz als einer hochkomplexen Materie, deren Beherrschung viel Fleiß, Selbstdisziplin und eine fundierte Belesenheit erfordert.

Interkulturelle Diskrepanzen lassen sich grundsätzlich auf die jeweils unterschiedliche Schwerpunktsetzung bei der Selbstprofilierung zurückführen. Die Vermittlung eines positiven und authentischen Berufsbildes erfolgt auf deutscher Seite grundlegend individual- und kompetenzorientiert, auf italienischer Seite eher gemeinschafts- und beziehungsorientiert. In diesem Zusammenhang fällt das weniger zugewandte (also freundlich lächelnde) Auftreten der italienischen Anwälte ins Auge, die insgesamt viel kontrollierter und beherrschter wirken als ihre deutschen Kollegen, die hingegen zuvorkommend und entspannt in die Kamera lächeln. Dies lässt sich wiederum mit der landesüblichen Auffassung in Verbindung bringen, dass die juristische Tätigkeit eine sehr ernste Angelegenheit ist. Fachliche Expertise wird in den deutschen Videos durch den Verweis auf akademische Grade (Doktortitel) und anerkannte Spezialisierungen (Fachanwaltschaft) glaubwürdig demonstriert, während in den italienischen Stichproben diese Angaben eine untergeordnete Rolle spielen. Als zentrale berufliche Werte stellen sich bei den deutschen Rechtsanwälten in erster Linie Gerechtigkeitssinn und Verantwortungsbewusstsein sowie Zielstrebigkeit und persönlicher Einsatz heraus. Bei den italienischen Anwälten stehen dagegen die Fähigkeit zum Zuhören, Ehrlichkeit und Vertrauen sowie eine ausgeprägte Teamfähigkeit deutlich im Mittelpunkt.

Kulturspezifische Tendenzen lassen sich auch im Bereich der Popularisierungsstrategien erkennen, mit denen in den untersuchten Videos eher emotionalisierend argumentiert wird. Wissensasymmetrien mit dem anvisierten Laienpublikum werden vor allem von den deutschen Anwälten explizit thematisiert, indem sie auf Alltagsbeispiele und allgemein gebräuchliche Redewendungen zurückgreifen oder versuchen, relevante juristische Fachbegriffe laienverständlich zu erklären. Dies belegt unter anderem die besondere Bedeutung, die der Popularisierung juristischen Fachwissens im deutschen Kontext beigemessen wird. Demgegenüber neigen die italienischen Rechtsanwälte weniger zu Strategien der populärwissenschaftlichen Wissensvermittlung, sondern beziehen sich eher – meist implizit – auf die anerkannte und herrschende Fachliteratur oder sie untermauern ihre Argumentation mit Zitaten führender Autoren der Rechtslehre und Rechtsphilosophie. Das bestätigt das stereotype Bild des Juristen als Hüter und Vermittler eines komplexen, weitgehend für den Laien opaken und unzugänglichen Wissens, dem im italienischen Kontext nach wie vor Respekt, Achtung, ja fast Ehrfurcht entgegengebracht wird. Es erklärt wohl auch, warum der Topos des Vertrauensverhältnisses zwischen Anwalt und Mandant so sensibel und zentral für die Argumentation der italienischen Anwälte ist. Denn sie müssen sich bei einer tendenziell misstrauischen Klientel, die durch die Komplexität des Rechts eingeschüchtert und verunsichert ist, möglichst klar, transparent und glaubwürdig akkreditieren.

Der Verweis auf das Argumentationsgeschick (als unabdingbare Kompetenz für eine erfolgreiche Strafverteidigung vor Gericht) und die Demonstration rhetorischer Gewandtheit (durch den Einsatz rhetorischer Fragen und alltagsnaher Metaphorik sowie durch den Rückgriff auf fachpersuasives Kausalisieren) deuten schließlich in den Videopräsentationen der zwei Strafverteidiger (Fallbeispiele 2 und 4) auf rechtsgebietsspezifische, kulturübergreifende Ausprägungen des Anwaltsbildes hin, die im Rahmen eines interkulturellen Vergleichs epistemischer Kulturen von besonderem Interesse sind. Auffällig ist, dass sie dieselbe Popularisierungsstrategie anwenden, indem sie zunächst erhebliche Ängste evozieren (falscher Vorwurf, Justizirrtum) und sich anschließend als ‚Retter in der Not‘ präsentieren.

VIII. Schlussbemerkungen

Der vorliegende Beitrag hat sich mit einer speziellen Form der Anwaltskommunikation befasst, und zwar mit biographischen Selbstdarstellungspraktiken von Rechtsanwälten – primär von Fachanwälten in Boutique-Kanzleien –, die das Video nutzen, um potenzielle Klienten zu adressieren. Die auf deutschen und italienischen Kanzlei-Webseiten verorteten Anwaltsvideos wurden mit Hilfe von vier Fragen sprach- und kulturvergleichend analysiert (siehe Ziffer IV). Hervorzuheben ist, dass in allen Anwaltsvideos das Visual Personal Branding eine besondere Rolle spielt. Es hat die Funktion, der Kanzlei ein sympathisches und freundliches Gesicht zu geben und Vertrauen zu erzeugen (vgl. Qyll 2021; Luttermann im Ersch.; Luttermann / Engberg 2023, 2024). Die erste Begegnung zwischen Anwalt und Mandant soll möglichst persönlich und nahbar sein und ein Gefühl von Glaubwürdigkeit hervorrufen (siehe Ziffern V bis VII). Das Medium verfügt über charakteristische kontextuelle Merkmale, um im zwischenmenschlichen Kontakt Vertrauen zu generieren. Dazu gehört, dass die Art des Kontaktes zwischen den Kommunizierenden einer face-to-face-Situation ähnelt, und zwar optisch wie akustisch.

In den nächsten Projektschritten wollen wir das Korpus vergrößern und die anwaltlichen Videovorstellungen anhand von Basisfaktoren typologisieren (siehe Ziffern III und IV). Darüber hinaus sollen die kulturspezifischen und kulturübergreifenden biographischen und berufsethischen Ausprägungen weiter bestimmt und gebündelt werden. Außerdem sollen vor allem Strategien der fachlichen Wissensvermittlung und Popularisierung sowie Verständlichkeit und Klarheit im Sprachgebrauch multiperspektivisch mit dem Rechtslinguistischen Verständlichkeitsmodell (vgl. Luttermann 2021: 111ff.) untersucht werden. Dabei spielt auch eine Rolle, wie Experten Rezeptionsprozesse aktivieren und steuern und welches Wissen sie auf Rezipientenseite voraussetzen.

Eine weitere Zielsetzung des Projekts besteht darin, dialogische Interaktionsprozesse zu fokussieren. Interaktive Elemente sind zunehmend auf den Webseiten eingepflegt, häufig in Form eines Reiters zu den Bewertungen von Kanzleileistungen oder zu Blogs (vgl. z.B. Bondi 2022; Diani 2023; Garzone 2014). Bei den Blogs interessiert uns in erster Linie, wie juristisches Fachwissen (rechtliche Konzepte, juristische Methodik usw.) dialogisch konstruiert und Bedeutung ausgehandelt wird. Dabei geht es auch um das Rechtsempfinden von Rechtslaien, welche Fragen sich ihnen dadurch stellen (etwa zu Fachtermini) und was ihre Erwartungen und Anforderungen an den Berufsstand sind. Rechtslinguistische Forschung kann mithin dazu beitragen, die Kommunikation des Rechts verständlicher zu machen und Brücken zwischen Kulturen und zwischen Menschen (hier: Rechtsanwälten und Mandanten) zu bauen.

IX. Literatur

Baldry, Anthony / Paul J. Thibault. 2005. *Multimodal Transcription and Text Analysis. A Multimedia Toolkit and Coursebook.* Equinox: London-Oakville.

Bernsmann, Klaus. 2013. *Verteidigung ist Kampf.* Vortrag auf dem 37. Strafverteidigertag Freibug. https://strafverteidigertag.de/rechtspolitik/verteidigung-ist-kampf/. Letzter Zugriff 1.8.2024.

Bolter, David / Richard Grusin. 1999. *Remediation. Understanding New Media.* Cambridge, MA: The MIT Press.

Bondi, Marina. 2022. Dialogicity in Individual and Institutional Scientific Blogs. *Publications* 10 (9), 1-20.

Brewer, Marlynn B. / Wendi Gardner. 1996. Who is this "We"? Levels of Collective Identity and Self Representations. *Journal of Personality and Social Psychology* 71, 83-93.

Busch, Albert. 2024. Fachpersuasion. Theorie, Praxis, Analyse. In: Albert Busch / Karin Luttermann (Hrsg.), *Professionskommunikation.* Hildesheim: Universitätsverlag, 39-77.

Busch, Albert / Karin Luttermann (Hrsg.). 2024. *Professionskommunikation.* Hildesheim: Universitätsverlag.

Diani, Giuliana. 2023. Stance Features in Legal Blogging. In: Patrizia Anesa / Jan Engberg (Hrsg.), *The Digital (R)Evolution of Legal Discourse.* Berlin: de Gruyter Mouton, 67-84.

Dudenredaktion. 2014. *Das Herkunftswörterbuch. Etymologie der deutschen Sprache*. 5. Auflage. Berlin: Dudenverlag.

Erll, Astrid / Ann Rigney (Hrsg.). 2009. *Mediation, Remediation, and the Dynamics of Cultural Memory*. Berlin: de Gruyter.

Garzone, Giuliana. 2014. Investigating Blawgs through Corpus Linguistics. Issues of Generic Integrity. In: Maurizio Gotti / Davide S. Giannoni (Hrsg.), *Corpus Analysis for Descriptive and Pedagogical Purposes. ESP Perspectives*. Frankfurt am Main: Lang, 167-188.

Hanimann, Joseph. 2013. Leidenschaft für die Hoffnungslosen. *Süddeutsche Zeitung*. https://www.sueddeutsche.de/politik/zum-tod-von-jacques-verges-leidenschaft-fuer-die-hoffnungslosen-1.1748058. Letzter Zugriff 1.8. 2024.

Keller, Rudi. 2009. Die Sprache der Geschäftsberichte. Was das Kommunikationsverhalten eines Unternehmens über dessen Geist aussagt. In: Christoph Moss (Hrsg.), *Die Sprache der Wirtschaft*. Wiesbaden: Springer, 19-44.

Knorr-Cetina, Karin. 1999. *Epistemic Cultures. How the Sciences make Knowledge*. Cambridge MA: Harvard University Press.

Koch, Peter / Wulf Oesterreicher. 2008. Mündlichkeit und Schriftlichkeit von Texten. In: Nina Janich (Hrsg.), *Textlinguistik. 15 Einführungen*. Tübingen: Narr, 199-215.

Kreuzbauer, Günther / Norbert Gratzl / Ewald Hiebl. 2007. Einleitung. In: Günther Kreuzbauer / Norbert Gratzl / Ewald Hiebl (Hrsg.), *Persuasion und Wissenschaft. Aktuelle Fragestellungen von Rhetorik und Argumentationstheorie*. Wien: LIT, 1-5.

Lakoff, George / Mark Johnson. 1980. *Metaphors we Live by*. Chicago: University of Chicago Press.

Liebert, Wolf-Andreas. 2016. Wissenskulturen. In: Ludwig Jäger / Werner Holly / Peter Krapp / Samuel Weber (Hrsg.), *Sprache – Kultur – Kommunikation. Ein internationales Handbuch zu Linguistik als Kulturwissenschaft / Language – Culture – Communication. An International Handbook of Linguistics as a Cultural Discipline*. Berlin: de Gruyter Mouton, 578-586.

Lombardi, Alessandra. 2024. Stellenanzeigen im Sprach- und Kulturkontrast. Zur fachkommunikativen Komplexität juristischer Stellenangebote als kulturbedinge Handlungspraktiken. In: Albert Busch / Karin Luttermann (Hrsg.), *Professionskommunikation*. Hildesheim: Universitätsverlag, 149-170.

Lombardi, Alessandra / Karin Luttermann. 2023. Legal Specialists Telling their Stories on the Internet. A Comparative Analysis of Professional Self-Portrayals on German and Italian Law Firm Websites. In: Patrizia Anesa / Jan Engberg (Hrsg.), *The Digital (R)evolution of Legal Discourse. New Genres, Media, and Linguistic Practices*. Berlin: de Gruyter Mouton, 53-66.

Luttermann, Karin. 1996. *Gesprächsanalytisches Integrationsmodell am Beispiel der Strafgerichtsbarkeit*. Münster: Lit.

Luttermann, Karin. 2017. „Unsere Stärke: *Sie*!". Zielgruppenansprache und Textbausteine in Stellenanzeigen als ein Konzept von Werbung. In: Martin Nielsen / Karin Luttermann / Magdalène Lévy-Tödter (Hrsg.), *Stellenanzeigen als Instrument des Employer Branding in Europa. Interdisziplinäre und kontrastive Perspektiven*. Wiesbaden: Springer VS, 55-80.

Luttermann, Karin. 2018. Kommunikativ-funktionale Analyse von werbenden Gebrauchstexten in der Wirtschaft. In: Kerstin Kazzazi / Karin Luttermann / Sabine Wahl / Thomas Fritz (Hrsg.), *Worte über Wörter*. Tübingen: Stauffenburg, 301-318.

Luttermann, Karin. 2021. Klare Sprache für eine verständliche Kommunikation im Rechtsbereich. Ein handlungspragmatischer Ansatz. In: Karin Luttermann / Albert Busch (Hrsg.), *Sprache und Recht. Konstitutions- und Transferprozsesse in nationaler und europäischer Dimension*. Berlin: Lit, 101-132.

Luttermann, Karin. 2024. Personalwerbung in Stellenanzeigen. Ein textpragmatischer Zugang. In: Albert Busch / Karin Luttermann (Hrsg.), *Professionskommunikation*. Hildesheim: Universitätsverlag, 121-148.

Luttermann, Karin. Im Ersch. Texte als kulturelle Entitäten. Eine handlungstheoretisch-qualitative Analyse von Stellenanzeigen im Recht. In: Hanna Acke / Nikola Vujčić (Hrsg.), *Sprache – Kultur – Kommunikation*. Hamburg: Lang.

Luttermann, Karin / Jan Engberg. 2017. Kulturkontrastive deutsch-dänische Textanalyse von sprachlichen Handlungen in juristischen Stellenanzeigen. In: Martin Nielsen / Karin Luttermann / Magdalène Lévy-Tödter (Hrsg.), *Stellenanzeigen als Instrument des Employer Branding in Europa. Interdisziplinäre und kontrastive Perspektiven*. Wiesbaden: Springer VS, 107-131.

Luttermann, Karin / Jan Engberg. 2023. Erklärvideos und Broschüren als Information und Mittel zum Aufbau von Verständlichkeit und Vertrauen – eine Fallstudie. In: Karin Luttermann / Jan Engberg (Hrsg.), *Popularisierung als Methode der Wissensvermittlung in der Rechtslinguistik / Popularisation as a Method of Knowledge Mediation in Legal Linguistics*. Berlin: Lit, 99-130.

Luttermann, Karin / Jan Engberg. 2024. Verständlichkeit und Vertrauen durch Popularisierung am Beispiel des Erbrechts. In: Pavla Schäfer / Milena Beloševič (Hrsg.), *Sprache und Vertrauen. Facetten der linguistischen und interdisziplinären Vertrauensforschung*. Berlin: de Gruyter, 165-183.

Mortara Garavelli, Bice. 2001. *Le parole e la giustizia. Divagazioni grammaticali e retoriche su testi giuridici italiani.* Torino: Einaudi.

Nielsen, Martin / Karin Luttermann / Magdalène Lévy-Tödter (Hrsg.). 2017. *Stellenanzeigen als Instrument des Employer Branding in Europa. Interdisziplinäre und kontrastive Perspektiven*. Wiesbaden: Springer VS.

Pöckel, Wolfgang. 1999. Kontrastive Textologie. In: Sylvia Reinart / Michael Schreiber (Hrsg.), *Sprachvergleich und Übersetzen – Französisch und Deutsch. Akten der gleichnamigen Sektion des ersten Kongresses des Franko-Romanistenverbandes (Mainz, 24.-26. September 1998)*. Bonn: Romanistischer Verlag, 295-302.

Qyll, Nicholas. 2021. *Visual Person Branding. Eine frame-analytische Betrachtung ikonischer Personenmarken*. Köln: Herbert von Halem Verlag.

Rolf, Eckard. 1993. *Die Funktionen der Gebrauchstextsorten*. Berlin: de Gruyter.

Rossbach, Oliver. 2019. Boutique-Kanzleien. Mit Spezialisierung zum Erfolg. In: Claudia Schieblon (Hrsg.), *Kanzleimanagement in der Praxis. Einführung und Management für Kanzleien und Wirtschaftsprüfer*. 4. Auflage. Wiesbaden: Springer Gabler, 69-82.

Schieblon, Claudia. 2019. Management in Kanzleien. In: Claudia Schieblon (Hrsg.), *Kanzleimanagement in der Praxis. Einführung und Management für Kanzleien und Wirtschaftsprüfer*. 4. Auflage. Wiesbaden: Springer Gabler, 1-12.

Stöckl, Hartmut. 2012. Werbekommunikation semiotisch. In: Nina Janich (Hrsg.), *Handbuch Werbekommunikation*. Tübingen: UTB, 243-262.

Stöckl, Hartmut. 2016. Multimodalität. Semiotische und textlinguistische Grundlagen. In: Nina-Maria Klug / Hartmut Stöckl (Hrsg.), *Handbuch Sprache im multimodalen Kontext*. Berlin: de Gruyter, 3-35.

Stukenbrock, Anja / Cornelia Bahr. 2017. Zur kommunikativen Leistung des generischen „du"-Gebrauchs in der sozialen Interaktion. In: Angelika Linke / Juliane Schröter (Hrsg.), *Sprache und Beziehung*. Berlin: de Gruyter, 149-182.

Stumpf, Marcus. 2017. Employer Branding versus Consumer Branding. (Stellen-)Anzeigen im Vergleich. In: Martin Nielsen / Karin Luttermann / Magdalène Lévy-Tödter (Hrsg.), *Stellenanzeigen als Instrument des Employer Branding in Europa. Interdisziplinäre und kontrastive Perspektiven*. Wiesbaden: Springer VS, 81-103.

Zhao, Jin. 2011. Kulturspezifik, Inter- und Transkulturalität von Textsorten. In: Stephan Habscheid (Hrsg.), *Textsorten, Handlungsmuster, Oberflächen*. Berlin: de Gruyter, 123-143.

Alida Maria Silletti

Les marqueurs introduisant un «ailleurs» discursif dans les publications de l'UE destinées au grand public, aux adolescents et aux enfants

Abstract

Cette recherche porte sur certains marqueurs parenthétiques de reprise interprétative (Murât / Cartier-Bresson 1987; Vassiliadou 2008; Gomez-Jordana / Anscombre 2015) introduisant une réflexion sur le dire et le dit: *c'est-à-dire*, *autrement dit*, *à savoir*, *en d'autres termes*, *soit*, *ou*. Afin de vérifier leur rôle en co(n)texte, nous analyserons trois publications / brochures de l'UE, adressées au grand public, aux adolescents et aux enfants, respectivement. Après avoir relevé la fréquence de ces outils, nous nous pencherons sur leur portée syntaxique et sémantico-pragmatique en nous appuyant sur la nature morphologique des segments A et B et sur leur relation sémantique par le biais des outils susmentionnés. Nous examinerons en particulier l'équivalence et la caractérisation, qui permettent aux sujets auteurs des trois ouvrages de définir, d'expliquer, de préciser ou de simplifier des contenus spécialisés à leurs destinataires, d'où leur reformulation et paraphrase. Nous nous intéresserons ainsi à la distinction entre langage ordinaire et terminologie technique (domaine juridique) en comparant la manière dont les mêmes sujets sont abordés en vue d'atteindre des publics différents, alternant la terminologie juridique de l'UE et les mots et expressions d'emploi commun correspondants.

This research deals with some parenthetic connectives of reformulation and interpretation (cf. Murât / Cartier-Bresson 1987; Vassiliadou 2008; Gomez-Jordana / Anscombre 2015) concerning a reflection on: *c'est-à-dire*, *autrement dit*, *à savoir*, *en d'autres termes*, *soit*, *ou*. In order to verify their role in co(n)text, the analysis will be focused on three publications by the EU addressed to adults, adolescents and children, respectively. After showing the frequency of these tools, attention will be paid to their syntactic and semantico-pragmatic values by taking into account A and B segments and their semantic relation *via* these tools. In particular, equivalence and characterisation will be examined, by which the authors may define, explain, specify or simplify specialised contents to the addressees by reformulations and paraphrases. Hence, we will focus on the distinction between ordinary language and legal technical terminology in the three books by comparing the way in which each subject is presented in order to target different audiences and by comparing EU legal terminology with the corresponding ordinary words and expressions.

I. Introduction

Cet article s'intéresse à certains outils de reformulation et de paraphrase visant à marquer un «ailleurs» discursif (Authier-Revuz 1984) au sein de trois publications rédigées et diffusées par l'UE *via* son site web à l'égard de trois cibles différentes: le grand public, les adolescents (15 ans et plus) et les enfants (9-12 ans). Notre but consistera à relever la présence des marqueurs parenthétiques de reprise interprétative de «dire», à savoir *autrement dit/ dit autrement*, *en d'autres termes*, *c'est-à-dire*, et des marqueurs qui introduisent, plus en général, une dénomination autre même par une explication de celle-ci. Tel est le cas d'*à savoir*, et d'*ou* et de *soit* d'équivalence. Deux relations sémantiques principales seront envisagées pour l'ensemble de ces marqueurs, l'équivalence et la caractérisation. Celles-ci s'inscrivent dans la volonté des rédacteurs des trois publications d'identifier en vue de définir, d'expliquer, de préciser ou de simplifier des contenus considérés comme spécialisés, en les reformulant et en les paraphrasant.

Les trois publications qui font l'objet de cette étude sont disponibles dans toutes les langues de l'UE, mais nous analyserons leur version française. Elles se différencient par cible ainsi que par contenus présentés: *Comment fonctionne l'Union européenne – Guide des institutions européennes à l'usage des citoyens* s'adresse au grand public; *L'Union européenne. Sa fonction et ses activités* vise les adolescents; *À la découverte de l'Europe!*

est destinée aux enfants. Nous imaginons que les thèmes abordés ont une influence tant sur les marqueurs de reformulation et de paraphrase introduisant un «ailleurs» discursif, et sur la relation sémantique qu'ils expriment, que sur les segments à définir, préciser, expliquer, simplifier.

Notre cadre théorique de référence s'appuie sur les travaux de Jacqueline Authier-Revuz (1984, 1995, 2020) à propos de la représentation du discours autre et sur les études sur la reformulation et la paraphrase (Fuchs 1982; 1994) au niveau des marqueurs (Gülich / Kotschi 1983; Murât / Cartier-Bresson 1987; Kleiber 1994; Authier-Revuz 1995; Vassiliadou 2008, 2013, 2017, 2019; Mongi 2009; Gomez-Jordana / Anscombre 2015). L'intérêt de mener cette recherche dans le cadre de la vulgarisation relève d'une intention plus générale de continuer à nous intéresser[1] de la manière dont le sujet vulgarisateur de discours de transmission de connaissances, notamment scientifiques et juridiques, s'emploie à rendre leurs contenus plus compréhensibles pour atteindre un public de plus en plus vaste. Or, si les signes graphiques et de ponctuation sont sans doute parmi les outils les plus immédiats et les plus fréquents,[2] la reformulation et la paraphrase *via* des marqueurs *ad hoc* explicites méritent également à notre avis d'être prises en compte surtout lorsque les destinataires appartiennent à des tranches d'âge différentes et sont mus par des exigences différentes en termes de connaissances déjà acquises, d'approche et d'intérêt à l'égard d'un texte écrit portant sur tel ou tel sujet.

Ainsi, notre but est d'analyser les «ailleurs» (Authier-Revuz 1984) par rapport au discours, interférant dans le fil du discours par le biais d'un point d'hétérogénéité qui, dans le corpus à examiner, relève d'une langue technique[3] différant de celle de rédaction du texte ou d'un autre discours, dont

---

[1] Voir, à ce propos, Silletti (2014) sur l'emploi des signes graphiques de reformulation dans le discours de vulgarisation scientifique, et Silletti (2018) pour une étude des marqueurs de reformulation et paraphrase dans le discours de vulgarisation de l'UE pour le grand public.

[2] On ne peut pas exclure que des raisons techniques et éditoriales, telles que des contraintes d'espace et de caractères, mènent les sujets auteurs à se servir de ces outils.

[3] Suivant Authier-Revuz (1984: 103f.), ces «ailleurs» peuvent concerner une autre langue, un autre registre discursif, un autre discours, une autre modalité de prise de sens, un autre mot, ou un autre sujet interlocuteur.

les concepts ou les termes employés demandent une reformulation pour qu'ils soient mieux compris par leurs destinataires.

II. Le corpus

Notre corpus est composé de trois brochures rédigées par la Commission européenne au sujet de l'UE, de ses institutions et de son fonctionnement, à l'usage de publics différents. *À la découverte de l'Europe!*, qui s'adresse à des enfants scolarisés entre la fin de l'enseignement primaire et le début de l'enseignement secondaire, porte sur une présentation générale de l'UE sous plusieurs aspects: son histoire; ses institutions et partenaires; ses enjeux futurs, avec en plus – ce qui est la partie la plus étendue – les caractéristiques naturelles, artistiques et géopolitiques des pays membres de l'UE. En effet, comme l'introduction le souligne, l'idée est d'entreprendre «un voyage plein d'aventures à travers le temps et l'espace» (p. 3) pour découvrir ce qu'il y a d'intéressant dans les pays de l'UE.

Les deux autres publications sont présentées comme des guides, l'attention étant plutôt focalisée sur les institutions européennes, notamment leur fonctionnement et leurs activités. Si *Comment fonctionne l'Union européenne – Guide des institutions européennes à l'usage des citoyens* «expliqu[e] le processus d'élaboration de la législation européenne avant de décrire plus en détail chacune des institutions de l'UE, ainsi que les agences et organes qui les soutiennent» (p. 3), *L'Union européenne. Sa fonction et ses activités* se compose de trois sections autour d'une présentation de l'UE, de ses domaines d'activité et des actions entreprises ou à entreprendre.

Puisque ces trois publications visent avant tout à faire connaître l'UE, ses institutions et ses pays membres, il est indispensable que les informations véhiculées soient tirées de sources fiables et constamment mises à jour au fur et à mesure que des changements interviennent (tel est le cas, à titre d'exemple, du nombre de pays de l'UE, des résultats des élections, des noms des représentants des institutions européennes). À ce propos, nous avons choisi leurs versions les plus récentes.[4]

	Destinataires	Nombre de pages	Nombre de mots
Comment fonctionne l'Union européenne – Guide des institutions européennes à l'usage des citoyens (2014)	Grand public	44	20 169
L'Union européenne. Sa fonction et ses activités (2019)	15 ans et plus	64	27 020
À la découverte de l'Europe! (2020)	9-12 ans	56	13 396

Tab. 1: Présentation du corpus

Le Tableau 1 montre que les trois brochures sont assez homogènes par nombre de pages (54-55 en moyenne) ainsi que, dans les deux premiers cas, par nombre de mots (20 169 *vs* 27 020). Quant à elle, *À la découverte de l'Europe!* se compose de moins de mots en raison du fait que les informations présentées y sont moins denses, mais surtout qu'elles sont enrichies d'illustrations pouvant ainsi mieux capter l'attention et faciliter la compréhension des enfants. Toutes les publications examinées sont cependant des «iconotextes» (Maingueneau 2015) mélangeant une partie langagière et une partie visuelle en proportion variable.[5]

III. La reformulation paraphrastique et ses marqueurs

L'étude des marqueurs de reformulation, au-delà de son application à des domaines distincts, suppose la prise en compte de la réflexivité métalangagière. Suivant Authier-Revuz (2020), la présente recherche s'inscrit dans les aspects spécifiques du fonctionnement des opérations métalangagières

---

4 Nous faisons notamment référence à avril 2020.

5 Pour une étude des relations entre éléments iconiques et textuels, nous renvoyons à Kress / van Leeuwen (1996).

fondamentales. Pour qu'il y ait un acte d'énonciation autre, une formulation «autre» du segment A, le «reformulé», par un segment B, le «reformulant», qui lui est sémantiquement équivalent, doit avoir lieu. Cette «image-substitut» (Authier-Revuz 2020: 200) est le résultat d'une reformulation paraphrastique. Dans ce cas, on a affaire à une relation de substituabilité par équivalence de sens entre deux séquences,[6] ce qui permet de rendre compte aussi bien de la compréhension, de la production et du choix entre toutes les formulations possibles que du point de vue de celui qui en est l'auteur, qui donne son jugement métalinguistique.

Si donc une reformulation suppose une formulation seconde que le sujet locuteur s'approprie (Loffler-Laurian 1984) et qui engendre une synonymie des deux expressions dans le contexte où elles apparaissent (Romero 2009), l'équivalence sémantique qui en résulte peut se manifester sous des formes différentes à partir d'un noyau sémantique commun pour les expressions linguistiques reliées (Fuchs 1982; Eshkol-Taravella / Grabar 2014). Des notions proches de et / ou associées à celle de reformulation sont ainsi celle de paraphrase (Fuchs 1982), présupposant une équivalence sémantique exacte entre A et B, mais également la glose (Steuckardt 2005), concernant un commentaire pour définir l'unité lexicale préalable, en A; la reprise (Vion 2006), consistant en une répétition assortie d'une modification des propos précédents; et encore le commentaire métalinguistique, l'ajout et la réinterprétation (Vassiliadou 2019). Ces notions comportent d'une part un flou terminologique (Vassiliadou 2019), d'autre part une formulation différente, non identique, du segment B par rapport à A.

Suivant Vassiliadou (2019), dans le cadre des discours de transmission de connaissances pour un public non expert, la reformulation[7] est une formulation effectuée une autre fois et le cas échéant autrement dans une visée d'éclaircissement et d'explicitation d'un propos antérieur sans pour autant

---

[6] La relation de substituabilité distingue, entre autres, la reformulation paraphrastique de la catégorisation métalangagière par le biais d'une nomination du fait de dire (Authier-Revuz 2020: 226).

[7] Nous renvoyons à Landolsi / Svensson / Norén (2019) pour la présentation des différentes définitions de la reformulation.

le répéter ou le confondre avec le premier segment (Riegel / Tamba 1987), pour exprimer une équivalence de sens. De même, en nous alignant sur Gülich / Kotschi (1983) et Rossari (1994, entre autres), nous distinguons deux types de reformulation. D'un côté, une reformulation paraphrastique, caractérisée par une équivalence sémantique entre les deux segments reformulés, sans changement de perspective énonciative, où les marqueurs reformulants peuvent apparaître – parmi lesquels *c'est-à-dire*, *autrement dit*, *en d'autres termes* – ou faire défaut – ce manque est alors comblé par des marqueurs (typo)graphiques. De l'autre côté, une reformulation non paraphrastique, où le sujet locuteur s'éloigne davantage de son discours initial et le connecteur reformulant – comme *en somme*, *enfin*, *de toute façon* – marque un changement de perspective énonciative, là où, au contraire, son absence empêche toute reformulation. Notre analyse ne portera que sur la reformulation paraphrastique pour étudier la nature du marqueur de reformulation, le rapport entre les deux formulations A et B et les informations véhiculées par celles-ci.

1. Les marqueurs en *dire* et en *dit*

Parmi les marqueurs introduisant une reformulation paraphrastique, nous examinerons *c'est-à-dire*, *à savoir*, *autrement dit*, *en d'autres termes*, *soit* et *ou* (pour ces deux derniers, relativement à leur valeur d'équivalence). Si l'ensemble de ces outils partage et sous-tend une reprise par un renvoi anaphorique, dans *c'est-à-dire* et *à savoir* ce renvoi est exprimé par *ce* – *à savoir* résultant d'une réduction de *c'est à savoir*, désormais littéraire (Vassiliadou 2008), et étant ainsi très proche, même dans sa formulation, de *c'est-à-dire* (Steuckardt 2006). Pour autant, aussi bien *c'est-à-dire* qu'*autrement dit* (dont l'élément anaphorique est en *autre(s)*, comme pour *en d'autres termes*) partagent le fait d'être des «marqueurs du dire»: ils recèlent le verbe «dire» (Gomez-Jordana / Anscombre 2015) et ils comportent une réflexion sur le «dire» et sur le «dit» (Authier-Revuz 1995), respectivement. Au-delà de cette parenté sémantique, en raison de la diffusion très élevée de *dire* en français, ces outils ne sont pas seulement des marqueurs de reformulation mais aussi des marqueurs de discours dont les emplois relèvent du contexte où ils figurent, tout comme des éléments et des lexèmes qui sont reliés d'un point de vue sémantico-grammatical.

Si, suivant Choul (1985), parmi les «fonctions classiques» (p. 95) de *c'est-à-dire*, figurent, entre autres, l'explication, la précision, la qualification sous forme d'équivalence connotée et la définition,[8] Murât / Cartier-Bresson (1987) attribuent à *c'est-à-dire* une fonction dialogique due à un besoin commun aux sujets locuteurs d'inter-locution et d'inter-compréhension, d'où des reprises, un rephrasage, une reformulation sous-tendant ce qui est repris. Le déictique «ce», indiquant une relation spatio-temporelle avec un antécédent (Kleiber 1994), le présentatif «c'est» et *dire* permettent à cet outil issu du latin,[9] composé d'éléments très fréquents dans le lexique français, d'exprimer l'explication. À partir du modèle latin, sa morphologie est due au figement de morphèmes grammaticaux et lexicaux pourvus d'une liaison structurelle interne élevée (Vassiliadou 2013). Murât / Cartier-Bresson (1987) remarquent également que la structure «*c'est à* + INF» est une forme de déonticité proche du modal «devoir» renvoyant à une norme d'expression connue et partagée par les sujets interlocuteurs.

Dans ces cas, *c'est-à-dire* introduit, dans B, une reprise de A. Pour autant, puisque A est «une manière (telle ou telle) de dire (B)», donc proche de la valeur d'équivalence et d'identité (Rey-Debove 1978), *c'est-à-dire* peut partager cette valeur avec *autrement dit*, avec *ou* d'équivalence (Tamba 1987), mais aussi avec *soit* pour signaler des équivalences métalinguistiques avec une commutation des termes en vue de les expliciter. Vassiliadou (2013) qualifie cette valeur de *c'est-à-dire*[10] d'«identico-équationnelle» (p. 3):[11] elle figure dans les marqueurs du même type d'autres langues romanes à partir des deux verbes «dire» et «être» et de la réutilisa-

[8] Choul (1985) fait également mention de la fonction de rectification, qui ne fera pour autant pas l'objet de notre étude.

[9] Vassiliadou (2013) souligne que les premières attestations de *c'est-à-dire* remontent au XVIIe siècle dans les dictionnaires du français.

[10] Lorsqu'elle traite de ce marqueur, Vassiliadou (2008, 2013, 2017) fait référence tant à *c'est-à-dire* qu'à *c'est-à-dire que*.

[11] Comme Vassiliadou (2013) le remarque, cet emploi de *c'est-à-dire* est répertorié dès le XIIe siècle pour introduire des gloses explicatives ou définitionnelles, entre autres, dans la Bible.

tion de morphèmes grammaticaux et lexicaux déjà présents dans la langue. Relativement à cette valeur d'équivalence de *c'est-à-dire* (et des autres marqueurs de reformulation examinés), Vassiliadou (2008) distingue les cas où *c'est-à-dire* introduit une véritable reformulation[12] de ceux où il signale une argumentation[13] ou précise une fonction.[14]

Cette auteure attribue à ce marqueur également une valeur d'identification: dans ce cas, *c'est-à-dire* introduit des définitions «intermédiaires» pouvant prendre la forme de gloses et se situant entre les définitions directes – les énoncés définitoires copulatifs (désormais EDC) (Riegel 1987) – et les gloses introduites par des marqueurs typographiques (Rebeyrolle 2005). Si en gros *c'est-à-dire* et *autrement dit* entrent dans un processus de définition, *c'est-à-dire* précise et restreint parmi plusieurs référents celui qui est le plus concret, correspondant à la définition en extension (Murât / Cartier-Bresson 1987)[15] et à une caractérisation de l'objet par sa décomposition en éléments plus petits (Loffler-Laurian 1983). En revanche, dans ce cas *autrement dit* créerait plutôt un dialogisme, exclu par rapport à *c'est-à-dire*. Même si, d'un point de vue syntaxique, *c'est-à-dire* est intégré dans la phrase, il peut porter, comme *autrement dit*, sur la reformulation d'éléments qui ont ou n'ont pas la même nature (contrairement à *ou*), voire sur des syntagmes plus complexes et sur d'entières propositions et phrases. Quant à leur position dans le discours, Vassiliadou (2008) souligne qu'*autrement dit* a tendance à résumer et ainsi à conclure un discours, contrairement à *c'est-à-dire*.

---

[12] On rappelle, à ce propos, l'exemple «C'est une zoonose, c'est-à-dire une maladie transmissible de l'animal à l'homme» (Vassiliadou 2008: 2), relevant d'une définition. Pour autant, dans cet emploi *c'est-à-dire* peut également introduire une paraphrase, une explication ou une exemplification.

[13] Tel est le cas de «Vous avez voté pour Le Pen, c'est-à-dire que vous acceptez sa politique» (Vassiliadou 2008: 2).

[14] Dans un exemple tel que «Le Président de la République, c'est-à-dire Jacques Chirac, a annoncé que les impôts baisseront en 2004» (Vasssiliadou 2008: 2).

[15] Les auteurs proposent l'exemple «Les langues romanes, c'est-à-dire le français, l'italien, etc., sont dérivées du latin» (Murât / Cartier-Bresson 1987: 12), là où *autrement dit* ne peut pas commuter avec *c'est-à-dire*.

Plus en détail, *autrement dit* relève de la médiativité:[16] il fait référence à une source de savoir qui diffère du sujet locuteur lui-même, à la mise en scène d'une altérité, à la présentation d'une autre nomination de A (Steuckhardt 2006), témoignée par *autre* (Mongi 2009) et commune aux cas où *autrement* est utilisé.[17] En tant que locution adverbiale, d'un point de vue syntaxique *autrement dit* (il en va de même pour *en d'autres termes*) peut introduire une proposition entière et être détaché de A par un point ou bien reformuler des éléments de nature même différente, des syntagmes plus complexes, d'entières propositions voire des phrases (Vassiliadou 2008). En termes sémantiques, *autrement dit* instaure une polysémie faible par rapport aux deux segments qu'il relie, d'où son inscription dans les «marqueurs de glose à métaterme, […] qui explicitent la nature métadiscursive de l'opération de glose par la présence d'un métaterme» (Steuckhardt 2006: 12).

2. Les autres marqueurs: convergences et différences

Le fait d'indiquer une autre nomination, une manière autre de poser A, permet aussi bien à *autrement dit* qu'à *en d'autres termes* de se différencier de *c'est-à-dire*, qui est plus neutre car il ne porte pas sur une altération du dire. Ainsi les deux premiers marqueurs peuvent-ils figurer en début de phrase pour reformuler un propos antérieur, souvent pour introduire une paraphrase conclusive, contrairement à *c'est-à-dire* (et à *à savoir*), qui apparaissent généralement au sein de la phrase pour reformuler immédiatement ce qui précède par une paraphrase explicative (Vassiliadou 2008). À cet égard, seuls *c'est-à-dire* et *à savoir* introduisent une spécification,

[16] On entend, par «médiativité», les sources de l'information qui sont véhiculées par un énoncé et la manière dont le sujet locuteur accède tant à ces sources qu'à cette information (Anscombre 2014: 8).

[17] Mongi (2009) identifie deux emplois principaux d'*autrement* en français contemporain comme marqueur unique, que nous rapprochons en termes sémantiques également aux cas où *autrement* se combine avec *dire*, dont *autrement dit* et *soit dit autrement*.

l'apport d'une information supplémentaire,[18] alors qu'*autrement dit* et *en d'autres termes* indiquent une manière équivalente ou «autre» de A.

Toutefois, ces quatre marqueurs peuvent commuter, chacun avec ses propres spécificités, pour combler un manque de référence temporelle par une identification plus complète (*c'est-à-dire*), par une spécification d'information vague (*à savoir*), ou par une information posée autrement (*autrement dit* et *en d'autres termes*).[19] Un autre cas de commutation de ces quatre marqueurs, auxquels il est possible d'ajouter *soit*, se vérifie lorsque A et B disent la même chose mais sous une formulation différente due au référent plutôt qu'au mot: tel est le cas des chiffres exprimés en nombres ou en pourcentages. Vassiliadou (2008) souligne également qu'*en d'autres termes* peut reformuler deux termes ou une proposition. Il peut même sous-entendre *dit en d'autres termes*, dont il serait une forme elliptique. Les contextes d'emploi d'*en d'autres termes* sont ainsi moins nombreux que ceux des autres marqueurs.

Pour sa part, *à savoir* appartient aux marqueurs de glose à métaterme (comme *c'est-à-dire*): il établit une équivalence sémantique entre A et B, mais *c'est-à-dire* se situe du côté de l'émission et comporte une nomination (en témoigne *dire*), tandis qu'*à savoir*, renfermant *savoir*, se place du côté de la réception et engendre une interprétation. De plus, ce dernier tend à introduire une nouvelle information alors que *c'est-à-dire* instaure une identité entre des savoirs déjà acquis par les sujets interlocuteurs (Vassiliadou 2008).

Quant à *ou* d'équivalence, l'étude de Tamba (1987) s'appuie sur l'analyse de Rey-Debove (1978: 49ff.) sur les «différenciateurs métalinguistiques entre des référents identiques différemment nommés», parmi lesquels cette dernière auteure cite *c'est-à-dire*, *autrement dit* et *ou*. Le terme introduit par *ou* peut être soit plus connu que le segment A, et dans ce cas on aura

---

[18] L'exemple proposé par Vassiliadou (2008: 9) est «Je suis né en Alsace, c'est-à-dire / à savoir à Schiltigheim pour être plus précis».

[19] L'exemple présenté est «Les manœuvres de Spirit doivent commencer cinq jours après son atterrissage, *c'est-à-dire* le 9 janvier» (Vassiliadou 2008: 9), où *à savoir*, *autrement dit* et *en d'autres termes* seraient possibles.

affaire à une glose, soit ressortir d'un domaine technique – la visée d'*ou* sera alors didactique, allant du terme connu vers ce qui relève d'un langage spécialisé. Dans ces cas, *ou* peut commuter avec *c'est-à-dire* et *autrement dit* pour introduire une équivalence entre les deux segments A et B. Pour autant, *ou* d'équivalence présente des restrictions morphosyntaxiques plus fortes que les deux autres marqueurs: il relie généralement des syntagmes nominaux, y compris les sigles; le terme en B est généralement en usage, par ailleurs dépourvu de déterminant; lorsque B est entre parenthèses, *ou* y est facultatif[20] (Tamba 1987).

En termes sémantiques, les deux segments reliés par *ou* peuvent être considérés comme des synonymes, mais leur valeur informative est différente car seulement l'une des deux appellations est connue par le sujet interlocuteur. De par cette valeur d'équivalence sémantique, *ou* peut relier deux dénominations de langues différentes (Tamba 1987).

3. Bilan provisoire

Pour résumer, nous empruntons à Steuckardt (2006) son classement des «marqueurs de glose à métaterme», parmi lesquels figurent *c'est-à-dire*, *à savoir*, *autrement dit* et *en d'autres termes*. D'un point de vue sémiotique, ces marqueurs portent sur le nom de signifié; d'un point de vue syntaxique, B est toujours lié à A par coordination et figure en mention; d'un point de vue pragmatique, la nouvelle nomination introduite par ces marqueurs concerne une équivalence par rapport à la première nomination. Ces quatre marqueurs, auxquels on peut ajouter *ou* d'équivalence et *soit* dans le même emploi, expriment donc une équivalence à la portée variable qui dépend de variations de la nomination inter- ou intralinguistiques, du système idéologique du sujet locuteur, ou encore d'aspects pragmatiques (Steuckardt 2006).

---

[20] Voici un exemple résumant l'ensemble de ces remarques: «on endort (ou «anesthésie») le patient» (Tamba 1987: 19).

IV. Analyse du corpus

Dans la transmission de connaissances spécialisées à un public non expert, toute reprise et / ou reformulation visent à une meilleure intelligibilité de A par le biais de sa reformulation (sous forme de définition/ explication, de paraphrase, d'exemplification, d'appellation autre) *via* B. Le sujet vulgarisateur doit adapter et orienter son dire vers ses destinataires, à savoir un public hétérogène qui veut se renseigner sur un domaine qu'il ne maîtrise pas ou pas entièrement en vue d'accroître ses connaissances. Tel est le cas des trois brochures et / ou des guides que nous allons examiner, que l'UE adresse à ses citoyens en les différenciant par âge et, implicitement, par savoirs possédés en amont. Nous supposons que la spécialisation et le degré de technicité des trois publications diminuent au fur et à mesure que la cible est constituée, respectivement, par le grand public, par des adolescents ou par des enfants. Aussi la typologie textuelle des textes informatifs et des textes de vulgarisation se combine-t-elle bien avec l'ajout d'illustrations, lesquelles, encore une fois, sont adaptées à la cible visée. En particulier, *À la découverte de l'Europe* est la brochure la plus riche en illustrations, ce qui est en corrélation avec un nombre de mots plus réduit par rapport au nombre de pages.

	Comment fonctionne l'Union européenne (P1)	*L'Union européenne. Sa fonction et ses activités* (P2)	*À la découverte de l'Europe!* (P3)	Total
C'est-à-dire	\	3	5	8
A savoir	11	\	\	11
Autrement dit[21]	7	\	\	7
En d'autres termes	5	1	3	9
Soit d'équivalence	4	1	\	5
Ou d'équivalence	3	2	2	7
Total	30	7	10	47

Tab. 2: Les marqueurs paraphrastiques dans le corpus

Comme le montre le Tableau 2, le nombre d'occurrences des six marqueurs paraphrastiques mentionnés dans les trois publications (désormais P1, P2 et P3) est très réduit, même absent. Si c'est le guide adressé au grand public qui contient plus de marqueurs, par nombre (30 au total) et par type, à l'exception de *c'est-à-dire*, c'est ce dernier outil qui est le plus récurrent dans les deux autres publications, avec huit occurrences au total (dont trois dans P2, cinq dans P3). *À savoir* et *autrement dit* ne figurent que dans P1, où ils sont les marqueurs les plus employés, avec 11 et sept occurrences, respectivement. Les trois autres marqueurs, dont les (rares) occurrences se répartissent dans les trois publications, sont plus nombreux dans P1.

1. *C'est-à-dire*

Les huit occurrences de *c'est-à-dire* dans le corpus confirment que, dans une situation proche de celle de l'enseignement – toutes les publications de l'UE pour enfants et pour adolescents sont généralement enrichies de suppléments pour les enseignants et pour les parents –, il introduit des reformulations paraphrastiques pour contourner ou pour éviter tout obstacle à la compréhension de la part des destinataires ciblés (Vassiliadou 2019).

[21] Nous tenons à préciser qu'aucune occurrence de *(soit) dit autrement* n'apparaît dans le corpus.

En effet, il est rare que ce marqueur exprime l'équivalence stricte entre termes. Il vise à introduire une explication, en mots du langage ordinaire, du terme ou de l'expression représentés par A. Pour autant, dans nos exemples *c'est-à-dire* exprime toujours l'équivalence.

En particulier, dans quatre cas, figurant dans P2 et dans P3, A, qui est le terme nouveau, est mis en relief d'un point de vue graphique soit par des guillemets (exemple 3) soit par un lien hypertexte (exemple 1) activable à partir de l'expression signalée. Cela prouve que le contenu de A ne fait pas partie des savoirs que les enfants et adolescents devraient posséder en amont. *C'est-à-dire* est toujours précédé d'un signe (typo)graphique, notamment la virgule (six cas) ou les parenthèses (les deux autres, dont l'exemple 2): ce qui est recelé par B est donc syntaxiquement accessoire, mais essentiel en termes sémantiques. Quant à l'information à reformuler, ce qui est introduit par *c'est-à-dire* est strictement lié tant à A qu'au public à atteindre. Ainsi, l'équivalence entre «tempéré» (exemple 3), entre guillemets et précédé par *dit* – signalant aux enfants que ce qui suit ne fait pas partie du langage ordinaire –, et «ni trop chaud ni trop froid» est adressée aux enfants alors que l'équivalence entre «majorité qualifiée» (exemple 1) et «55 % des États membres représentant au moins 65 % de la population totale de l'UE» est adressée aux adolescents. Ces derniers connaissent déjà le sens de «majorité» et accèdent donc à un savoir plus technique par le biais de l'explication qui leur est présentée.

Sous l'aspect morphosyntaxique, A est variable. Il peut concerner un syntagme nominal (trois cas, exemple 1), un adjectif (deux cas, exemple 3), un verbe (un cas, exemple 2) et même une proposition (deux cas, exemple 4). *C'est-à-dire* peut donc se combiner avec et lier tout type de syntagme:

(1) *Pour être adoptées, les décisions requièrent généralement une majorité qualifiée, c'est-à-dire 55 % des États membres représentant au moins 65 % de la population totale de l'UE. (P2, p. 53)*

(2) *Chaque année, le Conseil conclut (c'est-à-dire signe officiellement) un certain nombre d'accords entre l'Union européenne et des pays tiers, ainsi qu'avec des organisations internationales. (P2, p. 59)*

(3) *La plupart des pays d'Europe bénéficient d'un climat dit «tempéré», c'est-à-dire ni trop chaud ni trop froid. (P3, p. 12)*

(4) *[N]ous pouvons ainsi apprécier non seulement ce qui nous distingue, c'est-à-dire les différences et les spécificités de notre pays ou de notre région, mais également ce qui nous rapproche, c'est-à-dire tout ce que nous avons en commun en tant qu'Européens. (P3, p. 31)*

Ces exemples confirment que *c'est-à-dire* est le marqueur de reformulation paraphrastique par excellence. Le segment reformulant qu'il introduit peut prendre la forme d'une reformulation paraphrastique, d'une définition en extension, d'une simplification, d'une explication en vue d'éclairer le sens de A, d'une équivalence entre syntagmes différents.

2. *À savoir*

À savoir n'apparaît que dans le guide grand public (P1), où ses occurrences dépassent celles de *c'est-à-dire*. Elles portent sur l'expression de la relation sémantique d'équivalence, mais aussi sur celle de caractérisation. La caractérisation permet d'appréhender A par le biais de B non pas en termes d'identité mais plutôt de mise en relief *via* l'exemplification, la spécification, l'explication, en B, d'un élément permettant de caractériser A de manière généralement non univoque. Or, *à savoir* introduit une information supplémentaire, qui figure toujours en mention, séparée de A par des outils (typo)graphiques. Parmi ceux-ci, les plus utilisés sont la virgule double (huit cas), les parenthèses (deux cas) et les tirets doubles (un cas). Ces signes doubles marquent un isolement de B par rapport à A et concernent un élément accessoire d'un point de vue syntaxique mais dont la présence et le sens visent à accroître les connaissances des destinataires.

En particulier, dans cinq cas, *à savoir* introduit une équivalence par une sorte de définition en extension – dans quatre cas, il s'agit d'une identification de A par la spécification de ses composants dans B. Tel est le cas de l'équivalence posée entre «les hauts dirigeants politiques de l'UE» et leur identification par les «Premiers ministres et présidents» (exemple 5), ou de celle entre «le législateur de l'Union (exemple 6)» / «l'autorité budgétaire» (exemple 7) et «le Parlement européen et le Conseil»:

(5) *Le Conseil européen réunit les hauts dirigeants politiques de l'UE, à savoir les Premiers ministres et présidents, ainsi que son propre président et celui de la Commission. (P1, p. 12)*

(6) *La Commission envoie les propositions législatives aux parlements nationaux en même temps qu'au législateur de l'Union (à savoir le Parlement européen et le Conseil), afin qu'ils puissent procéder à des contrôles de subsidiarité. (P1, p. 23)*

(7) *Une autre fonction essentielle de la Cour des comptes européenne consiste à aider l'autorité budgétaire, à savoir le Parlement européen et le Conseil, en lui communiquant un rapport annuel sur l'exécution du budget de l'UE relatif à l'exercice précédent. (P1, p. 29)*

Dans l'exemple 8, bien qu'*à savoir* introduise une définition en extension, c'est également une précision qui apparaît par le biais de la subordonnée relative déterminative (Touratier 1980), ce qui justifie la présence des tirets doubles marquant une coupure plus forte que les virgules doubles, qui complète l'équivalence entre «Etats membres» (sous-entendant «de l'UE») et «les 28 pays»:

(8) *Ce sont les États membres – à savoir les 28 pays qui adhèrent à l'Union – et leurs citoyens qui forment l'essence même de l'UE. (P1, p. 3)*

Dans le dernier exemple où *à savoir* marque une relation d'équivalence entre A et B, il y a une définition en intension doublée d'une explication. Les sujets auteurs peuvent ainsi faire mieux comprendre ce qu'on entend par «cas de mauvaise administration de la part des institutions européennes» dans le cadre de la législation européenne:

(9) *En recevant et en examinant les plaintes, le Médiateur contribue à mettre au jour des cas de mauvaise administration de la part des institutions européennes et d'autres organes de l'UE, à savoir des cas dans lesquels une institution de l'UE manque à ses obligations ou les remplit de manière inadéquate, voire commet un acte répréhensible. (P1, p. 34)*

Or, hormis cet exemple, *à savoir* d'équivalence indique une identité entre deux expressions, où B recèle une définition en extension plutôt qu'une équivalence stricte entre termes. Dans tous ces cas, A est l'élément inconnu alors qu'*à savoir* introduisant B s'appuie sur les savoirs déjà acquis par les lecteurs pour les interpréter et pour y ajouter des informations, quoique vagues, en vue d'éclairer A (Vassiliadou 2008).

La visée explicative d'*à savoir* est cependant plus évidente lorsqu'il marque une caractérisation. Dans ces cas, c'est l'éclaircissement d'un élément inconnu recelé par A qu'*à savoir* opère en introduisant B par les traits qui le caractérisent, de façon souvent non univoque et approximative. Dans l'exemple 10, A est entre guillemets pour marquer le caractère non ordinaire, et donc sans doute inconnu, du terme «représentation» dans le cadre de la législation européenne. Le résultat n'est alors pas une équivalence mais une caractérisation explicative et clarificatrice, également marquée par les subordonnées relatives déterminantes dans B (exemples 10 et 11):

(10) *Chaque État membre dispose en effet à Bruxelles d'une «représentation», à savoir une équipe permanente qui le représente et défend ses intérêts nationaux sur la scène européenne. (P1, p. 16)*

(11) *La politique monétaire, qui porte sur la stabilité des prix et les taux d'intérêt, est menée de façon indépendante par la Banque centrale européenne dans la zone euro, à savoir dans les États membres qui ont adopté l'euro pour monnaie. (P1, p. 8)*

Pour autant, *à savoir* introduit toujours des contenus syntaxiquement accessoires: c'est ce qui émerge, entre autres, de l'emploi des parenthèses (exemple 12):

(12) *Le Conseil est un pôle de décision essentiel pour l'Union européenne. Il assume cette fonction en réunissant les ministres concernés (à savoir le ministre compétent de chaque gouvernement national) afin d'examiner, de convenir, de modifier [...]. (P1, p. 14)*

Enfin, *à savoir* introduit une information nouvelle qui exprime une caractérisation: dans l'exemple 13, A, «deux organes consultatifs», est spécifié par ses composants et par les éléments plus petits qui en font partie:

(13) *Aussi entretient-elle des contacts permanents avec un large éventail de groupes d'intérêts et deux organes consultatifs, à savoir le Comité économique et social européen (formé de représentants des employeurs et des syndicats) et le Comité des régions (formé de représentants des autorités régionales et locales). (P1, p. 20)*

3. Les marqueurs en *autre*: *autrement dit* et *en d'autres termes*

De par leur étymologie, *autrement dit* et *en d'autres termes* présentent *autre* et sous-tendent un renvoi anaphorique explicite à ce qui est différemment exprimé auparavant ainsi qu'une forme de dialogisme. Comme les outils qui précèdent, ces deux marqueurs peuvent exprimer tantôt une relation d'équivalence entre des mots ou des expressions qu'ils relient tantôt une relation de caractérisation dont l'interprétation et la perception du public diffèrent. Si *autrement dit* ne figure que dans la brochure grand public avec sept occurrences, *en d'autres termes* apparaît dans toutes les publications avec des proportions variables, en passant de cinq occurrences dans P1 à trois cas dans P3, voire à une seule occurrence dans P2. En revanche, *autrement dit* n'est représenté que dans P1: c'est par ces occurrences que nous allons entamer son analyse.

Au-delà de la relation sémantique exprimée par *autrement dit*, dont quatre cas d'équivalence et trois de caractérisation, les exemples relevés attestent des points communs d'un point de vue syntaxique ainsi que sémantico-pragmatique. En termes syntaxiques, ce marqueur montre une indépendance soulignée par une coupure plus forte que les autres outils au sein de la phrase. En effet, dans deux cas, il figure dans des incises séparées du reste de la phrase et du segment A par des tirets doubles et, dans trois cas, en début de phrase. Son antécédent, le segment A avec le propos qui y est exprimé, apparaît dans la phrase qui précède. Ainsi seulement dans deux cas *autrement dit* est-il précédé d'une virgule:

(14) *Le terme «Commission» désigne à la fois les «membres de la Commission» – autrement dit l'équipe d'hommes et de femmes désignés par les États membres et le Parlement pour gérer l'institution et arrêter ses décisions – et l'institution elle-même, avec son personnel. (P1, p. 19)*

(15) *Le Conseil conclut (autrement dit, signe officiellement) chaque année un certain nombre d'accords entre l'Union européenne et des pays tiers [...]. (P1, p. 15)*

En outre, *autrement dit* permet de relier, même d'un point de vue visuel, un terme ou une expression entre guillemets (exemple 14), relevant d'une terminologie spécialisée, notamment juridique, qui sont ainsi «exprimés autrement» dans B. L'expression «autre» contenue dans ce marqueur assure à B une meilleure intelligibilité car il relève de la langue commune, d'où sa réception plus aisée auprès des destinataires. On a ainsi affaire à une équivalence exprimée par une définition en intension proche d'un EDC (Riegel 1987) comprenant une décomposition de l'expression «membres de la Commission» en ses éléments et la fonction qu'ils remplissent. Un cas similaire relève de l'exemple 16, où *autrement dit*, en début de phrase, reformule une phrase entière en simplifiant le sens de A:

(16) *Dans tous les autres domaines d'action, les décisions demeurent du ressort des États membres. Autrement dit, la Commission ne peut proposer d'acte législatif dans un domaine non spécifié par un traité. (P1, p. 9)*

Encore *autrement dit* peut-il marquer une équivalence «1 à 1» entre A et B là où A est toujours en usage et relève du langage juridique et B, en mention, en est la traduction dans la langue commune. La reformulation par équivalence sémantique opérée par *autrement dit* est donc immédiate, comme le montrent, dans l'exemple 15, *conclut* et *signe officiellement*. Par ailleurs, il est intéressant de remarquer que dans l'exemple 2, qui est presque identique en termes lexico-sémantiques et syntaxiques à l'exemple 15, mais figurant dans P2, adressée aux adolescents, le sujet vulgarisateur a employé *c'est-à-dire* pour sceller l'équivalence entre les deux syntagmes verbaux, d'où l'interchangeabilité entre *c'est-à-dire* et *autrement dit*, mais également une réception différente de ceux-ci de la part des destinataires. Nous supposons que l'immédiateté de *c'est-à-dire* auprès des adolescents est la preuve de son emploi plus pédagogique et moins «spécialisé», appartenant à un registre moins formel qu'*autrement dit*.

Au-delà de ces cas d'équivalence, *autrement dit* peut introduire une caractérisation dans le but de préciser A en l'expliquant, dans B, par une simplification en langue courante, ainsi plus familière au public visé par P1. Tel est le cas du principe de subsidiarité (exemple 17) dans A, où *autrement dit* permet d'éclairer pour mieux comprendre le concept sous-tendant ce principe, notamment «subsidiarité»:

(17) *Les actions de l'UE doivent respecter le principe de* ***subsidiarité*** *– autrement dit, hormis dans les domaines qui relèvent de sa compétence exclusive,*

> *l'Union européenne intervient seulement si l'action envisagée à son niveau est plus efficace qu'une action menée au niveau national. (P1, pp. 7-8, gras dans l'original)*

Une caractérisation émerge également lorsque le but du sujet vulgarisateur est plutôt de faire comprendre, toujours par une simplification et une mise en œuvre, ce à quoi le segment A fait référence. Dans l'exemple 18, une reformulation est employée pour faire comprendre que la présidence du Conseil est tournante: une simplification et une exemplification soulignent ainsi que le gouvernement assurant la présidence du Conseil doit organiser et présider les réunions du Conseil – mais le rôle de la présidence tournante va même au-delà de ces tâches:

(18) *La présidence du Conseil – à ne pas confondre avec la présidence du Conseil européen – est assurée à tour de rôle par les 28 États membres pour une durée de six mois. Autrement dit, il incombe au gouvernement occupant la présidence d'organiser et de présider les différentes réunions du Conseil. (P1, p. 16)*

Encore, dans l'expression de la caractérisation, *autrement dit* peut donner des précisions par rapport à A: dans l'exemple 19, ce marqueur spécifie que le Conseil traite des problématiques identifiées dans les conclusions du Conseil européen dans le cadre de réunions des ministres:

(19) *Les conclusions du Conseil européen identifient les grandes problématiques à traiter par le Conseil, autrement dit lors des réunions des ministres. (P2, p. 12)*

Quant à *en d'autres termes*, les cinq occurrences dans P1 montrent que son fonctionnement est similaire à celui d'*autrement dit* en termes syntaxiques et sémantico-pragmatiques, tout en montrant des tendances peut-être plus tranchées. D'un point de vue syntaxique, le segment A est toujours séparé par une coupure (même (typo)graphique) forte du segment B *via* les tirets doubles (deux cas) ou le point final (trois cas) – dans ce dernier cas, le marqueur apparaît en début de phrase:

(20) *L'Union européenne se fonde sur l'état de droit. En d'autres termes, toute action entreprise par l'UE découle de traités que tous les pays de l'Union ont librement et démocratiquement approuvés. (P1, p. 3)*

(21) *La Cour des comptes européenne a pour rôle principal de veiller à la bonne exécution du budget de l'UE – en d'autres termes, de veiller à ce que les recettes et les dépenses de l'Union soient légales et régulières et à ce que sa gestion financière soit saine. (P1, p. 29)*

Les deux exemples présentés portent, l'un, sur une équivalence (c'est le seul cas d'équivalence d'*en d'autres termes* dans P1), l'autre, sur une caractérisation (quatre cas au total dans P1). Ils partagent la reformulation de phrases entières et des propos qu'elles recèlent (le segment A) plutôt que de syntagmes. Ainsi, il s'agit d'une sorte de réécriture, dans B, en vue, encore une fois, d'expliquer «autrement», s'appuyant sur le langage courant, la notion d'état de droit au sein de l'UE (exemple 20) et les fonctions de la Cour des comptes européenne. Cette remarque est également valable pour la seule occurrence d'*en d'autres termes* au sein de la publication pour adolescents:

(22) *L'Union européenne est fondée sur l'état de droit. En d'autres termes, toutes ses actions reposent sur des traités que l'ensemble de ses États membres ont adoptés volontairement et démocratiquement. (P2, p. 51)*

Dans cet exemple d'équivalence, *en d'autres termes*, en début de phrase, relie deux phrases dont la première est technique et la seconde est reformulée par des termes plus proches du public visé, mais le segment A est à peu près identique à celui de l'exemple 20. Les deux exemples (20 et 22) diffèrent par rapport au segment B: bien qu'il contienne les mêmes informations, il est présenté sous une forme syntaxiquement et lexicalement plus simple dans l'exemple 22.

Ces aspects à propos d'*en d'autres termes* sont davantage confirmés par la publication pour enfants: les trois occurrences de ce marqueur, qui véhiculent une relation d'équivalence, ne font qu'exprimer différemment, d'une manière plus simple et immédiate, ce qui figure dans le segment A:

(23) *Une majorité d'Européens travaillent dans le secteur des «services». En d'autres termes, ces personnes travaillent dans des magasins, des bureaux de poste, des banques, des compagnies d'assurances, des hôtels, des restaurants, des hôpitaux, des écoles, etc., soit en vendant des produits, soit en fournissant les services dont les gens ont besoin. (P3, p. 27)*

(24) *«Économique» signifie «se rapportant à l'économie», en d'autres termes, qui se rapporte à l'argent, aux affaires, au travail et au commerce. (P3, p. 31)*

Si dans l'exemple 23 la reformulation du secteur des services est obtenue par une liste d'exemples de métiers des services qui devraient être connus par les enfants et faire partie de leur quotidien – il pourrait même s'agir du métier de leurs parents – l'exemple 24 présente d'abord une première remarque métalinguistique (signalée par les guillemets) pour reformuler *économique*, ensuite une reformulation de *se rapportant à l'économie*, où encore une fois *en d'autres termes* introduit dans B une simplification par des exemples liés à la vie quotidienne des enfants et à des mots qu'ils devraient déjà connaître.

C'est donc l'effort du sujet vulgarisateur qui émerge d'*autrement dit* et d'*en d'autres termes* pour mieux approcher ses destinataires – un public adulte pour *autrement dit*, tout public pour *en d'autres termes* – des contenus spécialisés (et de la terminologie pour les exprimer) figurant dans les trois publications.

4. *Soit* et *ou* d'équivalence

Soit et *ou* sont les seuls marqueurs n'exprimant qu'une relation d'équivalence dans ce discours de transmission de connaissances spécialisées à un public non expert. Ils introduisent dans B un référent exprimé différemment et ils portent sur la reformulation d'éléments de même nature, se distinguant des marqueurs en *autre* par le fait de ne pas exprimer le dialogisme. *Ou* est présent dans les trois publications, bien que de manière limitée. Les trois exemples repérés dans P1, dont:

(25) *Ces «trios» ou «troïkas» de présidences élaborent pour le Conseil un programme de travail commun pour une période de 18 mois. (P1, p. 15)*

(26) *Il est assisté du Comité des représentants permanents ou Coreper. (P1, p. 16)*

confirment qu'il marque une équivalence entre référents syntaxiquement équivalents, en l'occurrence des syntagmes nominaux. La différence entre les deux référents reliés par *ou* relève toujours d'une sorte de traduction:

dans l'exemple 25, il s'agit du mot français (en fait un calque de l'italien) «trios» et de sa traduction par «troïkas» (calqué sur le russe), utilisé dans le jargon des experts du domaine, alors que dans l'exemple 26 – ainsi que dans la troisième occurrence d'*ou* – l'équivalence est obtenue par acronymie, entre le syntagme étendu «Comité des représentants permanents» et «Coreper», acronyme répandu auprès des experts. Ainsi B est-il le référent inconnu ou celui qui est connu et partagé par les spécialistes, tandis que A relève du connu et indique la dénomination la plus courante. Il en va de même pour les deux occurrences, par ailleurs identiques et concernant la même phrase dans deux chapitres différents, de ce marqueur dans P2:

(27) *Chaque année, à la suite d'une recommandation du Conseil, le Parlement européen décide s'il donne son approbation finale, ou «décharge», sur la manière dont la Commission exécute le budget de l'UE. (P2, p. 62)*

Dans cet exemple, *ou* marque une équivalence entre deux référents de même nature, notamment des syntagmes nominaux, dont «approbation finale» appartient à la langue courante, «décharge» au langage technique, comme le montrent par ailleurs les guillemets. Contrairement aux exemples précédents, dans l'exemple 28, c'est une démarche didactique qui permet d'aller du connu, A, vers le nouveau, B, par le biais de l'une des deux occurrences d'*ou* dans la publication adressée aux enfants:

(28) *La plupart de ces langues appartiennent à trois grands groupes ou «familles» linguistiques: ce sont les langues germaniques, slaves et romanes. (P3, p. 8)*

Dans cet exemple, «familles», entre guillemets, est l'appellation technique de «groupes», qui est censée être la plus connue et courante. Quant à lui, l'exemple 29 porte sur une traduction intralinguistique entre «Normands» et «hommes du Nord», son étymologie, et c'est en tout cas une visée didactique qui souligne cette équivalence entre les deux syntagmes nominaux reliés par *ou*:

(29) *Les Normands ou «hommes du Nord» sont des Vikings qui se sont d'abord établis en France (dans la région que l'on appelle «Normandie») avant de conquérir l'Angleterre en 1066. (P3, p. 22)*

En revanche, *soit*, dont les occurrences figurent dans P1 (quatre cas) et P2 (une occurrence), relie des éléments équivalents par le biais de chiffres, en les caractérisant de manière généralement approximative (en témoignent les adverbes «quelque» et «environ») pour souligner une équivalence à partir de référents exprimés différemment. Ainsi, dans l'exemple 30, il est précisé que les citoyens âgés de 18 ans révolus (ou de 16 ans en Autriche) dans l'UE s'élèvent à 380 millions environ:

(30) *Des élections ont lieu tous les cinq ans et tous les citoyens âgés de 18 ans au moins (16 ans en Autriche), soit quelque 380 millions de personnes, ont le droit de vote. (P1, p. 9)*

Dans l'exemple 31, une équivalence est exprimée deux fois entre un pourcentage et son chiffre correspondant:

(31) *Les votes favorables doivent représenter: au moins 55 % des États membres, soit 16 pays sur 28 et au moins 65 % de la population totale de l'UE, soit environ 329 millions de personnes sur près de 506 millions. (P1, p. 16)*

Dans la dernière occurrence de *soit* dans P1, où il exprime une équivalence en précisant A par le biais de B de manière toujours approximative, *une fois par mois environ* indique le moment dans lequel l'Eurogroupe se réunit informellement dans la plupart des cas:

(32) *[L]'Eurogroupe tient une réunion informelle la veille des sessions du Conseil «Ecofin», soit une fois par mois environ. (P1, p. 17)*

La seule occurrence de *soit* dans la publication adressée aux adolescents confirme qu'il indique une équivalence entre référents exprimés en chiffres appartenant à des grandeurs différentes:

(33) *Afin d'atteindre ces objectifs et de répondre aux divers besoins de développement de toutes les régions de l'UE, 259,7 milliards d'euros, soit un quart du budget total de l'UE, sont disponibles pour la politique régionale pendant la période 2014-2020. (P2, p. 23)*

Ces traits expliquent l'absence de *soit* dans la publication pour enfants, mais également dans P2, hormis l'exemple 33: son caractère est plus technique, comme le montre l'équivalence en chiffres et en pourcentages entre les deux segments A et B.

5. Les autres outils de reformulation et de paraphrase dans le corpus

L'analyse effectuée a mis en évidence que l'emploi des marqueurs de reformulation et paraphrase examinés est peu répandu, même parfois absent dans le corpus. En revanche, d'autres outils de reformulation paraphrastique y sont beaucoup plus fréquents. Nous les rappellerons brièvement. Le fait que la publication adressée aux enfants est en partie composée d'illustrations ne peut que confirmer que celles-ci y jouent un rôle essentiel. En effet, une reformulation langagière peut être remplacée par une illustration, c'est-à-dire une manifestation directe de l'élément à définir / expliquer.

Quant à *L'Union européenne. Sa fonction et ses activités*, adressée aux adolescents, un autre outil non langagier de vulgarisation y apparaît, à savoir des liens hypertexte.[22] Ceux-ci renvoient au segment qu'une reformulation «classique» permettrait d'indiquer par B. Cependant, ils ne s'activent lors de la consultation en ligne que si leur lectorat choisit de les consulter en les ouvrant sur la base de ses intérêts de lecture, d'où leur imprévisibilité formelle (Paveau 2017). À partir d'un mot ou d'un groupe de mots mis en valeur en discours et signalé(s) par la couleur et / ou le soulignement typographique, on assiste à un dédoublement de l'énoncé sur plusieurs strates de textes (Reboul-Touré 2003), à une multiplication des informations, bien que souvent complémentaires de celles du texte «de départ», et à une «matrice de textes potentiels» (Davallon / Jeanneret 2004: 45).

Dans P2, les 268 liens hypertexte sont presque tous de type interne (266 cas), c'est-à-dire ils renvoient à des «ailleurs textuels» limités au même portail, celui de l'UE.[23] Ils permettent ainsi d'ouvrir des contenus complémentaires de ceux qui sont présentés dans la brochure en ligne dans une visée informative et explicative. Par exemple, lorsque ce guide cite les

---

[22] Paveau (2017: 215) définit l'hyperlien ou hypertexte, qui apparaît toujours sous forme de URL et qui est typique du texte numérique, «une dimension majeure de l'écriture hypertextuelle […] contribuant à la forme des énoncés, l'élaboration de leur sens et leur mode de circulation».

[23] Les seules exceptions relèvent de renvois à des vidéos disponibles sur *YouTube*.

vingt-huit pays membres de l'UE en 2019 (P2, p. 7), un hyperlien renvoie à une fiche technique de synthèse à propos d'informations géopolitiques sur chaque pays. Les liens portent dans la plupart des cas sur des dénominations institutionnelles / techniques,[24] des thèmes-clés dans le cadre de la législation européenne,[25] des institutions / des portails,[26] des actions partagées et des mécanismes / systèmes communs,[27] des initiatives européennes et l'annonce de résultats obtenus,[28] l'invitation à participer à la vie de l'UE.[29] Au contraire, les deux liens externes renvoient à des institutions extra-européennes. Les hyperliens se combinent ainsi avec les outils de vulgarisation plus traditionnels pour introduire, comme ces derniers, des suppléments d'information.

Une autre stratégie de reformulation présente dans les publications examinées consiste à utiliser des outils introduisant une appellation autre, une démarche de dénomination (Loffler-Laurian 1983). Ceux-ci sont identifiés par des expressions telles qu'*également connu sous le nom / également appelé* et visent à introduire une reformulation: le segment A ressort généralement du connu alors que B, introduit par une marque d'appellation ou de nomination du type *appelé / dit / connu / nommé* – rappelons à ce propos l'exemple 3 –, relève de ce qui est inconnu. Pour autant, les outils les plus utilisés sont les signes (typo)graphiques, parmi lesquels ceux de ponctuation, qui accompagnent souvent également les autres marqueurs, comme il émerge des exemples présentés, et signalant une relation soit d'équivalence

---

[24] Tel est le cas de «marché unique»: «Grâce au marché unique (parfois aussi appelé «marché intérieur»), les personnes, les biens, les services et l'argent peuvent circuler dans l'UE» (P2, p. 18).

[25] «Les Européens partagent des valeurs qui sont énoncées dans les traités de l'UE et dans la charte des droits fondamentaux de l'Union européenne, qui garantissent des droits aux citoyens de l'UE» (P2, p. 36).

[26] «Le portail européen de la jeunesse fournit des informations sur ces initiatives et d'autres actions de l'UE en faveur des jeunes dans toute l'Europe, tandis qu'EURES, le portail européen sur la mobilité de l'emploi, aide également à mettre en relation les demandeurs d'emploi et les entreprises qui proposent un emploi» (P2, p. 45).

[27] «[L]es autorités de l'UE peuvent suivre les mouvements de produits alimentaires via le système TRACES (système informatique vétérinaire intégré)» (P2, p. 38).

[28] «Depuis juin 2017, les frais d'itinérance ont été supprimés» (P2, p. 39).

[29] «Sur le portail en ligne «Donnez votre avis», les citoyens peuvent s'abonner pour être informés par courriel» (P2, p. 58).

soit de caractérisation. Tel est le cas des virgules doubles, des tirets, des parenthèses, des guillemets, autant de signes doubles qui marquent une coupure variable dans la phrase pour signaler une reprise d'un élément en vue de le reformuler, de l'expliquer, de le paraphraser ou de le définir. Ces outils soulignent de manière plus immédiate, mais implicite et par inférence, la relation sémantique entre les segments A et B.

V. Conclusions

Au début de notre parcours, nous avions fait l'hypothèse d'une spécialisation et d'un degré de technicité des trois publications décroissants au fur et à mesure que les destinataires sont le grand public, les adolescents ou les enfants. Bien que ces ouvrages soient des brochures et / ou des guides adressés à un public non spécialisé, et que le nombre limité d'occurrences des marqueurs examinés ne permette pas de justifier entièrement notre hypothèse,[30] les outils paraphrastiques étudiés relient des segments différents et se répartissent de manière différente selon les publications, les thèmes abordés et les destinataires à atteindre. *C'est-à-dire*, qui figure dans P2 et P3, est le marqueur de reformulation paraphrastique le plus explicite et le plus transparent pour un public en formation, comme les enfants scolarisés et les adolescents. Il définit, explique, reformule en mots plus simples un propos qui précède, et les éléments renfermés dans A et dans B relèvent d'une terminologie moins spécialisée que celle qui concerne *autrement dit* dans l'expression de l'équivalence.

Ce dernier n'apparaît au contraire que dans P1 pour introduire des définitions et des explications de notions techniques présentées «autrement», dans un langage plus compréhensible et *via* des paraphrases. Pour sa part, *soit*, qui marque *per se* une équivalence entre grandeurs exprimées différemment, dont des pourcentages *vs* des données chiffrées, ne figure presque que dans P1. Au contraire, *c'est-à-dire* est le marqueur le plus employé

---

30 Par ailleurs, les publications de l'UE sont pour la plupart des traductions d'une langue source, généralement l'anglais, vers des langues cibles représentées par les autres langues de l'UE, y compris le français. Une rédaction en français-langue source aurait sans doute donné des résultats différents, non influencés par ce biais linguistique.

dans la publication pour enfants – alors qu'il fait défaut dans P1 – pour établir une équivalence «neutre» et complète soit en termes d'identité entre des référents différemment exprimés soit sous forme d'EDC et de définition en extension entre A, le terme ou l'expression inconnus, et B, sa reformulation sous forme de reprise interprétative univoque. Encore, les emplois d'*ou*, qui figure dans toutes les publications, portent sur une équivalence stricte entre éléments de la même catégorie grammaticale: si A recèle la dénomination étendue, ainsi transparente, B concerne son abrègement et relève du jargon des experts. Enfin, nous avons identifié des exemples de reprise du même concept ou terme à reformuler au sein de P1 et de P2, là où le marqueur reliant A et B devrait engendrer une perception différente de la part du public visé.

Ainsi, la réception des destinataires, mais également le type d'information changent dans l'emploi de tel ou tel marqueur de reformulation paraphrastique dans l'expression de la relation d'équivalence. Une équivalence stricte sera véhiculée *via ou*; pour une équivalence entre référents appartenant à des grandeurs différentes *soit* est le marqueur le plus approprié; une équivalence «neutre» sera véhiculée par *c'est-à-dire*. Encore une équivalence qui met l'accent sur un rephrasage du «dit» d'une manière «autre» est-elle du ressort d'*autrement dit*; une équivalence plus vague, visant une caractérisation, concernera *à savoir*. Enfin, une équivalence entre termes «autres», donc plus spécialisée, fera l'objet d'*en d'autres termes*. Cette distinction n'est pourtant pas tranchée, comme les cas de substituabilité entre marqueurs en témoignent.

Pour conclure, même si d'autres outils de reformulation et paraphrase sont beaucoup plus utilisés dans les trois publications examinées, l'analyse des six marqueurs de reformulation paraphrastique a permis de mieux focaliser l'attention sur la nature des segments A et B, mais surtout de montrer qu'un discours de transmission de connaissances s'adapte aux destinataires à atteindre à partir des marqueurs de reformulation et paraphrase employés. Par conséquent, si ce travail peut d'abord s'inscrire dans le domaine de la linguistique française, notamment l'étude syntaxique et sémantico-pragmatique des marqueurs de reformulation et paraphrase, il peut s'étendre à l'analyse des discours de vulgarisation juridique et institutionnel.

En effet, les trois brochures / guides examinés sont tous publiés dans le site institutionnel de l'Union européenne et partagent la volonté de l'UE de faire connaître à ses citoyens ses pays membres, ses institutions et ses activités, dans une sorte de discours (auto-)promotionnel qui est le propre des sites web de toute institution. Quoique provisoires, les résultats de ce travail pourraient donc tant contribuer à élargir les domaines d'étude envisagés à d'autres discours de vulgarisation qu'être un point de départ pour étendre cette recherche à d'autres langues et à leur comparaison.

VI. Références

Anscombre, Jean-Claude. 2014. Présentation. In: Jean-Claude Anscombre / Evelyne Oppermann-Marsaux / Amalia Rodriguez Somolinos (Eds.), *Médiativité, polyphonie et modalité en français. Etudes synchroniques et diachroniques*. Paris: Presses Sorbonne Nouvelle, 7-16.

Authier-Revuz, Jacqueline. 1984. Hétérogénéité(s) énonciative(s). *Langages* 73, 98-111.

Authier-Revuz, Jacqueline. 1995. *Ces mots qui ne vont pas de soi. Boucles réflexives et non coïncidences du dire*. Paris: Larousse.

Authier-Revuz, Jacqueline. 2020. *La représentation du discours autre. Principes pour une description*. Berlin: Mouton de Gruyter.

Choul, Jean-Claude. 1985. C'est-à-dire. L'expression métalinguistique de l'équivalence. *RAQL* 8 (3-4), 89-106.

Commission européenne. 2014. *Comment fonctionne l'Union européenne. Guide des institutions européennes à l'usage des citoyens*. Luxembourg: Office des publications de l'Union européenne.

Commission européenne. 2019. *L'Union européenne. Sa fonction et ses activités*. Luxembourg: Office des publications de l'Union européenne.

Commission européenne. 2020. *À la découverte de l'Europe!* Luxembourg: Office des publications de l'Union européenne.

Davallon, Jean / Yves Jeanneret. 2004. La fausse évidence du lien hypertexte. *Communication & Langages* 140, 43-54.

Eshkol-Taravella, Iris / Natalia Grabar. 2014. Paraphrastic Reformulations in Spoken Corpora. In: Adam Przepiórkowski / Maciej Ogrodniczuk (Eds.), *Advances in Natural Language Processing Lecture Notes in Computer Science. Proceedings of 9th International Conference on NLP*. Berne: Springer, 425-437.

Fuchs, Catherine. 1982. *La paraphrase*. Paris: PUF.

Fuchs, Catherine. 1994. *Paraphrase et énonciation*. Paris: Ophrys.

Gomez-Jordana Ferary, Sonia / Jean-Claude Anscombre. 2015. Introduction. Dire et ses marqueurs. *Langue française* 186 (2), 5-12.

Gülich, Elisabeth / Thomas Kotschi. 1983. Les marqueurs de la reformulation paraphrastique. *Cahiers de linguistique française* 5, 305-351.

Kleiber, Georges. 1994. Dénomination et relations dénominatives. *Langages* 76, 77-94.

Kress, Gunther / Theo van Leeuwen. 1996. *Reading Images. The Grammar of Visual Design.* Leuwen: Psychology Press.

Landolsi, Houda / Maria Svensson / Coco Norén. 2019 (Eds.), *La reformulation. À la recherche d'une frontière*. Uppsala: Uppsala Universitet.

Loffler-Laurian, Anne-Marie. 1983. Typologie des discours scientifiques. Deux approches. *Etudes de linguistique appliquée* 51, 8-20.

Loffler-Laurian, Anne-Marie. 1984. Vulgarisation scientifique. Formulation, reformulation, traduction. *Langue française* 64, 109-125.

Maingueneau, Dominique. 2015. Argumentation et scénographie. In: Carmen Pineira-Tresmontant (Ed.), *Discours et effets de sens. Argumenter, manipuler, traduire*. Arras: Artois Presses Université, 71-86.

Mongi, Kahloul. 2009. Autrement. Un connecteur autrement polyfonctionnel. *Langue française* 161, 147-163.

Murât, Michel / Bernard Cartier-Bresson. 1987. *C'est-à-dire* ou la reprise interprétative. *Langue française* 73, 5-15.

Paveau, Marie-Anne. 2017. *L'analyse du discours numérique. Dictionnaire des formes et des pratiques*. Paris: Herman.

Rebeyrolle, Josette. 2005. Une analyse discursive d'un type de reprise immédiate. La reprise autonymique, dans les énoncés définitoires. *Journal of French Language Studies* 15, 67-82.

Reboul-Touré, Sandrine. 2005. La glose entre langue et discours. In: Agnès Steuckardt / Aïno Niklas-Salminen (Eds.), *Le mot et sa glose*. Aix-en-Provence: Publications de l'Université de Provence, 75-91.

Rey-Debove, Josette. 1978. *Le métalangage, étude linguistique du discours sur le langage*. Paris: Le Robert.

Riegel, Martin. 1987. Définition directe et indirecte dans le langage ordinaire. Les énoncés définitoires copulatifs. *Langue française* 73, 29-53.

Riegel, Martin / Irène Tamba. 1987. Présentation. *Langue française* 73, 3-4.

Romero, Clara. 2009. La reformulation. Acquisition et diversité des discours. *Cahiers de praxématique* 52, 7-28.

Rossari, Corinne. 1994. *Les opérations de reformulation. Analyse du processus et des marques dans une perspective contrastive français – italien*. Berne: Lang.

Silletti, Alida M. 2014. Signes graphiques et reformulation dans le discours de vulgarisation scientifique. Analyse d'un corpus comparable français, italien, anglais. *Sintagma* 26, 23-35.

Silletti, Alida M. 2018. Outils de reformulation et de paraphrase dans les brochures de l'UE. *ÉLA, Études de Linguistique Appliquée* 192, numéro thématique coordonné par Chiara Preite / Alida M. Silletti (Eds.), *La terminologie et la construction / transmission des connaissances spécialisées dans le web*, 489-504.

Steuckardt, Agnès. 2005. Les marqueurs formés sur dire. In: Agnès Steuckardt / Aïno Niklas-Salminen (Eds.), *Les marqueurs de glose*. Aix-en-Provence: Publications de l'Université de Provence, 51-65.

Steuckardt, Agnès. 2006. *Du discours au lexique. La glose*. Séminaire ATILF, Nancy.

Tamba, Irène. 1987. *Ou* dans les tours du type. 'Un bienfaiteur ou évergète'. *Langue française* 73, 16-28.

Touratier, Christian. 1980. *La relative. Essai de théorie syntaxique (à partir de faits latins, français, allemands, anglais, grecs, hébreux, etc.)*. Paris: Klincksieck.

Vassiliadou, Hélène. 2008. Quand les voies de la reformulation se croisent pour mieux se séparer. À savoir, autrement dit, c'est-à-dire, en d'autres termes. In: Marie-Claude Le Bot / Martine Schuwer / Élisabeth Richard (Eds.), *La reformulation. Marqueurs linguistiques, stratégies énonciatives*. Rennes: PUR, 35-50.

Vassiliadou, Hélène. 2013. La formation de *c'est-à-dire (que)* et de ses correspondants dans les langues romanes. Quelques remarques. In: Emili Casanova / Cesáreo Calvo Rigual (Eds.), *Actas del XXVI congreso internacional de lingüística y de filología románicas*. Volume 2. Berlin: de Gruyter, 453-461.

Vassiliadou, Hélène. 2017. *C'est-à-dire (que)*, des emplois propositionnels aux emplois discursifs. Poursuite du débat sur les connecteurs et les marqueurs discursifs. In: Gaétan Dostie / François Lefeuvre (Eds.), *À l'articulation du lexique, de la grammaire et du discours. Marqueurs grammaticaux et marqueurs discursifs*. Paris: Honoré Champion, 399-414.

Vassiliadou, Hélène. 2019. Qui trop embrasse, mal étreint. Pour une conception stricte de la notion de reformulation. In: Houda Landolsi / Maria Svensson / Coco Norén (Eds.), *La reformulation. À la recherche d'une frontière*. Uppsala: Uppsala Universitet, 5-24.

Vion, Robert. 2006. Reprise et mode d'implication énonciative. *La linguistique* 42, 11-28.

Giuliana Diani

"All Brexplained!" – Popularising Brexit to Younger Generations

Abstract

The aim of this contribution is to discuss the popularisation strategies adopted in texts destined for children which deal with the topic of Brexit. Starting from the hypothesis that the age and the profile of the target reader have a strong bearing on the structure and nature of a text and that popularisation strategies might be adjusted in different ways, I will attempt to ascertain which popularisation strategies are used in relation to the age of the addressee. To this purpose I will concentrate on two books, *BREXIT: Britain's decision to leave the European Union* by Daniel Nunn (2016), and *I WANT TO LEAVE THIS BOOK!* by Richard David Lawman (2019), which address two different age groups. Consequently, the theme of Brexit is treated in different ways, both in terms of content and language. Attention is paid to examples that highlight popularisation strategies on the basis of the verbal and the visual elements characterising them. The basic methodological framework of this study is discourse analysis with reliance on notions taken from multimodality. This provides instruments suitable for identifying cases where the visual mode interacts with the verbal mode to support popularisation strategies.

I. Introduction

This contribution looks at popularisation of Brexit targeted at children. The aim is to analyse the popularisation strategies adopted in English texts destined for children which deal with the topic of Brexit. What follows is a description of the Brexit background. On 23 June 2016, the British electorate voted in favour of leaving the European Union (EU) in what has come to be known as the Brexit referendum. As journalist Alison Flood observed in a Guardian article (2019), children's book authors realised that there was nothing available to explain this important issue to young children.[1] The children's book author Daniel Nunn himself stated in an interview with Luke Sproule of the Oxford Mail newspaper in 2017,[2]

> I realised there was a desire from youngsters to understand the implications of the vote. It is a very big issue that they are going to hear about all the time. You cannot turn on the TV without hearing about it. I thought there must be some children who are quite worried about it but they still do not know the answers to a lot of questions. Hopefully, this [the book] will make it a lot less scary.

This statement explains the reason why Nunn decided to write the book entitled *BREXIT: Britain's decision to leave the European Union*, which was first published by Raintree in December 2016.

The importance of younger generations understanding Brexit is also emphasised by Richard David Lawman, the author of a Brexit children's picture book entitled *I WANT TO LEAVE THIS BOOK!*, published by WatAdventure on 31 October 2019, the day the UK was scheduled to leave the EU. In an interview reported in The Daily Express in October 2019, he said: "As a father to an inquisitive four-year-old, I started to think about how I would explain the current political landscape to my daughter and the answer was, I couldn't."[3] He called the book "the answer to my dilemma", and he felt it was important for younger generations to understand Brexit as an important piece of history.

Lawman's difficulty in explaining Brexit to young children finds confirmation in the results emerging from a survey of 1.000 parents, carried out by WatAdventure publisher releasing Lawman's picture book, which revealed that 70% of children were aware of the term Brexit. However, only 27% of parents felt confident in giving an explanation, while 32% admitted

---

1 The Guardian, 4th November 2019, *'No goose is an island'. The Brexit picture books for children of all ages.* https://www.theguardian.com/books/2019/nov/04/brexit-picture-books-for-children-of-all-ages-eu-animals (Last access 22.12.2022).

2 Oxford Mail, 1st February 2017, *Brexit for kids.* https://www.oxfordmail.co.uk/news/15062192.brexit-kids-book-launched-oxford-publisher/ (Last access 22.12.2022).

3 The Daily Express, 29th October 2019, *Brexit children's book to help parents explain UK's complex exit set for release.* https://www.express.co.uk/news/uk/1197343/brexit-news-eu-latest-childrens-kids-book-parent-explain-politics (Last access 22.12.2022).

that they felt so confused about the situation themselves that they could not clarify it for their kids.[4]

The fact that many children were aware of the word Brexit echoes the results emerging from BBC Radio 2's 500 Words story writing competition held in 2019, hosted by Zoe Ball's Radio 2 Breakfast Show. A total of 112.986 children from 25.000 UK schools entered the competition. Their writing was analysed by the team of *Children's Dictionaries & Children's Language Data* within the educational division of Oxford University Press and, as a result, the word Brexit was identified as the 2019 Oxford Children's Word of the Year. As reported by the team in the Oxford Corpus Children's Language Report 2019, it emerged that the word Brexit appeared a total of 418 times in the 2019 children's stories, with a total rise of 464% from the 89 occurrences in 2018 and of 1.488% from the 31 occurrences in 2017, when the word first appeared in the 500 Words stories. This result was commented on by Helen Freeman, Director of Publishing Operations and Home Sector at Oxford University Press, in a blog posted on 11 June 2019 by Oxford Owl (an award-winning primary platform developed by Oxford University Press).[5] She said that Brexit was the Children's Word of the Year

> not only because of its significant increase in use, but also because of the political and social awareness that children demonstrate in their stories and the incredibly inventive hooks and ways in which it inspired children to write about finding solutions to Brexit. (Freeman 2019)

Freeman's view confirms van Deth / Abendschön / Vollmar's (2011: 166) claim that

---

[4] Ginger Comms carried out the Omnibus survey on behalf of WatAdventure publisher in October 2019. Source: The Daily Express, 29th October 2019, *Brexit children's book to help parents explain UK's complex exit set for release.* https://www.express.co.uk/news/uk/1197343/brexit-news-eu-latest-childrens-kids-book-parent-explain-politics (Last access 22.12.2022).

[5] Oxford Owl blog post, 11 June 2019, *2019 Oxford children's word of the year: Brexit.* https://home.oxfordowl.co.uk/blog/2019-oxford-childrens-word-of-the-year-brexit/ (Last access 22.12.2022).

> children generally have what it takes to be young citizens: they express political opinions and attitudes, and they display basic political knowledge and orientations which are prerequisites of political involvement and participation.

The results emerging from the above competition reinforce van Deth / Abendschön / Vollmar's (2011: 148) further claim that "young children are increasingly considered not only as future citizens, but also as current citizens." Within the Brexit context, as the Young Citizens Foundation in an article entitled *Brexit and young people* (2018) stated: "For today's generation of school children – even those who are primary school – the process of Brexit will dominate their childhood years. They are the 'Brexit generation'".[6]

Over the last decades, the study of children's and adolescents' political knowledge and citizenship conceptions has attracted the main interest of political socialisation researchers.[7] Berti (2005: 69ff.), for example, showed that, although children have limited knowledge as a consequence of age-related cognitive limitations, the teaching of politics in the school curriculum for all grades can foster their political understandings. As research has revealed, political knowledge tends to increase with age across the primary school years, but individual variation among children of the same age has been found. Abendschön / Tausendpfund (2017: 204ff.) noticed that girls show a tendency to be less politically knowledgeable than boys. Van Deth / Abendschön / Vollmar (2011: 147ff.) found that children from ethnic minorities and lower socioeconomic residence areas show relatively less developed political orientations, and they do not improve as much over the course of a school year as other children.

Another area of research that has received scholarly attention is related to the sources of political socialisation. Families, schools and news media are considered important sources of political socialisation for children and adolescents. They, argues McLeod (2000: 46), are to be the "conduits in

---

6 Young Citizens Foundation 2018. *Brexit and young people.* https://www.youngcitizens.org/news/brexit-and-young-people (Last access 22.12.2022).

7 See Patterson (2019) for an extended discussion of this research literature.

transmitting to the neophyte citizens [children] what mature citizens knew and practiced." However, as Patterson (2019: 234) points out,

> many adults limit their discussion of politics with children, due to beliefs that children will not understand or be interested in politics or that discussion of political issues will be inappropriately divisive or upsetting for children.

Her view confirms previous studies: in a survey of elementary school-aged children carried out before the 2016 US presidential election, Cully / Golinkoff / Ribic (2016: 1ff.) found that more than 60% of children talked little with their parents about the election and 20% did not talk at all. This is also the result emerging from Patterson / Bigler / Pahlke / Spears Brown / Hayes / Ramirez / Nelson's (2019: 7ff.) study of elementary school students' perceptions of the 2016 election. They found that only 20% of children talked a lot with their parents about the election while more than 35% did not talk at all. Along the same lines, teachers were found to avoid discussions of politics within their classrooms (e.g., Hess / McAvoy 2014; Gindi / Erlich 2018).

News media (e.g., newspapers, television news) were also found to play a crucial role in informing young people about the world and in encouraging political participation. Although literature argues that children are not interested in the news, there is a growing body of research reporting on the effectiveness of news media in supporting "children's civic rights and engagement to ensure their informed voices are included in public debates" (Carter 2017: 417). In his book entitled *The Making of Citizens. Young People, News and Politics*, Buckingham (2000) offers an interesting analysis of the complexities of young people's interpretations of news, and their judgments about the ways in which key social and political issues are represented. On the other hand, Patterson (2019: 231ff.) analysed how picture books can inform young children about politics and influence their political engagement and aspirations.

As we have seen, children's understanding of politics has been extensively researched from a political socialisation perspective. The issue, however, still remains, as far as we know, an under-explored area of inquiry in connection with popularisation within a linguistic perspective. The present contribution attempts to help fill this gap in the research field by investigating how UK children understand Brexit and the European Union. For this purpose I will analyse the popularisation strategies associated with the dissemination of political knowledge in the following two books for children aged between 3 and 11 dealing with Brexit: *BREXIT: Britain's decision to leave the European Union* by Daniel Nunn (2016); *I WANT TO LEAVE THIS BOOK!* by Richard David Lawman (2019).[8] Attention will be paid to examples that highlight popularisation strategies on the basis of verbal and visual elements which will be characterised in relation to the age of the addressee.

The basic methodological framework of this study is discourse analysis with reliance on notions taken from multimodality. This provides instruments suitable for identifying cases where the visual mode interacts with the verbal mode to support popularisation strategies. The context of this study is provided by previous research which looked at the popularisation strategies associated with the dissemination of legal knowledge in texts for children (cf. Diani 2015, 2018). The next section gives an overview of research on popularisation of specialised knowledge addressing children. Section III provides a description of the books used for the study as well as the methodology adopted. The results will be reported in section IV, followed by concluding remarks in section V.

II. Popularisation of specialised knowledge for children

According to Calsamiglia / van Dijk (2004: 372), popularisation involves not only a reformulation of specialised knowledge, but also a "recontextualization" of scientific knowledge originally produced in specific contexts to which the lay public has limited access. The drafting of popularising texts is therefore seen as an instance of the linguistic, textual and discursive re-elaboration of specialised knowledge in a way that is comprehensible and relevant for new recipients, and in a discursive context, which is predictable though different from that of the original source (cf. Caliendo

[8] The book titles are written as they are in the original version.

2014: 7ff.). As stated elsewhere (cf. Diani 2018: 293), the recontextualisation of expert knowledge for various lay audiences necessarily affects several aspects of communication, which range from lexico-syntactic patterns to different discourse strategies. This is particularly evident when children are the addressees of knowledge transmission.

Popularising specialised knowledge addressing children is a fairly recent area of research in connection to popularisation from a linguistic perspective. Studies in the field have focused on popularisation strategies adopted in different genres and specialised domains. For example, Sezzi (2017) investigated popularisation as a form of remediation in history books for children in translation. Diani (2015; 2018) analysed the linguistic-discursive strategies for successful transfer and effective dissemination of legal concepts in texts destined for children, such as newspaper articles and information books from a cross-cultural perspective.

Other research that has focused on the ways in which specialised and culture-specific concepts are reconceptualised and recontextualised is that of Cappelli / Masi (2019), who investigated the discourse of travel guidebooks for children in English and Italian. Similarly, Bruti / Manca (2019) explored the strategies adopted to recontextualise specialised knowledge in English and Italian children's magazines, dealing with the topic of environmental education.

Parallel to strategies of recontextualisation of specialised knowledge adopted in print texts targeted at children, attention has also been given to this area of study in digital texts for children. Diani / Sezzi (2019) investigated verbal popularisation strategies on the two official websites of the European Union for children. Similarly, these two websites were explored by Silletti (2017), who analysed how verbal and visual elements interact to support popularisation strategies. Sezzi (2019) also illustrated how museum websites popularise art for children. What emerges from the cited research is that popularisation aimed at a juvenile audience involves recontextualisation of expert discourse for the lay audience, in the same way as that which targets adults. However, given that its specific addressees have limited background knowledge, and, arguably, cognitive abilities, concepts need to be made even simpler in popularisation for children than in popularisation for adults, though without being dumbed down to banality, as research has revealed.

The present study contributes to the above-mentioned research direction, by exploring how children's books popularise Brexit. As the two books under investigation address different age groups, the theme of Brexit is treated in different ways, both in terms of content and language. More specifically, the study addresses the following research questions:

i. Which popularisation strategies are used in the books in relation to the age of the addressee?
ii. How do the verbal and the visual interact (i.e. what is told in words and / or in images) in order to support popularisation?

III. Materials and method

The study is based on the analysis of two UK English books for children aged between 3 and 11 which set out what Brexit is. More specifically, *BREXIT: Britain's decision to leave the European Union* is written by Daniel Nunn and was first published in December 2016 by Raintree. It is for key stage 2 children (age 7 to 11), and it contains thirty-two pages with colour photographs on each page. Its cover blurb gives the following description:

> Through simple, informative text and photographs, this book explains to young readers the key institutions of the EU and what functions they perform, the arguments made by both the 'remain' and 'leave' campaigners and the immediate and likely long-term effects of the vote to leave.

The book is organised in eight thematic sections, five of which pose a question in the title and their answers are provided in the text of the section: *What is the European Union?*, *What were the arguments for staying in the European Union?*, *What were the arguments for leaving the European Union?*, *What happens next?*, *What do* you *think?*. Each section is accompanied by photographs (and one graph) and some words appearing throughout the text are in bold, whose meanings are shown in the glossary at the end of the book. As the author says in the volume: *Some words are shown in bold,* ***like this****.*[9] *You can find out what they mean by looking in the glossary.* Each page of the book consists of blocks of text on a green or white background and of a separate light blue small box framed with gold stars – the same as the European flag – containing explanations and extra information usually next to or superimposed on a photo they refer to, which is included on the page.

I WANT TO LEAVE THIS BOOK! is written by Richard David Lawman and illustrated by Katie Williams, and it was first published in 2019 by WatAdventure. It is a picture book for 3 to 5-year-old children translating Brexit into a story of animals. It contains thirteen double page spreads with colourful animals. The plot revolves around a group of animals who, after debating whether they should stay in the book or not, decide to leave but find themselves unable to agree on what type of story they want to be in.

To identify popularisation strategies, I refer to existing studies on the discursive practices which, in literature on popularisation, are identified as being used to facilitate a layman's access to specialised scientific knowledge. More specifically, I used Calsamiglia / van Dijk's (2004: 372ff.) classification of the following five forms of explanation. The first is *denomination* or *designation*, which consists in introducing new terms and indicating their specialised denominations. Closely linked to denomination is *definition*, which involves the explanation of unknown terms by means of a brief description of some general and specific properties of the referent. Another procedure is *reformulation* or *paraphrase*, marked by appositions, parentheses, dashes, quotes and metalinguistic expressions (e.g., *are called*). A fourth procedure is *generalisation*, which draws general conclusions from specific examples or cases. The last category is *exemplification* which provides specific examples of general phenomena.

All the discursive practices described above work on a lexical and syntactic level. There are other practices which, on the contrary, work on a cognitive one. They are classified under the label "analogy" or "association" (Calsa-

[9] In all excerpts taken from the book, bold is used as in the original.

miglia / van Dijk 2004: 376), and include linguistic similes and metaphors. In Lakoff / Johnson's (1980: 5) words, "the essence of metaphor is understanding and experiencing one kind of thing in terms of another." The 'other' element is usually cognitively familiar to the reader, being part of his / her background knowledge. A simile, on the other hand, is a type of metaphor which is easily indentifiable as it is accompanied by specific indicators such as *like*, *as*, *similar to* or *the same as*.

Considering that both books contain photos and illustrations, particular attention was also paid to the relation between text and images. With the advent of digital media technologies, communication tools have increased their degree of multimodality, defined by Kress / van Leeuwen (2001: 20) as "the use of several semiotic modes in the design of a semiotic product or event." In the past decade, extensive research has been conducted on linguistic and non-linguistic semiotic resources (cf. Lemke 1998; Kress 2000; Kress / van Leeuwen 2020), contributing "to an evolving 'inventory' of semiotic modal resources" (Jewitt 2008: 246).

In this study I will look at some prominent examples of how the verbal and the visual interact (i.e. what is told in words and / or in images) in order to support the procedures established by Calsamiglia / van Dijk (2004) and presented above. As regards the analysis of the visual mode, the framework I adopted is based on the grammar of visual design proposed by Kress / van Leeuwen (2020), concerning the functional semiotic accounts of the meaning-making resources of illustrations that were analysed in terms of the meanings constructed in them, based on Halliday's (1970: 143) three metafunctions of language: ideational, interpersonal, textual.

According to their approach, in a multimodal text, ideational or representational meaning, as they call it, refers to "the way images represent the relations between the people, places and things they depict, and the complex set of relations that can exist between images and their viewers" (Kress / van Leeuwen 2020: 179). Interpersonal meaning refers to the verbal and visual choices representing a particular social relation between the producer, the viewer and the object represented. Compositional or textual meaning refers to the way the visual elements "are integrated into a meaningful whole" (Kress / van Leeuwen 2020: 179).

In this study, I will investigate the dimensions of ideational and interpersonal meaning in the books under examination as they are of particular importance in children's knowledge construction. Due to space limitations, my discussion of ideational meaning addresses the notion of semiotic metaphor (cf. O'Halloran 1999) that contributes to text-image relations.[10] As regards interpersonal meaning in images, I only address some of the many aspects dealt with in Kress / van Leeuwen's (2020: 149ff.) analysis. I will limit it to investigating issues of visual modality, which refers to the extent to which images are "naturalistic" representations of reality, in that they depict reality as it is seen "naturally".

IV. Data analysis

This section analyses the two books, focusing on selected examples that highlight popularisation strategies on the basis of verbal and visual elements characterising them.

1. BREXIT: Britain's decision to leave the European Union

Starting with the book's title *BREXIT: Britain's decision to leave the European Union* (see Fig. 1), we can observe that the term Brexit – rendered in red and in a capitalised large bold font to catch the young readers' attention – is followed by a subtitle that zooms in on the main topic of the book: the Brexit referendum. This is represented through an illustration contributing to transmitting it. A voter's hand, whose shirt sleeve has the Union Jack flag on it, is inserting her / his ballot paper into the ballot box which

[10] The notion of semiotic metaphor adopted here derives from O'Halloran (1999: 348). Her notion is an extension of Halliday's grammatical metaphor that aims to determine how images and words integrate across verbal and visual modes. In her view, like grammatical metaphor, semiotic metaphor also involves a shift in the grammatical class or function of an element that takes place intersemiotically rather than intrasemiotically, as is the case for grammatical metaphor.

the words *leave* and *remain* are printed on. Her / his preference is marked with a tick in the box next to the word *leave*.

The book's title thus combines with the image and instantiates the shift from verbal to visual mode: the meaning of *Brexit* in the verbal mode is reflected in the visual modality through the use of an image containing the material process of putting a ballot paper into the ballot box. The illustration exemplifies an interesting use of image supporting popularisation strategy: it contributes to exemplifying the result of the Brexit referendum by inserting it into a realistic context, so it facilitates the correct interpretation of the image for the young reader.

Fig. 1: Front cover of the book

The book opens with an introductory section entitled *A very important decision* that anticipates some background information on the referendum, presented as *On 23 June 2016, the people of the United Kingdom voted in a very important* ***referendum***. The text then defines what a referendum is: *A referendum is held when the* ***government*** *wants the people to help them* *make an important decision*, and provides further information: *Everyone who votes in a referendum answers the same question.* The text is accompanied by a photograph of a ballot paper which has the goal of making it easier to understand the term *referendum*, which is not particularly transparent. The sentence *All voters in the referendum had to fill out a* ***ballot paper*** *like this one*, placed in a separate light blue box next to the picture, functions partly as description and caption heading. As can be seen, three words are highlighted in bold in order to select the most important concepts in the text.

The text then proceeds by introducing the young reader to the concept of *Brexit*. Interestingly, the author explains it by referring to a real-life situation (news): *The day after the referendum, people woke up to the news that Britain had decided to leave the European Union (EU). This was known as 'Brexit'*. The paraphrastic device used here is denomination (*known as*). This explanation is placed in a light blue box next to a photo of a newspaper headline where the word *Brexit* is written in capital letters and in a very large bold font. Its aim is to reproduce an image young readers have already stored in their memories so that they can relate it to a real context. *Brexit* is further described by saying that *The big question of the 23 June referendum was: should the United Kingdom remain a member of the European Union or leave the European Union? For months,* ***campaigners*** *had tried to persuade voters to choose either to 'Remain' or 'Leave'. Now it was time for the people to decide!*

The book then goes on to explain some of the background issues related to Brexit through the question / answer pattern (cf. Giannoni 2008: 212ff.) in the sections entitled *What is the European Union?, What were the arguments for staying in the European Union?* and *What were the arguments for leaving the European Union?*. Resorting to *wh*-questions in title sections is a common strategy of popularisation for children (cf. Diani 2015, 2018; Sezzi 2017; Silletti 2017; Bruti / Manca 2019; Diani / Sezzi 2019). It suggests a didactic function reflecting the audience the book is designed for, i.e. children who need to be taught the basic concepts of the topic discussed.

By using this type of question format, the author tries to draw the young readers' attention to the issue, so as to arouse their interest and curiosity on a specific topic (cf. Webber 1994: 257ff.). Tentatively, we may speculate about the use of this strategy on the basis of the function *wh*-questions express "an imbalance of knowledge between participants" (Hyland 2002: 530). Hyland's (2002: 535) argument is particularly convincing here as it confirms how such questioning helps "to construct readers as learners, and learning as a one-way transfer of knowledge" from expert to non-experts.

Brexit is disseminated through other popularisation strategies. There are three main paraphrastic devices used in the book: *definition*, *denomination* and *exemplification*, which are introduced throughout as part of the main text or in separate small boxes usually next to or superimposed on a photo these explanations refer to. They are mainly used in the section entitled *What is the European Union?* This is undoubtedly the most striking (albeit predictable) feature of this section as its aim is to introduce the young reader to the concept of the EU, exploring what the EU is, how it was formed, how it governs, its member states, its citizens. *Definition* is, for example, used to explain the term *single market*:

(1) *The European Union (EU) is a single market.* This means *that people and businesses can buy and sell things within the EU countries without restrictions.*[11]

On the other hand, *denomination* is used in order to give the young reader the precise name of concepts:

(2) *The history of the European Union (EU) began in 1957, when six countries decided to work more closely together. These countries were France, West Germany, Italy, Belgium, Luxembourg and the Netherlands. Together they created what* was called *the European Economic Community (EEC). Over the years, more and more countries decided to join the EEC. The United Kingdom joined in 1973. In 1993, the EEC became* known as *the European Union (EU).*

[11] In all excerpts taken from the book, non-italics is added for emphasis.

(3) *Many European countries also share a single* ***currency****. This* is called *the Euro. Britain does not use the Euro. It decided to keep the British pound instead.*

While the definition of the EU and its description are part of the main text block the section is made up of, the concept of the single currency, the Euro, is given in a separate light blue box as extra information, next to a naturalistic picture of Euro banknotes so that children can more easily understand it. This is because what they see in the image is also seen in reality. Similarly, the EU is exemplified visually by a colour map of the 28 countries it is made up of. The use of colour coding to create contrasts distinguishing different countries is most effective "as a model for shaping reality" (Kress / van Leeuwen 2020: 86), so that children can give concrete reference to the concept of the EU.

Moreover, *exemplification* is adopted as a strategy to offer a specific example of a more general concept, as illustrated in the following excerpts (*such as*, *for example*):

(4) *The countries of the European Union (EU) work together in many ways. They work together when making agreements with countries that do not belong to the EU (*such as *China and the United States). EU countries also cooperate in matters* such as *scientific research, education and security.*

(5) *Members of* ***governments*** *from all the EU countries meet at the Council of the European Union. Important decisions are made there. Who goes there depends on what is being talked about at the time.* For example*, if the Council is holding a meeting about farming, the* ***ministers*** *for farming from each of the 28 countries go there to talk together.*

These exemplifications that are part of the main text of the section are also supported visually. For example, the concept of scientific research is represented by a naturalistic photograph of two scientists researching over a microscope. The sentence taken from the book *The EU has helped scientists from all over Europe to work together*, placed in a light blue box next to the picture, serves to help understand the visual component. As for the members of governments from all the EU countries, a naturalistic picture of the 28 EU ministers who met together at the Council of the European Union in 2015 is provided. Again, a light blue box is placed on the photo in which the following is written: *Sometimes, the leaders of the 28 EU countries get together. They discuss important questions that will affect the future of Europe.* As observed elsewhere (cf. Diani / Sezzi 2020: 278), these pictures seem to fulfill an interpersonal function: not only do they gaze directly at the viewers, thus establishing an imaginary relationship with them, but they also function as a device used to attract the viewers' attention to one thing rather than another.

After the introductory section to the EU, the book moves on to talk about the key figures involved in the Brexit debate, namely David Cameron, Theresa May, Boris Johnson, Nigel Farage, because, as the author himself stated in an interview with Raintree Publisher for launching the book, "children want to know who those people are."[12] They are described as the leaders of the two campaigns, the *vote remain* and the *vote leave*, in the sections entitled *What were the arguments for staying in the European Union?* and *What were the arguments for leaving the European Union?*, respectively. Two of them are visually represented by photographs: David Cameron as the leader of the 'vote remain' campaign, and Nigel Farage as the leader of 'vote leave'. The sections provide the reasons that each campaign gave for staying in the EU or leaving the EU. Here is the text on the arguments for leaving the EU taken from the book:

(6) *The motto of the Leave campaign was 'Take back control'. They argued that leaving the EU would allow Britain to reduce the numbers of European people coming to live and work in Britain. They believed that this would mean more jobs for British people and that services such as hospitals and schools would be less crowded. The Leave* ***campaign*** *also believed that leaving the EU would allow Britain to save many millions of pounds' worth of money that currently goes to the EU. Instead of Britain giving that money to the EU, they argued that it could instead be spent on public services such as the National Health Service (NHS), schools and housing. Leave* ***campaigners*** *also believed that it would be better for Britain if it could make all of its own* ***laws****. [...] Finally, the Vote Leave campaign argued that Britain did not need to be part of the EU to get good* ***trade*** *agreements with other countries. They*

[12] The interview *Brexit for kids* took place on February 17th, 2017. https://www.youtube.com/watch?v=MJGGk2JDn3k (Last access 22.12.2022).

believed that Britain could ***negotiate*** *its own deals with non-EU countries as well as the other countries.*

As can be seen, the author writes as a journalist, using discourse strategies typically associated with journalistic discourse, which is characterised by reports of voices, and long, complex sentences (cf. Motta Roth / Scherer 2016: 183). He reports the voices from the 'vote leave' campaign by searching for objectivity, "attained by the *invoking of voices from social actors* that legitimise the news as they signal that the account is not just a one-sided view from the journalist" (Motta Roth / Scherer 2016: 183; italics in original). That the author is unbiased in his presentation of the 'remain' or 'leave' campaigns is echoed in an interview reported in the Oxford Mail newspaper in 2017, where he said: "We [the author and the editor] tried really, really hard to cut out anything biased. There were things I wrote that we reviewed because we thought they were a bit subjective" (see footnote 2).

In order to make the text easily understandable for its intended young readers, the author again supports popularisation through photographs. For example, the belief that leaving the EU would free up more money to spend on NHS hospitals is reinforced by a picture of ambulances outside a hospital entrance for accident and emergency. Similarly, the text introduces a picture of the Parliament building, and in a light blue box placed on it the young readers learn: *Leave campaigners wanted more of Britain's laws to be made at the Houses of Parliament in London instead of the European Parliament*. Thus, the image of the Parliament can be visually recognised by young readers as the place where UK laws are made with respect to European ones.

From the pros of staying in the EU or leaving the EU, the book shifts to a description of the referendum day in a section entitled *23 June 2016: referendum day*, where young readers are provided with very specific information on polling location, opening hours, the legal voting age, the number of people who voted and the final results. This last information is visually represented by a pie chart showing the percentage of votes for *leave* and for *remain* (*48.1% remain, 51.9% leave*). A light blue box containing extra information is positioned next to the graph: *The final results were 17.410.742 votes for Leave and 16.141.241 votes for Remain.*

Finally, in the section closing the book, entitled *What do you think?*, the author directly addresses the young reader through the pronoun *you*. A direct appeal to the reader is a popularising feature aimed at engaging the reader in the text and drawing him / her into the discourse (cf. Hyland 2005: 173ff.; Giannoni 2008: 212ff.). The pronoun *you* is used to involve the young readers in political issues as a result of the Brexit referendum. As the author says in the book: *Many people have said that the biggest winners or losers will be the next generation – people who are still at school today! So, now that you know more about the EU and the arguments to Remain or Leave: What do YOU think?* Note the use of emphasis on '*YOU*' in capitals that is added by choosing to italicise it as a word the author wants to particularly focus on.

The text also introduces reader engagement visually through an image of a schoolgirl with question marks over her head. This is further emphasised by the question the author poses to the young reader, written inside a light blue box next to the picture: *If you had been allowed to the vote in the referendum, would you have chosen to Remain or Leave?* The strategy of directly addressing children as readers foregrounds the highly interactive and reader-oriented nature of texts for children, whose main purpose is to involve its readership in the text and create a rhetorical effect of "closeness and involvement" as described by Breeze (2015: 16), who suggests that "the level of familiarity associated with the second person serves to involve the reader in the story."

The book concludes with a glossary section listing the words used in bold throughout. This makes the book resemble a textbook which presents itself as a reference work. Through a glossary, the child can work autonomously and without the help of an adult.

2. I WANT TO LEAVE THIS BOOK!

I WANT TO LEAVE THIS BOOK! is a picture book explaining Brexit through the story of colourful animals who argue whether or not to leave the pages of the book. As Arizpe / Styles (2003: 22) point out, "picture-books are composed of pictures and words whose intimate interaction creates layers of meaning." Their statement finds confirmation in the picture book under examination. Even the title on the front cover (see Fig. 2) represents an interesting relationship between word and image. The meaning of *leave* in the verbal mode is exemplified in the visuamonl component by a dog with a threatening facial expression grabbing a monkey's tail to prevent it from leaving. By using this semiotic metaphor, the child can understand the meaning of *leave* when he or she looks at the illustration. Like the Brexit book's title, the picture book's title is written completely in capitals and the hand-lettered typeface suggests a child's handwriting, giving it a human touch (cf. Serafini / Clausen 2012: 11).

Fig. 2: Front cover of the book

As Moya Guijarro observes (2014: 154),

> animal characters are frequently used in children's picture books. The animals are typically transformed into anthropomorphic beings with human attributes and motivation, as they are often able to speak, show feelings.

Most of these aspects are reflected in the picture book under scrutiny, where the main characters are able to speak through verbal processes in verbal language as well as material processes in the visual mode. This is well exemplified when the writer explains Brexit to children by introducing them to the concepts of *leave* and *stay* in this book. They are realised verbally through two declaratives uttered by the two main characters of the story, Jiblets, a monkey, and Sirius, a dog: *Well, we want to leave!*, shouted Jiblets, *Well, we want to stay!*, shouted Sirius.

The 'leave' and 'stay' supporters representing exclusive *we*, in the sense of 'us and not them', are visually depicted as two distinct groups of animals, each grouped into a page on one side of the double spread: on the left page the monkey, the highland cow and the anteater are the 'leave' supporters, while on the right page, the dog, the pig, the frog, and the hamster are the 'stay' supporters. On the left page, the words cried by Jiblets, the leader of the 'leave' supporters. *We could end up in the* ***BEST BOOK EVER!***[13] are faithfully echoed in the illustration through the use of a semiotic metaphor: he is throwing his hands in the air as a sign of joy while the other animals depicted on the right page – the 'stay' supporters – look at him suspiciously. Jiblets' state of happiness, described verbally by the adjective *best* and the adverb *ever*, is thus exemplified metaphorically through the use of an image containing a material process in the visual mode. Jiblets' excitement is also reflected in the way the words he utters are written: they are in capital letters, in a very large bold font, and slanting to give an idea of how they are pronounced.

Typography makes the text not only visible but also meaningful (cf. Gutjahr / Benton 2001: 2), having an evident multimodal interpersonal meaning. As van Leeuwen (2006: 154) points out, "typography can be seen as a

[13] In all excerpts taken from the book, bold caps are used as they are in the original.

semiotic mode – systematic, multimodal and able to realise not just textual, but also ideational and interpersonal meaning." This view is well exemplified by the use of the typeface and even size that triggers and illustrates emotional reactions to the characters within the narrative. As regards verbal language, there is an interesting change of simpler lexis in the picture book compared to the Brexit book: for example, *stay* is used rather than *remain*. Another interesting feature is the use of exclusive *we* in the double spread page which highlights the contrastive aspect 'us' vs 'you / them', and thus echoes the Brexit 'leave / remain' divide.

The picture book introduces the young reader to the concept of a referendum by resorting to the idea of a vote. The interrogative clause *Why don't we have a vote?* uttered by a pig anticipates the visual process that is depicted in the illustration: in the double spread all the animals with a white paper in their hand are queuing to vote. The first one to vote is Jiblets inserting his paper into a box that is placed on a big red armchair with the word *VOTE* printed on it. In the following double spread, the text announces the result of the vote. Here Mayor Gruft, the frog, standing on huge stack of papers used for voting, says: *The result of the vote, shall we all leave or stay in this book is [...]* ***LEAVE!***. The result cannot be fully understood without the picture. Here again, another semiotic metaphor can be identified. The illustration reflects the ***LEAVE!*** result in the visual component through the more concrete and tangible material process of the 'leave' supporters raising their arms up in the air as a sign of triumph and smiling, while the other animals representing the 'stay' supporters seem to be upset.

The state of being happy (by the 'leave' supporters) is also echoed in the way the word *leave* is written: in capitals and in a very large bold font followed by an exclamation mark. Here again, typography is multimodal, integrated with other semiotic means of expression such as colour (bold font), and expresses attitudes towards what is being represented (cf. van Leeuwen 2006: 143). As can be seen, semiotic metaphors are a recurrent feature throughout the story, confirming Moya Guijarro's (2016: 47) claim that using semiotic metaphors in children's tales facilitates the understanding of the story by young children. The story proceeds with the animals unable to agree on what type of book they want to be in. Arguments and chaos ensue, which are also reflected in the layout of their exclamations dotted irregularly over the pages.

Interestingly, separated from the story, the picture book is accompanied by a two-page section describing what Brexit is together with a glossary. The texts use language and sentence structure that bring them closer to the style of textbook writing. This is also reflected in the design of the page layout which is similar to a primary school textbook: the page consists of six coloured framed boxes containing handwritten texts. As can be seen, there is a change of the target reader: we have shifted from the very young children the picture book story addresses to the primary school children this informative section involves. The choice to include it derives from the author's interest in providing an "informative tool for parents to explain Brexit to their children", as he himself stated in an interview (cf. footnote 3).

The author introduces the concept of Brexit by saying: *IN JUNE 2016, THE BRITISH GOVERNMENT ASKED THE PUBLIC IF THEY WOULD LIKE TO STAY IN THE EUROPEAN UNION. HERE'S WHAT HAPPENED [...].*[14] In examining the typography, it becomes clear that the sentence (see the use of all caps) is designed to catch the child reader's attention and convey importance. What follows is a very simple description of the Brexit affair. Definitions are used to explain what the UK, the EU and a referendum are, as exemplified by the following excerpts taken from the book:

(7) *The United Kingdom of Great Britain and Northern Ireland is a sovereign country made up of England, Scotland, Wales and Northern Ireland. The UK joined the EU in 1973.*

(8) *The European Union is a special 'club' for 28 countries from the continent of Europe. In return for a membership fee, the EU will organize some laws, rules on trade and how people can move from country to country for all the members.*

---

[14] Caps are used as they are in the original.

(9) *What is a referendum? It's a public vote on a very important issue. Anyone who lives in the UK who is over 18 is allowed to vote in a secret ballot.*

Each definition is supported by a picture: a map of the European countries is placed between UK and EU definitions respectively, and a pie chart showing the percentage of votes for 'leave' and for 'remain' is placed next to the definition of referendum. A comment on the percentage figure is made: *It was very close!* The section also includes 'leave' and 'remain' arguments, suggesting the same format as used in *BREXIT: Britain's decision to leave the European Union*. But while in the latter, the organisation of the argumentation consists of four paragraphs in each of the sections devoted to them, in the picture book, the arguments are organised as lists of three bulleted points. As we can notice, the author uses the word *remain* rather than *stay*, which he preferred throughout the picture book story. A possible explanation could be the target reader this section addresses, mainly primary school children. The author is aware that children aged 7-11 want the recognition that they have moved beyond simpler lexis used for younger children.

The section concludes with a summary of the Brexit timeline, the key events in the UK's path from referendum to EU exit. The meaning of some words used in the Brexit timeline can be found in the glossary placed next to it. The term *BREXIT* is analysed as *BRITAIN + EXIT = BREXIT*. Compared to the glossary of the Brexit book consisting of 23 words listed in alphabetic order with very brief accompanying definitions, the glossary of the picture book only contains seven words extracted from the Brexit timeline, and they are listed in the order they are mentioned in the timeline. The words are *Parliament*, *General Election*, *Government*, *Political Party*, *Prime Minister*, *Deal*, *No Deal*, whose detailed definitions are provided.

V. Conclusions

The results emerging from the study provide evidence that in the two children's books under examination, a significant difference exists in the way Brexit is explained to children. *I WANT TO LEAVE THIS BOOK!* as a picture book relies on the visual mode to appeal to very young children with colourful characters providing a lot of different contributions and with justifications of wanting or not wanting to remain depicting the Brexit story. On the other hand, *BREXIT: Britain's decision to leave the European Union* is primarily based on the verbal mode, as the target age group it addresses (children aged 7 to 11) is looking to learn for itself. This may find an explanation in the use of long information texts, interspersed with photos. However, the study shows that both books use similar strategies to popularise Brexit. The picture book, although limited to the two pages of information at the back and separate from the story, features definitions and the question-answer pattern (*What is a referendum?*, *What happens next?*) that find a recurrent use in the Brexit book as well. Similarities are also found in visual representations supporting popularisation strategies.

Both books use semiotic metaphors to facilitate the understanding of the concepts transmitted. For example, in the Brexit book the concept of referendum is visually represented by an image of a ballot paper to be filled in and put into a ballot box. Similarly, in the picture book, there is an image of animals with a white paper in their hand queueing to put their papers into a box. This strategy corroborates the general view emerging from other studies that the metaphorical element "is cognitively familiar to the reader, being part of his/her background knowledge or everyday experience" (Garzone 2014: 85). Thus, as Garzone (2014: 85) observes,

> when metaphors are used in popularization the kind of knowledge that is usually presupposed on the part of the readers is simply a basic general sociocultural knowledge 'of the world'.

As research has demonstrated, the use of metaphors serves a pedagogical purpose (cf. Cameron 2003: 36ff.) because, as we have seen, it often involves concrete and familiar concepts to help readers understand topics they may find abstract and difficult to grasp. This is particularly evident in the dissemination of knowledge targeted at children, as observed by Vosniadou (1987: 882) who suggests that metaphorical thinking plays "an important role in the child's attempts to acquire new knowledge."

Another level of similarity can be observed in the visual representation of the 'leave' and 'remain' campaigns in both books. In the Brexit book, a photo of the leaders of each campaign is included (cf. David Cameron and Nigel Farage in the sections dealing with the arguments for staying and leaving the EU, respectively). Similarly, in the picture book, the two main characters of the story, Jiblets and Sirius, are the leaders of the 'leave' and 'remain' supporters, respectively.

It is commonly assumed that reading plays a fundamental role in the learning of concepts. Both books have an educational goal. In *BREXIT: Britain's decision to leave the European Union*, the way the text is structured encourages both verbal communication (in the form of the children's personal comments on the concepts explained in the text) and active participation of the young reader (i.e. the use of *you* in the text: *What do* you *think?*). On the other hand, as Lawman stated in an interview, in the picture book, the story "provides an entertaining and informative tool for parents to explain Brexit to their children" (cf. footnote 3). This view supports Patterson's (2019: 245) claim that

> picture books are an important source of learning for young children and can provide opportunities for communication between children and important socialization agents, such as parents and teachers.

As the books have shown, each mode of communication serves a different purpose: the image entertains while verbal language educates (cf. Buckingham / Scanlon 2004: 289f.).

Although the age and the profile of the target reader is different, both books trigger the question of how important it actually is to try to explain Brexit to children. This may be viewed within the broader context of citizenship education (cf. Davies 2014: 22ff.). As stated by Kisby / Sloam (2014: 52f.), "it offers a means for connecting young people to the political system, helping them to make sense of a complex political world." As research has shown, UK citizens have low levels of knowledge about the EU when compared to their counterparts elsewhere in Europe, and this lack of political knowledge is particularly pronounced amongst younger generations (cf. Sloam / Henn 2019: 17ff.). Thus, the two books seem to fill this gap by making, as Lawman said in an interview, "these complex political issues as digestible as possible to ensure that younger generations truly engage and understand the wider moral backdrop of these events" (see footnote 3).

Since this study is limited to two books, there are, of course, limitations to the generalisability of the results. Further research should explore how popularisation strategies are realised in other publications dedicated to political and civic issues targeting children so as to collect further supporting evidence of the trends that have emerged from the present study as well as of other tendencies within and beyond those discussed above.

VI. References

Abendschön, Simone / Markus Tausendpfund. 2017. Political Knowledge of Children and the Role of Sociostructural Factors. *American Behavioral Scientist* 61 (2), 204-221.

Arizpe, Evelyn / Morag Styles. 2003. *Children Reading Pictures. Interpreting Visual Texts*. London: Routledge.

BBC Radio. 2019. *BBC Radio 2 Breakfast Show's 500 Words 2019 Winners are Revealed at Windsor Castle*. https://www.bbc.co.uk/mediacentre/latest-news/2019/500-words-winners. Last access 22.12.2022.

Berti, Anna Emilia. 2005. Children's Understanding of Politics. In: Martyn Barrett / Eithne Buchanan-Barrow (Eds.), *Children's Understanding of Society*. Hove: Psychology Press, 69-103.

Breeze, Ruth. 2015. Or so the Government would have you Believe. Uses of *you* in Guardian Editorials. *Discourse, Context & Media* 10, 36-44.

Bruti, Silvia / Elena Manca. 2019. The Popularization of Environmental Issues in Children's Magazines. A Cross-Cultural Corpus Analysis. In: Meng Ji (Ed.), *Translating and Communicating Environmental Cultures*. London: Routledge, 182-201.

Buckingham, David. 2000. *The Making of Citizens. Young People, News and Politics*. London: Routledge.

Buckingham, David / Margaret Scanlon. 2004. Connecting the Family? 'Edutainment' Web Sites and Learning in the Home. *Education, Communication & Information* 4 (2-3), 271-291.

Caliendo, Giuditta. 2014. Introduction. In: Giancarmine Bongo / Giuditta Caliendo (Eds.), *The Language of Popularization. Theoretical and Descriptive Models / Die Sprache der Popularisierung. Theoretische und deskriptive Modelle*. Bern: Peter Lang, 7-19.

Calsamiglia, Helena / Teun van Dijk. 2004. Popularization Discourse and Knowledge about the Genome. *Discourse & Society* 15 (4), 369-389.

Cameron, Lynne. 2003. *Metaphor in Education Discourse*. London: Continuum.

Cappelli, Gloria / Silvia Masi. 2019. Knowledge Dissemination through Tourist Guidebooks. Popularization Strategies in English and Italian Guidebooks for Adults and for Children. In: Marina Bondi / Silvia Cacchiani / Silvia Cavalieri (Eds.), *Communicating Specialized Knowledge. Old Genres and New Media*. Newcastle upon Tyne: Cambridge Scholars Publishing, 124-161.

Carter, Cynthia. 2017. The Role of New Media in Fostering Children's Democratic Citizenship. In: Howard Tumbler / Silvio Waisbord (Eds.), *The Routledge Companion to Media and Human Rights*. London: Routledge, 416-425.

Cully, Christine French / Roberta Michnick Golinkoff / Sasha L. Ribic. 2016. *Highlights. The State of the Kid 2016*. https://www.highlights.com/sites/default/files/public/sotk_16_report-928.pdf. Last access 22.12.2022.

Davies, Ian. 2014. Defining Citizenship Education. In: Liam Gearon (Ed.), *Learning to Teach Citizenship in the Secondary School. A Companion to School Experience*. 3rd edition. London: Routledge, 18-30.

Diani, Giuliana. 2015. Exploring Knowledge Dissemination Strategies in English and Italian Newspaper Articles for Children. A Focus on Legal Issues. *Textus* 28 (2), 109-126.

Diani, Giuliana. 2018. Popularization of Legal Knowledge in English and Italian Information Books for Children. In: Jan Engberg / Karin Luttermann / Silvia Cacchiani / Chiara Preite (Eds.), *Popularization and Knowledge Mediation in the Law / Popularisierung und Wissensvermittlung im Recht*. Wien: Lit, 291-316.

Diani, Giuliana / Annalisa Sezzi. 2019. The EU for Children. A Case of Web-Mediated Knowledge Dissemination. In: Stefania M. Maci / Michele Sala (Eds.), *Representing and Redefining Specialised Knowledge. Variety in LSP*. Bergamo: CERLIS Series 8, 203-221.

Diani, Giuliana / Annalisa Sezzi. 2020. Scientific Websites for Children. Nurturing Children's Scientific Literacy through the Conflation of Multiple Semiotic Resources. *Journal of Visual Literacy* 39 (3-4), 273-291.

Flood, Alison. 2019. *No Goose is an Island. The Brexit Picture Books for Children of all Ages*. https://www.theguardian.com/books/2019/nov/04/brexit-picture-books-for-children-of-all-ages-eu-animals. Last access 22.12.2022.

Freeman, Helen. 2019. *2019 Oxford Children's Word of the Year. Brexit.* https://home.oxfordowl.co.uk/blog/2019-oxford-childrens-word-of-the-year-brexit/. Last access 22.12.2022.

Garzone, Giuliana. 2014. News Production and Scientific Knowledge. Exploring Popularization as a Process. In: Giancarmine Bongo / Giuditta Caliendo (Eds.), *The Language of Popularization. Theoretical and Descriptive Models / Die Sprache der Popularisierung. Theoretische und deskriptive Modelle*. Bern: Peter Lang, 73-110.

Giannoni, Davide. 2008. Popularizing Features in English Journal Editorials. *English for Specific Purposes* 27 (2), 212-232.

Gindi, Shahar / Rakefet Ron Erlich. 2018. High School Teachers' Attitude and Reported Behaviors towards Controversial Issues. *Teaching and Teacher Education* 70, 58-66.

Gutjahr, Paul C. / Megan Benton. 2001. *Illuminating Letters. Typography and Literary Interpretation*. Amherst: University of Massachusetts Press.

Halliday, Michael A. K. 1970. Language Structure and Language Function. In: John Lyons (Ed.), *New Horizons in Linguistics*. Harmondsworth: Penguin, 140-165.

Hess, Diana E. / Paula McAvoy. 2014. *The Political Classroom. Evidence and Ethics in Democratic Education*. New York: Routledge.

Hyland, Ken. 2002. What do they Mean? Questions in Academic Writing. *Text & Talk* 22 (4), 529-557.

Hyland, Ken. 2005. Stance and Engagement. *Discourse Studies* 7 (2), 173-192.

Jewitt, Carey. 2008. Multimodality and Literacy in School Classrooms. *Review of Research in Education* 32 (1), 241-267.

Kisby, Ben / James Sloam. 2014. Promoting Youth Participation in Democracy. The Role of Higher Education. In: Andrew Mycock / Jonathan Tonge (Eds.), *Beyond the Youth Citizenship Commission. Youth People and Politics*. London: Political Studies Association, 52-56.

Kress, Gunther. 2000. Multimodality. Challenges to Thinking about Language. *TESOL Quarterly* 34 (2), 337-340.

Kress, Gunther / Theo van Leeuwen. 2001. *The Modes and Media of Contemporary Communication*. London: Arnold.

Kress, Gunther / Theo van Leeuwen. 2020. *Reading Images. The Grammar of Visual Design*. 3rd edition. London: Routledge.

Lakoff, George / Mark Johnson. 1980. *Metaphors We Live By*. Chicago: University of Chicago Press.

Lawman, Richard David. 2019. *I Want to Leave this Book!* Manchester: WatAdventure Publishing.

Lemke, Jay L. 1998. Multiplying Meaning. Visual and Verbal Semiotics in Scientific Text. In: James R. Martin / Robert Veel (Eds.), *Reading Science. Critical and Functional Perspectives on Discourses of Science*. London: Routledge, 87-113.

McLeod, Jack M. 2000. Media and Civic Socialization of Youth. *Journal of Adolescent Health* 27 (2), 45-51.

Motta Roth, Désirée / Anelise Scotti Scherer. 2016. Science Popularization. Interdiscursivity among Science, Pedagogy, and Journalism. *Bakhtiniana* 11 (2), 171-194.

Moya Guijarro, Arsenio Jesús. 2014. *A Multimodal Analysis of Picture Books for Children. A Systemic Functional Approach*. London: Equinox.

Moya Guijarro, Arsenio Jesús. 2016. The Role of Semiotic Metaphor in the Verbal-Visual Interplay of three Children's Picture Books. A Multisemiotic Systemic-Functional Approach. *ATLANTIS. Journal of the Spanish Association of Anglo-American Studies* 38 (1), 33-52.

Nunn, Daniel. 2016. *Brexit. Britain's Decision to Leave the European Union*. Oxford: Raintree.

Nunn, Daniel. 2017. *Brexit for Kids*. https://www.oxfordmail.co.uk/news/15062192.brexit-kids-book-launched-oxford-publisher/. Last access 22.12.2022.

O'Halloran, Kay. 1999. Interdependence, Interaction and Metaphor in Multisemiotic Texts. *Social Semiotics* 9 (3), 317-354.

Patterson, Meagan M. 2019. Children's Literature as a Vehicle for Political Socialization. An Examination of Best-Selling Picture Books 2012-2017. *The Journal of Genetic Psychology* 180 (4-5), 231-250.

Patterson, Meagan M. / Rebecca S. Bigler / Erin Pahlke / Christia Spears Brown / Amy Roberson Hayes / M. Chantal Ramirez / Andrew Nelson. 2019. *Toward a Developmental Science of Politics* 84 (3), 7-185.

Serafini, Frank / Jennifer Clausen. 2012. Typography as Semiotic Resource. *Journal of Visual Literacy* 31 (2), 1-16.

Sezzi, Annalisa. 2017. History is Horrible. Especially in Schools. Remediating History Books for Children in Translation. In: Michela Canepari / Gillian Mansfield / Franca Poppi (Eds.), *The Many Facets of Remediation in Language Studies*. Beau Bassin: Lambert Publishing, 447-466.

Sezzi, Annalisa. 2019. Go on an Art Adventure. Popularizing Art for Children through Museum Websites. In: Marina Bondi / Silvia Cacchiani / Silvia Cavalieri (Eds.), *Communicating Specialized Knowledge. Old Genres and New Media*. Newcastle upon Tyne: Cambridge Scholars Publishing, 162-177.

Silletti, Alida. 2017. L'UE expliquée aux enfants. Le coin des enfants. In: Luciana Radhut-Gaghi / Denisa A. Oprea / Axel Boursier (Eds.), *L'Europe dans les Medias en Ligne*. Paris: L'Harmattan, 157-176.

Sloam, James / Matt Henn. 2019. *Youthquake 2017. The Rise of Young Cosmopolitans in Britain*. Basingstoke: Palgrave MacMillan.

Van Deth, Jan W. / Simone Abendschön / Meike Vollmar. 2011. Children and Politics. An Empirical Reassessment of Early Political Socialization. *Political Psychology* 32 (1), 147-173.

Van Leeuwen, Theo. 2006. Towards a Semiotics of Typography. *Information Design Journal* 14 (2), 139-155.

Vosniadou, Stella. 1987. Children and Metaphors. *Child Development* 58 (3), 870-885.

Webber, Pauline. 1994. The Function of Questions in Different Medical Journal Genres. *English for Specific Purposes* 13 (3), 257-268.

Young Citizens Foundation 2018. *Brexit and Young People*. https://www.youngcitizens.org/news/brexit-and-young-people. Last access 22.12.2020.

Autorinnen und Autoren / Contributors

Giuliana Diani is Professor of English Language and Translation at the University of Modena and Reggio Emilia, Italy. She holds an M.A. in Language Studies from the University of Lancaster, UK, and a Ph.D. in English Linguistics from the University of Pisa, Italy. She has worked and published on various aspects of discourse analysis and EAP, with special reference to language variation across academic genres, disciplines and cultures through the analysis of small, specialised corpora. Her recent work has centred on the analysis of the popularisation strategies adopted in print and in digital texts targeting young people and in law blogs.
e-mail: giuliana.diani@unimore.it

Jan Engberg is Professor of Knowledge Communication at the School of Communication and Culture, Section of German Business Communication, University of Aarhus, Denmark. His main areas of research interest are cognitive aspects of domain specific discourse and the relations between specialised knowledge and text formulation as well as basic aspects of communication in domain-specific settings, with a special focus upon the legal domain. He is especially interested in experts‘ and institutions' communication across knowledge asymmetries from the point of view of explanatory intention and prospective relations to addressees.
e-mail: je@cc.au.dk

Daniel Green is a lecturer at the Institute for English Business Communication at the Vienna University of Economics and Business (WU). He is also a lecturer at the Faculty of Law at Sigmund Freud Private University, Vienna (SFU), and has contributed to various research seminars on methods of computer-assisted statutory interpretation at the Department of Constitutional and Administrative Law at the University of Vienna. He studied English and History at the University of Vienna (Mag. phil.), as well as

Law at the University of Edinburgh (LL.M). He is the founding president of the Austrian Association for Legal Linguistics (AALL).
e-mail: daniel.green@wu.ac.at

Antonio Lazari is Professor of International Law, European Union Law and Comparative Law at the University of Pablo de Olavide of Seville, Spain. His main research interests area are the relationship between European identity and national identities, the international protection of cultural property and the legal and linguistic analysis of cross-fertilisation between national systems of administrative responsibility and the European Union paradigm of State liability.
e-mail: alazari@upo.es

Alessandra Lombardi is Associate Professor in German Language and Translation at the Catholic University of Brescia, Italy. She holds a Ph.D. in Translation Studies, with a specialisation in legal translation and legal linguistics. She is a member of the Research Centre on Specialised Languages (CERLIS) and co-founder of the Italy-Germany Networking Initiatives for Art Communication and Promotion (IGENI). Her main research interests are contrastive linguistics (Italian-German), LSP (text-)linguistics and LSP translation (focus on academic, legal and tourist texts), corpus-based terminology and terminography.
e-mail: alessandra.lombardi@unicatt.it

Karin Luttermann is Professor of German Linguistics at the Department of Linguistics and Literature at the University of Eichstätt-Ingolstadt, Germany. She is also a member of the Graduate School of the Faculty of Linguistics and Literature at the Catholic University of Milan, Italy. She heads the section *Language for Specific Purposes* of the Society for Applied Linguistics. She is member of the advisory board of the Austrian Association for Legal Linguistics and co-editor of the book series *Rechtslinguistik*. She has published widely and co-edited a number of books and special issues of journals within the field of language and law. Her main research in-

terests are the study of language use and comprehensibility in legal texts and discourses, popularisation of legal knowledge, and clear language.
e-mail: karin.luttermann@ku.de

Jon Christian Fløysvik Nordrum is Associate Professor at the Faculty of Law, University of Oslo. He is candidatus juris from the University of Tromsø (2004), Legum Magister, LL.M. from the New York University (2005), and philosophiae doctor, PhD law, from the University of Oslo (2017). His main interests are in the field legislative studies and legislative language, topics for which he is also responsible at the University of Oslo.
e-mail: j.c.nordrum@jus.uio.no

Chiara Preite is Associate Professor at the University of Milan La Statale, Italy, and she qualified as Full Professor in French Language and Translation in 2021. She holds an M.A. in Legal Translation at the University of Genoa, Italy, and a PhD in French Linguistics at the University of Brescia, Italy. Her main research interests lie in the fields of legal French, lexicology, lexicography and specialised lexicography, terminology, and popularisation of legal knowledge. She has published widely on these topics and is the author of the volume *Langage du droit et linguistique*, as well as the editor of several special issues on terminology, lexicography, and popularisation.
e-mail: chiara.preite@unimi.it

Patricia Rawinsky is a PhD student at the Catholic University of Eichstätt Ingolstadt. Her dissertation deals with the importance of pre-knowledge in specialised communication. In addition, she deals with current topics such as institutional web communication, translation into easy-to-read language and corpus-based discourse analysis with reference to politically and socially relevant texts. Her main research interests focus on legal linguistic communication, its possible optimisation and popularisation.
e-mail: patricia.rawinsky@freenet.de

Torunn Reksten is a plain language expert at the Language Council of Norway and Vice President of the Plain Language Association International (PLAIN). She holds a candidatus philologiæ degree from the University of Oslo (2002). In her work, she is in charge of implementing the plain language section of the Norwegian Language Act and serves on the Drafting Committees for three of the ISO-24495 standards on plain language.
e-mail: torunn.reksten@sprakradet.no

Janine Schaller-Bøyum is Head of Analysis and Evaluation at the Norwegian Ministry of Digitalisation and Public Governance. She holds a Magister Artium degree in German philology from the University of Wuppertal (2000) and a B.A. degree in Administration and Leadership in the Public Sector, University of Oslo (2016). She works, among others, with the Central Government Communication Policy, plain language and plain legal language.
e-mail: janine.schaller-boyum@dfd.dep.no

Alida Maria Silletti is Associate Professor of French language and translation at the University of Bari, Department of Political Science, Italy. Her main areas of research interest are French macro- and microsyntax, analysis of French political discourse, discourse of commemoration, discourse on European belonging, AI tools for education, strategies for an inclusive language and discourse of popularisation applied to the legal and administrative field, with a special focus on multimodality.
e-mail: alida.silletti@uniba.it

Ole Kristian Våge is Senior Adviser at the Department of Terminology, the Norwegian Directorate of Health. He holds a PhD degree in Linguistics and Terminology from the University of Bergen (2011). He works with digitalisation, semantic interoperability, and terminology in the public health sector in Norway.
e-mail: ole.kristian.vage@helsedir.no

Rechtslinguistik
Studien zu Text und Kommunikation
Studies on Text and Communication
hrsg. von Claire Kramsch (Berkeley), Claus Luttermann (Eichstätt-Ingolstadt) und Karin Luttermann (Eichstätt-Ingolstadt)

Karin Luttermann; Jan Engberg (Hg./Eds.)
Popularisierung als Methode der Wissensvermittlung in der Rechtslinguistik / Popularisation as a Method of Knowledge Mediation in Legal Linguistics
The focus of Legal Linguistics (Rechtslinguistik) has shifted from lexical, syntactic and terminological issues to expert-lay communication. This volume focuses on popularisation as a method of knowledge mediation in the law. It deals with different forms of communication (e.g., explanatory videos, brochures, websites), addressees (e.g., children, adolescents, adults), topics (e.g., empathy, emotions, trust), settings (e.g., courts, law firms, EU institutions), and finally, specific areas of law (e.g., inheritance law, criminal law, environmental law). The contributions, written in German and English, discuss theoretical issues and apply them practically to the corpus. The book is stimulating for anyone wanting to delve more deeply into the topic of popularisation.
Bd. 13, 2023, 404 S., 59,90, gb., ISBN 978-3-643-15421-7

Daniel Green; Luke Green (Eds.)
Contemporary Approaches to Legal Linguistics
The articles present research in the areas of contract interpretation, bijuralism, the European Reference Language System, clear language and communication in legal settings, issues in legal semantics, plain legal language in multilingual legislative drafting, legal language teaching, light verb constructions in legal German, forensic linguistic expert testimony, deontic modality in legislative drafting, migration and legal language, appeals in Russian and their qualification as language crimes, and graduation in the use of force statutes. The concepts, methods, and findings offer valuable insights into current research in legal linguistics.
vol. 12, 2022, 380 pp., 49,90, gb., ISBN 978-3-643-91387-6

Karin Luttermann; Albert Busch (Hg.)
Sprache und Recht: Konstitutions- und Transferprozesse in nationaler und europäischer Dimension
Dieser Themenband zur Schnittstellendisziplin *Rechtslinguistik* stellt eine spannende und fortdauernde Diskussion vor, die ihren Ausgang mit dem Symposium Rechtslinguistik zum 50. Jubiläum der Gesellschaft für Angewandte Linguistik (GAL) an der Universität Duisburg-Essen nahm. Der Band führt Wissenschaftler verschiedener (Teil-)Disziplinen und Praktiker zusammen und zeigt Entwicklungslinien in der Rechtslinguistik. Den Schwerpunkt bilden die Themenfelder *Recht und Konstitution*, *Recht und Forensik* sowie *Recht und Transfer*. Die Themen werden in fünfzehn Einzelbeiträgen, auch über nationale Bezüge hinaus, im europäischen Vergleich behandelt. Ziel ist es, den interdisziplinären Dialog an der Schnittstelle zwischen Sprache und Recht zu fördern, Forschungsperspektiven fortzuentwickeln und den Blick auf angewandte rechtslinguistische Zugänge zu weiten.
Bd. 11, 2021, 412 S., 44,90, gb., ISBN 978-3-643-14358-7

LIT Verlag Berlin – Münster – Wien – Zürich – London
Auslieferung Deutschland / Österreich / Schweiz: siehe Impressumsseite

Karin Luttermann; Kerstin Kazzazi; Claus Luttermann (Hg.)
Institutionelle und individuelle Mehrsprachigkeit
Das Buch führt die bisher weithin getrennt behandelten Typen der Mehrsprachigkeit – *institutionell* und *individuell* – zusammen, indem Verbindungslinien gezogen sowie Abhängigkeiten und gemeinsame Perspektiven gezeigt werden. Den Ausgangspunkt bildet die unterschiedliche Konzeptualisierung der erfahrenen Welt durch verschiedene Sprachen in nationalen, europäischen und internationalen Kontexten in Alltag, Schule, Beruf und Wissenschaft. Die Beiträge auf Deutsch und Englisch zeigen aus verschiedenen Blickwinkeln und auf unterschiedlichen Ebenen zwischen den Typen von Mehrsprachigkeit bestehende Verhältnisse. Sie laden ein zum Dialog über die Bedeutung und Funktion von Sprachen für Institutionen und für das Individuum.
Bd. 10, 2019, 422 S., 29,90 , br., ISBN 978-3-643-14192-7

Jan Engberg; Karin Luttermann; Silvia Cacchiani; Chiara Preite (Eds./Hg.)
Popularization and Knowledge Mediation in the Law. Popularisierung und Wissensvermittlung im Recht
vol. 9, 2018, 372 pp., 39,90 , br., ISBN 978-3-643-90924-4

Projekt Angewandte Linguistik (PAL)
hrsg. von Prof. Dr. Karin Luttermann (Universität Eichstätt-Ingolstadt), Prof. Dr. Christina Gansel (Universität Greifswald)

Christina Gansel; Sergej Nefedov; Irina Jesan (Hg.)
Kommunikative Praktiken in sozialen Kontexten
Sprachliche Mittel im Einsatz
Die Beiträge dieses Bandes gehen Themen und Perspektiven nach, die vor dem Hintergrund aktueller Diskussionen zur theoretischen Fassung von kommunikativen und sprachlichen Praktiken zusammengehalten werden. Gemeinsam ist ihnen, dass bei der Analyse kommunikativer und sprachlicher Praktiken von sozialen Handlungszusammenhängen ausgegangen wird.
Es werden Praktiken aus der Sphäre der Wissenschaftskommunikation, des Journalismus, der tradierten Kulturalität oder der historischen Herausbildung von Höflichkeitsstrukturen und Textsorten erfasst. Makro-, meso- und mikrostrukturelle Ebenen bilden jeweils einen Ausgangspunkt der Untersuchungen.
Bd. 3, 2019, 224 S., 39,90 , gb., ISBN 978-3-643-14307-5

Friedrich Markewitz
Das Schulprogramm als Textsorte zwischen Erziehungs- und Wissenschaftssystem
Eine systemtheoretisch-textsortenlinguistische Untersuchung
Bd. 2, 2019, 750 S., 84,90 , br., ISBN 978-3-643-14043-2

Christina Gansel; Karin Luttermann (Hg.)
Nachhaltigkeit – Konzept, Kommunikation, Textsorten
Bd. 1, 2020, 416 S., 39,90 , gb., ISBN 978-3-643-14688-5

LIT Verlag Berlin – Münster – Wien – Zürich – London
Auslieferung Deutschland / Österreich / Schweiz: siehe Impressumsseite